"*Ancient Jewish and Christian Scriptures* is a treasure trove of fascinating information and insight about a body of literature that in recent decades has attracted an enormous amount of scholarly and popular attention. This book is an extremely helpful and learned guide to the writings that constitute the Apocrypha and Pseudepigrapha, materials not included in the ancient rabbinic scriptural canon or the Christians' First Testament. Do these writings contribute to our understanding of biblical Jewish and Christian heroes and beliefs, concerning whom canonical texts have traditionally supplied the entirety of our source material, or should we reject the most extravagant claims made on behalf of the antiquity and reliability of this material? *Ancient Jewish and Christian Scriptures* clearly establishes that we should approach these materials with more nuanced questions in mind."

—Richard Kalmin, Theodore R. Racoosin Professor of Talmud and Rabbinics, Jewish Theological Seminary, and author of *Jewish Babylonia between Persia and Roman Palestine*

"As compelling as the Three Tenors, John J. Collins, Craig A. Evans, and Lee Martin McDonald combine their respective areas of expertise to update anyone interested in the latest thinking about scriptural canons. This brave, new operatic volume enchants with its complex repertoire of chapters addressing the diversity of ancient understandings about inspiration, acceptance, and reception. Anyone interested in the emergence of sacred scripture must read this book."

—Clare K. Rothschild, Professor of Scripture Studies, Lewis University, and Professor Extraordinary, Department of Ancient Studies, Stellenbosch University, and author of *Luke-Acts and the Rhetoric of History*

"It is hard to imagine assembling a finer 'dream team' to guide a reader through the process of canon formation and the broader use of (what would become) extracanonical literature in early Jewish and Christian circles than Collins, Evans, and McDonald. Their collaboration has produced a well-planned and coherent book that consistently pushes us beyond our obsession with the boundaries of canon and draws us into the contributions this larger body of literature—the deuterocanonicals, Pseudepigrapha, Dead Sea Scrolls, and early Christian 'Apocrypha'—have made to the shaping of both Judaism and Christianity through the centuries."

—David A. deSilva, Trustees' Distinguished Professor of New Testament, Ashland Theological Seminary, and author of *Introducing the Apocrypha: Message, Context, and Significance*

"This book succeeds eminently in presenting in a very lucid way what is known and unknown, accepted and debated regarding the Jewish and Christian collections of scriptures. Questions of canonicity are discussed from all angles by three outstanding experts."

—Emanuel Tov, J. L. Magnes Professor Emeritus of Bible, Hebrew University, Jerusalem

Ancient Jewish and Christian Scriptures

Ancient Jewish and Christian Scriptures

New Developments in Canon Controversy

John J. Collins, Craig A. Evans,
and Lee Martin McDonald

WESTMINSTER
JOHN KNOX PRESS
LOUISVILLE • KENTUCKY

© 2020 John J. Collins, Craig A. Evans, and Lee Martin McDonald

First edition
Published by Westminster John Knox Press
Louisville, Kentucky

20 21 22 23 24 25 26 27 28 29—10 9 8 7 6 5 4 3 2 1

Unless otherwise indicated, Scripture quotations are from the New Revised Standard Version of the Bible, copyright © 1989 by the Division of Christian Education of the National Council of the Churches of Christ in the U.S.A., and are used by permission. Quotations marked NETS are taken from *A New English Translation of the Septuagint*, © 2007 by the International Organization for Septuagint and Cognate Studies, Inc. Used by permission of Oxford University Press. All rights reserved. Scripture quotations marked NIV are from *The Holy Bible, New International Version*. Copyright © 1973, 1978, 1984, 2011 by Biblica, Inc.® Used by permission. All rights reserved worldwide. Scripture quotations marked RSV are from the Revised Standard Version of the Bible, copyright © 1946, 1952, 1971, and 1973 by the Division of Christian Education of the National Council of the Churches of Christ in the U.S.A., and are used by permission.

Chapter 1, "The Penumbra of the Canon: What Do the Deuterocanonical Books Represent?," was previously published in *Canonicity, Setting, Wisdom in the Deuterocanonicals* (edited by Géza G. Xeravits, József Zsengellér, and Xavér Szabó; Boston: de Gruyter, 2014). Reprinted by permission of the publisher; all rights reserved.

Book design by Sharon Adams
Cover design by Marc Whitaker / MTWdesign.net

Library of Congress Cataloging-in-Publication Data

Names: Collins, John J. (John Joseph), 1946-, author. | Evans, Craig A., author. | McDonald, Lee Martin, 1942- author.
Title: Ancient Jewish and Christian scriptures : new developments in canon controversy / John J. Collins, Craig A. Evans, and Lee Martin McDonald.
Description: First edition. | Louisville, Kentucky : Westminster John Knox Press, 2020. | Includes bibliographical references and index. | Summary: "This book examines the writings included in and excluded from the Jewish and Christian canons of Scripture and explores the social settings in which some of this literature was viewed as authoritative and some was viewed either as uninspired or as heretical. Through the writings of John J. Collins, Craig A. Evans, and Lee Martin McDonald, contemporary readers acquire a broader understanding of biblical Scripture and of Jewish and Christian faith inspired by Scripture"— Provided by publisher.
Identifiers: LCCN 2020016925 (print) | LCCN 2020016926 (ebook) | ISBN 9780664265977 (paperback) | ISBN 9781611649826 (ebook)
Subjects: LCSH: Bible—Canon.
Classification: LCC BS465 .C65 2020 (print) | LCC BS465 (ebook) | DDC 220.1/2--dc23
LC record available at https://lccn.loc.gov/2020016925
LC ebook record available at https://lccn.loc.gov/2020016926

Contents

Acknowledgments

We wish to thank Houston Baptist University and the Lanier Theological Library in Houston for the invitations to present lectures on some important issues in contemporary biblical scholarship, in the school year 2016–2017. We enjoyed the warm welcome and kind hospitality extended to us during our visit. We are especially grateful to Craig Evans for his role in arranging the lectures, for his contribution to this volume, and for facilitating its publication.

John Collins's article "The Penumbra of the Canon: What Do the Deutero-canonical Books Represent?" originally appeared in *Canonicity, Setting, Wisdom in the Deuterocanonicals* (edited by Géza G. Xeravits, József Zsengellér, and Xavér Szabó; Deuterocanonical and Cognate Literature Studies 22; Berlin: de Gruyter, 2014), 1–17. It is reprinted here by permission of de Gruyter.

Abbreviations

General

//	parallel(s)
§	section, paragraph
א*	original reading of Codex Sinaiticus
aka	also known as
alt.	altered
apud	citing a reference at second hand
B*	original reading of Codex Vaticanus
BCE	Before the Common Era
BHL	Bibliotheca Hagiographica Latina [MSS: http://bhlms.fltr .ucl.ac.be/]
BHL	*Biblia Hebraica Leningradensia*, ed. A. Dotan
c.	century
ca./c.	circa
CE	Common Era
chap(s).	chapter(s)
D	the Deuteronomist source in the Pentateuch
d.	died
diss.	dissertation
DSS	Dead Sea Scrolls
E	the Elohist source in the Pentateuch
ed(s).	edited by, editor(s), edition
e.g.	*exempli gratia*, for example
esp.	especially
ET	English translation
et al.	*et alii*, and others

etc.	*et cetera*, and the rest
fl.	flourished
fn.	footnote
fol.	folio
HB	Hebrew Bible
i.e.	*id est*, that is
J	the Yahwist source in the Pentateuch
lit.	literally
LXX	the Septuagint (the Greek OT, translation of HB)
MF	Muratorian Fragment = Canon Muratori
MS(S)	manuscript(s)
MT	Masoretic Text (of the OT)
NETS	*A New English Translation of the Septuagint.* Edited by A. Pietersma and Benjamin Wright. Oxford: Oxford University Press, 2014. http://ccat.sas.upenn.edu/nets/edition/
NIV	New International Version
NKJV	New King James Version
n(n). *or* n(n)	note(s)
no(s).	number(s)
NRSV	New Revised Standard Version
orig.	original
OT	Old Testament
P	the Priestly source in the Pentateuch
P	papyrus, with number or name, such as P^{46} or P.Oxy. *See papyri list below.*
pl.	plural
Q	*Quelle*, hypothetical *source* of Jesus' sayings and deeds used in Matthew and Luke
R.	Rabbi
repr.	reprint
rev.	revised
RSV	Revised Standard Version
ThD	doctor of theology degree
trans(s).	translated by, translator(s), translation
v., vv.	verse, verses
VACAT	blank (in a document)
vol(s).	volume(s)

Hebrew Bible / Old Testament

Gen	Genesis
Exod	Exodus
Lev	Leviticus
Num	Numbers

Deut	Deuteronomy
Josh	Joshua
Judg	Judges
Ruth	Ruth
1–2 Sam	1–2 Samuel
1–2 Kgs	1–2 Kings
1–2 Chr	1–2 Cronicles
Ezra	Ezra
Neh	Nehemiah
Esth	Esther
Job	Job
Ps/Pss	Psalm/s
Prov	Proverbs
Eccl	Ecclesiastes
Song	Song of Songs
Isa	Isaiah
Jer	Jeremiah
Lam	Lamentations
Dan	Daniel
Hos	Hosea
Joel	Joel
Amos	Amos
Obad	Obadiah
Jonah	Jonah
Mic	Micah
Nah	Nahum
Hab	Habakkuk
Zeph	Zephaniah
Hag	Haggai
Zech	Zechariah
Mal	Malachi

Old Testament Apocrypha

2 Esd	2 Esdras
1–4 Macc	1–4 Maccabees
Sir	Sirach, or Ben Sira
Wis	Wisdom of Solomon

Old Testament Pseudepigrapha

1–3 En.	*1–3 Enoch*
4 Bar.	*4 Baruch*
Let. Aris.	*Letter of Aristeas*

New Testament

Matt	Matthew
Mark	Mark
Luke	Luke
John	John
Acts	Acts
Rom	Romans
1–2 Cor	1–2 Corinthians
Gal	Galatians
Eph	Ephesians
Phil	Philippians
Col	Colossians
1–2 Thess	1–2 Thessalonians
1–2 Tim	1–2 Timothy
Titus	Titus
Phlm	Philemon
Heb	Hebrews
Jas	James
1–2 Pet	1–2 Peter
1–3 John	1–3 John
Jude	Jude
Rev	Revelation

NT-Related Extracanonicals

Acts Pil.	*Acts of Pilate*
BG	Berlin Gnostic Codex
Gos. Pet. (or: *Peter*)	*Gospel of Peter*
Gos. Thom. (or: *Thomas*)	*Gospel of Thomas*
Narr. Jos.	*Narrative of Joseph of Arimathea*
NHC	Nag Hammadi Codices

Dead Sea Scrolls

CD	Cairo Genizah copy of the *Damascus Document*
1QH[a]	*Hodayot[a] = Thanksgiving Hymns[a]*
1QM	*The War Scroll*
1QS	*Rule of the Community*
4QMMT	*Halakhic Letter*
4Q174	*4QFlorilegium*
4Q246	*4QAramaic Apocalypse*
4Q252	*Commentary on Genesis[a] = 4QGenesis Pesher[a]*

4Q471ᵇ	*A Self-Glorification Hymn*
4Q491	*4QWar Scrollᵃ*
4Q521	*4QMessianic Apocalypse*
4Q524	*4QTemple*
11QPsᵃ	*11QPsalmsᵃ*
11QTᵃ	*11QTempleᵃ*
11Q19	*Temple Scrollᵃ*
Scrolls	Dead Sea Scrolls

Papyri and Inscription

I.Eph.	an inscription found at Ephesus
P.Ant.	Antinopolis papyrus
P.Berol.	Berolinensis papyrus
P.Cair.	Cairo papyrus
P.Colog.	Cologne papyrus
P.Eger.	Egerton papyrus
P.Hamb.	Hamburg papyrus
P.Mert.	Merton papyrus
P.Oxy.	Oxyrhynchus papyrus
P.Ryl. Gr.	John Rylands Library, Greek papyrus
P.Vindob.	Vindobonensis papyrus, numbered

Rabbinic Works

Collections

b.	Babylonian Talmud
m.	Mishnah
t.	Tosefta
y.	Jerusalem Talmud

Josephus and Philo

Ag. Ap.	*Against Apion,* by Josephus
Ant.	*Jewish Antiquities*
J.W.	*Jewish War,* by Josephus
Life	*The Life,* by Josephus

Apostolic Fathers

Barn.	*Barnabas*
1–2 Clem.	*1–2 Clement*
Diogn.	*Epistle to Diognetus*

Ign. *Magn.*	*To the Magnesians*, by Ignatius of Antioch
Ign. *Phld.*	*To the Philadelphians*, by Ignatius of Antioch
Shepherd	*Shepherd of Hermas*

Other Early Christian Works

1 Apol.	*First Apology*, by Justin
Autol.	*To Autolycus*, by Theophilus of Antioch
Catech.	*Catecheses*, by Cyril of Jerusalem
Comm. Dan.	*Commentary on Daniel*, by Epiphanius
Comm. Gal.	*Commentaries on Galatians*, by Jerome
Comm. Matt.	*Commentaries on the Gospel of Matthew*, by Origen
Comm. Matt. Praefatio	*Commentaries on Matthew, Preface*, by Jerome
Dial.	*Dialogus cum Tryphone* (*Dialogue with Trypho*), by Justin
Ep.	*Epistula/Epistulae* (*Epistle/Epistles*) (several authors)
Haer.	*Adversus haereses* (*Against Heresies*), by Irenaeus
Haer.	*Haereses* (*Heresies*), by Philaster of Brescia
Haer.	*Refutatio omnium haeresium* (*Refutation of All Heresies*), by Hippolytus
Hist. eccl.	*Historia ecclesiastica* (*Ecclesiastical History*), by Eusebius
Hom. Luc.	*Homilae in Lucam* (*Homilies on Luke*), by Origen
Hom. Num.	*Homilae in Numbers* (*Homilies on Numbers*), by Origen
Klem.	*Klementia, Pseudo-Clementines*
Marc.	*Adversus Marcionem* (*Against Marcion*), by Tertullian
MF	Muratorian Fragment, Canon Muratori
Pan.	*Panarion* (*Adversus haereses*) (*Refutation of All Heresies*), by Epiphanias
Princ.	*De principiis* (*First Principles*), by Origen
Serm. Dom.	*De sermone Domini in monte* (*Sermon on the Mount*), by Augustine
Strom.	*Stromata* (*Miscellanies*), by Clement of Alexandria
Val.	*Adversus Valentianus* (*Against the Valentinians*), by Tertullian
Vir. ill.	*De viris illustribus* (*Concerning Distinguished Men*), by Jerome

Primary Source Collections

ANF	*Ante-Nicene Fathers*
LCL	Loeb Classical Library
NPNF[2]	*Nicene and Post-Nicene Fathers*. 2nd series
NTAM	*New Testament Apocrypha: More Noncanonical Scriptures.* Edited by T. Burke and B. Landau. Vol. 1. Grand Rapids: Eerdmans, 2016

OTP 1	*Apocalyptic Literature and Testaments*. Vol. 1 of *The Old Testament Pseudepigrapha* [*OTP* 1]. Edited by James H. Charlesworth. Garden City, NY: Doubleday, 1983
OTP 2	*Expansions of the "Old Testament" and Legends, Wisdom and Philosophical Literature, Prayers, Psalms, and Odes, Fragments of Lost Judeo-Hellenistic Works*. Vol. 2 of *The Old Testament Pseudepigrapha* [*OTP* 2]. Edited by James H. Charlesworth. Garden City, NY: Doubleday, 1985
OTPM	*Old Testament Pseudepigrapha: More Noncanonical Scriptures*. Edited by R. J. Bauckham, J. R. Davila, and A. Panayotov. 2 vols. Grand Rapids: Eerdmans, 2013
PG	Patrologia graeca [= Patrologiae cursus completus: Series graeca]. Edited by J.-P. Migne. 162 vols. Paris, 1857–1886
PL	Patrologia latina [= Patrologiae cursus completus: Series latina]. Edited by J.-P. Migne. 217 vols. Paris, 1844–1864

Secondary Resources

AB	Anchor Bible
ABD	*Anchor Bible Dictionary*. Edited by David Noel Freedman. 6 vols. New York: Doubleday, 1992
AGJU	Arbeiten zur Geschichte des antiken Judentums und des Urchristentums
ASBT	Acadia Studies in Bible and Theology
AYBRL	Anchor Yale Bible Reference Library
BBB	Bonner Biblische Beiträge
BETL	Bibliotheca Ephemeridum Theologicarum Lovaniensium
Bib	*Biblica*
BR	*Biblical Research*
BThZ	*Berliner Theologische Zeitschrift*
BZNW	Beihefte zur Zeitschrift für die neutestamentliche Wissenschaft
CBET	Contributions to Biblical Exegesis and Theology
CBQ	*Catholic Biblical Quarterly*
CBQMS	Catholic Biblical Quarterly Monograph Series
CBSC	The Cambridge Bible for Schools and Colleges
CanDb	*The Canon Debate*. Edited by Lee Martin McDonald and James A. Sanders. Peabody, MA: Hendrickson, 2002
CEJL	Commentaries on Early Jewish Literature
CRINT	Compendia rerum Iudaicarum ad Novum Testamentum
DJD	Discoveries in the Judaean Desert
DSD	*Dead Sea Discoveries*
ExpTim	*Expository Times*
FIOTL	Formation and Interpretation of Old Testament Literature

GCS	Die griechischen christlichen Schriftsteller der ersten [drei] Jahrhunderte
GRBS	*Greek, Roman, and Byzantine Studies*
HTR	*Harvard Theological Review*
IDB	*The Interpreter's Dictionary of the Bible*. Edited by George A. Buttrick et al. 4 vols. New York: Abingdon, 1962
JAC	*Jahrbuch für Antike und Christentum*
JAJSup	Journal of Ancient Judaism: Supplements
JBL	*Journal of Biblical Literature*
JSJ	*Journal for the Study of Judaism*
JSJSup	Supplements to the Journal for the Study of Judaism
JSNT	*Journal for the Study of the New Testament*
JSP	*Journal for the Study of the Pseudepigrapha*
JSPSup	Journal for the Study of the Pseudepigrapha: Supplement Series
JTS	*Journal of Theological Studies*
LNTS	The Library of New Testament Studies
NCB	New Century Bible
NEA	*Near Eastern Archaeology*
NedTT	*Nederlands theologisch tijdschrift*
NHS	Nag Hammadi Studies
NIBD	*New Interpreter's Dictionary of the Bible*. Edited by Katharine Doob Sakenfeld. 5 vols. Nashville: Abingdon, 2006–2009
NICNT	New International Commentary on the New Testament
NovT	*Novum Testamentum*
NovTSup	Supplements to Novum Testamentum
NTOA	Novum Testamentum et Orbis Antiquus
NTS	*New Testament Studies*
NTTS	New Testament Tools and Studies
NTTSD	New Testament Tools, Studies, and Documents
OECS	Oxford Early Christian Studies
OTL	Old Testament Library
PAST	Pauline Studies
RB	*Revue biblique*
REByz	*Revue des études byzantines*
RevQ	*Revue de Qumran*
SBLDS	Society of Biblical Literature Dissertation Series
SBLSCS	Society of Biblical Literature Septuagint and Cognate Studies
SBLTT	Society of Biblical Literature Texts and Translations
SECA	Studies on Early Christian Apocrypha
SNTSMS	Society for New Testament Studies Monograph Series
STAC	Studien und Texte zu Antike und Christendum

STDJ	Studies on the Texts of the Desert of Judah
StPB	Studia Post Biblica
SVTP	Studia in Veteris Testamenti Pseudepigrapha
TENTS	Texts and Editions for New Testament Study
TSAJ	Texte und Studien zum antiken Judentum
TUGAL	Texte und Untersuchungen zur Geschichte der altchristlichen Literatur
UBS	United Bible Societies
VC	*Vigiliae Christianae*
VCSup	Vigiliae Christianae Supplements
VTSup	Supplements to Vetus Testamentum
WBC	Word Biblical Commentary
WMANT	Wissenschaftliche Monographien zum Alten und Neuen Testament
WUNT	Wissenschaftliche Untersuchungen zum Neuen Testament
ZKG	*Zeitschrift für Kirchengeschichte*
ZNW	*Zeitschrift für die neutestamentliche Wissenschaft und die Kunde der älteren Kirche*

Introduction

JOHN J. COLLINS, CRAIG A. EVANS,
AND LEE MARTIN McDONALD

"All scripture is inspired by God and is useful for teaching, for reproof, for correction, and for training in righteousness, so that everyone who belongs to God
may be proficient, equipped for every good work," says 2 Tim 3:16–17. At first
glance, it might seem that this ringing endorsement is given to "all writing,"
everything that is written! But this would surely be absurd. Christian tradition
certainly distinguishes between "scripture," to which this endorsement applies,
and profane writing, which may be good, bad, or indifferent. We are accus-
tomed to assuming a clear distinction between "scripture," understood as the
material found in our printed Bibles, and other literature. What is found in our
Bibles is regarded as "canonical." But the situation in New Testament times was
considerably more complicated than this.

The word "canon" is borrowed from Christian theology. It denotes both a
fixed, definitive body of literature and a rule of faith. Already at the end of the
first century CE, Clement of Rome referred to "the glorious and venerable rule
[*kanōn*] of our tradition." The first use of the word "canon" to refer to a collection
of authoritative scriptures is variously credited to Eusebius (*Hist. eccl.* 6.25.3) or
to Athanasius, in his *Festal Letter* of 367 CE. To speak of a "canon" of scripture
before the fourth century CE is, strictly speaking, anachronistic.

Nonetheless, long before the word "canon" was adopted, some writings were acknowledged to be more authoritative than others in matters of religion. Toward the end of the first century CE, the Jewish historian Josephus wrote: "Our books, those which are justly accredited, are but two and twenty, and contain the record of all time" (Josephus, *Ag. Ap.* 1.37–39). At about the same time, a Jewish apocalypse called *Fourth Ezra* gave the number as twenty-four but may have been counting the same books differently. Lee McDonald's first two chapters in this volume discuss how the selection of these books, which we know as the Hebrew Bible, came about, also the order of the books, their division into three or four sections, and the possible criteria that may have underlain their selection and organization. But it would still be too simple to say that the canon of Jewish scripture had been closed by the end of the first century, or that these were the books to which 2 Timothy refers as "all scripture." First, by no means do all the books that we know as the Hebrew Bible claim to be inspired by God. The claim of inspiration is typical of the prophetic books and of the laws given to Moses on Mount Sinai, but there is no such claim in the historical books of the Bible, or in Psalms, or in the Wisdom books. Although one may, of course, choose to believe that these books are nonetheless inspired, with the possible claim of the author of Rev 1:1–3 and 22:18–19 (cf. Deut 4:2), that claim is not made in the books themselves, but later by believing communities that acknowledged them that way. Second, a larger corpus of literature was regarded as authoritative, at least by some people in ancient Judaism. John Collins's essays in this volume deal with three categories of additional literature that enjoyed some authority among ancient Jews.

The first of these is the collection of books known as "Apocrypha," or "deuterocanonical," in Christian tradition. These books were included in the ancient codices of the Greek Bible. At one time they were thought to have been part of the "canon" of Hellenistic Judaism. It is now apparent that there was no such canon, but that Hellenistic Judaism, like early Christianity, had an open-ended collection of Jewish scriptures. Not until the Reformation and the Council of Trent would a clear line be drawn between "canonical" books, found in the Hebrew Bible, and "deuterocanonical" books, found only in Greek codices.

A second category of noncanonical scriptures came to light in the nineteenth century in manuscripts buried in various monastic libraries. These scriptures were supposed revelations, attributed to ancient worthies such as Enoch, Ezra, and Baruch, who could not possibly have written them. Accordingly, they became known as Pseudepigrapha, or falsely attributed writings. It is apparent, however, that in ancient Judaism and early Christianity some of them were accepted as scripture, and many were accepted as inspired. These texts were preserved by Christians, often in languages that were unknown in the West, such as Ethiopic and Old Church Slavonic. It is not always clear whether they were of Jewish or Christian origin, but the Jewish origin of some of them was demonstrated beyond doubt when they were found in Aramaic or Hebrew among the Dead Sea Scrolls.

The third category of noncanonical scriptures is found in the Dead Sea Scrolls, a huge trove of Hebrew and Aramaic manuscripts found on the shores of the Dead Sea in the mid-twentieth century. These included many purported revelations that were previously unknown. Presumably they were accepted as revelations, at least by the people who preserved them.

The early Christians took over more revelatory Jewish texts than the 22/24 "canonical" books in the Tanak (TANAK is an acronym for *Torah* [the Law], *Nev'im* [the Prophets], and *Ketubim* [the Writings]), or Hebrew Bible. They also wrote new scriptures based on the experience of the early church. The development of the Christian scriptures is described in Lee McDonald's third and fourth chapters. His focus is not only on why the books were written, but also on when they began to be acknowledged as scripture and form a NT canon. In his fourth chapter, on the origins and dating of the New Testament, McDonald discusses a subject that is getting more attention in recent scholarship: whether the authors of the NT were consciously aware of writing sacred scripture when they penned their writings. Also of special interest is the continuing debate over the dating of the famous text known as the Muratorian Fragment. Was it written sometime in the late second century or early third century, in the fourth century, or was it a fraudulent text written to anchor a fourth- or fifth-century list of religious texts believed to be sacred scripture *at that time* as a second-century list? New arguments are now emerging that point to a later dating of this text. Some scholars contend that this text is reflective of second-century thinking, but there is no evidence of that or its influence until the late fourth or early fifth centuries. McDonald further adds more recent consideration of the criteria that led to the formation of the New Testament canon.

Craig Evans contributes two chapters, reviewing the early Christian literature that some churches regarded as sacred or that in some ways competed with or supplemented the older writings that were widely regarded as authoritative. Many of these writings, which were mostly produced in the second and third centuries, have been classified as apocryphal or pseudepigraphal. The general public has always found them fascinating, wondering if they contained additional information about Jesus and his apostles. Many popular books, some novels, and some supposed works of scholarship have been published that claim to reveal new truth about Christian beginnings. In the last generation or so, the scholarly community has also expressed new interest in these writings. This interest, fueled in part by new discoveries, is such that one cannot dismiss these writings in a sentence or two, as did Rudolf Bultmann long ago.[1]

In his first chapter Evans surveys all the extracanonical Christian literature that in one way or another was regarded as authoritative and therefore as candidates for acceptance in churches. By "acceptance in churches," he means that the leaders of Christian churches allowed something to be read to the congregation. This was the true test of canonicity in the early church, long before councils were convened and leaders formally debated the question of which writings were authoritative and what writings were not. These writings include gospels; books

---

1. R. Bultmann, *The History of the Synoptic Tradition* (Oxford: Blackwell, 1972), 374.

of acts, each usually focusing on one or two apostles; letters attributed to various apostles, even Jesus; and apocalypses. Evans explores the motives, goals, agenda, and influence of these writings.

According to Evans, a few of the works that we today identify as New Testament pseudepigrapha were read in some churches in the second and third centuries. Indeed, there is evidence that some books eventually recognized as canonical were not read in all churches. Some of these writings, which today are included in the New Testament, were referred to as "books spoken against," in Greek, *antilegomena* (ἀντιλεγόμενα). These included the Letter to the Hebrews, whose authorship was unknown; the brief letters known as 2 and 3 John; the letters of James and Jude, whose authorship and value were questioned; and the Apocalypse, whose meaning was not well understood and whose authorship was uncertain.

What all of this shows is that the canon of the New Testament was not recognized immediately and universally in the Christian churches. Nor was the canon recognized early. A good case can be made that several of the New Testament writings, such as the three Synoptic Gospels, the book of Acts, and the letters of Paul—or at least most of them—were recognized by many churches as authoritative as soon as they began to circulate though not called "scripture" at that time; yet acceptance of all twenty-seven writings that came to make up the New Testament canon was a long and complicated process.

In his second chapter Evans, in much greater detail, discusses two of the most talked-about and debated early extracanonical gospels: *Gospel of Peter* and *Gospel of Thomas*. Both of these gospels are said by some to date to the first century and to be independent of the New Testament Gospels. Along with many scholars, Evans finds that very doubtful and thinks that they should be dated no earlier than mid-second century, though he acknowledges that they are very important as witnesses to significant developments in the Eastern church. The *Gospel of Peter* develops Matthew's Easter apologetic by increasing the number of witnesses to the resurrection of Jesus. In doing this, the author tries to answer the criticisms of skeptics who, like Celsus, find the church's resurrection testimony weak and unconvincing.

In marked contrast to the *Gospel of Peter*, the *Gospel of Thomas* shows little interest in narrative or miracle; rather, it focuses on the ascetic and esoteric dimension of Jesus' teaching. The Thomasine portrait of Jesus seems to reflect a rivalry between the gospel authority of the West, centered in the apostles Matthew and Peter (the latter perhaps linked to the Gospel of Mark), and the gospel authority of the East, centered in the apostle Thomas. If so, the *Gospel of Peter* and the *Gospel of Thomas* may document a significant regional and political dimension in the church's struggle to define its canon of scripture. Although the church finally chose to exclude both the *Gospels of Peter* and *Thomas* (and the author and readers of the latter may never have intended *Thomas* to be read publicly in churches), the debate surrounding these writings played an important role in the development of the church's thinking. The ongoing scholarly debate regarding these two important writings continues.

What all of this shows, at the very least, is that interest in the canon of scripture has not waned—not in scholarly circles and not in the general public. The present book tries to identify the most important issues, as well as the progress that has been made; at the same time the authors try to show where the discussion will take us in the years ahead.

Chapter 1

The Penumbra of the Canon
What Do the Deuterocanonical Books Represent?

JOHN J. COLLINS

The deuterocanonical writings (Tobit, Judith, Ben Sira, Wisdom of Solomon, 1–2 Maccabees, Baruch, plus the additions to Daniel and Esther) owe their existence as a category to the Council of Trent (1546) and the polemics of the Reformation era. The Protestant Reformers had adopted Jerome's principle of *Hebraica veritas* and acknowledged only the books found in the Hebrew Bible as inspired scripture in the Old Testament. The Council of Trent reacted by affirming the larger canon of the traditional Catholic Church: "If any one receive not, as sacred and canonical, the said books entire with all their parts, as they have been used to be read in the Catholic Church and as they are contained in the old Latin Vulgate, . . . let him be anathema." The designation "deuterocanonical" is attributed to Sixtus of Siena (1520–69), in recognition of the fact that their canonicity was disputed.[1] A few centuries later B. F. Westcott scathingly remarked: "This decree of the Council of Trent was ratified by fifty-three prelates, among whom there was not one German, not one scholar distinguished by historical learning, not one who was fitted by special study for the examination of a subject in which the truth could only be determined by the

1. Brown and Collins, "Canonicity," 1035; Dorival, "Category of 'Deuterocanonical Books'?," 1.

voice of antiquity."[2] In fact, the Council fathers relied on tradition from the age of Augustine—when councils at Hippo (393 CE) and Carthage (397 CE) had affirmed the larger canon, which had also been endorsed at the Council of Florence in 1442—as the basis of union between Rome and the Coptic Christians. The Tridentine canon was identical to the list issued by the Council of Hippo, except that the Council fathers appear to have misunderstood the meaning of 1 and 2 Esdras, which they identified as the proto-canonical books of Ezra and Nehemiah.[3] The omission of 2 Esdras was significant since it deprived the Catholic Bible of a major apocalypse, and also of a book for which the primary text was not Greek but Latin.

The disagreement between Catholics and Protestants in the Reformation era reflected much older disputes in the early church. When Melito of Sardis was asked for "an accurate statement of the ancient books" in the late second century CE, he had to send to Palestine for an answer. His list is confined to the Hebrew canon, but without Esther. Others were more inclusive. Tertullian was aware that the book of *Enoch* was not accepted by the rabbis, but nonetheless argued: "Since Enoch by the same scripture has also made proclamation concerning the Lord, nothing whatever must be rejected by us which pertains to us" (*On Women's Dress* 1.3). Clement of Alexandria cited Tobit, Sirach, and the Wisdom of Solomon as scripture, and Judith and 2 Maccabees as historical sources. Origen accepted Susanna as part of the text of Daniel, although he knew it was not in the Hebrew, because Susanna "is found in every church of Christ." Tobit could not be used in disputation with Jews, but it could be read within the churches (*Letter to Africanus* 13).

The popular use of the codex in early Christianity was an important factor in the definition of a canon. The great fourth-century codices, Vaticanus and Sinaiticus, include the books of Tobit, Judith, Ben Sira (Ecclesiasticus), the Wisdom of Solomon. Sinaiticus further includes 1 and 2 Maccabees, and the fifth-century Codex Alexandrinus adds 3–4 Maccabees and the *Psalms of Solomon*.[4]

Athanasius and Jerome recognized only the twenty-two books of the Hebrew canon, counting the Book of the Twelve as one, and combining 1–2 Samuel, 1–2 Kings, 1–2 Chronicles, Ezra–Nehemiah; Jerome also combined Jeremiah and Lamentations, plus Ruth and Judges, so the twenty-two books are counted as thirty-nine in modern Christian Bibles. Jerome translated the additional books as well, although he distinguished them as apocryphal in his prefaces. Since the prefaces were not always copied or heeded, the Western church came to regard all the books of the Vulgate as part of scripture.

Augustine had a decisive influence on the Western church. He listed forty-four books but included Lamentations and Baruch as parts of Jeremiah.[5] The

2. Thus Charles, *Apocrypha and Pseudepigrapha*, 1:x, n. 1, citing Westcott, *Bible in the Church*, 257.

3. Charles, *Apocrypha and Pseudepigrapha*, 1:9.

4. Harrington, "Old Testament Apocrypha," 198–99.

5. Brown and Collins, "Canonicity."

Gelasian Decree (= *Decretum Gelasianum*) at the end of the fifth century recognized Tobit, Judith, the Wisdom of Solomon, Sirach, 1–2 Maccabees, and the additions to Esther, Daniel, and Jeremiah. The Tridentine fathers, then, could claim the support of a long, if not quite consistent, tradition.

A CANON IN JUDAISM?

Underlying all these debates was the history of the formation of a canon, or list of authoritative books, in Judaism. Ben Sira's grandson, in the prologue to his translation of his grandfather's work in the late second century BCE, speaks of "the Law and the Prophets and the others that followed them." It is clear, however, that the third category of "other writings" was open-ended. The Dead Sea Scrolls also provide abundant attestation of the importance of the Torah and the Prophets. A fragmentary line in 4QMMT has been reconstructed to read "the book of Moses and the books of the Prophets and David."[6] David was often regarded as a prophet, and the Psalms as prophecies. The New Testament references to the scriptures similarly refer either to "the law and the prophets" or, in a single case in Luke 24:44, "the law . . . , the prophets, and the psalms."[7]

In general, however, the Dead Sea Scrolls have complicated rather than clarified our picture of authoritative scriptures in Judaism around the turn of the era. On the one hand, there was considerable textual variation in the admittedly authoritative Torah, and there is some question as to whether a book like the *Temple Scroll* would have been regarded, by some people, as Torah.[8] On the other hand, there was a much larger corpus of writings in circulation than was previously known. These included prophetic or pseudo-prophetic works ascribed to Ezekiel, Jeremiah, and Daniel, but also wisdom compositions and halakhic texts. Some works that did not eventually become part of the Hebrew canon, such as the books of *Enoch* and *Jubilees*, appear to have been viewed as authoritative by the people who collected the Dead Sea Scrolls. Remarkably, however, the only deuterocanonical books found at Qumran are Tobit, which is attested in both Hebrew and Aramaic; Ben Sira (Sirach), of which Hebrew fragments were found at both Qumran and Masada; and the Letter of Jeremiah, of which a small Greek fragment was found.[9] We should not, of course, be surprised that works originally composed in Greek (Wisdom of Solomon, 2 Maccabees) would not have found their way to Qumran, but noteworthy are the

---

6. 4QMMT C 10 (composite text); Qimron and Strugnell, eds., *Miqsat Maʿase Ha-Torah*, 59. Note, however, the caveats of Ulrich, "Non-Attestation of a Tripartite Canon in 4QMMT"; and Lim, "Authoritative Scriptures and the Dead Sea Scrolls," 312–13. Lim argues that the reference is to the deeds of David rather than to the Psalms.

7. Barton, *Oracles of God* (1986 edition), 35.

8. VanderKam, "Questions of Canon," 104.

9. For a convenient summary, see Flint, "Noncanonical Writings," 90–93. English translations of the various fragments can be found in Abegg, Flint, and Ulrich, *Dead Sea Scrolls Bible*.

absence of 1 Maccabees, Judith, Baruch, and the additions to Daniel. (Esther is not attested in the Scrolls at all).[10]

For a long time it was assumed that the larger collection of Greek and Latin scriptures reflected the canon of Alexandrian Judaism. The idea that Alexandrian Judaism had a distinct canon was debunked by Albert C. Sundberg in his 1964 book, *The Old Testament of the Early Church*.[11] It is clear from the testimony of Philo that the Torah, or Pentateuch, was the primary scriptural authority. The prologues to Ben Sira and 2 Maccabees also acknowledge the prophets; but while these prologues were written in Greek, they may well reflect Judean rather than Alexandrian views. Many of the writings that survive from Egyptian Judaism either bear the names of their actual authors or were written under Gentile pseudonyms; consequently they were not likely to be considered as "scripture." According to Philo, the Therapeutae had a consecrated room into which they took nothing "but laws and oracles delivered through the mouth of prophets and psalms and anything else which fosters and perfects knowledge and piety."[12] This corresponds quite well to the prologue to Ben Sira. The Law and the Prophets were well-known categories (even if the texts and contents were still open to some debate), but the third category of "other writings" was fluid. It is to this third category that the deuterocanonical writings belong.

It is apparent, then, that the notion of canon, in the sense of a fixed list of authoritative scriptures, is anachronistic for Judaism in the Second Temple period. In the words of John Barton, "The picture that has emerged is of a number of books whose status had never been seriously in doubt, but with a very large penumbra of other books about which opinions varied widely and which were no doubt quite unknown to some communities even at periods when others valued them highly."[13]

Only at the end of the first century CE do we find authoritative books limited to a specific number. In his tract *Against Apion*, Josephus writes: "We do not possess myriads of inconsistent books, conflicting with each other. Our books, those which are justly accredited, are but two and twenty, and contain the record of all time" (*Ag. Ap.* 1.37–39). He goes on to specify the twenty-two books as the five books of Moses, thirteen books of the prophets, and four books containing psalms and precepts. The prophets are said to have written "the history of the events in their own times." This category incorporated what we could call the historical books, probably including Esther and Job and surely including Daniel. Josephus was concerned with these books as reliable historical sources, but he implies that they are also reliable guides to life. His argument is obviously apologetic. The books may not be myriad, but they are surely not consistent. In this passage Josephus does not acknowledge the existence of other Jewish books besides these, but he makes demonstrable use of 1 Esdras and 1 Maccabees in his

---

10. On the variable status of Esther, see Dorival, "Category of 'Deuterocanonical Books'?," 7.
11. Sundberg, *Old Testament of the Early Church*, passim.
12. Philo, *De vita contemplativa* [*On the Contemplative Life*] 25.
13. Barton, *Oracles of God* (1986 edition), 80.

histories, and also of the *Letter of Aristeas*, which was never regarded as canonical. The statement about the twenty-two books presumably reflects some current, authoritative opinion, but it does not reflect his own practice. Steve Mason infers that he did not regard these later books as equal in authority to the twenty-two,[14] but he also admits that he treats the "apocryphal" sources "the same way that he treats biblical material."[15] He felt no obligation to limit himself to the twenty-two books or to regard all other Jewish books as unreliable.

There is a second witness to the notion of a specific number of authoritative books in *4 Ezra*, written a few years later than *Contra Apionem*, by Josephus. The fictional setting of this apocalypse is in the period after the Babylonian destruction of Jerusalem. Not only was the temple destroyed but also, according to *4 Ezra*, the Law was burned. Ezra is commissioned and inspired to replace the written scriptures. Over the course of five days, he dictated to five scribes, and they wrote ninety-four books. Then the Most High spoke to Ezra: "Make public the twenty-four books that you wrote first and let the worthy and the unworthy read them; but keep the seventy that were written last, in order to give them to the wise among your people. For in them is the spring of understanding, the fountain of wisdom, and the river of knowledge" (*4 Ezra* 14:47). It is usually assumed that Ezra's twenty-four books correspond to Josephus's twenty-two, counted differently. (Josephus may have combined Judges with Ruth, and likewise Jeremiah with Lamentations.) But *4 Ezra* regards the "apocryphal" literature that is withheld from the masses as of higher value than the public scriptures.

THE NOTION OF A CANON

What then is the significance of the distinction of the 22/24 books? It is customary in scholarship to refer to them as the "canon" that emerged at the end of the first century CE. The word "canon," however, is borrowed from Christian theology, where it denoted both a definitive corpus of literature and a rule of faith.[16] The Greek word, derived from the Semitic *kaneh*, or "reed," means a measuring rod, and came to mean the standard or norm by which things are judged or evaluated. As early as the end of the first century CE, Clement of Rome referred to the "glorious and venerable rule [κανών] of our tradition."[17] The first use of the term to refer to a collection of authoritative scriptures is variously credited to Eusebius,[18] although he preferred other terms; or to Athanasius, in his *Festal Letter* of 367 CE, in which he refers to "canonized" writings.[19] "In these books

14. Mason, "Josephus and His Twenty-Two Book Canon," 121.
15. Mason, "Josephus and His Twenty-Two Book Canon," 126.
16. Ulrich, "Notion and Definition of Canon."
17. McDonald and Sanders, Introduction to *CanDb*, 12. Paul uses the word in 2 Cor 10:13, 15, 16, but the reference is not to a list of books.
18. Eusebius, *Hist. eccl.* 6.25.3. Eusebius more frequently refers to "covenanted books." See McDonald and Sanders, Introduction to *CanDb*, 12.
19. McDonald and Sanders, Introduction to *CanDb*, 12–13.

alone," wrote Athanasius, "is proclaimed the doctrine of godliness. Let no one add to or subtract from them."[20] Nonetheless, he also recognized seven books that were not "canonized" but could be used for the instruction of catechumens. These included several of the deuterocanonical books: the Wisdom of Solomon, Sirach, Judith, and Tobit, but he also placed Esther in this category, and he added the *Didache* and the *Shepherd of Hermas*.[21] (He still arrived at the number of twenty-two canonical books in the Old Testament by counting Ruth as a separate book.) He thus recognized a broader category of scripture, which included books that should be read (ἀναγιγνωσκόμενα), even if they were not "canonized." Only the canonized books were recognized as "divine" or "divinely inspired." These were recognized on the grounds that they were "handed down to our ancestors" by "those who were eyewitnesses from the beginning and assistants of the Word." In other words, Athanasius relied on apostolic tradition.

Athanasius formulated his canon in the context of conflict in Alexandria concerning what was authentic Christianity. He repeatedly denounces Arians, Melitians (followers of Melitius of Lycopolis), Jews, and simply heretics. Two groups are especially prominent in his thirty-ninth *Festal Letter*: "'teachers,' particularly Arians, who according to Athanasius invent their own ideas rather than submit to biblical truth, and Melitians, who according to Athanasius publish false apocryphal books to deceive unsuspecting Christians."[22]

As David Brakke has argued, "By excluding certain Christian writings from his canon, Athanasius hoped to reduce the influence of apocalyptic and visionary ideas that supported the Melitian claim to be the true church of the martyrs."[23] The delimitation of the canon was part of an ongoing dispute about authority in the church. It served to consolidate the authority of the bishop and the institutional church against that of charismatic teachers who formed study circles in Alexandria. The parties in this struggle have sometimes been dubbed "academic" and "institutional" Christianities.[24] In the words of Rowan Williams, "The 'Catholic' model of the church [came] to be allied with the idea of a monolithic social unit and the policy of religious coercion."[25] Athanasius wanted a limited canon in order to deprive teachers like Arius or the Melitians of a basis of authority. So he writes about the excluded books:

> Even if a useful word is found in them, it is still not good to trust them. . . . Let us command ourselves not to proclaim anything in them nor even to speak anything in them with those who want to be instructed, even if there is a good word in them, as I have said. For what do the spiritual scriptures lack that we should seek after these empty voices of unknown people?[26]

20. Athanasius, *Epistulae festales* (*Festival Letters*) 39.6.
21. Brakke, "Canon Formation," 397.
22. Brakke, "Canon Formation," 398.
23. Brakke, "Canon Formation," 399.
24. Williams, *Arius*, 82–91.
25. Williams, *Arius*, 87.
26. Athanasius, *Epistulae festales* (*Festival Letters*) 39.

A decade later, in his *Festal Letter* of 367, he specifically condemned books ascribed to Enoch, the *Testament of Moses*, and the *Martyrdom and Ascension of Isaiah; Enoch* was rejected because there were no scriptures before Moses, while the legitimate writings of Moses and Isaiah could be found in the canonical scriptures. To quote Brakke again, the attempt to establish a closed canon "was not merely a battle over book lists; it was even more a conflict among authoritative persons and the social institutions and practices that surrounded them."[27]

Athanasius did not have the last word on questions of canonicity. Augustine viewed the issue from a calmer perspective. He argued for a larger collection of scriptures, on the basis of the following criterion:

> Among the canonical scriptures he [the interpreter of scripture] will judge according to the following standard: to prefer those that are received by all the catholic churches to those which some do not receive. Again, among those which are not received by all, he will prefer such as are sanctioned by the greater number of churches and by those of greater authority to such as held by the smaller number and by those of less authority.[28]

He also appealed to a criterion of authenticity. The writings of *Enoch* could not be accepted because of the extreme antiquity of their supposed author.[29] In the case of the deuterocanonical books, he was at a loss to explain why they were not part of the Jewish canon.

> The reason for the omission, I confess, escapes me; except that I conceive that even those writers to whom the Holy Spirit unquestionably revealed matters which were rightly accorded religious authority may have written sometimes as men engaged in historical research, sometimes as prophets under divine inspiration. And the two kinds of writing were so distinct that it was decided that the first kind should be attributed to the writers themselves while the other kind was to be ascribed, as we might say, to God speaking through them.[30]

This suggestion does not carry conviction. Josephus had viewed the twenty-two "canonical" books primarily as historical records. Augustine's appeal to popular acceptance, however, was probably an important factor in the authority of scriptures from the beginning.

THE CONTEXT OF CANON FORMATION IN JUDAISM

Should we posit a similar conflict over authority behind the listing of twenty-two or twenty-four authoritative books in ancient Judaism?

---

27. Brakke, "Canon Formation," 417.
28. Augustine, *De doctrina christiana* (*Christian Instruction*) 2.8.12.
29. Wyrick, *Ascension of Authorship*, 354–55.
30. Augustine, *City of God* 18.38.

For long, this development was attributed to a supposed "council of Jamnia," but this idea has been thoroughly debunked.[31] The deliberations of the rabbis at Jamnia bore little resemblance to the later church councils, and the rabbinic passages that refer to them only concern the disputed status of a few books. The idea that the Torah, the Prophets, and the Writings make up a total of twenty-four books is well attested in rabbinic writings.[32] Michael Fishbane has argued that there was an "axial transformation" in Judaism that involved "making the movement from a culture based on direct divine revelations to one based on their study and reinterpretation."[33] So he writes in his study of rabbinic myth-making: "Prior to its canonization in ancient Judaism, the biblical corpus was an open collection of texts and traditions. . . . By contrast, the myths and mythopoesis found in the Midrash are based on a closed, canonical Scripture, whose every word and phrase can serve as the basis of new mythic inventions."[34] What was true of the rabbis was not necessarily true of all Jews everywhere,[35] but the rise of a rabbinic culture based on study and interpretation can hardly be disputed.

The roots of this transformation can certainly be found in the Second Temple period. Fishbane finds them already in Ezra, who is introduced as "a scribe skilled in the law of Moses" (Ezra 7:6) and is said to have "set his heart to study [lidrosh, לִדְרוֹשׁ] the law of the LORD, and to do it, and to teach the statutes and ordinances in Israel" (7:10).[36] Ezra, however, does not engage in explicit exegesis, even though exegetical activity may be implied. The Dead Sea Scrolls provide much clearer illustrations of a culture based on interpretation. The Torah was the well dug by the "penitents of Israel," according to CD 6.4, from which the Interpreter of the Law derived the statutes by which they should live. The command in Isaiah to go to the desert to prepare the way of the Lord is interpreted in 1QS 8.15 as referring to "the study [midrash, מִדְרָשׁ] of the Torah, which he commanded through the hand of Moses." Moreover, the Scrolls show that concern for the correct interpretation of the Torah was not just a preoccupation of this sect. The publication of 4QMMT made clear that the basic reason why this sect separated from the rest of Judaism was the conflict of interpretations, especially with the Pharisees, that raged in the Hasmonean era (and not the Hasmonean usurpation of the high priesthood, as earlier scholarship had supposed).[37] This should have already been clear from the Damascus Document, which specifies some of the issues in dispute: "But with those who remained steadfast in God's precepts, with those who were left from among them, God established his covenant with Israel forever, revealing to them hidden matters

31. Lewis, "Jamnia Revisited."
32. Leiman, Canonization of Hebrew Scripture, 51–56.
33. Fishbane, "From Scribalism to Rabbinism," 440.
34. Fishbane, Biblical Myth, 25–26.
35. See Najman, "Vitality of Scripture," 501–2, critiquing Fishbane.
36. Fishbane, "From Scribalism to Rabbinism," 441.
37. J. Collins, Beyond the Qumran Community, 88–121.

in which all Israel had gone astray: his holy Sabbaths and his glorious feasts, his just stipulations and his truthful paths and the wishes of his will which a man must do in order to live by them" (CD 3.12–16). The sectarians claimed new revelation, but the subject of the revelation was the interpretation of the Torah. In 4QMMT, when they appealed to the ruler of Israel, probably the high priest, the appeal was that he study the books of Moses and the Prophets and David, and appreciate that the interpretations proposed by the sectarians were correct.

But was there sectarian disagreement also on the extent of authoritative scripture? A reasonable case can be made that the Essenes, or the sectarian movement known from the Dead Sea Scrolls, regarded the books of *Enoch* and *Jubilees* as authoritative: *Jubilees* is cited in the *Damascus Document*, and the books of *Enoch* were preserved in multiple copies. Yet in 4QMMT the appeal to the high priest is based on the Torah of Moses, the Prophets, and David, which were apparently the scriptures recognized by all Judeans. The evidence of MMT must be qualified, however, in two respects. First, James VanderKam has argued that "we cannot be sure about the identification of Torah when it appears in a Qumran text as a designation of a body of literature."[38] Such books as the *Temple Scroll*, *Jubilees*, and *Reworked Pentateuch* may well have fallen under the rubric of Torah. Likewise, a host of previously unknown writings found at Qumran could have been regarded as prophecy. Also, 4QMMT does not cite any of these writings in its appeal. But a second consideration requires that we consider the purpose of 4QMMT: it was intended to be a conciliatory document, designed to influence the high priest. That purpose would not have been served by appealing to scriptures that he did not recognize. The authority of scriptures that were accepted by the Essenes may still have been an issue in sectarian disputes, and the Pharisees, or the rabbis after them, may have refused to recognize scriptures that were peculiar to their sectarian rivals.

We do not know who first decided that only twenty-two (or twenty-four) books should be properly accredited. Josephus states that this is a matter of agreement in the early 90s of the first century. If we dispense with the postulate of a Council of Jamnia, as we must, then it is likely that this position was held by at least one party before 70 CE. Sid Leiman suggested "that the Hagiographa was canonized and closed under the aegis of Judah Maccabee shortly after the death of Antiochus IV (164/163 BCE)."[39] He based his argument on the statement in 2 Macc 2:14–15 that Judas had collected "all the books that had been lost" during the war, and also on the inclusion of Daniel. Whether Judas Maccabee would have endorsed the book of Daniel, which is famously cool to the armed rebellion, may be disputed; in any case there is no evidence that the Hagiographa, or Writings, were closed before the end of the first century CE. Equally implausible, for some of the same reasons, is the suggestion of Philip Davies that "the fixing of a canonical list was almost certainly the achievement of the

---

38. VanderKam, "Questions of Canon," 108.
39. Leiman, *Canonization of Hebrew Scripture*, 30.

Hasmonean dynasty," at least if the canonical list is supposed to correspond to the twenty-two books listed by Josephus.[40] It is not implausible that the Hasmoneans acknowledged the authority of the Torah and the Prophets, and perhaps also the Psalms (David). One may infer from 4QMMT that the high priest was expected to recognize these as authoritative scriptures. But there is no evidence that the Writings had been limited to a fixed number before the turn of the era.

The most plausible candidates for the role of canonizers are the temple hierarchy or the Pharisees. Roger Beckwith argued at length that the canon was constituted by books that were laid up in the temple.[41] Temples usually had libraries, and the one in Jerusalem cannot have been an exception. Josephus reports that a copy of the Torah from the temple was taken to Rome and carried in the triumphal march.[42] He also claims that Titus gave him copies of holy books (*Life* 148), and these too are likely to have come from the temple. It is not implausible that a standard collection of authoritative writings was kept in the temple, but it is by no means assured that it included all of the twenty-two books to which Josephus referred. As we have seen, most references to authoritative writings in this period mention only the Torah and the Prophets, sometimes adding the Psalms. The Sadducees, who included much of the priestly class, allegedly recognized only the Torah.[43] The alternative view, that the twenty-two books were the canon of the Pharisees, was argued by Frank Moore Cross. Josephus, he argued, "echoes his own Pharisaic tradition and specifically the canonical doctrine of Hillel and his school."[44] Underlying this position is the assumption that the rabbis were the successors of the Pharisees and naturally would have adopted Pharisaic views. By the time Josephus wrote, the rabbis were the main spokesmen for Palestinian Judaism. Again, the argument is plausible but not entirely conclusive. It would seem, however, that the delimitation of the canon originated either with the Pharisees or with the temple authorities. Since the latter were presumably Sadducees, a Pharisaic origin is more likely. Even the apocalyptic author of *4 Ezra*, writing close to the end of the first century CE, had to acknowledge the separate status of the twenty-four books, even if he believed that the source of wisdom lay in other revelations.

Of the making of books there is no end, wrote Qoheleth (cf. Eccl 12:12), and the rabbis seem to have agreed. But the desire for limitation cannot have been the only consideration. The fact that the books of *Enoch* and *Jubilees* did not find a place in the rabbinic canon was surely based on sectarian considerations. In addition to the apocalyptic character of these books, they advocated a 364-day calendar, and this may have been enough to render them unacceptable to the temple authorities and also to the Pharisees. The omission of 1 Maccabees is probably also ideological, and strongly argues against the view that the Hasmo-

40. Davies, "Jewish Scriptural Canon," 50.
41. Beckwith, *Old Testament Canon*, 80–86.
42. Josephus, *J.W.* 7.5.5–7; §§148, 150, 162.
43. Josephus, *Ant.* 18.16; Beckwith, *Old Testament Canon*, 88.
44. Cross, "Stabilization of the Canon," 221.

neans were instrumental in assembling the canon. The Pharisees had a turbulent relationship with the Hasmonean dynasty and were fiercely critical of John Hyrcanus and Alexander Jannaeus. Even when they were given free rein by Salome Alexandra and Hyrcanus II, they were unlikely to canonize the praise of the dynasty. One could perhaps allow a less ideological explanation of the exclusion of the books of Maccabees by arguing, in Augustinian fashion, that they were historical accounts rather than religious instruction, but by that criterion several of the canonical books would also be called into question. Moreover, 2 Maccabees, at least, has a very clear theological dimension. In that case, however, the narrative was composed in Greek, and so it would not have been considered for inclusion in the Hebrew canon. The same could be said of the Wisdom of Solomon, which would probably have seemed suspect to the rabbis because of its veneer of Hellenistic philosophy.

Of the apocryphal, or deuterocanonical, books, only Ben Sira was controversial among the rabbis. A tradition attributed to Rabbi Akiba claimed that "one who reads the outside books such as the books of Ben Sira and the books of Ben La'aga" has no share in the world to come.[45] According to midrash *Qoheleth Rabbah*, "Whoever brings into his house more than the twenty-four books introduces confusion into his house," and Ben Sira is mentioned as an example. Nonetheless, we read in *b. Sanhedrin* 100b: "R. Joseph said: Even though the rabbis withdrew the book of Ben Sira, we expound all the good passages contained in it."[46] The book is cited several times in the Talmud and the midrash.[47] Sid Leiman suggested that Ben Sira was regarded as "uninspired canonical literature,"[48] but that category is exceedingly problematic. Ben Sira may have been popular and regarded as good to read, at least in part, but it was not accorded the same status as the so-called canonical books. We might compare the attitude of Athanasius to the seven books, including Ben Sira, that were recommended for reading even though they were not canonical.

It does not appear, then, that the rabbis had any ideological quarrel with Ben Sira. It may be that his book was not canonized because it was transparently the work of a human author of a relatively late period. Daniel could be accepted because it was supposed to have been composed centuries earlier, at the time of the Babylonian exile. It is somewhat ironic that Ben Sira's candor about his authorship may have thwarted his desire to have his work accepted among the "other writings" that carried authority in Jewish tradition.

It is doubtful that the rabbis would have any ideological quarrel with Tobit, Judith, or Baruch, or with the Additions to Esther and Daniel. Some of them may not have been known widely enough by the mid to late first century CE, but they were all well enough known to be translated into Greek, and Tobit had

45. See *j. Sanhedrin* 28a; cf. *m. Sanhedrin* 10:1; Leiman, *Canonization of Hebrew Scripture*, 86–87.
46. Leiman, *Canonization of Hebrew Scripture*, 95.
47. Leiman, *Canonization of Hebrew Scripture*, 96–97.
48. Leiman, *Canonization of Hebrew Scripture*, 100.

circulated in both Hebrew and Aramaic. As John Barton has observed, "[Ulti-mately] all attempts to find a hermeneutical significance in the fact that certain books are 'in the canon,' . . . have turned out to be a wild goose chase."[49] Philip Davies has argued that "the Jewish scriptural canon is not a careful selection of ancient Hebrew literature but represents more or less all that there was."[50] The first part of that statement may well be true; the books that became canoni-cal were those traditionally accepted in circles that enjoyed authority after 70 (rather than the product of a systematic sifting of all extant literature). But they were certainly not "all that there was." They were only a small sampling of the books that circulated in the late Second Temple period.[51]

Whatever motivation lay behind the distinction of twenty-two or twenty-four books by Jewish religious authorities in the first century CE, it had the unfortu-nate consequence that other books were not preserved in Hebrew. Consequently, the presumed Hebrew originals of 1 Maccabees and Judith were lost, and even that of Ben Sira, and the Hebrew and Aramaic of Tobit have only been recovered in fragments. It has been claimed, by Shaye Cohen, that the rabbis of Jamnia brought an end to Jewish sectarianism.[52] But they did so at a price, by suppress-ing much of the variety, and even of the literature, that had flourished in the period before 70.

Why were the deuterocanonical books preserved by Christianity? If it is dif-ficult to explain why so many writings were not included in the rabbinic canon, it is no less difficult to understand why the deuterocanonical books, rather than others, were accepted by Catholic Christianity. We must emphasize that the deuterocanonicals do not constitute a coherent corpus. They include books of different genres that originated in different times and places. Moreover, the list of books that were accepted, or excluded, varied down to the time of Augustine. At no point were these the only noncanonical books of Jewish origin that Chris-tians read for profit or pleasure. Most of the Jewish Pseudepigrapha have come down to us in translation through Christian churches. The designation of the deuterocanonical books as "canonical" is partly a matter of popularity and partly an assertion of ecclesial control. It is no doubt significant that no apocalyptic books were included, although, as we have seen, the omission of 2 Esdras may have been due to confusion on the part of the Tridentine fathers. The Christian churches were far enough removed from the conflicts of the Hasmonean era to appreciate the historical value of the books of Maccabees. The Wisdom of Solo-mon was congenial to the Christian theologians of Alexandria.

The books eventually accepted as deuterocanonical were books that did not give offense to Christians, although there were many more books of which that

49. Barton, *Oracles of God* (1986 edition), 82.

50. Davies, "Jewish Scriptural Canon," 48.

51. Davies adds, in the next sentence, "This is not to say that no other literary works existed"; but then what does it mean to say that the canonical books were "more or less all that there was"? Davies, "Jewish Scriptural Canon," 48.

52. Cohen, "Significance of Yavneh," 27–53.

could be said. It is tempting to suppose that they also reflected "common Judaism," rather than any definite sect, and won broad acceptance in Judaism before they were taken over by Christians, even if they were not accepted as canonical in Jewish tradition. This may be true of Ben Sira and Tobit, but it is too simple as a generalization. First Maccabees, at least, was a partisan book, and it was not accepted as authoritative by the rabbis. The Wisdom of Solomon represents a Jewish tradition enriched by Hellenistic philosophy that flourished in the Hellenistic Diaspora, but it was hardly representative of Palestinian Judaism.

Perhaps the main lesson to be learned from the existence of deuterocanonical literature as a category is that any canon is an artificial construct. There is no clear qualitative distinction between "canonical" and "noncanonical" literature, and the dividing line between the two categories has always been ragged. As John Barton put it, there has always been a penumbra of books about which opinions varied widely. Not all canonical books enjoy equal authority in practice, and there is a fuzzy edge between minor biblical books and influential apocrypha. It is in that gray area of books that are more or less authoritative, or authoritative for some Christians but not for others, that the deuterocanonical literature belongs.

Chapter 2

Beyond the Canon
The Recovery of the Pseudepigrapha

JOHN J. COLLINS

In the year 1773, a Scottish explorer named James Bruce brought back to Europe three Ethiopic manuscripts of a book of *Enoch*. He gave one to the king of France, gave one to the Bodleian Library at Oxford, and kept the third, which eventually found its way to the Bodleian Library.[1] The name of Enoch was well known, of course, from Genesis. According to Gen 4:17, Cain had a son named Enoch. The name appears again in Gen 5:18, where it refers to a son of Jared, in the seventh generation from Adam. This Enoch was father of Methuselah. He "walked with God [*Elohim*]" and then "he was not," for God took him (5:22, 24). The Epistle of Jude cites a prophecy of this *Enoch*, in the seventh generation from Adam. Greek fragments of a book of *Enoch* were preserved in the writings of George Syncellus, who wrote in the ninth century CE. The book of *Enoch* was accepted as canonical prophecy in the Ethiopian church, but it remained virtually unknown in the West.[2]

Nonetheless, there was no great rush to discover the content of the manuscripts Bruce brought back. Almost fifty years passed before an English translation was

---

1. J. Bruce, *Travels to Discover the Source of the Nile*, vol. 2, chap. 7.
2. See Nickelsburg, *1 Enoch 1*, 109.

published by Richard Laurence, under the title *The Book of Enoch, the prophet: an apocryphal production, supposed to have been lost for ages; but discovered at the close of the last century in Abyssinia; now first translated from an Ethiopic ms. in the Bodleian Library.*[3] Laurence also published the first edition of the Ethiopic in 1838.[4] The book was not greeted by any great uproar, but it laid the foundations of a new view of Judaism in the centuries before Christ.

Already in 1832, a German scholar named Friedrich Lücke signaled the significance of the new discovery when he published his commentary on the book of Revelation.[5] Lücke prefaced his commentary to Revelation with an introduction to "the entire apocalyptic literature," by which he meant the books of Daniel, *1 Enoch, 4 Ezra,* and the Jewish *Sibylline Oracles.* Daniel, of course, was well known since it is included in all the canons of Christian scripture, and its similarity to Revelation was clear. *Fourth Ezra,* which was preserved in Latin,[6] and the Greek *Sibylline Oracles* were also known. Only with the publication of *1 Enoch,* however, did it become clear that these were not isolated works but part of a distinctive genre, which Lücke called "apocalyptic." Over the course of the nineteenth century the corpus of apocalyptic writings was expanded by a series of discoveries in monastic libraries. The discoveries included apocalypses of Baruch in Syriac and Greek, an apocalypse of Abraham in Old Church Slavonic, an apocalypse of Isaiah in Ethiopic, and another book of *Enoch,* also in Old Church Slavonic. These works were all originally written either in a Semitic language, Hebrew or Aramaic, or in Greek. Most appeared to be Jewish in origin, although some had evidently been edited by Christians, to varying degrees. Most appeared to date from the centuries around the turn of the era, although some were of uncertain provenance. But taken together, they provided a substantial corpus of literature that was very different from the Hebrew Bible on the one hand, and the literature of the rabbis on the other. It seemed clear that these books could not actually have been written by the people whose names they bore, many of whom, like Enoch and Abraham, were supposed to have lived in hoary antiquity. Accordingly, they became known as "The Pseudepigrapha," which means "writings falsely ascribed."[7] But in view of the number of such compositions, it was also apparent that pseudepigraphy, the attribution of books to people who did not actually write them, was not just forgery but must have been a literary convention.

It may be well to pause here to recall what was known of ancient Judaism before this corpus came to light. According to Jewish tradition, prophecy had ceased in Judah in the Persian period (roughly the 5th and 4th centuries BCE). The books of the Writings, such as Psalms and Proverbs, are often hard to date,

3. Laurence, *Book of Enoch.*
4. Laurence, *Libri Enoch prophetae versio aethiopica.*
5. Lücke, *Versuch einer vollständigen Einleitung.*
6. Hamilton, *Apocryphal Apocalypse.*
7. On the origin of the category, see Reed, "Modern Invention of 'Old Testament Pseudepigrapha.'"

or to tell when they were written. In the rare case where a book of the Writings refers to a historical setting, such as the book of Esther, that setting is also in the Persian period. Fortunately, a larger collection of writings was preserved in the Greek Bible. The additional books were regarded as Apocrypha (books hidden away) by the Reformers, but most of them were preserved as canonical in the Catholic Church.[8] These included the books of Maccabees, which shed important historical light on the Hellenistic period; the Wisdom book of Ben Sira, which could be dated to the second century BCE; and some works that showed the influence of Greek philosophy and were evidently written in Greek, such as the Wisdom of Solomon and *4 Maccabees*. Much light was also shed on the period around the turn of the era by the historical writings of Josephus and by the writings of Philo, a Jewish philosopher who lived in Alexandria in the time of Christ. Very little of this literature had survived in Hebrew. Fragments of Ben Sira would eventually come to light at the end of the nineteenth century, but before that the text was mainly known from its Greek, Syriac, and Latin translations, plus a few quotations in rabbinic writings. Beyond that, knowledge of ancient Judaism depended on the Mishnah, Talmud, and midrash, which were all compiled centuries later (beginning with the Mishnah about 200 CE), although they might preserve earlier traditions that had been handed down orally.

The worldview of this literature was remarkably consistent. It was shaped by the books of Deuteronomy and Leviticus. At its core was the covenant between God and Israel, made through Moses on Mount Sinai. If Israel kept the law, the people would prosper and live long in the land. If not, the curses of the covenant would take effect. There were, to be sure, variations in the ways in which the covenant was understood. By the turn of the era, we increasingly find references to the world to come, and so the ideal of long life in the land became qualified. In some cases, understanding of the law was inflected through Greek philosophy. Some strands of Judaism insisted on stricter observance of the commandments than did others. Nonetheless, the emphasis on the Torah as the core of Judaism was pervasive.[9] The focus was this-worldly. As Deuteronomy put it:

> Surely, this commandment that I am commanding you today is not too hard for you, nor is it too far away. It is not in heaven, that you should say, "Who will go up to heaven for us, and get it for us so that we may hear it and observe it?" . . . No, the word is very near to you; it is in your mouth and in your heart for you to observe. (Deut 30:11–14)

The world disclosed by *1 Enoch* and the corpus of related writings was very different. The first section of *1 Enoch* is the Book of the Watchers (*1 En.* 1–36).[10] The opening scene includes the passage cited loosely in the Epistle of Jude:

---

8. See my essay: J. Collins, "Penumbra of the Canon."
9. See my book: J. Collins, *Invention of Judaism.*
10. Nickelsburg, *1 Enoch 1*, 129–332; J. Collins, *Apocalyptic Imagination*, 58–75.

> The Great Holy One will come forth from his dwelling, and the eternal God will tread from thence upon Mount Sinai. He will appear with his army; he will appear with his mighty host from the heaven of heavens. All the watchers will fear and quake, . . . and all the ends of the earth will be shaken. (1:4–5)

Here Sinai is not the mountain of the law, but the mountain of theophany, as it had been in the earliest biblical traditions.

The theophany scene in *1 Enoch* 1 is similar to many such scenes in the Bible (Deut 33:2; Judg 5:4–5; etc.) where the Lord is associated with a mountain to the south of Israel, except that here it does not recall a manifestation of God in the past but hopes for one in the future. What follows in the Book of the Watchers is less familiar. In Gen 6, we are told that "the sons of God" saw that the daughters of men were fair and took wives for themselves. This led to the existence of Nephilim, legendary giants. In Genesis, the union of divine (or semi-divine) beings with human women explains an odd tradition, that there were giants on earth in days of old. In *1 Enoch*, it has far more serious implications. The "sons of God" are here called watchers, a term known from the book of Daniel, where the angel who appears to Nebuchadnezzar in his dream is called "a watcher, a holy one" (Dan 4:13). When they come down and "go in" to the women, they teach them sorcery and charms, and they reveal to the women the cutting of roots and plants. It is possible to distinguish different strands in the revelations of the watchers. One leader, Shemihazah, teaches sorcery and spells. Another, Asael, "taught men to make swords of iron and weapons and shields and breastplates and every instrument of war," and how to work metals. He also taught women the art of makeup and seduction. Other watchers taught human beings the signs of the stars and heavenly bodies. The upshot, we are told, was much godlessness on earth. At this point the archangels intervene and ask God to act. God warns Noah to hide himself because a deluge is about to come on earth. Before that, Asael is bound hand and foot and cast into the darkness, while Shemihazah and the others who mated with human women are bound under the earth until the day of judgment, when they will be led away to a fiery abyss. Then the earth is cleansed by the flood.

Thus far the story of the watchers might be viewed as an expansion of the biblical story. In Genesis, the story of the flood comes shortly after the episode of the sons of God, but the two are not explicitly connected. The story of the watchers fills in a gap in the biblical account by linking those two and depicting the action of the watchers as grave sin. But the Book of the Watchers does not end there. The watchers ask Enoch to intercede for them. In Genesis, Enoch appears before the episode of the "sons of God" (Gen 6), and he was no longer alive when Noah was born. According to Genesis, Enoch had "walked with God," the Hebrew word *Elohim*, which is grammatically plural. In *1 Enoch*, this is taken to mean that "his works were with the watchers, and with the holy ones were his days" (12:2); in other words, he consorted with angels.[11]

---

11. VanderKam, *An Apocalyptic Tradition*, 31.

Enoch now takes the petition of the watchers and ascends to heaven with it. Biblical prophets were traditionally supposed to have stood in "the council of the LORD" (Jer 23:18), and they presumably ascended to heaven to do so. But nowhere in the Hebrew Bible do we find a description of an ascent, except in the case of Elijah, who was taken up in a whirlwind. But Elijah did not return (not yet, at any rate). The ascent of Enoch in the Book of the Watchers is the oldest account we have in Jewish tradition of a trip to heaven, though we are not told that he comes back.[12] He is taken up on the clouds, and he gives an extended description of the heavenly palace. There he sees "a lofty throne, and its appearance was like ice, and its wheels were like the shining sun, . . . and from beneath the throne issued rivers of flaming fire" (*1 En.* 14:18). The great Glory sat on the throne. Hs apparel was whiter than snow, and fire encircled him. "Ten thousand times ten thousand stood before him," but he needed no counselor (*1 En.* 14:22).

Like the prophets of old, Enoch is given a commission and entrusted with a message to take back to the watchers (*1 En.* 15:2–16:4). He is told to tell them: you should petition on behalf of men, not men on behalf of you. God reminds the watchers that they had been holy ones and spirits, living forever. As such they had no need of wives since they did not need to procreate. But they lusted after human women and defiled themselves. Their offspring would now become evil spirits on the earth. Enoch, then, is the opposite of the watchers. They were heavenly beings who gave up heaven for sex. Enoch typifies the righteous human being, who gives up earth for heaven, to consort with the angels. Enoch evidently does not subscribe to the Deuteronomic ideal of long life in the land, to see one's children and one's children's children.

The Book of the Watchers does not say that Enoch returned to earth after his divine audience. Rather, he is given a tour of the ends of the earth.[13] In the course of his travels, he sees many cosmic mysteries, such as the storehouses of the winds and the foundations of the earth. Much of what he sees concerns the provisions already made for a final judgment. He sees a fiery chasm where the fallen angels will be punished. He sees the chambers where the souls of the dead await the judgment. He sees a place in the center of the earth where God will sit when he comes to judge the world. He even sees the garden of Eden, where Adam and Eve had been. The lesson to be learned from his travel is that everything is under control, although this may not be apparent on earth. Deuteronomy 30:12 says that human beings do not need to go up to heaven and come down. The whole presupposition of the book of *Enoch* is that one *does* need to go up to heaven to find out what is really going on, or at least one needs to have access to instruction by someone who has had that experience.

Even though Adam and Eve are mentioned in the course of Enoch's travels, and their sin is acknowledged, they are not the ones responsible for the spread of

---

12. See my essay: J. Collins, "Journeys to the World Beyond in Ancient Judaism."
13. Bautch, *Study of the Geography of 1 Enoch 17–19.*

evil on earth.[14] That is the result of the descent of the watchers. The world is out of joint because of the activity of supernatural beings, whether the watchers or their demonic descendants, forces beyond human control. Equally, the world can only be set right by divine, or angelic, intervention. Repentance and fidelity to the covenant are not enough. In fact, the covenant is conspicuously absent from the Enochic writings (except for a passing reference in *1 En.* 93:6, in a section of *1 Enoch* called The Apocalypse of Weeks).[15] Again, the view of the world is in sharp contrast to that of Deuteronomy and the mainline Jewish tradition.

AFFINITY WITH DANIEL

As Lücke already recognized in 1832, the biblical books with which *Enoch* has most in common are Daniel and Revelation.[16] In the case of Daniel, we have already noted the reference to holy ones and watchers. Daniel is the only book in the Hebrew Bible that mentions angels by name (Gabriel and Michael). The Book of the Watchers knows the four archangels: Michael, Raphael, Gabriel, and Sariel or Uriel. Most striking is the similarity between the throne scenes in the Book of the Watchers and in Dan 7. In Daniel, too, the divine figure on the throne has clothing white as snow, his throne is fiery flames, and he is surrounded by tens of thousands. The heavenly host is called the holy ones of the Most High. At least in this case, the two books seem to share a common tradition, one that is also attested in another noncanonical composition, *The Book of Giants*, which is found among the Dead Sea Scrolls.[17]

But there is also a more fundamental resemblance. In Dan 7, Daniel has a dream in which he sees the four winds of heaven stirring up the great sea, and four great beasts coming up out of it. The imagery here is drawn from ancient Near Eastern mythology, in which a god imposes order on the world by killing a sea monster.[18] The fullest version of this myth is the Babylonian creation story, *Enuma Elish*, in which the god Marduk does battle with the monster Tiamat. In the Canaanite tradition, known to us from texts found at Ugarit in 1929, the god Baal does battle with Yamm, the Sea personified. No such story is told in the Bible, but such a story was evidently known in Israel, because we find allusions to it in poetic texts.[19] In Job 26:12 we read that God "by his power . . . stilled

14. See Stuckenbruck, "Origins of Evil in Jewish Apocalyptic Tradition."

15. Nickelsburg, *1 Enoch 1*, 50–56; Collins, *Invention of Judaism*, 70–76.

16. On the relation between *1 Enoch* and Revelation, see Stuckenbruck with Mathews, "Question of Influence."

17. Stuckenbruck, "Daniel and the Early Enoch Traditions," esp. 382–84; Stokes, "Throne Visions of Daniel 7"; Trotter, "Tradition of the Throne Vision."

18. For full discussion see my essay: J. Collins, "Stirring Up the Great Sea: The Religio-Historical Background of Daniel 7," in *Seers, Sibyls and Sages*, 139–55; and my commentary in *Daniel*, 280–94. The ancient myths' relevance to Dan 7 has been challenged by Newsom in her works: *Daniel*, 217–20; and "Reuse of Ugaritic Mythology." I respond to Newsom's critique in my essay "Canaanite Myth and Daniel 7."

19. See the classic treatment by Day, *God's Conflict with the Dragon and the Sea*.

the Sea; by his understanding he struck down Rahab." Again, in Isa 51:9–11, the prophet calls on the arm of the Lord to awake, as in days of old: "Was it not you who cut Rahab in pieces, who pierced the dragon?" Israel evidently had its own version of the combat myth, and Rahab was a name for the dragon. It was not necessarily the only name. Isaiah 27:1 projects the combat into the future: "On that day the LORD with his cruel and great and strong sword will punish Leviathan the fleeing serpent, Leviathan the twisting serpent, and he will kill the dragon that is in the sea." A name much like Leviathan, Lotan, appears in the Ugaritic texts.

The myth of the sea monsters in Daniel is different from the myth of the fallen angels in *Enoch*, but they share the idea that the state of the world is due to forces beyond human control. An angel tells Daniel that the four great beasts are kings who will arise on the earth, but that is evidently not the whole story. As beasts rising from the sea, they are embodiments of supernatural power. Again, they cannot be overcome by merely human means. In Dan 7 they are destroyed in a heavenly trial scene, presided over by the Ancient of Days, whose robes are white as snow. Then the kingdom, or sovereignty on earth, is given to "one like a son of man," who comes with the clouds of heaven. In the Hebrew Bible, YHWH the God of Israel is described as riding the clouds almost seventy times. In the older Canaanite myths from Ugarit, the "rider of the clouds" is Baal. In Daniel, it is most probably the archangel Michael. Daniel 10–12 tells of conflict between the angelic "princes" of Persia and Greece and Michael, prince of Israel. In the end, it is Michael who arises in victory.[20]

Both Daniel and *Enoch* evidently draw on many traditions that are not explicit in the Bible itself. We have very little literature from ancient Israel, so it should not surprise us that there was more traditional lore in circulation. Both also presuppose a view of the world where supernatural forces play an important role, whether these are conceptualized as fallen angels or as beasts rising from the sea. Both look to angelic forces to set things right on earth. Neither operates within the context of the traditional covenant. Daniel makes one brief reference to the covenant in chapter 11, where he refers to those who violate it. But the course of history is not determined by Israel's fidelity to the covenant. Also, the reward of the just is not to live long in the land, as it had been in Deuteronomy. Daniel is the only text in the Hebrew Bible that speaks unambiguously about the resurrection of the dead. The destiny of the righteous teachers, who are the heroes of the book, is everlasting life, to be like the stars forever (Dan 12:3).[21] The later chapters of *1 Enoch* also speak of immortality with the stars, and they make explicit that this means fellowship with the angels: "You will shine like the luminaries of heaven, . . . and the portals of heaven will be opened to you, . . . for you will be companions to the host of heaven" (*1 En.* 104:2–6).[22]

---

20. J. Collins, *Daniel*, 304–10.
21. J. Collins, *Daniel*, 393–94.
22. Nickelsburg, *Resurrection, Immortality*, 141–62; Stuckenbruck, *1 Enoch 91–108*, 569.

THE SIMILITUDES OF ENOCH

The affinities between Daniel and the book of *Enoch* appear most clearly in the second section of *1 Enoch*, known as the Similitudes (chaps. 37–71).[23] The Similitudes are visions of Enoch in the heavenly realm. In one of them

> I saw one who had a head of days, and his head was like white wool. And with him was another, whose face was like the appearance of a man, and his face was full of graciousness like one of the holy angels. (46:1)

The latter figure is subsequently referred to as "that Son of Man":

> This is the Son of man who has righteousness, and righteousness dwells with him. And all the treasuries of what is hidden he will reveal, for the Lord of Spirits has chosen him. (46:3)

This "Son of Man" is evidently meant to be the same figure as the one like a son of man in Daniel 7. The Gospels often speak of Jesus as "the Son of Man," who will come on the clouds of heaven. Here in the Similitudes we have the only other text from antiquity that uses this expression for a figure who is, in effect, a savior figure. We are told that

> he will raise the kings and the mighty from their couches, and the strong from their thrones. . . . He will overturn the kings from their thrones and their kingdoms, because they do not exalt him or praise him, or humbly acknowledge whence the kingdom was given to them. (*1 En.* 46:4)

His name was named (i.e., he was created) before the world was made, but he was hidden. God revealed him to the righteous. Those who believe in him will be saved. He is the Anointed One, or Messiah (*1 En.* 52:4), even though he is never said to appear on earth. He will sit on the throne of glory at the judgment (62:2). Those who believe in him will be saved and will share his lot in eternal life (71:16).

The Similitudes of *Enoch* are extant only in Ethiopic. The Ethiopian church has always assumed that "that Son of Man" is Jesus. Some modern scholars have also suspected that the text is Christian.[24] But it would be quite extraordinary for a Christian text not to make the identification with Jesus explicit. Instead, *1 Enoch* 71:14 appears to identify Enoch with the Son of Man.[25] When Enoch ascends to heaven at the end of his life, he is greeted by an angel who tells him: "You are the [a] Son of Man that was born for righteousness, and righteousness dwells with you." The passage seems to be an addition to

---

23. The fullest commentary is that of Nickelsburg and VanderKam, *1 Enoch 2*, 2–332.
24. Most notably Milik, *Books of Enoch*, 89–98.
25. This passage is extremely controversial. See the essays in *Enoch and the Messiah Son of Man*, ed. Boccaccini.

the Similitudes.[26] Perhaps it was meant to counter the Christian identification of the Son of Man as Jesus. Possibly the passage means that Enoch is *a* son of man who has righteousness, like *the* Son of Man, but not necessarily identical with him. It is quite inconceivable, however, that a passage seeming to identify the Son of Man with Enoch could have been written by a Christian. The Similitudes is certainly a Jewish work, from the first century CE.

The Similitudes does not refer to the law of Moses at all. One might argue that it would be anachronistic to do so; after all, Enoch supposedly lived long before Moses. But other Jewish texts of the period imply that the Torah was observed already by the patriarchs. (The book of *Jubilees* is a good example.) The Similitudes is exceptional in placing its emphasis on faith in a heavenly savior rather than on observance of the law. It shows why the Pseudepigrapha are of great interest to Christians and are often regarded as problematic by traditional Jews.

4 EZRA

Not all Pseudepigrapha or apocalypses pay as little attention to the law of Moses and the covenant as does the Enoch literature. The apocalypses *4 Ezra* and *2 Baruch*, written after the destruction of Jerusalem in 70 CE, are essentially meditations on the apparent failure of the covenant.[27] (They are set in the aftermath of the first destruction of Jerusalem by the Babylonians, which serves as an allegory for the destruction by Rome.)[28] *Fourth Ezra* is especially poignant. The first half of the book is taken up with a dialogue between Ezra and the angel Uriel. Ezra admits that Israel sinned, but he asks, pointedly, "Are the deeds of those who inhabit Babylon any better? Is that why it has gained dominion over Zion?" (3:28). Or again, "Why have you given over the one to the many, and dishonored the one root beyond the others, and scattered your only one among the man? And those who opposed your Torah have trodden down those who believed in your covenant" (5:28–29). Moreover, like all humanity, Israel is afflicted with an "evil heart," because of the sin of Adam, and is incapable of keeping the covenant. "O Adam, what have you done? For though it was you who sinned, the fall was not yours alone, but ours also who are your descendants" (7:48). Note that Ezra, unlike Enoch, does not attribute the state of the world to demonic forces, but it is still beyond human control.[29]

The angel struggles to provide a satisfactory answer. Eventually Ezra is overwhelmed by visions of the deliverance that is to come.[30] One of these, in chapter 13, describes a man who ascends from the sea on a cloud and takes his stand on

---

26. See J. Collins, *Apocalyptic Imagination*, 232–36.
27. M. Stone and Henze, *4 Ezra and 2 Baruch*.
28. Najman, *Losing the Temple*; Daschke, *City of Ruins*, 103–39 (on *4 Ezra*), 141–74 (on *2 Baruch*).
29. See my essay "Enoch and Ezra," in *Apocalypse, Prophecy and Pseudepigraphy*, 235–50.
30. See esp. M. Stone, *Fourth Ezra*; Hogan, *Theologies in Conflict in 4 Ezra*.

Mount Zion to do battle with the nations. This figure is clearly an adaptation of Daniel's "one like a son of man," but he is also identified with the Davidic messiah.

The most interesting part of *4 Ezra*, however, comes in the conclusion. Ezra complains to God that "thy law has been burned and so no one knows the things which have been done or will be done by thee" (14:21). He asks God to inspire him to write "the things that were written in the Law." He is then instructed to take five scribes, and he is given a fiery liquid to drink. Then he pours forth wisdom for forty days, and the scribes write it down, for forty days. In all ninety-four books are written. Ezra is told:

> Make public the twenty-four books that you wrote first and let the worthy and the unworthy read them, but keep the seventy that were written last, in order to give them to the wise among your people. For in them is the spring of understanding, the fountain of wisdom and the river of understanding. (14:45–47)

The twenty-four books that were written first are generally recognized as those that make up the canon of the Hebrew Bible. Josephus, roughly contemporary with *4 Ezra*, gives the number as twenty-two, but he was probably just counting the books differently.[31] What is striking in *4 Ezra*, however, is that the other seventy books are the ones that contain the fountain of wisdom. These books are apocrypha, in the sense that they are hidden away and not given to the public at large. The hiding may be a literary fiction. If these books are what we call the Pseudepigrapha, as seems likely, then most of them were not yet written in the time of Ezra. What is clear, however, is that they have even higher status than the canonical Torah. Indeed, it may well be argued that, from the perspective of *4 Ezra*, these additional books *are* Torah.[32] *Fourth Ezra* affirms the Torah as a guide to life, but the Torah is no longer just the law of Moses, or even the Hebrew Bible. The canonical revelation needs to be supplemented with the higher revelation found in the apocalyptic pseudepigrapha.

THE IMPORTANCE OF THE PSEUDEPIGRAPHA

Whatever we now think of the wisdom contained in the Pseudepigrapha, there is no doubt whatever about their importance as a source for Jewish beliefs and ideas around the turn of the era, or for the world of Jesus and his disciples.[33] This is a world populated by angels and demons, where human beings can ascend to the heavens to gain perspective on life on earth, learning where life on earth is but a prelude to everlasting reward and punishment in the hereafter. In light of this literature, we can make sense of the stories of exorcism in the Gospels. Most

31. Josephus, *Ag. Ap.* 1.39.
32. Hogan, "Meanings of *tôrah* in 4 Ezra."
33. Henze, *Mind the Gap*.

crucially, we can understand why the followers of Jesus believed, after his death, that he would come again on the clouds of heaven, as the Son of Man foretold in the book of Daniel. As Paul makes clear in 1 Cor 15, the belief that Jesus rose from the dead was only possible in the context of an apocalyptic worldview, where resurrection from the dead was to be expected. "If there is no resurrection of the dead, then Christ has not been raised" (1 Cor 15:13). A great German New Testament scholar, Ernst Käsemann, said that "apocalyptic was the mother of Christian theology."[34] Christianity did not arise, as some Jewish sects did, because of disputes about the interpretation of the law. Rather, it arose because the followers of Jesus believed they had received a new revelation that contained the promise of resurrection and salvation in a world beyond.

It is not surprising, then, that the Pseudepigrapha were preserved by Christians, who translated them into several languages. They were not, however, preserved by the rabbis. We can only guess as to why this was. As I have emphasized in this essay, many of the Pseudepigrapha expressed apocalyptic hopes of divine deliverance. Whether these writings contributed to the Jewish revolts against Rome in 66 and 132 CE is a matter of controversy. It is reasonable to suppose, however, that people came to regard these hopes as delusory. According to rabbinic tradition, the great rabbi Akiba had hailed Simon bar Kosiba, the leader of the revolt in 132 CE, as the messiah, the fulfillment of the prophecy of Balaam's oracle, "A star shall come out of Jacob" (Num 24:17). Accordingly, bar Kosiba became known as bar Kochba, son of the star. Another rabbi, however, greeted this pronouncement with skepticism: "Akiba, grass will grow between your cheeks and he still will not have come."[35] Hopes of deliverance were too often disappointed. It may also be that the rabbis rejected the apocalypses precisely because they were popular with the Christians. The apocalyptic worldview was what gave rise to the Christian movement. The rabbis reacted by concentrating their focus on the law and the Hebrew scriptures. Perhaps the simplest explanation is that the rabbis who reshaped Judaism after the failure of the revolts were primarily descendants of the Pharisees, who had always been more disposed to legal interpretations than to visionary experience. In any case, the Pseudepigrapha became a casualty of the parting of the ways between early Christianity and rabbinic Judaism.

THE MODERN CONTROVERSY

In the wake of the rediscovery of the Pseudepigrapha, a great German scholar, Wilhelm Bousset, published a reconstruction of Jewish religion around the time of Christ that was largely based on this literature.[36] Bousset was especially fascinated by the *Enoch* literature, which he found fantastic, bizarre, and foreign to

---

34. Käsemann, "Beginnings of Christian Theology," 40.
35. *J. Ta'anit* 68d; Vermès, *Jesus the Jew*, 134.
36. Bousset, *Religion des Judentums.*

the biblical tradition. His work was greeted by a storm of protest. Jewish critics, especially, objected to the prominence accorded to this material and to the lack of a systematic treatment of the "normative Judaism" of the rabbis. A Jewish scholar named Felix Perles claimed that Bousset had missed "the center of Jewish religion," which he took to be the focus on observance of the law.[37] Bousset, he claimed, reduced Judaism to a *"praeparatio evangelica"* by highlighting the aspects of Judaism that were taken up in Christianity. Bousset responded that we must distinguish between the "religion of the scribes," which became dominant after 70 CE, and the popular piety of the earlier period. He argued that Perles had failed to understand the richer and more diverse life of Jewish popular religion before the destruction of Jerusalem.[38] Few scholars would now argue that the Pseudepigrapha preserve the popular religion, although they may reflect aspects of it. They are, after all, literary works, and they themselves are the work of scribes. But Bousset had a valid point about the richness and variety of Judaism before the destruction of the temple, much of which was lost in the wake of the destruction.

The debate about the significance of the Pseudepigrapha, however, was not settled a hundred years ago. George Foot Moore, a Harvard professor and a Christian, published a classic study of Judaism in 1927–30 that remained authoritative for half a century.[39] Moore took the side of Perles and the critics of Bousset. The Pseudepigrapha were of peripheral importance because they were rejected by mainline Jewish tradition.[40] Other scholars pointed out, against Moore, that the so-called mainline Jewish tradition found in the rabbinic writings was formulated several centuries after the destruction of Jerusalem, and they argued that Moore's view of Judaism was theological rather than historical.[41] As in the history of Christianity, the views that eventually became authoritative in Late Antiquity and in the Middle Ages were not fully formed already in the time of Christ. This debate continues, in modified form, down to the present.

There is also a long-standing debate as to whether, or how far, the Pseudepigrapha should be accepted as an authentic representation of Judaism at all. All these texts were preserved by Christians rather than by Jews. Some scholars argue, reasonably enough, that they should first be understood in the contexts in which they were preserved.[42] At the same time, it is incontrovertible that many of these writings were originally composed in a Jewish context. That issue was settled decisively by the discovery of the Dead Sea Scrolls, which include substantial fragments of *1 Enoch* in Aramaic and Hebrew fragments of the book of *Jubilees*, another major text that is preserved in full only in Ethiopic. The Dead Sea Scrolls also include a range of texts that are similar in kind to the Pseudepig-

---

37. Perles, *Bousset's "Religion des Judentums."*
38. Bousset, *Volksfrömmigkeit und Schriftgelehrtentum.*
39. Moore, *Judaism in the First Centuries.*
40. Moore, "Christian Writers on Judaism."
41. F. Porter, Review of Moore, *Judaism in the First Centuries.*
42. So esp. Kraft, "Pseudepigrapha in Christianity"; Kraft, "Pseudepigrapha in Christianity Revisited."

rapha; some of them are probably Pseudepigrapha themselves, in the sense that they were ascribed to ancient figures who did not actually write them. (This issue is clouded by the fragmentary state of the Dead Sea Scrolls.) There can no longer be any doubt that many writings of the kind we now have in the Pseudepigrapha were produced in Judea, in Hebrew and Aramaic, during the centuries before the destruction of Jerusalem.

It remains true that the origin of some of the pseudepigraphic books is open to question.[43] Christians as well as Jews could compose books in the names of Old Testament figures. It is not unusual to find one or two clearly Christian statements in works that otherwise appear to be Jewish. These statements were presumably inserted by scribes to make the works more suitable for Christian devotional use. In some cases, the Christian elements are extensive. The more extensive the Christian elements, the more difficult it becomes to reconstruct an underlying Jewish work. The most controversial work in this regard is the *Testaments of the Twelve Patriarchs*, which is preserved only in Greek, although some related material is found in Aramaic in the Dead Sea Scrolls. No one doubts that many Jewish traditions are preserved in the *Testaments*, but in recent years scholars have come to accept the work in its present form as Christian.[44]

WHAT IS AT STAKE? WHY DOES IT MATTER?

What is at stake in these debates about the origin of the Pseudepigrapha? It seems to me that the issues are significant, both for Jews and for Christians.

On the Jewish side, at issue is the uniformity of Judaism. For many Jews, both observant and nonobservant, Judaism is by definition the religion based on the law of Moses, and many Christians share that assumption. Some scholars are reluctant to accept as Jewish any works that are not concerned with the distinctive marks of Jewish particularism.[45] If we accept the Pseudepigrapha as evidence for Judaism in the pre-Christian period, it was a good deal more varied than that. As I have already asserted, there can really be no doubt that some of the Pseudepigrapha, most notably *1 Enoch*, are Jewish works, written well before the rise of Christianity, and the law of Moses is not central to *1 Enoch*. This does not necessarily mean that all Pseudepigrapha attributed to Old Testament characters are Jewish, but it does mean that there are enough authentic Jewish works in the Pseudepigrapha to show that Judaism was a variegated religion in the period before 70 CE.

On the Christian side, the issue is the relation of Christianity to Judaism. People tend to view this in either of two ways. Some scholars operate on the assumption that continuity with Judaism validates Christianity as part of the

---

43. The most thorough attempt to investigate this subject is that of Davila, *Provenance of the Pseudepigrapha*.
44. De Jonge, *Testaments of the Twelve Patriarchs*; de Jonge, *Pseudepigrapha of the Old Testament*.
45. E.g., Himmelfarb, "*3 Baruch* Revisited," esp. 52.

stream of revelation, so to speak. As Martha Himmelfarb has argued, some scholars want to claim as Jewish certain books of the Pseudepigrapha that resemble Christianity in significant ways, in order to provide Christianity with a usable past.[46] Christianity was a viable option within the Jewish tradition.

Other scholars take exactly the opposite position. Here the assumption is that Christianity was decisively different from Judaism, and this difference is nowhere more evident than in attitudes to the Jewish law. This view is especially prominent in strands of Christianity that accord primary importance to the Pauline writings.

My own interest in this question is historical rather than theological. The theological validity of Christianity does not depend on continuity with Judaism. Neither does it depend on independence from Judaism. From a historical perspective, both continuity and discontinuity are in evidence. Christianity ultimately broke decisively with Judaism on the centrality of the Jewish law. But even this move was an option within the Judaism of the late Second Temple period.[47] Paul was a radical Jew, as Daniel Boyarin has characterized him,[48] but he was a Jew, nonetheless, and his position is intelligible as representing one extreme of an inner-Jewish debate. But there is lots of continuity too. The continuity, however, is largely with the apocalyptic strand of Judaism that we find in the Pseudepigrapha. That strand was by and large rejected by the rabbis, but it remains nonetheless an authentic part of the history of Jewish tradition.

46. Himmelfarb, "3 Baruch Revisited," 51.
47. J. Collins, Invention of Judaism, 159–81.
48. Boyarin, Radical Jew.

Chapter 3

Nonbiblical Literature in the Dead Sea Scrolls

JOHN J. COLLINS

Before the discovery of the Dead Sea Scrolls seventy years ago, in the vicinity of Qumran, near the Dead Sea, we did not have much firsthand information about Judaism around the turn of the era. For the period between the Hebrew Bible and the Mishnah, we had the Apocrypha, and also the Pseudepigrapha that had been recovered in the nineteenth century; but except for those works that had originally been composed in Greek, this literature was all preserved in translation, by Christians, and doubts persisted as to whether it was authentically representative of Judaism. Even the writings of Philo and Josephus, who were incontrovertibly Jewish, were transmitted by Christians. We had almost no literature in Hebrew or Aramaic later than the books of Ben Sira and Daniel in the early second century BCE, and earlier than the rabbinic writings that began to be edited in the late second century CE.

The Dead Sea Scrolls altered this situation radically.[1] We now have hundreds of texts, albeit in fragmentary form, written in their original languages. These include fragments of every book in the Hebrew Bible except Esther,

---

1. See my essay "What Have We Learned?"

and they shed invaluable light on the formation of the Hebrew canon.[2] But the fact that nearly all the canonical books were preserved does not necessarily mean that the people who preserved this literature distinguished between canonical and noncanonical books in the way that we do. The books of *Enoch* and *Jubilees* were preserved in multiple copies. Some of the books we know as biblical, such as Chronicles and Ezra–Nehemiah, are barely represented at all. Frank Moore Cross famously said that it would have taken only one more hungry worm to erase the books of Chronicles from the record of the Scrolls. Some parts of the Bible—the Torah, Prophets, and Psalms—were evidently important and were subjects of commentary, but the Writings, other than Psalms, do not seem to have enjoyed equal authority. Instead, we find a wide-ranging corpus of other writings, many of which had been unknown before the discovery of the Dead Sea Scrolls. It is this wider corpus of literature that concerns us in this essay.

DIFFERENT KINDS OF LITERATURE

The nonbiblical literature found in the Dead Sea Scrolls is of different kinds.

The very first batch of scrolls found in Cave 1 included a rule book for a community, which was originally dubbed "the Manual of Discipline" but later became known as *Rule of the Community*, or by its Hebrew title *Serek ha-Yahad*.[3] Because of this, the assumption was made early on that the Scrolls as a corpus were the library of the community described in this *Rule*. The "Manual" had clear points of contact with another rule for a community, a rule called the *Damascus Document*, which had been found in the Cairo Genizah at the end of the twentieth century. Fragments of that document soon showed up in Cave 4 at Qumran. While the two rule books differed in some respects, the presence of both among the Scrolls strengthened the impression that the Scrolls belonged to a sectarian group, to a movement with its own rituals of admission and expulsion. From a very early point, that movement was identified with the sect of the Essenes, known from the writings of Philo and Josephus and from a short description by Pliny the Elder.[4]

I do not propose to enter here into the recent debates about the identification of this movement. Let it suffice to say that I think the consensus view is correct, that the organization reflected in the Scrolls is that of the Essenes. According to Josephus, there were two orders of Essenes, one of which married and one of which did not.[5] The two main rule books found at Qumran can be understood

---

2. See esp. Lim, *Jewish Canon*, 119–47.

3. For the story of the discovery, see J. Collins, *Dead Sea Scrolls*, 1–32.

4. On the nature and identity of the sectarian movement, see J. Collins, *Beyond the Qumran Community*.

5. Josephus, *J.W.* 2.160. The various accounts of the Essenes are conveniently collected in Vermès and Goodman, *Essenes according to the Classical Sources*.

as reflecting this duality. The *Damascus Document* refers explicitly to women and children, while the *Community Rule* does not. Like the Essenes, the movement described in the Scrolls consisted of many communities, spread throughout the land.[6] The ruins found at Qumran can be reasonably interpreted as those of one Essene community. Whether it was the most important one, or the "mother-house," we do not know.

In view of the size of the corpus of the Scrolls, it seems to me unlikely that they were all contained in the library of the settlement at Qumran. It does appear, however, that the collection has a sectarian character. Several writings—such as the *pesharim*, or biblical commentaries—are clearly related to the rule books. Absent from the Scrolls are the books of Maccabees, which glorify the Hasmonean heritage, and anything that could be ascribed to the Pharisees. I suggest that the Scrolls represent the combined libraries of several Essene settlements, taken to Qumran for safekeeping at the time of the war against Rome. This would explain why several copies of the rule books, with differences in detail, were found in the caves; the different editions of the rule book may have been in force in different communities. To be sure, this is a hypothesis. We cannot prove how the Scrolls came to be placed in the caves near Qumran. But I think this is a plausible hypothesis, more plausible than one supposing that all these scrolls (nearly a thousand in all) were in the library of a single community.

The way in which we explain the provenance of the Scrolls has implications for another question: How well do the Dead Sea Scrolls represent Judaism around the turn of the era? The scrolls that contain the rule books, and others in the initial batch of scrolls from Cave 1, were predominantly sectarian. As more and more of the scrolls from Cave 4 became known, however, it became apparent that many of them were not especially sectarian in character.[7] These scrolls include a corpus of literature in Aramaic that does not fit the sectarian profile.[8] The Aramaic texts do not refer to any sectarian institutions of the kind described in the *Community Rule*, and they betray no awareness of the kind of sectarian disputes attested in 4QMMT. The Aramaic literature seems to have subsided in the period after the Maccabean revolt. All the properly sectarian literature is written in Hebrew. This is not to say that all the literature written in Hebrew *is* sectarian. Several wisdom texts found at Qumran, most notably *4QInstruction*, also lack reference to sectarian institutions or disputes.[9] Even texts that were composed within the sect, for sectarian purposes, may shed light on other strands of Judaism. Some writings reflect disputes with other parties in Judaism about the interpretation of the Mosaic law. These too are sectarian writings, but at least they give us an indication of the kinds of issues that were being disputed at the time. But no one can be a sectarian all the time. The members

6. Josephus, *J.W.* 2.124; Philo, *Quod omnis probus liber sit* [*That Every Good Person Is Free*] 76; CD 7.6; 1QS 6.1–8. J. Collins, *Beyond the Qumran Community*, 65–69.

7. Newsom, "'Sectually Explicit' Literature from Qumran."

8. Berthelot and Ben Ezra, eds., *Aramaica Qumranica.*

9. Goff, *Discerning Wisdom.*

of the sectarian communities also had in their possession books that had been written before these communities were formed at all. They had essentially the same Torah, Prophets, and Psalms as other Jews of the time. They also preserved older writings, like the books of *Enoch* and *Jubilees*, which do not appear to have been written within the sect, but which the members evidently found congenial.

Before the discovery of the Dead Sea Scrolls, there had been a debate about the character of Judaism around the turn of the era. Some scholars assumed that the kinds of interests reflected in the Mishnah and Talmud, which were largely concerned with the interpretation of religious law, were already dominant. Others looked rather to the Pseudepigrapha and the apocalyptic writings, which showed relatively little concern for legal issues, but speculated about the heavens and about the course and end of history. The Scrolls provided support for both sides of this debate. On the one hand, it is now apparent that interpretation of the law was a major factor in the formation of this movement. This appears especially in a text called 4QMMT, or "some of the works of the law," which outlines some twenty issues on which the author's party, designated as "we," disagrees with some other group, designated as "they" and usually thought to be the Pharisees.[10] The issues in question concern minutiae of the law. For example, one issue is "the purity of liquid streams": if you pour water from one vessel into another, and the second vessel is unclean, does the impurity travel upstream? The "we" group invariably takes the stricter position. We would not have guessed from the Pseudepigrapha that issues of this sort were important to at least some Jews around the turn of the era.

But if the Scrolls show that issues of legal interpretation were important, they also show that the kind of apocalyptic speculation known from the Pseudepigrapha was alive and well. Especially important here was the preservation of the books of *Enoch*—all sections of *1 Enoch* except the Similitudes, in the original Aramaic. No longer could there be any suggestion that these writings were not authentically Jewish. In fact, the Scrolls disclosed that there was a flourishing Jewish literature in Aramaic at one time. Many of the Aramaic writings, including the books of *Enoch*, appear to be older than the sectarian movement known from the Scrolls and in many cases date from a time before the Maccabean revolt. These include an Aramaic document about Levi, which is largely concerned with priestly instruction but which also narrates an ascent of Levi to heaven.[11] They also include a paraphrase of Genesis, known as the *Genesis Apocryphon*, which includes a lengthy digression on the beauty of Sarah, which seems to have been written simply for entertainment.[12] This Aramaic literature shows a great interest in dreams and visions, which are also important ingredients in apocalyptic literature.[13] It is not greatly concerned with religious law, except for specifically priestly law in the case of Aramaic Levi.

10. Qimron and Strugnell, eds., *Miqsat Maʿase Ha-Torah.*
11. M. Stone, Greenfield, and Eshel, *Aramaic Levi Document.*
12. Machiela, *Dead Sea Genesis Apocryphon* [1Q20].
13. Perrin, *Dynamics of Dream-Vision Revelation.*

It is not the case, however, that the different kinds of writing, legal and apocalyptic, can be neatly separated along linguistic lines. There is also a strong apocalyptic component in the Hebrew scrolls.[14] This was apparent already when the first scrolls from the Dead Sea area were published. The *Community Rule* includes a famous treatise on the Two Spirits of Light and Darkness, and the *War Scroll* sets out arrangements for a final battle between these spirits and their followers. Both of these compositions are likely to derive from the sect, as they envision a polarized world of light and darkness. But the Hebrew scrolls also include some compositions that are not so obviously sectarian and may have been part of the common Jewish heritage of the time.

In the remainder of this essay, I will present a few examples of this noncanonical literature to suggest its importance for anyone who wants to understand either Second Temple Judaism in general or the segment of it that we call the New Testament. I will consider one Aramaic writing and then two Hebrew ones.

The Son of God Text

The first of these is a text variously known as "the Son of God text" or "the Aramaic Apocalypse." We must be hesitant in assigning the text to a genre, such as "apocalypse," since both the beginning and the end are missing. This text was presented in a lecture at Harvard by J. T. Milik in December 1972, but it was not formally published until Émile Puech edited it twenty years later.[15] In the meantime, it had already become controversial on the basis of Milik's lecture.

The text consists of two columns of nine lines each. The first column is torn vertically, so that one-third to half of each line is missing, but the second column is substantially intact. There was at least a third column, since the second one ends in midsentence, and it is possible that there was another column before column 1. The fragmentary opening verse says that someone "fell before the throne." The following verses are apparently addressed to a king and refer to "your vision." There are references to afflictions and carnage, and to the kings of Assyria and Egypt. The second half of line 7 reads, "will be great on earth." Line 8 says that "all will serve," and line 9 declares, "By his name he will be named."

Column 2 continues as follows:

> "Son of God" he shall be called, and they will name him "Son of the Most High." Like sparks which you saw, so will be their kingdom. For years they will rule on earth, and they will trample all. People will trample on people and city on city, VACAT until he raises up the people of God (or: until the people of God arises), and all rest from the sword. His kingdom is an everlasting kingdom and all his ways are truth. He will judge the earth with truth and all will make peace. The sword will cease from the earth, and all cities will pay him homage. The great God will be his strength. He will make war on his behalf, give nations into his hand and

14. J. Collins, *Apocalypticism in the Dead Sea Scrolls*.
15. Puech, "[4Q246.] 4QApocryphe de Daniel ar."

cast them all down before him. His sovereignty is everlasting sovereignty, and all the depths . . .

Many scholars argue that the VACAT at the beginning of the fifth[?] line is the key to the interpretation. They reason that everything before this point in the text is negative, and everything after it is positive.[16] Accordingly, they think that the figure who is called Son of God must be a negative figure, perhaps a Syrian king such as Antiochus Epiphanes, whose attempt to suppress the traditional Jewish cult led to the Maccabean revolt. Hellenistic kings were often accorded divine honors. The Seleucids often claimed to be "god" or "god manifest" (θεὸς Ἐπιφανής), as in the case of Antiochus Epiphanes, or son of a specific god such as Zeus or Apollo. But "Son of God" or "Son of the Most High" are not attested as Seleucid titles and instead point to Jewish tradition. (The Roman emperor Augustus was called "son of God [divi filius],"[17] but the Qumran text is almost certainly earlier than the time of Augustus.) Moreover, when a Gentile king assumes pretensions to divinity in biblical texts, we are left in no doubt that those claims are false. For example, in Dan 11 the king (Antiochus Epiphanes) "shall act as he pleases. He shall exalt himself and consider himself greater than any god and shall speak horrendous things against the God of gods" (Dan 11:36). But at the end of the chapter Daniel declares, "He shall come to his end, with no one to help him" (11:45). In the Aramaic text, however, the divine titles are not disputed.

But the assumption that the VACAT must mark the turning point of the text is false in any case.[18] Ancient texts are not so simple as this. Rather, it is characteristic of ancient texts that they go over the same ground in different ways. For example, in Daniel 7, the kingdom is given first to "one like a son of man," then to "the holy ones of the Most High," and finally to "the people of the holy ones of the Most High."[19] In Dan 12:1, Michael (patron angel of Israel) arises in victory, and we might expect that this is the turning point in the eschatological battle, but it is followed by a time of anguish that is almost unprecedented. It is too simple to suppose that an ancient text like this follows a simple sequential order.

By far the closest parallel to the titles "Son of God" and "Son of the Most High" is found in the Gospel of Luke, in the Annunciation scene.[20] The angel tells Mary: "He will be great and will be called Son of the Most High, and the Lord God will give to him the throne of David his [father]; . . . he will be called the Son of God" (Luke 1:32, 35). In this case there is no doubt at all about the significance of the titles. They are titles of the Davidic messiah: the Lord God

---

16. E.g., Cook, "4Q246." See my response to Cook's article: "Background of the Son of God Text."

17. Knohl, Messiahs and Resurrection, 58–61. Knohl dates 4Q246 to the Roman era.

18. For a fuller statement of this argument, see J. Collins, Scepter and the Star, 171–90.

19. J. Collins, Daniel, 312–19.

20. Henze, Mind the Gap, 80–81.

will give to him the throne of David his father. In the Old Testament, the king is explicitly told in Psalm 2: "You are my son; today I have begotten you." In 2 Sam 7, God tells David, through the prophet Nathan, that his son will be as a son to God: "I will be a father to him, and he shall be a son to me" (7:14).[21] Son of God and Son of the Most High are messianic titles, even though they are not widely attested. There is a controversial reading in another text from Qumran, the so-called *Rule of the Congregation* (1QSa), which has been taken to refer to God "begetting" the messiah, but the reading is disputed. The messiah is clearly called the son of God in the apocalypse of *4 Ezra* (7:28; note also the use of Ps. 2 in *4 Ezra* 13).[22] The Aramaic text from Qumran is a further important witness to the currency of this terminology.

In Ps 2 and 2 Sam 7, the figure who is called son of God is a human king, even though he is said to be begotten by God. There is no reason to suppose that anyone believed that kings of Judah were born from virgins. To be begotten by God was quite compatible with having a human father. In the Aramaic text, too, there is no suggestion of miraculous birth. The titles are honorific and indicate a close relationship with God, who is said to be his help and to fight on his behalf. This was in accordance with the traditional royal ideology of Judah, as we find it in the Psalms. The difference is only that it is projected into the future, since the line of David had been broken. The New Testament would draw on this language to indicate the messianic role of Jesus, but it would also try to differentiate Jesus from the traditional kings by the stories of the virgin birth, which heightened the claim to be begotten by God.

Should we infer that the author of the Gospel of Luke knew this Aramaic text from the Dead Sea Scrolls? This cannot be proven, and scholars have been hesitant to suggest it. But if the Gospel showed this level of correspondence to a biblical text, no one would hesitate to recognize it as an allusion. It is difficult to believe that this close a correspondence is coincidental. In any case, the Aramaic text sheds invaluable light on the cultural context within which Luke was operating and the language on which he drew.

4Q521

There is no reason to regard the son of God text as a sectarian composition. It was simply part of the literary heritage preserved by the sectarians. The date is uncertain. It is surely later than Daniel since it seems to allude to it at several points. Many scholars assume that all Aramaic compositions predate the formation of the sect, but this is not necessarily so. It could have been written at any time in the late second or early to mid-first century BCE. (The manuscript is dated to the last third of that century.)[23]

---

21. On the idea that the king was son of God, see A. Collins and J. Collins, *King and Messiah as Son of God*, esp. 1–24.

22. J. Collins, "Interpretation of Psalm 2."

23. Puech, "[4Q246.] 4QApocryphe de Daniel ar," 166, suggests a date around 25 BCE.

Another apparently nonsectarian text of great interest for the New Testament is 4Q521, dubbed "the messianic apocalypse," although it is clearly not an apocalypse in form.[24] Again, it is fragmentary, but it seems to be a psalm or hymn rather than an account of a revelation.[25] This text is written in Hebrew. The longest fragment reads as follows:

> . . . Heaven and earth will obey his messiah, [and all th]at is in them will not turn away from the commandments of holy ones. You who seek the Lord, strengthen yourselves in his service. Is it not in this that you will find the Lord, all who hope in their hearts? For the Lord will seek out the pious and call the righteous by name, and his spirit will hover over the poor and he will renew the faithful by his might. For he will glorify the pious on the throne of an eternal kingdom, releasing captives, giving sight to the blind and raising up those who are bo[wed down]. Forever I will cleave to [those who] hope, and in his kindness. . . . The fru[it of a] good [wor]k will not be delayed for anyone and the glorious things that have not taken place the Lord will do as he s[aid], for he will heal the wounded, give life to the dead and preach good news to the poor and he will [sat]isfy the [weak] ones and lead those who have been cast out and enrich the hungry. . . .

This composition draws heavily on Ps 146, which declares blessed those "whose help is the God of Jacob, . . . who made heaven and earth, the sea, and all that is in them" (146:5–6). God "executes justice for the oppressed, . . . gives food to the hungry, . . . sets the prisoners free, . . . opens the eyes of the blind, [and] . . . lifts up those who are bowed down" (146:7–8). It also draws on Isa 61:1–2: "The spirit of the Lord GOD is upon me, because the LORD has anointed me; he has sent me to preach good news to the oppressed, to bind up the brokenhearted, to proclaim liberty to the captives, and release to the prisoners; to proclaim the year of the LORD's favor, and the day of vengeance of our God."

The text from Qumran departs from Ps 146 at two significant points. It introduces a "messiah" whom heaven and earth will obey. It also speaks of giving life to the dead. Grammatically, the Lord is the subject who will perform the actions listed in the later part of the passage, including raising the dead. The Lord, of course, is normally the one who raises the dead. The Jewish prayer the Eighteen Benedictions blesses God in the second benediction as the one who makes the dead live.[26] It is surprising, however, to find God preaching good news to the poor. That is the work of a prophet or messenger.[27]

The introduction of the "messiah" at the beginning of the passage arises from the fact that the author is combining Ps 146 and Isa 61.[28] In Isa 61, the one who is anointed is the prophet, who is sent to preach good news to the poor. I

---

24. Puech, "[4Q521.] Apocalypse Messianique."

25. Niebuhr, "4Q521 2 II—Ein Eschatologischer Psalm."

26. Hultgren, "4Q521, the Second Benediction of the Tefilla"; Hultgren, "4Q521 and Luke's Magnificat and Benedictus"; Singer, *Authorized Daily Prayer Book*, 44–45.

27. J. Collins, *Scepter and the Star*, 131–41.

28. Henze, *Mind the Gap*, 68–74.

suggest that this is also the role of the "messiah" in the Qumran text. The actions are still the works of the Lord, but they are performed through the agency of a prophetic messiah.

Prophets are not often said to be "anointed" or "messiahs" in the Hebrew Bible, but there is some basis for it. In 1 Kgs 19:16 Elijah is told to anoint Elisha as prophet after him, but the actual anointing is not reported. In the Dead Sea Scrolls, however, the prophets of old are called "anointed ones" in CD 2.12 and 1QM 11.7. In the present context, the identification of the "messiah" as a prophet is suggested by the claim of the prophet in Isa 61 that the Lord has anointed him.

A herald is also called a messiah in another Hebrew text from Qumran, the *Melchizedek Scroll*.[29] That scroll cites Isa 52:7: "How beautiful upon the mountains are the feet of the messenger who announces peace, who brings good news, who announces salvation." It then identifies the herald as "the one anointed of the spirit, about whom Daniel said . . ." Daniel mentions an anointed one twice: in Dan 9:25, in the context of the restoration of Jerusalem after the exile; and in 9:26, which says that an anointed one will be cut off. Modern scholars interpret the references in Daniel as to two high priests: Joshua, who was involved in the rebuilding of the temple in the late sixth century BCE; and Onias III, who was murdered shortly before the Maccabean revolt. The scroll, however, is trying to read all scripture as one system of interlocking references, identifying a figure mentioned in one prophet with one mentioned in another. The expression "anointed of the spirit," again, is derived from Isa 61, which associates the anointing of the prophet with the spirit.

The anointed figure in Isa 61 is not said to give life to the dead. Neither is this usually said of the Davidic messiah. Resurrection often follows the earthly career of the messiah, but he is not said to raise the dead. In later Jewish tradition we find the notion that "the dead will first come to life in the time of the Messiah," but again, he is not the agent who brings it about. Rather, "the resurrection of the dead comes through Elijah" (end of *m. Sotah* 9.15; *y. Sheqalim* 3.3). Elijah was said to raise the dead during his historical career (1 Kgs 17), as also Elisha (2 Kgs 4). According to a medieval Jewish text, *Pesikta de Rab Kahana* 76a, "Everything that the Holy One will do, he has already anticipated by the hands of the righteous in this world, the resurrection of the dead by Elijah and Ezekiel, the drying of the Dead Sea by Moses."

It seems likely, then, that the messiah in 4Q521, whom heaven and earth obey, is a prophet like Elijah, if not Elijah redivivus. Elijah's command of the heavens was legendary. In the words of Ben Sira, "By the word of the Lord he shut up the heavens, and also three times brought down fire" (Sir 48:3). The two olive trees in Revelation 11, who have authority to shut up the sky so that no rain may fall and to turn the waters into blood, are usually identified as Elijah and Moses.

---

29. See my article: "Herald of Good Tidings."

The most fascinating parallel to 4Q521, however, comes from the New Testament. In a passage that is attested in Matthew and Luke, and usually assigned to the Sayings Source Q, John the Baptist sends his disciples to inquire of Jesus: "Are you the one who is to come, or are we to wait for another?" Jesus answers: "Go and tell John what you hear and see: the blind receive their sight, the lame walk, the lepers are cleansed, the deaf hear, the dead are raised, and the poor have good news brought to them." Both Gospel passages (Matt 11:2–5; Luke 7:22) go on to identify John with the messenger sent to prepare the way in Mal 3:1. Matthew describes the works in question as "the works of the messiah."

The "works of the messiah" in Matthew 11 could easily be taken to suggest that Jesus was the eschatological prophet, or Elijah redivivus. The Gospels are at pains to identify John the Baptist as the herald or messenger.[30] There are indications in the Gospels, however, that Jesus was sometimes thought to be Elijah or a similar prophet. In Mark 6:14–15 Herod hears that various people identify Jesus as John raised from the dead, Elijah, or "a prophet." Again, in Mark 8:27–28, Jesus asks, "Who do people say that I am?" He is told: "John the Baptist; and others, Elijah; and still others, one of the prophets."

The parallel between the text from Qumran and the New Testament is intriguing since both go beyond Isa 61 in referring to the raising of the dead. This can hardly be coincidental. If the author of the Sayings Source did not know 4Q521, he must at least have known a common tradition. The Elijah-like eschatological prophet had a clear basis in scripture and was not a peculiarly sectarian idea. In fact, the expectation of an anointed prophet is atypical of the sectarian Dead Sea Scrolls. The *Community Rule* refers to the coming of a prophet and the messiahs of Aaron and Israel, but it does not say that the prophet would be anointed. Here again these scrolls provide a window on popular belief in Judea around the turn of the era. There was no strict orthodoxy in the matter of messianic expectation, but there were plentiful traditions that could be combined in various ways.

A Throne in Heaven?

The last text I will discuss here is found in five very fragmentary Hebrew manuscripts.[31] One of these is part of the scroll of *Thanksgiving Hymns*, or *Hodayot*, from Cave 1, which was one of the first scrolls discovered, but its significance was not recognized until the other copies came to light. The first copy to attract scholarly attention was published in 1982 as part of the *War Scroll*.[32] The text spoke of a throne in the council of the gods, and the speaker claimed to dwell, or to have taken a seat, in heaven. The editor, Maurice Baillet, thought that only an angel could make such an exalted claim, and he dubbed this composi-

30. See Marcus, "John the Baptist and Jesus."
31. The most complete synopsis is provided by Wise, "*Mi kamoni ba'elim.*"
32. Baillet, *4Q482–4Q520*, 26–30.

tion "The Canticle of Michael." Morton Smith, a notoriously caustic scholar who taught for many years at Columbia University in New York, derided this interpretation.[33] An archangel, Smith argued, would not need to boast. He had been created an archangel and could take his throne in the heavens for granted. The speaker in this text is a mere parvenu, one who claims to be reckoned with the gods but evidently is not at home in the heavens. The speaker must be an exalted human being. The idea of a human being who is enthroned in heaven immediately suggests a parallel with the ascension of Jesus.[34]

It is apparent that one recension of this text was part of the *Thanksgiving Hymns*, which is surely a sectarian composition. Whether it was originally composed for that context is unclear. But the compositional history of the text need not concern us here. The fragment published by Baillet is translated as follows by Géza Vermès:

> . . . the righ[teo]us exult [in the streng]th of His might
> and the holy ones rejoice in . . . righteousness
> . . . He has established it in Israel
> Since ancient times His truth and the mysteries of His wisdom
> (have been) in all . . . power
> . . . the council of the poor into an eternal congregation
> . . . the perfect . . . eternity a throne of strength in the congregation of gods
> so that not a single king of old shall sit on it,
> neither shall their noble men . . .
> My glory is incomparable, and apart from me none is exalted.
> None shall come to me for I dwell . . . in heaven, and there is no . . .
> I am reckoned with the gods
> and my dwelling-place is in the congregation of holiness.
> [My] desire is not according to the flesh,
> [and] all that I value is in the glory of the place of holiness.
> Who is counted despicable on my account,
> and who is comparable to me in my glory? . . .
> Is there a companion who resembles me? There is none!
> I have been taught and no instruction resembles [my instruction] . . .
> Who shall attack me when I op[en my mouth]?
> And who can contain the issue of my lips?
> Who shall summon me to be destroyed by my judgment? . . .
> For I am reckoned with the gods,
> and my glory is with the sons of the King.[35]

Another copy of this remarkable composition asks, "Who is like me among the gods?"[36] The question echoes Exod 15:11, which asks the Lord, "Who is like you . . . among the gods?" For a human being to apply this question to himself seems almost blasphemous.

33. Smith, "Deification in 4QM[a]."
34. Smith, "Two Ascended to Heaven."
35. Vermès, *Complete Dead Sea Scrolls*, 342–43.
36. In 4Q471[b]; Vermès, *Complete Dead Sea Scrolls*, 343.

In the edition of this text found in the *Thanksgiving Hymns*, it is designated a psalm (*mizmor*) for the *maskil*. The *maskil* in this context is probably a liturgical leader. It is likely, then, that this psalm was chanted in community. This raises the possibility that each member of the community would apply it to himself. The idea that the whole community could have a throne in heaven gets some support from a line in 4Q521, that God will honor the pious on the throne of an eternal kingdom. Nonetheless, since the claims made in this psalm are so exceptional, it is difficult to believe that they do not refer to a specific individual. Christians may identify with Christ, to a degree, and rejoice in the thought of Christ enthroned in heaven, but they do not identify with him without remainder. As Philip Alexander, who has written an important book on Jewish mysticism, put it, the speaker is "someone special. His experience is not something that anyone can achieve, though he can still lead others into a state of closer communion with the heavenly host."[37]

The idea that members of the sectarian community can enter into fellowship with the heavenly host, or angels, is not in itself unusual. The claim is commonly made in the *Thanksgiving Hymns*. Consider, for example, this passage from column 11 of the Thanksgiving Scroll:

> I thank you, Lord, because you saved my life from the pit, and from the Sheol of Abaddon have lifted me up to an everlasting height, so that I can walk on a boundless plain. And I know that there is hope for someone you fashioned out of dust for an everlasting community. The depraved spirit you have purified from great offense so that he can take a place with the host of the holy ones, and can enter in communion the congregation of the sons of heaven.[38]

But the speaker in this hymn, and in others of the *Thanksgiving Hymns*, retains a sense of modesty. He may be lifted up to the angelic host, but he remembers that he was fashioned out of the dust and that he had to be purified from great offense. There is no such modesty in the so-called Self-Glorification Hymn under consideration. It is possible that the speaker claims to have endured suffering. One line, omitted in the translation above, has been reconstructed to read, "Who bears all sorrows like me? And who suffers evil like me? There is no one."[39] He also says that he has been instructed. All of this is compatible with the idea that the speaker is an exalted human.

But who might this person be? The only individual who comes to mind in the context of the Scrolls is the so-called Teacher of Righteousness, a sectarian leader who was certainly revered by his followers. But the Teacher is often thought to be the author of one section of the *Thanksgiving Hymns* (1QHᵃ 10–16).[40] While

37. Alexander, *Mystical Texts*, 88.

38. Trans. García Martínez and Tigchelaar, *Scrolls Study Edition*.

39. See 4Q491 fragment 11, line 9; trans. García Martínez and Tigchelaar, *Scrolls Study Edition*, 2:981.

40. Douglas, "Teacher Hymn Hypothesis"; Wise, "Teacher's Movement," esp. 102–7.

these hymns make strong claims of exaltation, they are also conscious of their author's lowly origin and basic unworthiness. Some, including myself, have suggested that the speaker is an entirely imaginary person, such as an eschatological high priest.[41] But then the references to his earthly career are difficult to explain, especially if he claims to have endured evil. Another possibility is that this hymn was put on the lips of the Teacher after his death, that his followers imagined him enthroned in glory, much as the early Christians believed that Christ was enthroned.[42] In the end, we can only speculate. What seems clear enough is that this psalm affirms the possibility that a righteous human being could be taken up and enthroned in heaven. Even if the speaker in this hymn is exceptional, he represents an ideal that his followers could hope to emulate, even if in a lesser degree.

There are some parallels for such an idea in ancient Judaism. The Son of Man in the Similitudes of *1 Enoch* sits on the throne of glory at the judgment, as his counterpart in the Gospel of Matthew does in the judgment scene in 25:31. The Enochic Son of Man is a heavenly figure, not an exalted human being. But in an epilogue to the Similitudes, Enoch is taken up to heaven and greeted as either *the* or *a* son of man who has righteousness. It is not clear whether Enoch is being identified with the Son of Man or is being told that he is like the Son of Man. Moreover, Enoch is told that his followers too will share his destiny: "With you will be their dwelling and with you their lot, and from you they will not be separated forever and ever" (*1 En.* 71:16–17). The heavenly glory of the Son of Man is an ideal to which Enoch and his followers, in different degrees, can aspire.

Later Jewish tradition went further. A mystical work called *Sefer Hekalot*, or *3 Enoch*, reports the ascent to heaven of one Rabbi Ishmael.[43] Ishmael was greeted by a figure called Metatron, a kind of heavenly viceroy, who has many names, including Enoch son of Jared.[44] Metatron tells him how he (Enoch) was taken up from the generation of the flood and how "the Holy One, blessed be he, made for me a throne like the throne of glory" (*3 En.* 10:1). His enthronement had its dangers, however. Another Jewish mystic, known as Aher ('Aḥer), the Other, also ascended to heaven, and when he saw Metatron he exclaimed, "There are indeed two powers in heaven." Then Metatron was given sixty lashes of fire and made to stand on his feet (*3 En.* 16:4–5).

Sefer Hekalot is dated many centuries later than the Dead Sea Scrolls, but it represents the culmination of a long tradition. The so-called Self-Exaltation text from Qumran shows how the idea that a human being could be taken up and enthroned in heaven was already current before the turn of the era. Once again, the text opens at least a small window onto the world in which the New Testament took shape.

41. J. Collins, *Scepter and the Star*, 159; Eshel, "'Speaker' of the Self-Glorification Hymn."
42. Wise, "*Mî kamoni ba'elîm*," 218.
43. Alexander, "3 (Hebrew Apocalypse of) Enoch."
44. See the study by Orlov, *Enoch-Metatron Tradition*.

CONCLUSION

In this essay I have not raised the hoary questions whether Jesus or John the Baptist might have spent time with the Essenes at Qumran or been influenced by their ideas. I think it is highly unlikely that they did. The Essenes represented one extreme in Jewish religious life at the time, one that was obsessed with purity and the attempt to separate from the rest of impure humanity. Jesus and John the Baptist came from the other end of the spectrum, much less concerned with purity and more with human relations. I doubt that either Jesus or John the Baptist would have lasted through a novitiate at Qumran.

But the significance of the Dead Sea Scrolls is not limited to the religious ideals of the Essenes, and not all the Scrolls reflect a sectarian mentality. The Scrolls are a trove of the Jewish religious literature at the time. They may not give us the full spectrum. As I mentioned at the beginning, some things are conspicuously lacking. But they still preserve a range of writings and ideas that were not peculiarly sectarian but reflected the common Judaism of the time. The importance of the Scrolls for understanding Jesus or the New Testament lies in this broader sampling of the Judaism of the time. Here we find, somewhat randomly to be sure, ideas, phrases, and motifs that reappear in the New Testament, although they may be adapted in various ways. The New Testament did not spring forth from the Hebrew Bible as Athena was said to have sprung from the head of Zeus. More than two hundred years intervened between the last books of the Hebrew Bible and the first of the New Testament. For a long time, that was a dark age, illuminated only by some Greek writings and inferences from later traditions. Then in the nineteenth century the darkness was penetrated a little by the recovery of the Pseudepigrapha. We are fortunate that in our time considerable new light has been shone on this era by the discovery of the Dead Sea Scrolls.

Chapter 4

Recognizing Jewish Religious Texts as Scripture

LEE MARTIN McDONALD

There is now considerably more focus on questions regarding the formation of the Bible than earlier, and we are closer to resolving some vexing problems in this complex topic than was possible earlier. The following examination focuses more specifically on why the Hebrew Bible's scriptures were written and when they were recognized as sacred scripture and eventually formed a biblical canon. Scholars are aware that far more discussion and research has been focused on the latter issue (when) than the former (why). In what follows, I will also discuss both of these issues but also some important related questions including how and when they were organized in their current shape and order.

WHY THE JEWISH SCRIPTURES WERE WRITTEN

Eventually all of the books or texts that now comprise the Hebrew Bible (HB) and the Christian Old Testament (OT) were viewed as sacred scripture, but initially that was not the case. The Former Prophets or earlier historical books (Joshua, Judges, 1–2 Samuel, and 1–2 Kings) and the later historical books (1–2 Chronicles, Ezra–Nehemiah, and Esther) do not clearly reflect a prophetic stance, namely, delivering the word and will of God, in the same way that the Latter Prophets (Isaiah, Jeremiah, Ezekiel, and the Twelve) do. The Latter Prophets often introduce their texts with "The word of the LORD came to me saying . . ." or such like (e.g., Jer 1:4; Hos 1:1; Mic 1:1; Hab 1:1; Zeph 1:1; Mal 1:1; etc., but see also Deut 1:3, 6), but other ancient biblical texts are not so obvious.

It is not uncommon for some biblical scholars today to assume that when biblical texts were written, their authors were consciously aware of writing scripture, that is, divine revelation, rather than producing literary texts that told an important story for the Israelite nation. Eva Mroczek has highlighted the anachronistic tendencies that often lie behind such investigations. She notes that biblical scholars often assume that ancient authors were interested in "book" or "scripture" when they wrote. She correctly identifies many of the faulty assumptions of several contemporary scholars[1] and is well aware that such designations as Bible, biblical, canon, noncanonical, pseudepigraphal, and apocryphal are, of course, later anachronistic terms employed to describe a reality that was unfamiliar both to those who wrote the ancient texts and those who read or heard them. While the notion of scripture was present among many Jews in the late Second Temple period, fixed sacred collections or listings of rejected texts were not. There is little evidence for any notions of canon, biblical or nonbiblical, in Second Temple Judaism (up to 70 CE) or in early Christianity in its first two centuries. However, this does not answer many questions with which modern scholars busy themselves, such as how those who wrote religious texts or those who read or heard them understood those texts in Second Temple Judaism or early Christianity. When the notion of a fixed number of sacred books emerged by the end of the first century CE in Josephus (twenty-two in *Ag. Ap.* 1.37–43) or in *4 Ezra* (twenty-four in 14:44–46), the numbers themselves were sacred or iconic and did not bring clarity to which texts were in view or even their genre.[2] For some Jews, the fixing of a specific number of sacred texts into a collective whole (the HB) came in the late second century (*b. Baba Bathra* 14b) and for most Christians even later. Discussions and debates about specific books in that collection varied, however, for much longer.

There are multiple reasons why the Jewish sacred texts were produced. Some authors wrote to preserve a story that gave the Israelite nation its identity, some were written to advance wisdom among the people, some were produced to bring a warning to the nation or to offer hope in desperate times, some were written to advance piety and for use in worship or liturgies. The authors of the Hebrew scriptures wanted to tell the story of Israel's origin and rise to prominence, then its decline and failure as a nation, including the implications of that story. Three major components to that story are reflected, especially in the prophetic texts that now comprise the Hebrew scriptures. James A. Sanders reminds us that the essential core components of that story have to do with Israel's sojourn in Egypt

---

1. Mroczek, *Imagination in Jewish Antiquity*, 19–46, 128–29, and 184–89.
2. For an interpretation of these texts, see McDonald, *Old Testament*, 341–56.

and exodus from that land, their wilderness wanderings, and their entrance into Canaan. This story was eventually expanded to include the giving of the law at Sinai, the origin of humanity, and the birth of the Israelite nation. The story concludes with the nation's failure to maintain control of its land, temple, and nation as well as the prophetic voice that explained both why the nation failed and how it could have a renewed hope. There are many early examples of this core story that various prophets cited as justification for divine judgment against the nation. This story is referred to in several places outside the Pentateuch (e.g., Josh 24:2–13; 1 Sam 12:8; Jer 23:7–8; Amos 2:4, 9–12; Mic 6:4–5; Ps 106:7–46; and elsewhere); and the writers remind the people of what God has done for them and what their response to the Lord should be. Sanders goes on to say that this story forms the basis for prophets in reminding the nation of its failure to respond appropriately to God's activity among them.[3]

The current text of Torah likely originated in the sixth or fifth century BCE, though its story of the exodus, wanderings, and entrance doubtless were present in memory and oral tradition circulating in the nation earlier.[4] The period that others have called the origin of "early Judaism" begins after the devastation of the kingdoms of Israel in the north (722–721 BCE) and in the south (587–586 BCE). James A. Sanders has recently summarized this time as follows:

> Israel in the north was totally annihilated because of Assyrian foreign policy that forced peoples to migrate around the 8th to 7th c. BCE empire and integrate, thus losing their Israelite identity. But some Israelites escaped south to Jerusalem and Judah and were able to keep their basic identity through integration with their Judahite cousins there. This caused amalgams of the epics and traditions of north and south which are identified in the Pentateuch as a southern source J, and a northern source E (= JE), Deuteronomy, and the basic "histories" that are found in Joshua–Judges and in Samuel–Kings. They tell a story of God's rule over his chosen people, first through patriarchs, then judges, prophets, and kings, up to the exile.[5]

In telling this story, the authors of the biblical books did something remarkable: they acknowledged the failure of Israelite people that led to the demise of their nation. They also agreed that their failure was not due to the weakness of their God, but rather to their own failure and disobedience as the people of God. The historical, prophetic, wisdom, and poetic writings were all composed

---

3. J. A. Sanders (*Monotheizing Process*, 13–19) makes a good case that these important events were shaping Israel's history and identity and lists numerous texts to illustrate his point.

4. Carr, *Formation of the Hebrew Bible*, esp. 102–79, 252–303. Carr describes the history of the formation of the HB and discusses aspects of the Documentary Hypothesis (JEDP), which he presents and challenges at various places, especially testing whether the sources suggest Yahweh (J) first or Elohim (E) first. See also Du Toit, *Textual Memory*, who draws parallels between oral tradition and memory relating to other ancient libraries; she suggests that patterns of archival practices from the great libraries of Ashurbanipal and Alexandria were models that influenced the formation of the Hebrew Bible.

5. This quote, from J. A. Sanders's forthcoming article "Judaism," describes Israel's complex history and the emergence of Judaism from its inception in the 6th c. BCE to the present.

to address particular issues facing the Israelites and to some extent to emphasize the call to obey the God who brought them out of the land of Egypt. This story called the Israelite nation into existence, and the earliest strands of that story were not initially preserved in writing, but rather it was transmitted by memory in oral tradition long before it was written down in the Torah or Pentateuch.[6] When the primary elements of that story were written, they were likely stored in the temple (the book of Deuteronomy?) and later discovered in the temple during the days of Josiah (2 Kgs 22:8–13; 23:1–25 // 2 Chr 34:8–33; 35:1–19).

The notion that the will of God is conveyed in sacred books is quite ancient and has parallels in Mesopotamia and Egypt and Greece and subsequently among the Israelites.[7] Scribal activity was highly valued in antiquity and often viewed as a sacred activity.[8] Similarly, the notion that prophetic individuals were inspired by God to convey the will of God, whether orally (Elijah) or in writing (e.g., Isaiah), contributed to the notion of sacred scripture that was emerging in ancient Israel. For centuries, Second Temple Jews and later early Christians were interested in divinely inspired *texts*, but not initially in a specific number of those texts, that is, not in a fixed collection of sacred scripture texts. Only in the second century CE is this notion coupled with a specific collection of sacred texts that comprise the Jewish scriptures (*b. Baba Bathra* 14b) and first in the early church father, Melito of Sardis (ca. 170 CE). In neither case are these examples reflective of widespread perspectives in rabbinic Judaism or early Christianity, but rather the beginning of such thought among Jews and Christians.

Some ancient texts cited in Numbers and in Joshua to 2 Chronicles appear to have been viewed as prophetic texts, but they were eventually lost. They were cited in an authoritative manner and appear to have functioned like scripture for the Israelite nation temporarily, but by about 500–450 BCE these texts were no longer cited and somehow were lost, whether during the destruction of Jerusalem, the exile, or perhaps in natural disasters such as earthquakes, fires, and floods. It is also possible that when ancient religious texts were no longer deemed relevant to the ongoing life of the nation of Israel, they simply were no longer copied or preserved after about 450–400 BCE. These lost ancient texts mentioned in the HB/OT include the following:

In the Law or Torah: "Book of the Wars of the Lord" (Num 21:14). In Joshua, 2 Samuel, and 1–2 Kings, we find the following: "the Book of Jashar" (Josh 10:12–13; 2 Sam 1:18–27); "the book of the Annals of the Kings of Judah" (1 Kgs 14:29; 15:7, 23; 22:45; 2 Kgs 8:23; 12:19; 14:18; 15:6, 36; 16:19; 20:20; 21:17, 25; 23:28; 24:5); "the book of the Annals of the Kings of Israel" (1 Kgs 14:19; 15:31; 16:5, 14, 20, 27; 22:39; 2 Kgs 1:18; 10:34; 13:8, 12; 14:15, 28; 15:11, 15, 21, 26, 31); "the book of Acts of Solomon" (1 Kgs 11:41). In Chronicles, Ezra, and Nehemiah we find the following: "the book of the Kings of Israel"

---

6. Carr has convincingly argued this point in *Formation of the Hebrew Bible* and in his earlier *Tablet of the Heart*.

7. I have argued this in *Old Testament*, 39–41.

8. See Bar-Ilan, "Writing in Ancient Israel."

(1 Chr 9:1; 2 Chr 20:34); "the book of the Kings of Judah and Israel" (2 Chr 16:11); "the book of Kings of Israel and Judah" (27:7); "the Annals of the Kings of Israel" (33:18); "the records of the seer Samuel" (1 Chr 29:29); "the records of the seer Gad" (29:29); "the records of the seer Nathan" (29:29); "the history of the prophet Nathan" (2 Chr 9:29); "the prophecy of Ahijah the Shilonite" (9:29); "the visions of the seer Iddo" (9:29); "the records of the prophet Shemaiah and the seer Iddo" (12:15); "the Annals of Jehu the son of Hanani, which are recorded in the Book of the Kings of Israel" (20:34); "the records of the seers" (33:19); "the story of the prophet Iddo" (13:22); "the Commentary on the Book of the Kings" (24:27); a book written by the prophet Isaiah son of Amoz, containing the history of Uzziah (26:22); a "vision of the prophet Isaiah son of Amoz in the Book of Kings of Judah and Israel" (32:32; cf. Isa 1:1); "the Annals of King David" (1 Chr 27:24); the annals of the ancestors of King Artaxerxes (Ezra 4:15); "the book of the Annals" (Neh 12:23); and an *additional book* titled "Laments" in 2 Chr 35:25, which is not a reference to Lamentations, but rather to a book evidently produced by or for Josiah, a book now lost.[9]

In several of these references, writings are attributed to prophets or seers, as in the case of "records of the *seer* Samuel" (e.g., 1 Chr 29:29; cf. 1 Sam 9:9, 11, 18, 19; 1 Chr 9:22; 26:28). Similarly, a second source for the account of the activities of David is the "records of the *prophet* Nathan" (1 Chr 29:29; 2 Chr 9:29; 29:25); we also see books by the *prophet* Iddo, who saw the end of Solomon's reign (2 Chr 13:22), the *prophet* Shemaiah and the *seer* Iddo (12:15). Also Iddo is mentioned later: the acts of Abijah are written in the "story of the *prophet* Iddo" (13:22), and the acts of Manasseh, along with the "words of the *seers*," are recorded in the "annals of the Kings of Israel" (33:18), and "records of the *seer* Gad" (1 Chr 29:29; cf. 1 Chr 21:9 and 2 Sam 24:11).

We do not know the contents of these lost books; yet we have some indication from a few of the citations, as in the case of the two references to the Book of Jashar. More importantly, the references to prophets and seers are about those who were believed to have received a message from God that they communicated to the people. It is possible that initially the records or annals were only understood as histories, but such texts eventually were welcomed as sacred scripture among the Jews and were called the "[former] prophets." Such texts were included in the Jewish scriptures, as we see in the cases of Joshua, Judges, 1–2 Samuel, 1–2 Kings, 1–2 Chronicles, Ezra, Nehemiah, and Esther. What one concludes about the lost writings is difficult to say since for the most part we only know some of the stories that are included in them and not their

---

9. The "Book of the Acts of Solomon" and the "Book of the Annals of the Kings of Israel," as well as the "Annals of the Kings of Judah," likely existed in the courts of Samaria and Jerusalem, respectively, and are referenced. The authors and editors of 1–2 Kings doubtless used independent sources that circulated during the Deuteronomistic period of Israel's history. See my discussion of these sources in McDonald, "Lost Books," 581–87, here 581–84. See also Davila, "Quotations from Lost Books," providing the available or suggested texts of these quotations from the texts, as in the case of the "Book of Jashar" (Josh 10:13), or OT references to the books mentioned.

whole contents, but the context in which several of the stories are cited suggests that the stories at least functioned in an authoritative manner in Israelite religious communities. That kind of function is not far from the notion of scripture.[10]

It also is difficult to know the extent to which the ancient Israelite community accepted these lost texts as scripture, but some of them may have functioned either as scripture or as trusted sources for the faith and life of various Jewish sects *before* the second century CE. There are many other known texts that have survived antiquity and that at one time functioned as authoritative religious texts for some Jews. These are commonly identified today as Jewish apocryphal and pseudepigraphal texts, but initially both Jews and eventually some Christians welcomed them as sacred religious texts. Initially in antiquity, they were not viewed as extraneous or noncanonical texts.

Chapman observes that other texts besides the Law of Moses were cited in antiquity as religiously authoritative texts. He shows that at a certain (later) stage of the nation's history, not only the Law but also some "prophets" formed a "twin criteria of right belief," and he cites as evidence 2 Kgs 17:13 and Jer 26:16–18, in which Micah's prophecy (Mic 3:12) is cited to King Hezekiah. See also Jer 26:3–5, in which that prophet admonishes the people to "heed the words of my servants the prophets." It is not always clear which prophets are in view in Chapman's texts, but he correctly shows that a broader collection of sacred prophetic texts was welcomed than simply the law of Moses. He also cites Zech 7:12, which refers to the "former prophets" who prophesied in Israel; and Ezra 9:9–12, in which commands from Exodus 34:11 and Deut 7:1–5 are cited. The prayer of Daniel (Dan 9:5–10) also reflects the nations' failure to heed the Lord's commandments and the laws "set before us *by his servants the prophets*" (emphasis added).[11] I add to this Ezra's reference to the prophecies of Haggai and Zechariah, uttered to the Jews regarding the restoration of the temple (Ezra 5:1–2).

Again returning to the question at hand, there is little doubt about why some books were written and became authoritative for the Israelite nation. Torah, Prophets, and some of the Writings (or Ketuvim) addressed and reflected the most important stories and perspectives of the Jewish people and gave them their identity and mission. While most of the HB/OT writings had a long history of acceptance both in Judaism and later in the early churches, some of the canonical writings continued to be ignored or debated for centuries, such as Song of Songs, Ecclesiastes, Esther, Wisdom of Solomon, and Sirach (Wisdom of Jesus ben Sira, or Ecclesiasticus). However, some religious texts initially welcomed by some Jews were, for various reasons, no longer deemed important to

---

10. See Davila, "Quotations from Lost Books."

11. Chapman, "Canon, Old Testament," here 103. He also refers to several of the now-lost books listed above to support his view that both lawbooks and some prophetic texts served as sacred authoritative resources among the people of Israel before and during the exilic period.

the nation, and eventually they were excluded from sacred collections of texts. Besides the lost works listed above, many apocryphal and pseudepigraphal texts that were eventually excluded have survived and are a source of considerable and fruitful inquiry today.

As we see in the variety of religious texts discovered at Qumran and elsewhere in the Judean Desert, most of those writings were not sectarian or just local but rather were texts circulating in Palestine in late Second Temple Judaism, finding acceptance and recognition by a broader collection of Palestinian Jews of that era. A number of these popular religious texts were not later included in the HB books, but for a time they informed Jewish faith and values in the first centuries BCE and CE. Well into the third and fourth centuries CE, the rabbinic sages questioned and debated the sacred status of some of the books that were later included in the HB. The most commonly disputed HB books among the rabbis included these: Ecclesiastes (*m. Yadayim* 3:5; *b. Berakhot* 48a; *b. Shabbat* 100a; *Ecclesiastes Rabbah* 1.3; 11.9; *Leviticus Rabbah* 23; *Avot of Rabbi Nathan* 1; cf. Jerome on Eccl 12:14); Esther (*m. Megillah* 4:1; *b. Megillah* 7a; *b. Sanhedrin* 100a; cf. *t. Megillah* 2.1a; 2 Macc 15:36; Josephus, *Ant.* 11.184–296);[12] Ezekiel (*b. Shabbat* 13b; *b. Hagigah* 13a; *b. Menahot* 45a; cf. Jerome, *Epistle* 53.8; and Sir 49:8); Proverbs (*b. Shabbat* 30b); Ruth (*b. Megillah* 7a); Song of Songs (*m. Yadayim* 3:5; *m. Eduyyot* 5:3; *t. Sanhedrin* 12.10; *t. Yadayim* 2.14; *b. Sanhedrin* 101a; *b. Megillah* 7a).[13]

Despite the variety of religious texts circulating in Palestine in Second Temple Judaism, the Torah or Pentateuch was always at the heart of the Jewish scriptures and the most frequently cited religious texts among the broader prophetic collection. The Former and Latter Prophets generally are viewed as having functioned as commentary on the Torah; they provided the rationale for later prophetic warnings and admonitions to the nation. In regard to the collection later called the Writings, or Ketuvim, Morgan suggests that they formed a bridge between the Prophets and the primary rabbinic tradition, that is, the Mishnah, Tosefta, and the two Talmudim (Talmuds).[14] While the groupings of individual sacred books into two parts (Law and the Prophets) or three parts (Law, Prophets, and Writings) varied in Judaism of Late Antiquity, the Torah, or Pentateuch, was always first. The sequence of the Prophets and Writings was seldom stable until the codex was used for transmitting the Jewish scriptures (5th c. to 6th c. CE), but the order of books varied even after that. There are between fifty-two and ninety variations in the order of the Ketuvim alone. The three "Major Prophets" (Isaiah, Jeremiah, and Ezekiel) and the "Minor Prophets" (the "Twelve") were not always in the same sequence. Also, there is little agreement on the historical

---

12. For a helpful listing of early church fathers who rejected or minimized the use of Esther, see Dunne, *Esther and Her Elusive God*, 96–100. He also includes rabbinic references to the absence or rejection of Esther in synagogal use.

13. For more examples, see Lewis, "Jamnia Revisited," here 154–57.

14. This is argued at length in Morgan, *Text and Community*.

sequence of the Twelve, though many scholars now appear to place Amos in first place and Hosea second.[15] We should also note that only two of the catalogs before the sixth century CE have the OT concluding with the Twelve and with Malachi at the end (Mommsen and Isodore). Many of the *Christian* OT catalogs end with Daniel or Esther or 1–2 Maccabees; a number of variables are in the endings of the canonical lists.[16] Similarly, those who offer rationales for the *current* order of the collection of Writings are not convincing. Timothy Stone, for example, contends that the Ketuvim, or Writings, have a greater association with the Law and Prophets than with themselves, and he offers arguments for a greater coherence, integration, and logic in the current order of the Ketuvim and its overall message.[17] The difficulty in affirming such positions, however, is the lack of evidence to support them, including the lack of rabbinic or earlier Jewish sources to support such arguments. Why are those arguments not found in antiquity, whether among rabbinic sages or early church fathers? Those who argue for the current order in the Writings do not adequately answer that question.

The recognition of some sacred religious texts in a scriptural fashion likely took place no later than the seventh century to the sixth century BCE and possibly earlier, but *why* some of the religious texts are included in the HB is often vague, such as Esther and Song of Songs. It is not clear why several of the HB books were included or why many of the more than ninety Jewish religious texts were not finally included in the HB. The canonization of the HB appears to have been largely a process of limitation and rejection of religious texts that had earlier informed Jewish faith but later, for a variety of reasons, no longer did. The rabbinic sages whose influence shaped the final scope of the HB canon recognized a smaller collection of sacred texts that they believed reflected the nation's most important religious perspectives. Similarly, church decisions about the scope of their First Scriptures, or Old Testament, also appear largely to have been a process of narrowing rather than expanding the texts that informed the faith of early Christianity. There is little evidence for widespread rejection of the so-called pseudepigraphal religious texts before the second century CE and even less evidence for the rejection of the so-called apocryphal, or deuterocanonical, texts. It is likely that most, if not all, of the *known* early Jewish religious literature initially functioned as sacred texts for *some* Jews, as we can see in the variety of texts discovered at Qumran often without clear or obvious distinctions from the so-called canonical texts. Acceptance of the sacred and authoritative status of some of this literature in several early churches continued for centuries, even well after church councils began to deliberate their status in the late fourth century.

15. It is not clear why the Former Prophets (Joshua to Kings) were identified as "prophets" unless it was believed that prophetic figures wrote them. Their genre, however, is clearly different from the Latter Prophets.

16. See a list of canon catalogs in McDonald, *Old Testament*, 489–97.

17. See T. Stone, *Compilational History of the Megilloth*, 1–8 and 80–117. Note that "integrated" is taken from his page 5; see also Seitz, *Goodly Fellowship of the Prophets*; and Steinberg, *Die Ketuvim*, 444–54.

Torah[18] (or Pentateuch),[19] the usual designation for the first five books of the Hebrew Bible (HB), is logically in the first place in both the Jewish and Christian Bibles because of its focus on the beginning of humanity and the unfolding of Israel's story. It tells Israel's prehistory, from its Primal History (Gen 1–11) to the patriarchal history, beginning with Abraham as the father of the nation (Gen 12–50); then forward to the death of Moses (Deut 34), the giver of the law of God. The freeing of the nation from Egypt (Exod 1–18), the wilderness sojourn (Numbers), and the entrance of the Israelites into the land of Canaan (cf. Gen 50:24; Num 34–35; Deut 30:1–10; 31:1–8; 34:1–4; and Joshua) show the central role YHWH had for the nation and later form the foundational prophetic arguments against the nation when it failed. The account gave clarity about the nation's rise and eventual destruction, yet also offered hope for renewal in their return to honoring and obeying YHWH.

The Torah, or Pentateuch, is the foundation for understanding both the Former and Latter Prophets and also much of what is designated as poetic and Wisdom literature. Collins suggests that the prominence of laws in the Pentateuch is likely what gave rise to the translation of Torah as "Law," but he acknowledges that the Pentateuch contains much more than laws.[20] The Pentateuch and the Former Prophets often refer to the "law of Moses" as laws commanded by God and given to Moses (e.g., Deut 1:3–6; Josh 8:31–32; 23:6; 1 Kgs 2:3; 2 Kgs 14:6; 23:25); this is similar to what we see later in the Chronicles, Ezra, and Nehemiah, which refer to the law or book of Moses (e.g., Ezra 3:2; 6:18; Neh 8:1, 13–18). Even later, Sirach (ca. 180 BCE) refers to writings attributed to Moses as "the book of the covenant of the Most High God, the law that Moses commanded us" (Sir 24:23). According to Collins, the tradition that Moses wrote all five books of the Pentateuch likely had its origin in the reference to Moses as the author of Deuteronomy (see Deut 1:3–6), and this eventually was

---

18. *Torah* (תּוֹרָה) is not only a reference to the first five books of the Hebrew and Christian Bibles; it eventually also became a reference to the entire corpus of Jewish sacred literature, including the "Oral Torah," that is, religious texts subsequent to the Hebrew Bible. While *Torah* is almost always translated as "Law" (νόμος, *nomos*) in the LXX and in the NT, its more appropriate meaning is "teaching," "instruction," or "guidance," as we see in the HB at Mal 3:22 (= Mal 4:4 ET). It is sometimes used in reference to wisdom texts as well (Ps 119, Proverbs, Sirach) and in the later "rewritten Bible" texts at Qumran (e.g., *Commentary on Genesis*ᵃ, 4Q252; and the *Temple Scroll*ᵇ, texts that often refer to themselves as Torah). For a discussion of this, see Hindy Najman, "Torah and Tradition," in *Eerdmans Dictionary of Early Judaism* (ed. J. J. Collins and D. C. Harlow; Grand Rapids: Eerdmans, 2010), 1316–17; and Schwartz, "Torah."

19. The term "Pentateuch"—from πέντε (*penta*, five) and τεῦχος (*teuchos*, book), forming πεντάτευχος, referring to the first "five books" in the HB—is attributed to Moses, though in its current form that is highly unlikely. In the third century CE, Tertullian and Origen adopted the term "Pentateuch" to refer to the first five books of the Christian scriptures. The Jews generally adopted the term *Torah* for this collection, yet sometimes referred to it also as the *khāmesh* (Heb. = חָמֵשׁ), the term for "five." Torah is regularly translated in the LXX as *nomos* and in English as "law," but Torah is much more than law. "Law," or *nomos*, does not catch the full significance of the term "Torah," as we saw in n. 18 above, but it came to be a reference to commandments and laws, especially in the Hellenistic period, when God was increasingly referred to as a "lawgiver" or "legislator" (νομοθέτης).

20. J. Collins, *Introduction to the Hebrew Bible*, 3rd ed., 50.

extended to all of the books in the Pentateuch.[21] Coogan observes that neither Deuteronomy nor any of the other pentateuchal books say that Moses wrote those books, and Moses is often spoken of in the third person and not the first person.[22] Later (as in *b. Baba Bathra* 14a and 15a) all five books of the Pentateuch are attributed to Moses, a view that likely circulated not much later than Ezra and Nehemiah (500–450 BCE), who frequently refer to the laws of Moses including to several books of the Pentateuch (e.g., Ezra 3:2–4; 6:18–22; 7:6; Neh 1:7–8; 8:1, 14; 9:6–8, 12–22; 10:29–32; 13:1–2).

Torah also tells the story from the beginning of creation to the selection of a people through whom the purposes of God will be carried out. As that story unfolds in the Former Prophets, or history books, it also tells of the nation's failure, destruction, and reconstitution or renewal. The various parts that form this story lead to the conclusion that Israel is responsible for living in obedience to the Lord God of Israel, YHWH. Because Christianity began as a religious sect within Judaism, its first sacred scriptures (the OT) were similar to those embraced by their contemporary Jewish siblings, though sometimes welcoming books not later included in the HB, and those they had in common were regularly welcomed in a different sequence and order than is found in the later HB canon. Most of these scriptures and some not in the HB (e.g., Wisdom, Enoch, and others) are cited authoritatively throughout the church's Second Testament, the New Testament, although the writers employ a different hermeneutic for understanding those scriptures in new situations facing the churches.

Recent reexaminations of Deuteronomistic History (essentially Deuteronomy to 2 Kings) have affected traditional understandings of the formation of the Pentateuch and subsequently also the development of the HB itself. When Julius Wellhausen introduced the Documentary Hypothesis in his *History of Israel* (1878) to explain the origin and sources of the Pentateuch, he identified new terminology for what he thought were the major sources that comprise the Pentateuch: J, E, D, and P; these sources are identified by the divine names of YHWH (J) and Elohim (E), those that reflect the Deuteronomistic History (D), and finally those reflecting Priestly traditions (P). In short, these sources are believed not only to show the origin and development of the Pentateuch; they can also be seen in the Former Prophets.

More recently, questions have been raised about the existence of the E source since it appears only in fragmentary sections of the Hebrew scriptures, but there are also questions about its reflection of the northern tribes' designation for God, Elohim. In fact, much of Wellhausen's hypothesis has been reexamined, and new proposals are beginning to emerge that suggest different understandings of the sources and formation of the Pentateuch and the Deuteronomistic

---

21. J. Collins, *Introduction to the Hebrew Bible*, 3rd ed., 50.
22. Coogan, *Old Testament*, 50–51.

History.[23] It is not yet clear what *new* formation theories will emerge to take the place of the older Wellhausen interpretations, but the traditional views of JEDP are still reflected in current HB/OT scholarship. While many have thought that questions about the sources of much of the HB/OT (Pentateuch and Deuteronomistic History) are settled, some contemporary scholars are now challenging aspects of the traditional Documentary Hypothesis.[24]

The postulated JEDP sources likely have unrecoverable oral and even written antecedents; yet there are antecedent sources that influenced the Deuteronomistic History's story, sources initially repeated from memory and later put into written form. Despite these recent challenges to Wellhausen's theory, Coogan concludes that the Documentary Hypothesis continues to provide "the best explanation of the data that careful analysis uncovers, data that include repetitions, similarities, inconsistencies, and contradictions."[25]

Because of the relatively small number of Jews who returned to their homeland without a temple and its cultus, it was a natural move for them to give priority to their sacred texts, especially Torah.[26] Torah, and to some degree also some "prophets" (e.g., 2 Kgs 17:13; Ezra 5:1; 6:14; 9:11; Neh 6:7; 9:30), gave hope and direction to the remnant of Jews who returned to their homeland. From this time and onward, it appears that the Jewish people became "a people of the book." Following the rebuilding of their temple (Ezra 5:2–6:18; cf. 2 Chr 36:23), there was a renewed focus on priestly functions in the Jewish homeland,[27] but the prominence of sacred texts remained. While the law or

23. See, e.g., Stackert, *Prophet like Moses*, who challenges Wellhausen's reconstructions and understanding of religion of ancient Israel. In a more radical fashion, Nicholson, *Judaean Diaspora*, suggests that the book of Deuteronomy was not what was found in the temple in Jerusalem during Josiah's reign (2 Kgs 22–23). He claims that Deuteronomy was written by Judean exiles in Babylon in the 6th c. BCE, that the Deuteronomistic school saw itself as writing scripture, and that the history of Joshua to 2 Kings was viewed as theodicy rather than history.

24. Julius Wellhausen presented his theory in 1889 in his *Die Composition des Hexateuchs und der historischen Büchern des Alten Testaments*; in recent years, OT scholars have begun challenging this theory and have revised many of the previously "assured results" of the earlier generations. For discussions of this, see Carr, *Formation of the Hebrew Bible*, 256–303, 337–38; and Coogan, *Old Testament*, 49–58.

25. Coogan, *Old Testament*, 51; see his more complete and helpful summary of J E D P on 49–55, esp. his more complete discussion of the Priestly source (P) and the exilic edition of the Deuteronomistic History (404–13), plus discussion of 1–2 Chronicles, Ezra–Nehemiah, Psalms, Proverbs, and other texts (444–71). See also J. Collins, *Introduction to the Hebrew Bible* (1st ed.; 2004), 47–64, 159–78, 427–442; see also the same sections in his 2nd ed. (2014), 49–67, 177–81; he offers not only a lucid clarification of Wellhausen's Documentary Hypothesis, but also a critique of it, with implications for future developments. Also helpful and engaging is Gerstenberger, *Israel in the Persian Period*, who examines the postexilic literature (Ezra–Nehemiah, Haggai–Zechariah, and Malachi, as well as the continued shaping of Deuteronomy and the Psalms), offering a coherent description of the often-elusive history of the Achaemenid period. On this, see also Yee, Page, and Coomber, *Fortress Commentary on the Bible*. Finally, see also a different perspective in Chapman's summary and critique of the Documentary Hypothesis in his "What Are We Reading?," here 335–37.

26. J. A. Sanders, "Canon: Hebrew Bible."

27. Morgan, *Text and Community*, 33–36.

commandments of Moses did not appear to play much of a major role in the nation before or near the end of Israel's monarchy, the festivals and foundational references in the Torah to the exodus, wanderings, and entrance into the land did have great influence: they formed the basis for the Former and Latter Prophets to warn and judge the nation.

In a related question, were the biblical authors aware of writing sacred scripture when they wrote? In other words, were they prompted to write out of a belief that they were writing inspired texts with a divine origin? The authors of the Hebrew scriptures occasionally tell their readers why they wrote. For example, Jeremiah (1:1–4) claims that he is writing the "word of the LORD" that came to him (1:2, 4, 11, 13, passim), but see also Hosea (1:1–2), Amos (1:1–3), Micah (1:1–3), Malachi (1:1), and other prophets who wrote to the people, believing that what they wrote was the will of God for the nation, whether in dealing with their lack of faithfulness to YHWH or how they were treating the weak among them (Hosea and Amos). Israel's prophets often challenged questionable actions of evil kings or the nation's inappropriate dealings with the widows, orphans, and strangers among them. The specific reason for writing some texts is often unclear in the text itself, but occasionally the reason may be discerned. For example, the Wisdom literature may have been written simply to share guidance on practical living as a reflection of reverence for the Lord. Some of the Hebrew scriptures were written to remind the nation Israel of the story of its origin and identity (the Pentateuch), or to account for the nation's rise and fall (several of the Former and Latter Prophets), as well as the opportunity for its renewed status and hope in difficult circumstances (several of the Writings). The prophets often reminded the nation of elements in their story—such as exodus, wanderings, and entrance into the land—that had important implications for their behavior and how ignoring that story and its implications could affect their prosperity and future.[28]

The story that defined Israel's identity and responsibility to YHWH existed long before it was written down (e.g., 1 Sam 2:27–28) and later expanded. That account was preserved in the writings familiar to us now and eventually was consciously recognized as sacred scripture, often after it was written and functioned as a sacred text in the nation. Collins shows how the story was penned after the events described in the text. In Gen 12:6, for example, "At that time the Canaanites were in the land," which shows that this text must have been written later. Similarly, he notes that Gen 36:31 mentions "the kings who reigned in the land of Edom before any king reigned over the Israelites," which clearly reflects a time after the monarchy had been established.[29]

Although some of the books appear to have been written consciously as a "word from the LORD," that was not always the case. Some of the biblical books

---

28. In *Monotheizing Process* (13–19) J. A. Sanders makes a good case that these important events were shaping Israel's history and identity; he lists numerous texts to illustrate his point.

29. J. Collins, *Introduction to the Hebrew Bible* (2nd ed., 2014), 50.

were likely recognized as sacred texts considerably later than their writing. The Samuels, Kings, Chronicles, Ezra, Nehemiah, Esther, and Song of Songs are more historical information or poetic expression and not obviously sacred texts that consciously came to the authors as a "word from the LORD," such as we see in the case of the Latter Prophets. Were these historical books written initially as history that eventually came to be recognized as scripture? Was this later recognition the consequence of the nation's recognition that those texts told the story of the nation's birth, rise to power, and eventual decline because its people refused to obey and serve YHWH? In other words, do those texts try to explain the nation's failure and demise (esp. in the cases of 2 Kings, Chronicles, and Ezra–Nehemiah) and to justify the prophetic words against the nation? While some biblical writers appear to be aware of writing the will of God, as we see in the Latter Prophets, that is not as clear in the Former Prophets or in some of the poetic and Wisdom literature.

Since the biblical authors do not use the term "scripture" for their writings, were they always aware of the divine origin of what they were writing? This is, of course, at the heart of the notion of scripture. Could an author write "scripture" without being aware of writing a sacred text? As we saw in the examples above and will see later in the New Testament writers, the answer appears to be yes. The authors of Deuteronomy (1:3; cf. Josh. 1:7–8) and the Latter Prophets were more aware of writing sacred texts. However, conscious awareness of writing scripture is not always obvious in some of the Former Prophets or in some of the Writings. The story that the scriptures told existed first as an oral story remembered, one that gave identity to a community of people, and eventually it was put into writing, perhaps when later scribes realized the significance of that story for their nation. Religious texts that were not finally included in the Hebrew Bible (HB) no doubt functioned as authoritative religious texts or scripturally for a time for some Jews and some early Christians before they were excluded from the emerging collections of sacred scripture.

WHEN WERE THE HEBREW SCRIPTURES RECOGNIZED AS SCRIPTURE?

When were Israel's sacred texts recognized as scripture and read to the people of Israel as a divine message? For our purposes, the influence that Israel's foundational story had on the nation of Israel began perhaps as early as the tenth century BCE (or earlier?), but apart from a few reflections such as we see in 1 Kgs 2:3 (ca. 620 BCE), Torah's sacred texts apparently had little influence or impact on the nation. There are very few references to the "law of Moses" or its influence on the nation before the time of Josiah (621–620 BCE; cf. 2 Kgs 22–23). Jeremiah was believed to be the author of the Kings (so *b. Baba Bathra* 15a), with its frequent references to the "law of Moses" or the "word of the LORD." This suggests that the scribes who were involved in the final editing of

Deuteronomistic History after Jeremiah gave greater attention to the Torah and in some instances also to some of the prophets. There are frequent references to the law of Moses in the later Deuteronomistic period (2 Kings), that is, the commandments, statutes, and ordinances in the Torah; this appears some thirteen times in 2 Kings from 10:31 to 23:25, and especially in chapter 17.

Multiple references to the law of Moses are similarly found in 2 Chronicles, but only two times in 1 Chronicles (16:40; 22:12). The Chronicles repeat the same story of the history of the kings of Israel, but with a different focus. However, there are numerous references to the law or the law of Moses in Chronicles, Ezra, and Nehemiah. The Latter Prophets make frequent references to the law of Moses as well as to the exodus, wanderings, and entrance stories noted above (e.g., Jer 23:7–8; Amos 2:9–10; 3:1–2; 9:7; Mic 6:4–5), and similar references occur in other postexilic canonical writings (e.g., 2 Chr 7:12–22; Pss 78:8–12; 135:8–12; 2 Esd 4:4–27). Again, however, before Josiah and the subsequent destruction of Jerusalem and the temple (587–586 BCE) and the deportation to Babylon, there is little evidence that the Torah, or law of Moses, was the basis for regulation of life and activities among the Jews, or that it had much influence in the nation of Israel except for the brief time during Josiah's reign.

The evidence for determining the precise dating of most of the HB/OT books is lacking, likely due to how the story of Israel's formation and history was initially transmitted orally and from memory and not in texts. The Torah *as we now have it* probably dates at the earliest from about the late seventh century BCE, but more likely from the late sixth century or early fifth. The Former Prophets (Joshua, Judges, Samuels, and Kings) date perhaps from roughly the tenth century to the sixth or fifth century BCE. These texts tell the story of Israel's good leaders and kings, yet also the bad ones; combined, they lay the ground for understanding why the nation prospered at first but ultimately failed.

The primary evidence for recognizing Jewish religious texts as sacred scripture began largely with the discovery of Deuteronomy (most likely that text) in the temple in the time of Josiah (ca. 621 BCE; 2 Kgs 22:3–13). This recognition significantly advanced during the exilic period and especially by the time of Ezra and Nehemiah, when there was no monarchy or temple or cultus in the postexilic period. By the time of Sirach (ca. 180 BCE), the Law and a collection of prophets were surely functioning as authoritative religious texts among the Jews. Subsequently, as we see in Sirach (38:34b–39:3; 39:6; 49:9–10, which mentions Job and the Twelve Prophets, and other prominent texts and individuals featured in chaps. 44–50), several kinds of texts are mentioned; especially in the Prologue to Sirach (130 BCE), a collection of the laws of Moses, some unspecified "prophets," and "others" were functioning as sacred texts among the Jews. The growth of this collection of sacred texts is supported by the discovery of the Dead Sea Scrolls at Qumran in the late 1940s and early 1950s and elsewhere in the Judean Desert. Finally, we see the multiple citations of HB texts as scripture in the NT and in Josephus, both of which support the presence of a larger and influential body of sacred scriptures among the Jewish and early Christian communities in the first century CE.[30]

However, if our question is about when these religious texts functioned as sacred scripture and when these texts emerged as a *fixed* sacred collection of scriptures, the answer at present must be more vague and more challenging. It is easier to focus on the end of that process for the Jews than its beginning. There are two first-century-CE Jewish references to a *fixed* number of scriptures, and both appear around 90–100 CE: Josephus, in his work *Against Apion* (1.37–43), speaks of twenty-two books that comprise the Jewish scriptures; and the pseudonymous author of *4 Ezra* 14:44–46 speaks of twenty-four books that could be read publicly and seventy others that could be read by the wise. Unfortunately, in neither of these cases do the authors identify the books that comprise their sacred collections.

Josephus identifies the Jewish sacred books by category or genre as five books of Moses, thirteen prophets, and four books that contain "hymns to God and precepts for the conduct of human life." Strangely, he lists thirteen prophetic books, unlike the later-designated eight prophets that include the Former Prophets (Joshua, Judges, Samuels, and Kings) and Latter Prophets (Isaiah, Jeremiah, Ezekiel, and the Twelve). His additional four books (*Ag. Ap.* 1.40) do not provide an easy inclusion of Song of Songs and Lamentations. Were these final four books earlier a part of a larger prophetic corpus that eventually formed what became known as the Writings (Ketuvim)? We do not know if Josephus's list is identical with the books that later shaped the HB canon, though this is a popular notion. Josephus does not identify the books in his list despite the number of those books matching the number of letters in the Hebrew alphabet, twenty-two. But the twenty-four books in *4 Ezra* fits the count of letters in the Greek alphabet. Josephus does not mention all the books in the later HB, but he cites most of them in *Jewish Antiquities* 1–11. It is likely that the number twenty-two in Josephus reflects more the completeness and sacredness of the Jewish scriptures than the specific books that are in his collection.[31] Neither Josephus nor *4 Ezra* identify the *tripartite* biblical canon (Tanak) that later forms the HB canon, nor does either twenty-four or twenty-two match the number of books in the later HB. Books need to be combined to come to either number (e.g., Ruth with Judges, Ezra with Nehemiah, the Twelve as one volume).

The specific identity of the HB books and their tripartite order appears for the first time in the middle to late second century CE *baraita* (Jewish interpretations, as in *b. Baba Bathra* 14b), but the Tanak order was not the most common way of referring to the Jewish scriptures until centuries later. Before then, the most common Jewish designation for the Jewish scriptures was the "Law and the Prophets."

30. I have discussed the evidence for this development at length in *Old Testament*, 121–59, 268–95.

31. I discuss the significance and prominence of these numbers at length in *Old Testament*, 223–27 and 341–56.

The early Christians, who eventually welcomed all the HB scriptures and other books besides, did not generally follow the *tripartite* divisions in the HB. For the most part, they adopted a *quadripartite* order for their OT scriptures: Pentateuch, history, poetry and wisdom, and Prophets. This raises the questions of whether they *invented* that order, as is often supposed, or adopted it from a preexisting order more commonly found in the LXX. The early Christians *generally* adopted the LXX translation for their OT scriptures: the LXX also included additional so-called apocryphal, or deuterocanonical, books, but likely in a different order. Since no known church father made an argument for the quadripartite order in the Christian OT canon, it appears more likely that this order was inherited or adopted rather than invented by the church. It is likely that Christians simply inherited that order from texts of the LXX. We do not have any pre-Christian LXX texts available to demonstrate this, but the so-called Christian order is not necessarily Christian. Any diaspora Jew could have adopted a similar order. While the quadripartite order is certainly conducive to the Christian proclamation since the OT used by some Catholic and Protestant Christians (not Orthodox) ends with Malachi, which looks forward to the coming of Elijah (Mal 4:4–5; cf. Matt 11:13–14), there is no reason why diaspora Jews looking forward to hope for their nation and the demise of nations controlling their homeland (Persia/Rome) could not have adopted that same order. The earliest Christian OT canon lists are generally quadripartite but generally do not end with Malachi; those lists that do end with Malachi (Mommsen and Isodore) are few, and that order may be a Christian invention.[32]

Barton is doubtless correct when he concludes that "there is never any suggestion [in the church fathers] that any particular order is the 'proper' one or has any special authority, still less that the preferred arrangement has any hermeneutical importance."[33] The current order of *some* Christian OT canons ends with Malachi, and that may be a Christian invention, as James A. Sanders contends;[34] but the usual quadripartite order in modern Bibles is not uniformly found in antiquity, and no ancient collection clearly ends with Malachi before the Mommsen or Cheltenham catalog (359) and the catalog attributed to Bishop Isodore of Seville (620–635), and only rarely thereafter. Again, there is no rationale offered for that order. Before the fourth century, when it was uncommon to include all the biblical books in a codex, a so-called *pandect* Bible, there was no value attached by the church fathers to any particular order of the HB or OT books.[35] Long after that, the practice of putting all of the books of the church's scriptures in one volume was rare until the production of the Paris pandect Bibles in the thirteenth century. At that time, with the use of the magnifying glass that had

32. I have listed these in *Old Testament*, 491–97. See also my arguments for this in "The Reception of the Writings and Their Place in the Biblical Canon."
33. Barton, *Oracles of God* (2007 edition), 90.
34. James A. Sanders, "'Spinning' the Bible."
35. So argues Barton, *Oracles of God* (2007 edition), 91.

only recently been invented and the production of thinner pages, the text of the church's scriptures could be reduced in size so that all of the OT could fit into a single volume with thinner pages.[36] The notion of a "Bible," a complete collection of all the church's sacred books (Greek pl., *biblia*, "books") in one volume, became more common after the emergence of the pandect Bibles. After the circulation of the Paris Bibles, the order of the Bibles generally followed the order of books in the Latin Vulgate.

The most consistent aspect of the order of the Jewish scriptures in late Second Temple Judaism and in the first scriptures of early Christianity is that the Pentateuch is consistently in first place in scriptural references, as indicated by the phrase "the Law and the Prophets," and the same is true in the early canon lists or catalogs of those scriptures, such as in the Bryennios catalog (100–150 CE), the *b. Baba Bathra* catalog (ca. 150–180 CE), and the earliest Christian lists (Melito and Origen—see below), but there is considerable variation in the order of the rest of the books in the surviving manuscripts and in the ancient scripture catalogs. This suggests, as noted above, that outside of the usual pentateuchal order, the sequence of the OT books was not an important issue in the early churches. It is likely that the Pentateuch was the only part of the Jewish scriptures that was fixed before the first century CE, with the possible exception of the collection of the Twelve Minor Prophets that circulated together much earlier but not always in the same uniform sequence.

The collection of recognized scriptural texts was larger in the last centuries BCE and the first centuries CE than what was eventually included in the HB canon or in later Christian OT canons. While accepting the widespread recognition of most of the current books in the HB canon in the first century CE, Barton correctly concludes: "It seems to me that the body of texts widely regarded as 'Scripture' in our period [NT era] was probably a lot larger than the present limits of even the Greek canon allow."[37] He and other scholars recognize the acceptance of *1 Enoch* as a scriptural text, and likely the acceptance of other books besides what we know as the apocryphal, or deuterocanonical, texts. Some church fathers—especially Jerome and Cyril, who both lived in Palestine—*generally* adopted the HB Jewish scriptures and their order (Tanak), though not completely; Jerome comes closest to it. In the Christian catalogs of OT books, Daniel is almost always listed among the Major Prophets (Isaiah, Jeremiah, Ezekiel, and Daniel). Jerome alone places Daniel in the latter part of his OT canon, a position the Writings have in the HB canon. However, Jerome places Ruth with Judges, unlike the rabbinic listings of Ruth.

Widespread popularity and use appear to account for the acceptance of most of the books that comprise the HB and Christian OT canons. This is also true in Catholic and Orthodox OT biblical canons that accept all the HB books and other

---

36. For a discussion of this, see Liere, *Medieval Bible*, 95–98.
37. Barton, *Oracles of God* (2007 edition), 92.

OT-related scriptures as well. While there are still differences in the Christian OT canons (Catholic, Greek and Russian Orthodox, Protestant, and Ethiopian), they all presently agree on the HB books. Again, the order of these collections varies, as we see in the multiple conclusions of the OT canons such as the Eastern, Russian, and Oriental Orthodox churches' Old Testaments. Also some of the changes seen in the various canon lists may reflect the early transmission of them in rolls or in second- and third-century codices that technologically could not include all the church's sacred books in one volume at that time.

Jesus appears to have been aware of or familiar with several ancient noncanonical Jewish texts, including Sirach (Sir 28:2–5; cf. Mark 11:25; Luke 11:4; Matt 6:12), *1 Enoch* (97:8–9; cf. Luke 12:16–21; see also *1 En.* 69:27–29; cf. Matt 19:28; 25:31), *Psalms of Solomon* (4:2–3; cf. Luke 18:10–14); and shows familiarity with others as well such as 2 Maccabees (possibly also 1 Maccabees), and *likely* the *Testaments of the Twelve Patriarchs*, and the *Testament of Job*.[38] Although Jesus cites more than half of the HB/OT books, and more frequently Deuteronomy (some 15 or 16 times), Isaiah (some 40 times), and the Psalms (some 13 times),[39] he also cites Daniel and Zechariah and several other HB books, but did not cite or allude to Song of Songs, Ruth, Lamentations, Ecclesiastes, Esther, Ezra and Nehemiah, and *possibly* Chronicles.[40] Several early Christians made use of or cited not only most of the HB books, but also several Jewish apocryphal and pseudepigraphal writings. Some early Christians welcomed several apocryphal and pseudepigraphal works like scripture, especially Wisdom of Solomon, Sirach, *1 Enoch*, but others also.[41] Melito of Sardis (ca. 170 CE) produced the earliest known *Christian* collection of OT scriptures, and his list is similar to though not identical with the collection now present in the Protestant OT. However, he omits Esther and also the Twelve likely by accident, but adds Wisdom of Solomon. Melito's order of the Christian OT scriptures is unlike either the HB or later Christian OT order. Although he went to Palestine to learn which books comprise the church's first scriptures, the order in his list has no other parallels in antiquity and is likely reflective of an emerging Christian OT canon in the second century (see his list in Eusebius, *Hist. eccl.* 4.26.13–14). Jerome lists the OT books in his *Preface to the Books of Samuel and Kings* (*Prologus in libro Regnum*, ca. 394, Bethlehem, Palestine) much like the HB order. While Jerome's list is like Jewish lists that have the Writings at the end and his order numbers them as twenty-two instead of the HB's twenty-four, he places Ruth after Judges, as in most Christian orders, and appears to include Lamentations with Jeremiah but acknowledges that some place it in the Hagiographa (Ketuvim). He places it with Jeremiah and counts

---

38. DeSilva, *Jewish Teachers*, 254–55. He lists others as well. See also more examples in McDonald, *Old Testament*, 301–9.

39. C. A. Evans, "Scriptures of Jesus," here 185–86.

40. C. A. Evans, "Scriptures of Jesus," 185–86, compares the references that Jesus makes to the OT scriptures with the quotation of biblical texts in noncanonical writings from Qumran.

41. I list these in *Old Testament*, 229–35.

the books as twenty-two instead of twenty-four. Jerome's important description of the OT books and their order is as follows:

> As, then, there are twenty-two elementary characters by means of which we write in Hebrew all we say, and the compass of the human voice is contained within their limits, so we reckon twenty-two books, by which, as by the alphabet of the doctrine of God, a righteous man is instructed in tender infancy, and, as it were, while still at the breast. The first of these books is called *Bresith*, to which we give the name Genesis. The second, *Elle Smoth*, which bears the name Exodus; the third, *Vaiecra*, that is Leviticus; the fourth, *Vaiedabber*, which we call Numbers; the fifth, *Elle Addabarim*, which is entitled Deuteronomy. These are the five books of Moses, which they properly call *Thorath*, that is, *law*.
>
> The second class is composed of the Prophets, and they begin with *Jesus* the son of Nave, who among them is called Joshua the son of Nun. Next in the series is *Sophtim*, that is, the book of Judges; and in the same book they include Ruth, because the events narrated occurred in the days of the Judges. Then comes Samuel, which we call First and Second Kings. The fourth is *Malachim*, that is, Kings, which is contained in the third and fourth volumes of Kings. And it is far better to say *Malachim*, that is Kings, than *Malachoth*, that is Kingdoms. For the author does not describe the Kingdoms of many nations, but that of one people, the people of Israel, which is comprised in the twelve tribes. The fifth is Isaiah, the sixth, Jeremiah, the seventh, Ezekiel, the eighth is the book of the Twelve Prophets, which is called among the Jews *Thare Asra*.
>
> To the third class belong the *Hagiographa*, of which the first book begins with Job, the second with David, whose writings they divide into five parts and comprise in one volume of Psalms; the third is Solomon, in three books, Proverbs, which they call *Parables*, that is *Masaloth*, Ecclesiastes, that is *Coeleth*, the Song of Songs, which they denote by the title *Sir Assirim*; the sixth is Daniel; the seventh, *Dabre Aiamim*, that is, *Words of Days*, which we may more expressively call a chronicle of the whole of the sacred history, the book that amongst us is called First and Second Chronicles; the eighth, Ezra, which itself is likewise divided amongst Greeks and Latins into two books; the ninth is Esther.
>
> And so there are also twenty-two books of the Old Testament; that is, five of Moses, eight of the prophets, nine of the Hagiographa, *though some include Ruth and Kinoth (Lamentations) amongst the Hagiographa,* and think that these books ought to be reckoned separately; we should thus have twenty-four books of the old law. And these the Apocalypse of John represents by the twenty-four elders, who adore the Lamb, and with downcast looks offer their crowns, while in their presence stand the four living creatures with eyes before and behind, that is, looking to the past and the future, and with unwearied voice crying, Holy, Holy, Holy, Lord God Almighty, who wast, and art, and art to come. (*NPNF*[2] trans., emphasis added)

Like the earliest Jewish collections of scriptures, the Christian collections vary considerably in their order or sequence.

For centuries there was considerable fluidity in the surviving collections of the Jewish and Christian scriptures. The lack of full agreement among the rabbis

over the books included in the Jewish scriptures and their order in the second
and later centuries CE can be seen in the doubts about Esther, Ecclesiastes, Song
of Songs, Ezekiel, and Wisdom of Solomon noted above. Scholars are aware
that some rabbinic sages continued to welcome Sirach as scripture for centuries
before dismissing it.[42] Some of the doubts about some HB texts are reflected in
the early church fathers, especially Esther, which is omitted by several church
fathers including Athanasius, well into the fourth century.

Scholars who argue for an earlier closure of the HB/OT often appeal to
the prologue to Sirach, 2 Macc 2:13–15, Philo, 4QMMT, and Luke 24:44,
but a careful analysis of these texts does not reflect a clear tripartite canon
before or during the first century CE.[43] Even if there was an emerging Jewish
scriptural canon at the end of the first century CE (Josephus and the author of
4 Ezra), that is not a major focus of the majority of rabbinic sages until much
later. The same can be said of the early church. For example, the author of
Heb 1:1 begins with a reference to God having spoken "to our ancestors . . .
by the prophets" and then throughout cites texts from the Pentateuch, the
Prophets, Psalms, and Wisdom of Solomon without distinction (see Heb 1:3
citing Wis 7:25). All these works are cited as scripture and are introduced as
"prophets." There are no scriptural designations for these cited texts like "as
the scripture says" or "it is written" throughout the book except in Heb 10:7,
a quote from Ps 40:7. Apparently the only closed divisions of books that were
widely accepted in the first century were Torah, or Pentateuch, and the Twelve
(Minor Prophets). It is difficult to argue that there was a third division of Jewish scriptures in the first century CE since even the parameters of the second
division, "Prophets," is not yet clear. For the rabbinic Jews, the formation of
the HB canon took centuries, and disagreement over its shape continued even
later. For instance, the Karaite Jews (8th c. CE, Babylon) chided rabbinic Jews
and their successors in the ninth to eleventh centuries because they recognized
the Tanak scriptures instead of only the Torah (Pentateuch). Before the ninth
century CE it is unlikely that Jews in the Diaspora accepted the rabbinic traditions that were written only in Hebrew and Aramaic or only the books in the
HB canon instead of the books in the LXX. The Diaspora Jews, who spoke
only Greek or Latin until well into the ninth century CE, would have adopted
the LXX books as their scriptures.[44]

The now widely accepted HB canon was not universally accepted in the sec-
ond century CE, and Christians have never fully agreed on the scope of their
OT canon, though all eventually agreed on all the books in the HB canon.
Initially several church fathers raised questions about the sacred status of Esther,
Song of Songs, and Ecclesiastes, though eventually the majority welcomed them
and all the HB books, and some church fathers also welcomed books that we

42. This is discussed in McDonald, *Old Testament*, 378–418.
43. McDonald, *Old Testament*, 163–75 and 268–94. Also see Lim's careful discussion of these
frequently cited texts: Lim, *Jewish Canon*, esp. 25–34, 94–165.
44. In "Split Jewish Diaspora," Edrei and Mendels argue this convincingly.

now identify as apocryphal, or deuterocanonical. Although Jerome favored only the books in the HB canon, Augustine accepted the apocryphal, or deuterocanonical, books, and that view held sway in most churches until the Reformation period. Well into the third century and even later, some churches continued to accept *1 Enoch* as scripture, as did Tertullian and initially Origen. Many also accepted the *Shepherd of Hermas* as well as the *Epistle of Barnabas*, as we see in Irenaeus and Codex Sinaiticus.

While I do not believe that Protestants necessarily should change the scope of their biblical canon, which would cause more divisions than it would be worth, I do think it is important to read the apocryphal and pseudepigraphal writings that informed the thinking of many Second Temple Jews and many early Christians as well as others throughout church history.[45] There is considerable value in being informed by *all* the books that influenced the faith of many early Christians, including those books not now included in the Protestant canon. In this literature biblical scholars continue to find invaluable information that has relevance for understanding both the biblical literature and its socio-historical context.

The term "scripture" was not used throughout much of ancient Israel's history and is likely first found in its absolute sense of sacred scripture in the *Letter of Aristeas* (likely ca. 130–100 BCE), which states: "So we are exhorted through *scripture* also by the one who says thus, 'Thou shalt remember the Lord, who did great and wonderful deeds in thee.'"[46] Nevertheless, the *function* of religious texts as scripture is much earlier and likely begins during the later Deuteronomistic period. According to James Barr, that was the time when the *notion* of scripture actually began to take a central place in the life of the nation of Israel.[47] He concludes that it was only with the Deuteronomistic movement and the reforms of Josiah that the religion of Israel began to be built around a collection of sacred scriptures. Although the story of the nation's exodus, wilderness wanderings, and entrance into the land of Canaan existed much earlier than the notion of scripture, that story likely did not have the function of sacred scripture until later. There are few references to the law of Moses in the historical books from Judges through 1 Kings (most agree that the current form of Joshua is likely late 7th or early 6th century BCE); then, as noted earlier, after that time references to the Law and some references to prophets began to appear regularly. The Pentateuch *as we now have it* cannot be dated much before the sixth or at the latest fifth century BCE, but what is in it contains and reflects considerable rewriting with the use of multiple sources—especially J and E from an earlier period (950 BCE) and D (7th century?)—before it functioned widely as scripture following the addition of the P material.[48]

---

45. Metzger offers a helpful summary of the influence of these writings throughout church history. See Metzger, "Apocryphal/Deuterocanonical Books," esp. viii–xi.

46. §155, *OTP* 2:23, emphasis added.

47. Barr, *Holy Scripture*, 7.

48. For a helpful summary of scholarship on this, see Coogan, *Old Testament*, 50–56; and similarly, with more detail, J. Collins, *Introduction to the Hebrew Bible*, 3rd ed., 49–66.

In the next chapter I will focus more specifically on the critical issues related to the formation of the Jewish scriptures into a fixed biblical canon along with several recent issues that challenge traditional notions of canon formation. These issues include the early church's adoption of the fluid collection of Jewish scriptures before its separation from Judaism, including the order and divisions of those scriptures and the challenge of finding reliable criteria for determining the scope of the HB and OT canons.

Chapter 5

Forming Jewish Scriptures as a Biblical Canon

LEE MARTIN McDONALD

Without question, one of the more challenging questions to solve is the origin and fixing of the Jewish scriptures into what we now call the Hebrew Bible (HB), or Tanak, and the Christian Old Testament (OT). Below I will examine some of the more important issues related to this question and how recent scholarship is addressing them. The following focuses on the fixing of this collection of scriptures for Jews and Christians and the complexity involved for the three main bodies of Christians who have never agreed on the scope or function of that literature.

INTERPRETING ISRAEL'S PRIMARY STORY AS SCRIPTURE

The Former and Latter Prophets are often viewed as providing interpretations of Israel's primary story in Torah (exodus, wanderings, and entrance into the promised land) that gave rise to the nation's identity (see, for instance, 1 Sam 12:8; Amos 2:4, 9–12; Hos 12:2–4).[1] For later generations, the Writings explained

---

1. See many examples of this listed in J. A. Sanders, *Monotheizing Process*, 13–19.

the significance of the earlier sacred traditions from which hope and renewal for the Jews emerged and clarified to them how to be a faithful Jew when not in one's homeland or living under control of a foreign power. Since there are no *known* Jewish translations of these texts into Greek until the first quarter of the second century CE, it is possible that the sacred status of *some* of these books was not fully affirmed before then. Rajak suggests that since Lamentations was not translated into Greek before 70 CE, its scriptural status may have been in doubt earlier.[2]

Although the HB canon separates Daniel from the Latter Prophets and places it in the Writings, the early Christians, with rare exceptions, regularly placed Daniel at the end of their Major Prophets, namely, Isaiah, Jeremiah, Ezekiel, Daniel. Long ago Wildeboer and others after him argued that Daniel's inclusion in the Writings and not in the Prophets in the HB was because the Prophets had already been closed when Daniel was written.[3] Further, because of the emergence of the belief in the cessation of prophecy in the time of Ezra and Nehemiah (ca. 450–400 BCE) or later during early Greek rule over Palestine, some believe that Daniel, which was written later (ca. after 165 BCE), could not have been included among the Prophets because they were already closed by then. Wildeboer assumed that in the second century BCE there was a widespread belief that prophecy had ceased after the death of Malachi and that nothing more could be added to the Prophets, not even Daniel. He also assumed that *before* the second century CE, the term "prophets" was the same as "the Prophets" in the HB canon. The belief in the cessation of prophecy is illustrated in a *later* rabbinic text in *b. Sotah* 48b:

> But, said R. Nahman: Who are the former prophets? [The term "former"] excludes Haggai, Zechariah, and Malachi who are the latter [prophets]. For our Rabbis have taught: When Haggai, Zechariah and Malachi died, the Holy Spirit departed from Israel; nevertheless they made use of the *Bath Kol*. (*b. Sotah* 48b, Soncino trans.)

The belief that the Prophets were a closed and fixed collection because of the widespread notion of the cessation of prophecy before Daniel was written appears to ignore the evidence of Daniel's status in the literature at Qumran, the NT, Josephus, the early church fathers, and even some rabbinic sages. This evidence uniformly recognizes Daniel *as prophetic literature*. It also reflects a belief in Judaism of Late Antiquity that the Spirit was still active in the Jewish nation despite a popular belief that prophecy had ceased and the presence of the Spirit was gone. This notion of the Spirit's absence is first stated in 1 Macc 4:45–46; 9:27; and 14:41, but it was not a uniform belief among all Jews then or later.[4]

---

2. See Rajak, *Translation and Survival*, 312–13.
3. See Wildeboer, *Canon of the Old Testament*, 4. See also Leiman, *Canonization of the Hebrew Scripture*, 26, who argues similarly.
4. For a discussion of this, see McDonald, *Old Testament*, 175–86.

The residents of Qumran, the early Christians, Josephus, and most early church fathers all included Daniel among the prophets. For example, among the Dead Sea Scrolls at Qumran we read, ". . . as is written in the book of Daniel, the prophet" (Dan 12:10; 11:32; cf. 4Q174 1–3.ii.3; trans. García Martínez and Tigchelaar, 1:355).[5] Anderson and Barton observe that at Qumran the phrase "as it is written in the book of the prophet Daniel" appears multiple times.[6] In the NT, Jesus refers to Dan 11:31 and 12:11 with the words, "as was spoken of by the prophet Daniel" (Matt 24:15). Josephus also regularly refers to Daniel as a prophet who prophesied (*Ant.* 10.245–46, 249) and even concludes that he was "one of the greatest of the prophets" who authored several books and "was wont to prophesy future things, as did the other prophets" (*Ant.* 10.266–267), a possible reference to later additions to Daniel in the LXX.

In the second century CE, when introducing Dan 7:24 and subsequently 7:7–8, the author of *Epistle of Barnabas* (4.4) begins: "For also the prophet says . . ." Later in the rabbinic tradition Daniel continued to be referred to as a prophet among the prophets Haggai, Zechariah, and Malachi. For example, even after the Tanak was formed, Daniel held a place among the Prophets, as we see in a Babylonian talmudic text:

> Moreover, he spoke thus even of Daniel, who was greater than he. And whence do we know that Daniel was greater than he? From the verse, And I Daniel alone saw the vision: for the men that were with me saw not the vision; but a great quaking fell upon them, so that they fled to hide themselves. "For the men that were with me saw not the vision": now who were these men?—R. Jeremiah—others say R. Hiyya b. Abba—said: Haggai, Zecharia and Malachi. (*b. Sanhedrin* 93b, Soncino trans.)

Similarly, in *y. Megillah* 2.2a, Daniel is placed alongside Jeremiah and praised among the prophets as follows: "And may mortal men [such as Jeremiah and Daniel] cut these [titles of praise] out of the prayer to God?" Said R. Isaac bar Eleazar, "The prophets knew full well that their God is honest, and they were not going to flatter him" (*y. Meg.* 2.2a, trans. Neusner). It appears that Daniel was placed among the Writings, or Hagiographa, *for the first time* in the mid- to late-second-century-CE *baraita* text, *b. Baba Bathra* 14b noted above, but the residents of Qumran, Josephus, the early Christians, and several rabbinic sages regularly placed Daniel among the "prophets" and not in a separate category. With only one exception (see Jerome, *Preface to the Books of Samuel and*

5. The same can be said about the Psalms that were also included among the prophetic writings at Qumran. After numbering David's compositions (Psalms), the author of 11QPs^a 27.2–11 concludes: "All these he [David] composed through prophecy which was given him from before the Most High." See Flint, "Noncanonical Writings," here 116–17. Lim is not convinced that Psalms was counted among the Prophets at Qumran; see Lim, "'All These He Composed through Prophecy.'" This may be drawing a fine line between "a prophet" and writing psalms in the "spirit of prophecy." It is not clear whether such distinctions were made in antiquity.

6. G. Anderson, "Canonical and Non-canonical," here 151. See also Barton, *Oracles of God* (2007 edition), 40–42.

Kings), the church fathers and even the Jewish Bryennios catalog (ca. 100–150 CE) followed the usual pattern of placing Daniel among the Prophets. Barton summarizes the most important arguments against Wildeboer's (and Leiman's) rationale for placing Daniel in the Writings and identifies weaknesses of their reasoning.[7]

The evidence that the tripartite biblical canon of the HB was fixed by the end of the first century CE is presently insufficient and unconvincing.[8] It appears that the most prominent and cited books among the Writings, Daniel and Psalms, were cited as prophetic literature. Leiman has observed that in rabbinic literature both David (Psalms) and Daniel are frequently cited as נְבִיאִים (*Nevi'im*, prophets). He cites many references to the Law and the Prophets without reference to the Writings well into the Amoraic period, when the third part of the Tanak was identified more frequently.[9]

THE JEWISH SCRIPTURES AS A BIBLICAL CANON

There is no evidence that the HB canon was closed before the end of the first century CE and there was no known rabbinic council that made that decision. Josephus and *4 Ezra* are the first to limit the books to twenty-two and twenty-four, respectively, plus the seventy others in *4 Ezra* for the wise. There is likewise no clear reference to the tripartite biblical canon such as we see in the HB before its presence in the Babylonian *baraita b. Baba Bathra* 14b. This suggests that a tripartite collection of scriptures was not a widely held view at the time it was written since the rabbis continued to speak of their scriptures as the Law and the Prophets or Moses and the Prophets well into the fourth century and they even debated its parameters that late, as we saw above. There is an earlier Tosefta text that mentions the reading of the Ketuvim, or *Hagiographa*, but such texts are rare before the later *Talmudim*.[10] This suggests that the development of the Writings as the third part of the Jewish scriptures *began* in the second and third centuries CE and that the tripartite HB canon was not widely acknowledged among a majority of the rabbinic sages until even later.

Leiman suggests that the expansion of the Jewish scriptures into a three-part HB is based on a liturgical expansion rather than a canonical one, but it is difficult to distinguish the authority attributed to the Jewish scriptures in a canonical context from writings used in a liturgical context. Both function like or as scripture. He cites many references to the Law and the Prophets without reference to

---

7. Barton, *Oracles of God* (2007 edition), 25, 35–40.

8. So argues J. Collins, *Seers, Sybils and Sages*, esp. 14.

9. Leiman, *Canon and Masorah*, 58–67, 168 fn. 288. See also Leiman, *Canonization of the Hebrew Scripture*.

10. Here is that text: "The reciter opens with verses from the Torah, and closes with verses from the Torah, and recites from the Prophets and Hagiographa [Ketuvim] in between" (*t. Rosh HaShannah* 2.12G).

the Writings (or Ketuvim) well into the Amoraic period, when the third part of the Tanak was identified more frequently.[11]

Several of the later-designated Writings are cited as Torah or Law or are included among the "prophets" in the NT, as noted above. Also, the tripartite Tanak distinctions are not found in Jewish literature before the middle to end of the second century CE (*b. Baba Bathra* 14b), and the Tanak divisions are not obvious in Qumran literature, NT literature, or Josephus. It therefore seems obvious that those distinctions were not functional in the first century CE. Again, since the Jewish scriptures were all initially transmitted in individual rolls or scrolls, it is difficult to find consistency or stability in the order or sequence of them, apart from the Law, until the rabbis begin to make use of the codex centuries later. The Bryennios catalog is the earliest known Jewish scripture catalog and may date from 100–150 CE; it is quite similar to Epiphanius's Jewish list (ca. 374–377), and it also does not follow the HB Tanak order.

THE DIVISIONS AND ORDER OF THE HEBREW BIBLE AND OLD TESTAMENT CANON

In recent times considerable focus has been placed on the order of the books in the biblical canons of Jews and Christians. It is difficult to find that interest in antiquity, and it appears that this question is mostly a modern one rather than a historic ancient concern. The considerable variety of orders in both Jewish and Christian manuscripts and scripture catalogs suggests that the matter was not yet settled or considered important in antiquity for Jews or Christians. Much has been made over the completion and order of the HB canon, based on Luke's and Matthew's reference to the blood of Zechariah (Matt 23:35 and Luke 11:51), but that argument has not been convincing.[12] The argument goes thus: since Abel represents the first book of the HB canon (Genesis) and Zechariah the last (2 Chronicles), Jesus had the whole scriptural collection in view. They argue that Chronicles was the last book of the OT canon seen both by internal and external evidence, but this has been significantly challenged in both areas.[13] While Chronicles is in the last place only in *b. Baba Bathra* 14b, it does not reappear in last place in the HB canon until its last-place position in the tenth-century Aleppo and Leningrad codices. Other *Jewish* catalogs or manuscripts of HB books generally conclude with Esther; none of the known Christian canon catalogs concludes the OT canon with Chronicles. The argument that the HB scriptures concluded with Chronicles, based on the Matthew and Luke references to

---

11. Leiman, *Canonization of the Hebrew Scripture*, 58–67.

12. For a more complete discussion of these texts, see Gallagher, "Blood from Abel to Zechariah"; also McDonald, *Old Testament*, 286–94.

13. For a careful assessment of the place of Chronicles in the Bible and its significance in the canon formation, see Gallagher, "End of the Bible?"

Zechariah, is therefore unconvincing.[14] While ending the HB with Chronicles conveniently ties the two collections of the church's scriptures together, it is not found in the earliest canonical catalogs up through the medieval period, and concluding the OT canon with Malachi is rarely found in any Christian OT canon. Similarly, the identity of the Zechariah in Matthew and Luke is not easily made the same as the Zechariah in Chronicles, including the way that he died. Ancient interpretations of Luke 11:48–51 and Matt 23:35 never conclude that Jesus referred to the beginning and end of the OT canon.

Some scholars (Seitz and Chapman especially) argue that using the Tanak order is the best way to examine the Hebrew scriptures and understand them in the early Christian churches. That notion, however, is a modern conclusion, not based on evidence from antiquity.[15] Although some scholars claim that the HB canon order is the most appropriate way to understand the HB writings not only for Jews but also for Christians,[16] there is no evidence for this order before the Christians and Jews separated in the first and second centuries CE, and it is difficult to make a case for understanding the NT based on any order of the HB biblical canon.[17]

As we have seen, it is not clear that the usual order of the OT books in Christian manuscripts is necessarily later than the HB order or that the early church *invented* the usual quadripartite order for its OT. There is nothing in it, as noted above, that Diaspora Jews with a messianic hope would object to. It is more likely, as F. F. Bruce concluded long ago, that the quadripartite order in the Septuagint might not have been a Christian innovation, but rather one of several arrangements adopted by Jews in the Diaspora. He also observes that the current order in English Bibles is derived from the Latin Vulgate and is closer to the LXX than to the HB.[18] What suggests that he may be right is that the early church fathers do not make anything of or argue for the quadripartite order of their OT canon, or any order for that matter; also, with exceptions from those who lived in Palestine (Jerome and Cyril), most Christians did not follow the tripartite order and never made an argument for or against it.

Also, arguments for an early order of the HB scriptures based on the Prologue to Sirach (ca. 130–100 BCE) are likewise unconvincing since the Prologue never identifies the books or their order or divisions in the Jewish scriptures apart from the designation "the Law and the Prophets," the latter of which is a broad and

14. Gallagher, in "Blood from Abel to Zechariah," offers a careful assessment and refutation of arguments for the order and conclusion of the Jewish scriptures based on these Matthew and Luke texts.

15. See my "Reception of the Writings."

16. For arguments supporting the tripartite order of the HB canon, see Seitz, *Goodly Fellowship of the Prophets*; Seitz, *Prophecy and Hermeneutics*; Steinberg, *Ketuvim*; Steinberg and T. Stone, eds., *Shape of the Writings*; and T. Stone, *Compilational History of the Megilloth*.

17. For a discussion of this along with Chapman's argument for the HB tripartite order, see Chapman, "Reclaiming Inspiration for the Bible." Also see Chapman, "Second Temple Jewish Hermeneutics"; Chapman, "Canon, Old Testament"; and Chapman, "Canon Debate."

18. F. Bruce, *Books and the Parchments*, 81–82.

unidentified collection of books in a prophetic corpus. The Prologue refers to "others" with the Law and the Prophets but does not identify the others, which could well have included some of what we now call noncanonical writings or even canonical writings.[19]

The arguments for the Tanak order of the HB canon are arbitrary and not broadly reflective of early Christianity or even Judaism of Late Antiquity. The fourth-century rabbinic tradition usually refers to its scriptures as the "Law and Prophets" or "Moses and the Prophets"; the tripartite order was still not universally welcomed among early rabbinic Jews at that time. The ancient Christians appear to have no known *standard* order for their OT books, though most followed a *broadly* quadripartite order that generally did not end with the Twelve. The current order of the HB canon, the tripartite HB that ends with Chronicles, is not the only order that can be found in antiquity.[20] Until the tenth century, that appears to be a minority position.

So far as is known, no ancient or medieval Christians engaged in arguments for the order of their OT, with the possible exception of Epiphanius, who perhaps made an unusual argument for four "pentateuchs" of five books each and two additional books (Ezra–Nehemiah and Esther) in his OT canon, but even he did not end the OT scriptures with Malachi. His helpful explanation reads as follows:

> For the names of the letters [of the Hebrew alphabet] are twenty-two. But there are five of them that have a double form, for *k* has a double form, and *m* and *n* and *p* and *s*. Therefore in this manner the books also are counted as twenty-two; but there are twenty-seven, because five of them are double. For Ruth is joined to Judges, and they are counted among the Hebrews (as) one book. The first (book) of Kingdoms is joined to the second and called one book; the third is joined to the fourth and becomes one book. First Paraleipomena [1 Chronicles] is joined to Second and called one book. The first book of Ezra is joined to the second [Nehemiah] and becomes one book. So in this way the books are grouped into four "pentateuchs," and there are two others left over, so that the books of the (Old) Testament are as follows: the five of the Law—Genesis, Exodus, Leviticus, Numbers, Deuteronomy—this is the Pentateuch, otherwise the code of law; and five in verse—the book of Job, then of the Psalms, the Proverbs of Solomon, Koheleth, the Song of Songs. Then another "Pentateuch" (of books) which are called the Writings [Ketuvim], and by some the Hagiographa, which are as follows: Joshua the (son) of Nun, the book of Judges with Ruth, First and Second Paraleipomena, First and Second Kingdoms, Third and Fourth Kingdoms; and this is a third "pentateuch." Another "Pentateuch" is the books of the prophets—the Twelve Prophets (forming) one book, Isaiah one, Jeremiah one, Ezekiel one, Daniel one—and again the prophetic "Pentateuch" is filled up. But there remain two other books, which are (one

---

19. For arguments against identifying "others" as the Tanak Writings, see Lim, *Jewish Canon*, 99–102. He also discusses Sir 39:1–3 and adds that the grandson of Sirach surely included his grandfather's work among that collection of "others."

20. See arguments for this position by Dorival, "L'apport des Pères de l'Église." He shows how patristic canon lists reflect several Jewish arrangements and also that the Tanak order was not the only order known in ancient Judaism.

of them) the two of Ezra that are counted as one, and the other the book of Esther. So twenty-two books are completed according to the number of the twenty-two letters of the Hebrews. For there are two (other) poetical books, that by Solomon called Most Excellent, and that by Jesus the son of Sirach and grandson of Jesus—for his grandfather was named Jesus (and it was) he who composed Wisdom in Hebrew, which his grandson, translating, wrote in Greek—which also are helpful and useful, but are not included in the number of the recognized; and therefore they were not kept in the chest, that is, in the ark of the covenant.[21]

The OT canon catalogs seldom end with Malachi, the usual order in contemporary Catholic and Protestant OT canons, but not in the Greek or Russian or Oriental Orthodox OT canons or in the HB canon. It is difficult to find any consistent logical or rational Jewish or Christian arguments to support either the current HB tripartite or the Christian quadripartite orders of the HB or OT scripture canons.

While the ending of the OT with Malachi is likely a Christian innovation, the ancient Christians did not offer a theological rationale for their usual quadripartite arrangement of the OT canon, and initially they did not conclude their OT canon with Malachi. The Greek and some Russian Orthodox OT canons conclude with Daniel and its additions. The thirteenth-century "Paris Bibles"[22] often conclude with the Twelve Minor Prophets and with Malachi in last place *in the Twelve*, yet sometimes end with 1–2 Maccabees. The Paris Bibles generally follow the order and text in the Alcuin Bibles, which now is the order in the modern Vulgate.[23]

21. This translation of Epiphanius, *On Weights and Measures* 4, is from Dean, ed., *Syriac Version*.

22. For a discussion of the specific books and their order in the Paris Bibles, see Light, "Thirteenth Century and the Paris Bible." The Paris Bibles have many variations in their texts, which are expected in handwritten manuscripts, but they generally follow the Alcuin Bibles (ca. 800 CE) that were influenced by the Theoldulf (bishop of Orleans, ca. 750–821) and Italian recensions (Light, "Thirteenth Century and the Paris Bible," 387). The new Paris Bibles were designed to be portable, were produced on thinner pages and with much smaller letters, and were perhaps even to be read by using magnifying devices recently invented. This made it feasible to produce portable small-print "pocketbook" size scriptural texts in a single volume for students, priests, and professors in universities. These portable Bibles generally ranged from 10½ by 7¼ inches to as small as 6⅓ by 4⅓ inches, not unlike modern portable Bibles, thus making the contents of the church's scriptures more accessible. For a helpful discussion of this, see de Hamel, *Book: A History of the Bible*, 114–39. See also his discussion and several illustrations of these manuscripts in his chapter "Books for Students." For an informed discussion of the Alcuin Bibles, see M. Brown, "Spreading the Word." Perhaps the antecedent or model for Alcuin's Bible was the nine-volume Bible of Cassiodorus (ca. 485–580). The Alcuin Bibles were produced in Tours at the rate of some three copies a year. By 900, Alcuin's edition of the Bible was slowly becoming the norm throughout Europe. It formed the basis of the Paris Bibles (13th c., small letters, thin pages). "These assumed the size and character of the Bibles used today, namely, small, affordable, portable, densely written, single-volume Bible" (M. Brown, "Spreading the Word," 176).

23. That order is thus: Octateuch (Genesis–Ruth), 1–4 Kings (1–2 Samuel and 1–2 Kings), 1–2 Chronicles, Ezra, Nehemiah, 2 Ezra (= 3 Ezra), Tobit, Judith, Esther, Job, Psalms, Proverbs, Ecclesiastes, Song of Songs, Wisdom, Ecclesiasticus (Sirach), the major Prophets (Isaiah, Jeremiah, Lamentations, Baruch, Ezekiel, Daniel), the Twelve Minor Prophets, ending with Malachi, followed by 1–2 Maccabees.

Although the early Christians likely did not invent the quadripartite order, their concluding the OT with the Twelve that ends with Malachi may well be a Christian innovation; yet it is difficult to find arguments for it until modern times. The quadripartite order common to most Christian scriptures was likely inherited from an expression of Judaism in Palestine, or perhaps from the LXX before the Christian separation from Judaism (62–135 CE). In other words, the quadripartite order may have existed before the tripartite order emerged in rabbinic Judaism, but it is nonetheless possible that ending the OT canon with Malachi is a Christian innovation since there is little evidence of it until later in the history of Christianity.

What is obvious in the early churches is the fluidity of the parameters of their OT scriptures and their order. For example, from the first century onward, *1 Enoch* was cited as scripture in Jude 14, and portions of that text, or traditions from it, circulated in Galilee in the first century and appear familiar to Jesus.[24] This is also the case in much of early Christianity through the mid-third century, when Irenaeus, Tertullian, and initially Origen cited *1 Enoch* as scripture.[25] After Origen, *1 Enoch*'s favorable status diminished in most churches, though not completely. Centuries later, leaders in the church were still referring to *1 Enoch* even after most churches were no longer reading it. For example, *Enoch* is listed in the rejected "apocryphal" category in the ninth-century Stichometry of Nicephorus (ca. 850) and not to be read in churches. There would, of course, be no need to list it at that late period if no one was reading it. It continues to remain in the Ethiopian biblical canon, which likely dates from the late fourth century to sixth century CE.[26] This, of course, reflects the lack of universal agreement on the scope and order of the church's OT canon, though by the fourth century there was broad but never universal agreement on the scope of the church's first scriptures. Most churches then accepted all the books in the HB canon, but some also welcomed some apocryphal, or deuterocanonical, books in their Bibles.

---

24. Jesus' familiarity with Enoch can be seen, for example, in the reference to the coming Son of Man "sitting on his throne of glory" (Matt 19:28, cf. 25:31; cf. *1 En.* 62:2–3, "how he sits on the throne of his glory"), which is found only in *1 Enoch* outside the NT. There are other examples, as I have shown in my article: McDonald, "Parables of Enoch."

25. See, e.g., Jude 14 alongside *1 En.* 1:9; then *Barn.* 4.3 cites *1 Enoch* as scripture (γέγραπται); *Barn.* 16.5–6 is a summary of *1 En.* 106:19–107, esp. 91:13 (γέγραπται); cf. also *1 En.* 89:56–74. See Athenagoras, *Embassy for the Christians* 24; cf. *1 En.* 15:3. Clement of Alexandria, *Selections from the Prophets* 2.1, includes *Enoch* among the prophets without distinction. Irenaeus (130–200) cites *1 Enoch* as scripture in *Haer.* 4.16.2; cf. *1 En.* 12:13; see also Irenaeus, *Haer.* 4.36.4. He understood Gen 5:21–24 and 6:1–4 in the light of *1 Enoch*. Tertullian specifically cites *1 Enoch* as scripture with the words "I am aware that the Scripture of Enoch . . ." (*De cultu feminarum* 1.1). Later, in reference to *1 Enoch*, he says, ". . . our assertion of [the genuineness of] this Scripture" (*De cultu feminarum* 1.3; 3.1); and finally, "But since Enoch *in the same Scripture* has preached likewise concerning the Lord . . ." (*De cultu feminarum* 3.1.1–3, emphasis added). Origen also initially included *Enoch* as a prophet and a part of the scriptures (*On First Principles* 1.3.3 and 4.4.8), but later in *Against Celsus* 5.54–55 he rejects its scriptural status.

26. I have noted several citations of and verbal parallels with *1 Enoch* in early Christianity, along with positive and negative comments about its reception in the churches. See McDonald, "Parables of Enoch," here 357–62.

The ability to establish the identity and scope of the so-called Old Testament Apocrypha, however, is challenging. This collection of Jewish religious texts dates mostly from 200 BCE to 100 CE. Originally "apocrypha" (ἀπόκρυφα) referred to what was "hidden" or "hidden away" and "kept secret" or "not to be spoken [ἀπόρρητον]," and such designations had no negative connotations, as we see in Origen (ΒΕΠΕΣ [= Βιβλιοθήκη Ελλήνων Πατέρων καὶ Εκκλησιαστικῶν Συγγραφέων] 16.355.5–6 and 16.329.26–28). It is not altogether clear why "apocrypha" came to be used for the texts in question here and why they are not identified as "apocrypha" in the Catholic and Orthodox traditions, but rather as "deuterocanonical" (Catholic) or "noncanonical Old Testament Scriptures" or simply "readable" or "things that are readable publicly" (ἀναγιγνωσκόμενα), in contrast to "things not readable publicly" or "unreadable" (μὴ ἀναγιγνωσκόμενα) sacred texts.

For the Orthodox, these "readable" texts are on a lower level than the Tanak books. Such books are regularly identified as "Apocrypha" among Protestant Christians. Both Catholic and Orthodox reserve "Apocrypha" for rejected or heretical books not readable in church liturgies. In their Apocrypha are writings that Protestants regularly put in their Pseudepigrapha. Loren T. Stuckenbruck suggests that the notion of "apocrypha" as secret documents without negative connotations likely has its origin in Dan 12:4–9; 4 Ezra 14:23–26, 46–47; and 2 Baruch, writings which include revelatory messages that were to be kept secret for a time.[27] In the case of 4 Ezra, the unknown author tells of Ezra's desire to restore his nation's scriptures that were lost in the destruction of Jerusalem (587–586 BCE). After the author receives the "holy spirit" (14:22) and as the work is about to begin with the help of five men and for "forty days,"[28] the author says God commanded Ezra to make some of the writings public but to keep others "secret" and deliver them only to the wise (14:23, 26). After "forty days" the task is finished (14:23, 36, 42), and God again tells Ezra to make the twenty-four books public, but to "keep the seventy that were written last, in order to give them to the wise among your people" (14:46–47). The "seventy" hidden or set-apart books for "the wise" likely included both apocryphal and pseudepigraphal texts, some of which continue in many Christian Bibles today. There was nothing negative associated with this literature in first-century-CE Judaism or in early Christianity. Many in the early churches believed that these "additional books" in the LXX were inspired by God and so were welcomed as scripture.

27. Stuckenbruck, "Apocrypha and Pseudepigrapha," here 184–87.
28. "Forty" is a common number of days or years mentioned in biblical and nonbiblical texts in antiquity. It often refers to divinely inspired or directed activity that occurs in the Jewish religious texts, such as 40 days of rains that led to the flood in Noah's day (Gen 7:12, 17), Moses on Mount Sinai 40 days and 40 nights (Exod 24:18), 40 years of wilderness wanderings (Exod 16:35), Elijah at Mt. Horeb 40 days and 40 nights (1 Kgs 19:8), Jesus' temptations during 40 days (Luke 4:2), Jesus' post-resurrection appearances for 40 days (Acts 1:3), and also Ezra's recovery of the lost biblical literature in the destruction of Jerusalem in 587–586 BCE (4 Ezra 14:23, 36, 42–45), plus other 40s in the Scriptures.

Orthodox Christians add Ps 151, 3 Maccabees, and 1 Esdras (*3 Ezra*) to the collection that Catholics call "deuterocanonical" texts. They sometimes refer to them as "noncanonical Old Testament" writings, but following Athanasius's thirty-ninth *Festal Letter* (in 367), they more commonly use "readable" for the disputed texts.[29] Reading religious texts in liturgies was a significant factor in recognizing their scriptural status in the early churches. Rather than reading "canonical" texts in worship, it appears that texts read in worship became canonical, namely, they functioned as scripture in the churches.

Although Catholic and Orthodox Christians accept these disputed texts in their liturgies, the Orthodox receive them on a secondary or lower level of authority than the books in the Hebrew Bible/Tanak.[30] Initially, many Protestant Christians welcomed these texts and encouraged reading some of them well into the nineteenth century and, following the practice of Martin Luther, included them in their Bibles, grouped together *between* the Old and New Testaments. Their re-inclusion in some Protestant ecumenical Bibles returned in the mid-twentieth century. Orthodox and Catholic Christians include these books inside their Old Testament scriptures among books of similar genres (history, prophets, poetry, and wisdom literature).

Ethiopian Christians have a similar collection of additional books, as Catholics and Orthodox Christians do, along with some of the so-called pseudepigraphal books (*Jubilees*, *1 Enoch*, and *4 Ezra*). It is not clear that the Ethiopians' canon of the Bible was ever closed, despite the consistent number of eighty-one books in their canon lists; they lacked agreement on which books are in their "broader" or "narrower" collections.[31] This is comparable to the Armenian scripture canon, which includes the HB/Tanak, yet also *4 Ezra*, Judith, Tobit, Sirach, 1–4 Maccabees, plus *Testaments of the Twelve Patriarchs, Deaths of the Patriarchs*, and the story of *Joseph and Aseneth*.[32] The books in ancient lists and manuscripts have considerable overlap, but they still vary in the scriptural lists and in the books included in the manuscripts throughout most of church history in the East and West.

In the evidence that has survived antiquity, the church fathers do not include all the disputed writings in their scripture lists or catalogs and in what is replicated in the surviving LXX manuscripts.[33] Thus far arguments for accepting the boundaries or scope of the LXX in the standard Rahlfs-Hanhart edition are

29. "Noncanonical Old Testament," in De Regt, "Biblical Text in the Slavonic Tradition"; "readable," Pentiuc, *Eastern Orthodox Tradition*, 322–24; Pentiuc, "Canon," 341–43.

30. Oikonomos, "Deuterocanonicals in the Orthodox Church," here 20–23.

31. Asale, "Ethiopian Orthodox Tweahedo Church Canon."

32. Nersessian, *Bible in the Armenian Tradition*, 24–26, 79–85.

33. "Septuagint" and the "Seventy" are both mentioned in Origen's letter to Julius Africanus (*Ep. to Africanus* 3, 5). Eusebius also speaks of the "seventy" (LXX) translators of the Hebrew scriptures into Greek (*Hist. eccl.* 6.16.1); later Augustine speaks of the LXX as the Greek translation "that is now by custom called the Septuagint" (*City of God* 18.42). Jerome later used "Septuagint" for the Greek OT (*Ep.* 71.5, *To Lucinius*). Thereafter it was a standard designation in churches. See McDonald, *Old Testament*, 218–23.

unconvincing. Barton and Collins observe the broad variety of interpretations of these texts and are aware of their mixed and fluid reception in antiquity and even in the present. They conclude that these books constitute a "penumbra" of books that were either highly valued or sharply rejected both in antiquity and throughout church history.[34] Since 3 Ezra is not in the LXX, it is strange that the Russian Orthodox Christians welcome it among their "noncanonical Old Testament" scriptures. It is also challenging to obtain a clear Orthodox position on the scope of their Bible, and no ecumenical council made such a decision.

The following evidence reflects how the early church fathers encouraged Christians to read some of these writings and even welcomed some of them as scripture. Some church fathers, Origen and Augustine especially, cited several apocryphal texts as scripture and defended this practice. Others had reservations about their scriptural status (Athanasius), but nonetheless they encouraged Christians to read them in private, though not as scripture.[35] Jerome, Cyril, Rufinus, and other Eastern church fathers rejected their scriptural status in part because they did not exist in Hebrew. Jerome did not make a new translation of them for his new Vulgate except in the cases of Judith and Tobit, but Origen, knowing that most of the apocryphal books did not exist in Hebrew, welcomed and used several of them as scripture and defended this practice (*Ep. to Africanus* 4.12–14). However, Jerome and Cyril advised Christians *not* to read them except with considerable caution (Jerome, *Ep.* 107.12); yet Cyril welcomed Baruch and Epistle of Jeremiah, but said about all others: "Have nothing to do with the apocryphal writings" (Cyril, *Catech.* 4.35).

For Catholics, recognition of the scope or boundaries of the church's scripture canon became an essential ingredient in the Roman Catholic Church's theological position at the Council of Trent (April 8, 1546). After listing the books that comprise the biblical canon, the authors of the reports of that council add: "But if any one receive not, as sacred and canonical, the said books entire with all their parts, as they have been used to be read in the Catholic Church, and as they are contained in the old Latin vulgate edition; and knowingly and deliberately contemn [*sic*] the tradition aforesaid; let him be anathema."[36]

This is the first time an anathema was pronounced on all who do not accept the Old Testament books in the updated old Latin Vulgate Bible, and accept the books *without distinction* in regard to the Tanak (or HB books) and the deuterocanonical books that are translated either from the Hebrew Tanak or the Greek LXX texts.[37]

While Protestants do not accept the apocryphal, or deuterocanonical, writings as part of their OT and do not use them in establishing church doctrine, occasionally they publish Bibles with these writings and locate them between

34. Barton, *Oracles of God* (2007 edition), 80; and J. Collins, "Penumbra of the Canon."
35. Oikonomos, "Deuterocanonicals in the Orthodox Church."
36. P. Schaff and D. Schaff, *Creeds of Christendom*, 2:82.
37. Kerber, "Canon in the Vulgate Translation of the Bible," here 176–81.

the two Testaments. Rejection of the apocryphal books was not immediate among all Protestant churches, and some of their Bibles included them long after the Protestant Reformation. The first editions of the King James Bible, for example, included these books between the two Testaments. Luther, of course, did not include the apocryphal books in *his own* biblical canon and was especially opposed to 2 Maccabees because of its support for the Catholic doctrine of purgatory (see 2 Macc 12:38–45); yet he included them in his Bible due largely to popular support for them. This is not unlike Jerome's inclusion of them in his Vulgate translation. Since the final form of the OT canon had not yet been settled by the first century, when the church was born, it is understandable that for centuries there was fluidity in the shape of the church's OT canon.

The continuing debate in the church over the scope of their OT scriptures continued well into the late fourth and early fifth centuries and beyond, as we see in the well-known debate between Augustine and Jerome and even later.[38] Augustine won that debate on the popular level, and Jerome's translation of the OT scriptures included the very apocryphal books that he rejected, but he did not make a new translation of them.[39] Augustine was the most ardent advocate for including the apocryphal books in the church's OT canon and retaining the LXX as the church's inspired and OT canon. In support of his position, Augustine appealed to the "seventy" translators mentioned in the *Letter of Aristeas* and claimed that they carefully translated even obscure passages and that they arrived at exactly the same translations of their portion despite working separately. He writes:

> . . . As far as the Old Testament is concerned, the authority of the Septuagint is supreme. Its seventy writers are now claimed in all the more informed churches to have performed their task of translation with such strong guidance from the Holy Spirit that this great number of men spoke with but a single voice. It is generally held and indeed asserted by many who are not unworthy of belief, that each one of these wrote his translation alone in an individual cell and nothing was found in anyone's version which was not found in the same words in the others; if so, who would dare to adapt such an authoritative work, let alone adopt anything in preference to it? (*De doctrina christiana* 2.53–54)[40]

Although Jerome rejected the scriptural status of the apocryphal books and rejected the LXX as the *Vorlage* of his translation, he did not oppose reading some of the apocryphal books in the churches. He simply rejected their recognition as scripture and their use in establishing church doctrine.[41] Jerome had allies

---

38. Liere, *Medieval Bible*, 77; also see his introduction, 2–3.
39. For a discussion of this, see Gallagher, "Old Testament 'Apocrypha.'"
40. Green, *Saint Augustine: On Christian Teaching*, 42–43. For a careful examination of Augustine's OT canon, see Gallagher, "Augustine on the Hebrew Bible."
41. For a helpful discussion of this, see Gallagher, "Old Testament 'Apocrypha.'"

in his rejection of the apocryphal books, as we see in Cyril of Jerusalem (*Catech.* 4.35; ca. 394) and Hilary of Poitiers, who chose only the HB canon books, but noted that some included Tobit and Judith (*Prologus ad librum Psalmorum* §15, ca. 350–65). At the same time, Athanasius limited the OT canon mostly to the books in the HB but included 1–2 Esdras and the Epistle of Jeremiah (= chap. 6 of Baruch) but excluded Esther. He concluded his OT canon with Daniel. In his day some churches welcomed apocryphal books circulating in the LXX, especially Wisdom of Solomon, Sirach/Ecclesiasticus, Tobit, Judith, 1–2 Maccabees, Baruch, Epistle of Jeremiah, and 1–2 Esdras.

Variations in the OT canons of early Christianity can be seen in the fourth- and fifth-century codices. For example, Codex Vaticanus includes Sirach, Judith, Tobit, Baruch, and Epistle of Jeremiah. Codex Sinaiticus includes Tobit, Judith, 1 and 4 Maccabees, Wisdom, Sirach, and Prologue to Sirach; Codex Alexandrinus includes Tobit, Judith, Ps 151, 1–4 Maccabees, Wisdom, and Sirach. Codex Claromontanus includes Wisdom, Sirach, 1–3 Maccabees, Tobias (Tobit). We repeat here that while there is considerable agreement on the books included in the church's OT canon, there has never been complete agreement on its scope or in its order or how to understand, welcome, or reject the disputed writings in question. Nonetheless, all the major churches (Orthodox, Catholic, and Protestant) recognize the scriptural status of all the Tanak (HB) books.

THE EARLY CHURCH'S FIRST SCRIPTURES

As a Jewish sect, the earliest followers of Jesus were generally familiar with most of the contemporary Jewish religious texts and welcomed many of them as their own sacred scriptures. They regularly interpreted those OT scriptures in a *pesher* fashion[42] in support of their understanding of Jesus their Messiah (e.g., Matthew's example, "Out of Egypt I have called my son" (Matt 2:15; cf. Hos 11:1). The Jewish scriptures are generally identified in the NT as "Moses and the prophets," "Law and the prophets," or simply "the Law," but once as "Moses, the prophets, and the psalms" (Luke 24:44; cf. 24:27,[43] "all the prophets").[44]

The scope of the Jewish scriptures—that is, the books that comprise it—is not identified either in late Second Temple Judaism or in the New Testament,

---

42. *Pesher* (Heb. = "interpretation" or "realization"; pl., *pesharim*) is a form of biblical interpretation that is much like *midrash* yet sees the fulfillment of a scriptural passage in the context of its own interpreters and community. *Pesher* interpretation was popular at Qumran and in the NT and early Christianity. It has parallels with allegorical interpretation in that it often contemporizes the scriptural texts to current events or circumstances.

43. For a discussion of the importance of Luke 24:27 for understanding 24:44, see C. A. Evans, "Scriptures of Jesus"; and Lim, *Jewish Canon*, 163–65.

44. There were two primary designations for the early church's scriptures: the "law and the prophets." The "prophets" included a broad collection of texts that later rabbinic Jews divided to form their tripartite biblical canon.

but the parameters of that collection can be *broadly* discerned from citations of scriptural references in the Dead Sea Scrolls, the NT, and Josephus. As those references or citations and parallels show, the books that later comprised the Hebrew Bible (HB) scriptures are among the most cited scriptural texts in the first century CE among Jews at Qumran and among Christians, especially Deuteronomy, Isaiah, and the Psalms.

In a first-century-CE Jewish milieu, the church was born with a notion of scriptural authority that was well ingrained in Jesus' early followers. This can be seen in the many NT scriptural texts supporting affirmations about Jesus and the will of God, yet also in the practice of writing theology with scriptural support ("writing with scripture"). The followers of Jesus did not begin their journey of faith with an exegesis of those scriptures, but rather with an overwhelming encounter with Jesus, after which they went to their scriptures in search of affirmative scriptural texts that identified Jesus as their promised Messiah. Their motivation in the first place came not from their recognition or exegesis of the authority of scripture but rather from their encounter with Jesus. They did not start their journey of faith from an exegesis of the biblical texts, but from their experience with Jesus, and they sought scriptural support from those texts for what they came to believe about him from that experience. The followers of Jesus came to believe that he was the anticipated messianic figure who, they believed, would free them from Gentile oppression (Acts 1:6–7). However, the early Christians' recognition of Jesus as Lord (Rom 10:9) and the good news that they proclaimed about him (1 Cor 15:3–8) were both soon rooted in the church's recognized scriptures.[45] *Most* of the scriptural texts that affirmed their faith were in what we now call the HB, or OT scriptures.

The scriptures to which the early churches most frequently appealed included Deuteronomy, Isaiah, and the Psalms, though the early Christians regularly cited or showed familiarity with both canonical and so-called noncanonical Jewish scriptural texts that they believed supported their proclamation. These texts included *1 Enoch*, Wisdom of Solomon, Sirach, and several others.[46] Unfortunately, there are no Christian lists of OT scriptures until near the end of the second century, when Melito listed them. Melito's listing of OT scriptures and later Origen's (ca. 220–30; cf. *Selecta in Psalmos*; and Eusebius, *Hist. eccl.* 6.25)[47] reflect the popularity of some so-called apocryphal texts that were not included in the church's OT scriptures. Melito's catalog, cited by Eusebius (*Hist. eccl.*

---

45. I have addressed this issue at length in McDonald, *Old Testament*, chap. 9.

46. I have discussed some of these other texts in McDonald, "Scriptures of Jesus"; McDonald, "Parables of Enoch"; McDonald, *Forgotten Scriptures*, 123–50.

47. Origen accepted several apocryphal books in his listing of the OT scriptures. In his response to the rebuke paid him by Julius Africanus for accepting additional books beyond those in the HB canon, Origen defended his use of Bel and the Dragon, Song of the Three Children, Additions to Esther, and Judith (Origen, *Ad Africanus* 13). Elsewhere he quoted and approved of the Wisdom of Solomon and Sirach/Ecclesiasticus (*Hom. Num.* 18), and he specifically identifies the Maccabees (presumably 1–2 Maccabees) as "the Scriptures, the word of God" (*Princ.* 2.1.5).

4.26.14) is much like but not exactly like the eventual OT canon, and it considerably overlaps with the collection of books later included in the HB canon.[48]

The ancient churches eventually accepted all the books that now comprise the HB canon, yet some churches continued to accept other books as well. The early Christian canonical lists or catalogs often show both the similarities to, and the lack of agreement on, the full scope of the OT canon. A few books now in the Ethiopian biblical canon were also welcomed in *some* churches well into the fourth and fifth centuries and even now, especially *1 Enoch*, *Jubilees*, Tobit, Ps 151, Wisdom of Solomon, and Sirach. The Ethiopian Church was isolated from the rest of the churches for almost a thousand years as Christians in Ethiopia lived under the dominance of the Islamic religion. Until the sixth century, Ethiopian Christians had regular contacts with their fellow Christians in the east and west, but thereafter not for almost a thousand years. Their larger biblical canon (eighty-one books) likely reflects early Christian canons in the fourth to the sixth centuries outside of Ethiopia, when communications with churches to the east and west were more open, especially in Syria.[49] Ethiopian Christians have the largest OT canon, which likely reflects ancient notions of the OT outside their homeland. All the additional books that they recognize were imported from outside their country. In other words, they imported translocal texts circulating in some (likely Syrian) churches elsewhere.

THE CRITERIA FOR ESTABLISHING
THE HEBREW BIBLE CANON

The criteria employed to establish the HB canon are gleaned mostly from later rabbinic texts and from examples in the Dead Sea Scrolls, but this does not suggest that all Jews or Christians in antiquity agreed with all of the books in the HB-Tanak. As noted above, in the rabbinic period some Tannaitic and Amoraic sages expressed doubts about the sacred status of some books, especially Esther, Song of Songs, Ecclesiastes, Ezekiel, and Wisdom of Jesus ben Sira (Ecclesiasticus/Sirach).

48. I note here that the inclusion of "Wisdom" in this text is likely Wisdom of Solomon. Scholars regularly debate whether "Wisdom" is an alternative name for Proverbs, but most argue that it is a reference to the book Wisdom of Solomon. The Greek here is Σολομῶνος Παροιμίαι ἡ καὶ Σοφία. The popularity of Wisdom of Solomon (Wisdom) among the early Christians suggests that ἡ καὶ Σοφία refers to Wisdom of Solomon. Scholars translate these words as "or also Wisdom" or "that is Wisdom," referring to Proverbs by another name; or "also Wisdom" as a reference to Wisdom of Solomon. Those choosing καὶ as an explicative ("even") often cite the prominence of Proverbs in Eusebius who, in reference to Irenaeus (*Hist. eccl.* 4.22.8), magnifies Solomon's Proverbs as the "all virtuous wisdom." However, I choose the latter as a reference to the popular pseudonymous book in early Christianity that is also cited in the NT (cf. Rom 2:4 with Wis 11:23; cf. Heb 1:2–3 with Wis 7:22; 7:25, 26; and 8:1) and cited Σοφία as "Wisdom" regularly in the church fathers. In antiquity, the designation "Wisdom" is generally a reference to Wisdom of Solomon, not another reference to Proverbs.

49. See Cowley, "Canon of the Ethiopian Orthodox Church"; and Isaac, "Bible in Ethiopic."

There was uncertainty about the scriptural status of several biblical books not only by some rabbinic sages but also by some early church fathers. The following criteria are seldom explicitly stated but rather are inferred in some ancient texts.

The precise criteria used by Jews and subsequently by Christians to establish the scope of their scriptures are difficult to establish with precision, and it is not clear how soon such criteria were adopted. Leiman has suggested four criteria from the ancient rabbis for selection of books in their scripture canon, namely (1) books believed to have been written after the cessation of prophecy were excluded (cf. *t. Sotah* 13:2-4) and that addresses a criterion of date (cf. 1 Macc 4:45-46; 9:27; 14:41; and Josephus, *Ag. Apion* 1:40-41); (2) books written in Greek were automatically excluded (2 Maccabees); (3) books written in Hebrew that challenged halakic teaching of the rabbis (Jubilees' calendar at variance) were excluded; and (4) books with uncertain canonical status (Sirach) eventually were rejected.[50] Added to this is the question whether anonymity of authorship was considered in determining the final shape of the HB canon. If the author of the book included his name, as in the case of Sirach (see its prologue), the work was rejected.[51] These appear to have been prominent issues among the rabbinic sages, but not earlier. Doubtless also is the criterion of adaptability that James A. Sanders has brought forward many times over the years: was the text adaptable to ever new and changing situations? Some of these criteria are supported in the rabbinic tradition, but not all.

We might also ask whether a book's canonicity was related to its theological conformity to Torah, or to its usefulness in Jewish liturgy, or even to its perceived moral content. Silver has suggested that in some cases the matter was settled on the basis of size. He explains: "The decision to include or exclude [was] sometimes made for reasons as superficial as a scribe finding empty space available at the end of a scroll he had just copied, and filling it with something he liked."[52] However, he does not offer specific arguments to support this suggestion.

Eugene Ulrich has suggested a set of criteria to determine which books among the writings discovered at Qumran were viewed as sacred scripture. There was clearly a collection of scriptures circulating at Qumran, but it is challenging to identify those texts among the larger collection of the Dead Sea Scrolls (DSS), and thus far no final answer is available. It is likely that citations and multiple copies of individual manuscripts among the Dead Sea Scrolls are important clues regarding the sacredness of DSS documents. For example, Torah, Isaiah, the Twelve, Psalms, and Daniel were all viewed as sacred scripture, and multiple copies of each of these books were found there. Ulrich lists six criteria that may help in understanding whether some books found at Qumran were viewed as sacred

50. Leiman, "Inspiration and Canonicity," 61–63 and the fnn on 317–18, and his *Canonization of Hebrew Scripture*, 131–35, offer examples from rabbinic sources for these criteria.

51. For a discussion of authorship and anonymity in the canonization process, see Wyrick, *Ascension of Authorship*.

52. Silver, *Story of Scripture*, 134.

scripture. He suggests the following: (a) whether a document was found among a recognized collection of canonical scriptures; (b) whether formulas were used explicitly to introduce a text; (c) whether a book is explicitly quoted *as* scripture, that is, whether it is cited with the words "as the scripture says" or "it is written"; (d) whether multiple copies were made of a book; (e) whether a commentary was written on a book; and (f) whether a book was translated into vernacular languages.[53] These criteria are helpful in suggesting that a broader collection of scriptures than was later accepted in the HB was considered at Qumran. Ulrich posits that if most of these conditions were true of a document, its scriptural status at Qumran was likely. There is, however, no clear means of applying all these criteria to all the books that were later included in the HB, but some of them may be helpful.

Ulrich's criteria, while suggestive, are not determinative, as he admits. He goes on to show that the criterion identified above as *a* is not applicable to all of the documents at Qumran, but that criterion *b* is obviously in place since all books identified among the Law and the Prophets were recognized as sacred scripture. In criterion *c*, he shows that Isaiah and the Minor Prophets are quoted 9 times (in each of the two categories *a* and *b*) and the pentateuchal books (not counting Genesis) and Ezekiel are cited 1 to 5 times (each). Psalms and Daniel are each cited 2 times; and Jeremiah, Proverbs, and *Jubilees* are each cited once. Ulrich adds that the Former Prophets and the rest of the Ketuvim are never *cited* except for one time in the prophetic oracle in 2 Samuel 7. Item *d* is also suggestive since several books exist in multiple copies: Psalms (36), Deuteronomy (30), Isaiah (21), Genesis (20), Exodus (17), *Jubilees* (14), Leviticus (13), *1 Enoch* (12 or 20?), Minor Prophets (8), Daniel (8), Numbers (7), Jeremiah and Ezekiel (6 times each), Tobit (5). He also notes that the Former Prophets and the Writings (4 or fewer copies) are fewer in number than the *Community Rule*, the *Damascus Document*, the *Hodayot*, and the *War Scroll*. For *e*, Ulrich notes that only the Torah and the Prophets (specifically, Isaiah, the Minor Prophets, and Psalms) had commentaries written on them. Finally, regarding translations, *f*, only Torah and possibly *1 Enoch* were translated into Greek, and only Leviticus and Job were translated into Aramaic (Targumim). A Greek translation of the Minor Prophets was discovered at Naḥal Ḥever. From all of this and the translated texts, Ulrich concludes that Torah and the Prophets, including Psalms and Daniel, were all clearly recognized as scripture. He adds that Job and Proverbs might also qualify, but the rest of the books were "known" to the Qumran covenanters and may or may not have been acknowledged as scripture.[54] Apart from the Psalms and Daniel, however, there is little evidence that the residents of Qumran recognized the rest of the Writings (Ketuvim) as scripture, and certainly not Esther. Again, these criteria were discussed concerning the literature discovered at Qumran; we cannot be certain that later rabbis employed any of these criteria in order to determine the precise scope of the Hebrew Bible.

---

53. E. Ulrich, "Jewish Scriptures," esp. 116–17.
54. E. Ulrich, "Jewish Scriptures," 117–18.

As others have recognized, in some cases there appears to be no qualitative difference between some books that made it into the Jewish biblical canon and some that did not. For example, based on content alone, a case could be made for including Sirach and the Wisdom of Solomon instead of Ecclesiastes and Song of Songs. Similarly, it is unknown why Esther never mentions the name of God except in the additions to Esther but it was included while *Jubilees* and various *Testaments of the Patriarchs* were excluded. Ultimately, the books that were finally included in the HB were found by the Jewish community to be useful in defining and shaping its identity, faith, and life *at a given point in time*. It is difficult to be more precise than that. Some Dead Sea Scrolls scholars, especially Eugene Ulrich and Emanuel Tov, now claim that the older designations of "biblical" and "nonbiblical" scrolls are changing. This means that what earlier were called post-biblical scrolls, such as 4QRP (= "Reworked Pentateuch," but now 4QP) and 11QPSa (= "Reworked Pentateuch" but now 11QPS), are increasingly recognized as "scriptural" texts amid the many pluriform texts discovered at Qumran.[55] Ulrich appropriately observes that the book and not the text of the book was what was recognized as sacred scripture at Qumran. There was no "standard text" at Qumran or elsewhere until considerably later, but clearly there were "scriptures." The books do not always have the same text as those that later comprised the MT Hebrew Bible, but they overlap considerably with the later HB canon. Most of the books discovered at Qumran were translocal (nonsectarian) and were transported into Qumran.

With regard to the canonical *text* of the HB scriptures, James A. Sanders has observed that although there were always limits on how much change could take place in a text without objection, nevertheless in later generations the sacred texts often took on meanings that the original authors never intended.[56] A text could hardly continue as an authoritative document if it was not perceived to have some continuing relevance to the people it served. To bridge the gap between the text and succeeding generations, hermeneutics were employed to make the biblical texts relevant to contemporary believers who were facing ever-new circumstances and for whom, it was believed, the scriptures continued to be relevant. In this regard, Sanders speaks of the "hermeneutic triangle" that allows for the continuing relevance of the sacred texts, namely, "the tradition or text being cited, the new situation being addressed, and the hermeneutic by which the old was adapted to speak to the new."[57] Hermeneutics played a significant role in allowing the widely welcomed ancient sacred religious texts to have a continuing relevance for both Jews and Christians. Before such hermeneutics was developed, some texts simply did not continue to meet the test of relevance, and so they fell into disuse and were no longer copied for synagogue or church use (e.g., *Eldad and Modad*).

55. E. Ulrich, *Dead Sea Scrolls*, 187–99.
56. J. A. Sanders, "Scrolls and the Canonical Process," here 17–19.
57. J. A. Sanders, "Scrolls and the Canonical Process," 12.

The continuing adaptability and relevance of the biblical literature in new and changing contexts demonstrated its usefulness, but some texts ceased having a relevant function and no longer contributed to the religious life of the nation, as in the case of the so-called lost books mentioned above. Some of the apocryphal and pseudepigraphal books were useful to some Jews and to some Christians for a while and were cited in several contexts, but eventually and perhaps for various reasons they were no longer copied or transmitted. Some were even denounced in the later church catalogs of scriptural and rejected texts.

One of the most common hermeneutics employed to advance the continuing relevance of an ancient text was the use of allegory, not to focus on the text's plain or obvious meaning, but rather to seek in it a more spiritual meaning that symbolized different aspects of the text and also emphasized what was deemed important to later communities that read it. The book of Esther, for example, never mentions God and appears to be a historical reflection of the time when Jews were in Eastern Dispersion, but the book has historically been allegorized in antiquity to make it relevant. Perhaps the most allegorized or spiritualized book in the OT is Song of Songs. Contrary to its most obvious romantic meaning, it is regularly allegorized to make the text relevant to current and new situations. The book was originally produced as a nontheological volume that closely parallels Near Eastern poetry celebrating human love.

This obvious interpretation of the book led to voiced questions about its acceptance in both Jewish and Christian biblical canons. See, for example, how Song of Songs was viewed in *m. Yadayim* 3:5; *m. Eduyyot* 5:3; *t. Sanhedrin* 12.10; *t. Yadayim* 2.14; *b. Sanhedrin* 101a; *b. Megillah* 7a. Many communities of faith today simply ignore the Song of Songs altogether. It was not referred to or cited in the NT or in Josephus's writings, and Jews and Christians seldom referred to it in antiquity except in arguments for its sanctity. When the romance and sexual aspects of the book (e.g., 7:7–9) are no longer spiritualized to represent the love between YHWH and Israel (or the Church),[58] the text is generally ignored. The rabbis were prone to allegorize the book early on and make the female in the book represent the following: the house of Torah study, Moses, Joshua, an individual woman, a local court, the Sanhedrin, a group of righteous Jews, the Jewish community in the Diaspora in Syria, or even more commonly the community of Israel as a whole. According to the Mishnah, during a celebration on the Day of Atonement the daughters of Jerusalem wore white raiment that had been immersed (i.e., to make them ceremonially clean), and they went forth to dance in the vineyards. The rabbis then cited Song 3:11 as follows:

58. Reportedly, Rabbi Akiba in the second century CE is the first to spiritualize the message of the Song of Songs. This tradition is based on a talmudic interpretation (*y. Sheqalim* 6.1) of perhaps *m. Yadayim* 3:5. Hananiah, nephew of Joshua, is said to relate the praise of the man's body in Song 5:14 to the Ten Commandments and their interpretation in rabbinic discussion. For a discussion of this, see Carr, "Song of Songs as a Microcosm," here 175n5.

Likewise it saith, Go forth ye daughters of Sion, and behold king Solomon with the crown wherewith his mother hath crowned him in the day of his espousals and in the day of the gladness of his heart. In the day of his espousals—this is the giving of the Law; and in the day of the gladness of his heart—this is the building of the Temple. May it be built speedily, in our days! Amen. (*m. Ta'anit* 4:8, Danby, *Mishnah*, 201)

Likewise, in the Tosefta we see the following:[59]

Similarly you say: Under the apple tree I awakened you (Song 8:5), said the Holy Spirit. Set me as a seal upon your heart (Song 8:6), said the congregation of Israel. For love is strong as death, jealousy is cruel as the grave (Song 8:6), said the nations of the world. (*t. Sotah* 9:8, Neusner, *Tosefta*, 875)

The early church fathers Hippolytus and Origen reinterpreted Song of Songs to refer to the love between Christ and the church, yet also the love between God and an individual person. For example, in Origen's commentary on Song 2:5, we read:

If there is anyone anywhere who has at some time burned with this faithful love of the Word of God; if there is anyone who has at some time received the sweet wound of him who is the chosen dart, as the prophet says: if there is anyone who has been pierced with the love-worthy spear of his knowledge, so that he yearns and longs for him by day and night, can speak of naught but him, would hear of naught but him, can think of nothing else, and is disposed to no desire nor longing nor yet hope, except for him alone, if such there be, that soul then says in truth: "I have been wounded by charity."[60]

Allegorizing this and other books allowed for their continued acceptance in both the synagogue and the churches, but careful historical-critical approaches to it have led some clergy to ignore Song of Songs altogether. Since open discussions of sexuality, which a literal rendering of the text suggests, are often viewed as out of place in Jewish synagogues and Christian churches, the book is frequently ignored. Carr concludes that because of the allegorizing of Song of Songs, both the synagogue and church have functionally decanonized it by seldom referring to it.[61]

---

59. Carr also shows other examples of allegorizing the Song of Songs in *b. Shabbat* 88; *b. Yoma* 75a; *b. Sukkah* 49b; and *b. Ta'anit* 4a. See a complete list in Carr, "Song of Songs as a Microcosm," 175–76.

60. Translation from Lawson, *Origen: Song of Songs*, 198; cited by Carr, "Song of Songs as a Microcosm," 178.

61. Carr, "Song of Songs as a Microcosm," 184–85. He goes on to speak of the "recanonization" of the book in the postmodern and post-critical world, in which each interpreter reads the text for oneself and in which the stigmas formerly attached to discussions of sexuality no longer exist.

FINAL OBSERVATIONS

It is not always clear why some books were included in the HB and others were not. Why Sirach and Wisdom of Solomon were excluded but Esther, Ecclesiastes, and Song of Songs were included is seldom clear. Their continued use and readers' ability to reinterpret them in relevant ways for succeeding generations must have had some influence on their inclusion in the HB. There were, as we saw, questions and even debates among the rabbis about the sanctity of several doubtful books.

Most of the Jewish religious leaders who survived the destruction of the temple in 70 CE were Pharisees, and consequently they had a more significant role in influencing the eventual decisions made about the parameters of the HB/Tanak. For some of them, these issues were largely settled by the middle of the second century CE, though occasionally discussions of the sanctity of some of the Ketuvim continued to the fourth century. The most commonly posited criteria for the canonization of the books in the HB included the date of the writing, anonymity of its author,[62] whether the language in which a text was composed is Hebrew or Aramaic, and the adaptability of the text to ever-changing circumstances.

Fewer books were finally included in the HB scriptures than in most of the Christian OT canons. The Christian canon included books that were recognized by some Jewish religious sects before the church's separation from Judaism. Nothing new was added to the Christian OT after the third century; yet at the end of the fourth century, some churches welcomed several books, including some of the deuterocanonical or apocryphal writings, as sacred scripture. By the middle of the fourth century, most of the pseudepigraphal writings (e.g., *1 Enoch*) were rejected as pseudonymous texts, but several of these continued to be read in various churches for centuries.

Unlike *some* adherents of Judaism in the first centuries BCE and CE, the early Christians did not believe that the age of prophecy had ceased but rather that in the ministry of John the Baptist and Jesus, the outpouring of the Spirit was fully present, as also in the church on the day of Pentecost. This belief made it easier for Christians to acknowledge a new literature as inspired scripture along with their earlier OT scriptures.

The formation of the Jewish scriptures was *largely* finished by the end of the second century CE, but even after this collection was identified (*b. Baba Bathra* 14b), disputes continued over the fringes of those scriptures for centuries. No formal council decision was made about the scope of the scripture canons of Jews or Christians for centuries longer. Most of the disputes were over books in the Writings.

Melito's sequence, or order, of books also does not follow the later and now more usual Tanak order, but neither does an earlier antecedent, the Jewish Bry-

---

62. For a discussion of the role of authorship in canon formation, see Wyrick, *The Ascension of Authorship*.

ennios catalog.[63] The presence of three different orders of the Jewish scriptures in the second century (Tanak, Bryennios, and Melito) suggests that the Hebrew scriptures and their order had not yet been settled in the second century CE. It is unclear how normative a list of sacred scriptures and its order were for either rabbinic or diaspora Jews in the second century.

The Tanak canon, as Sundberg has shown, had an impact on some Christians *after* the third century CE, especially in Jerome, who wrongly considered it to be the canon of Jesus and of the apostles,[64] but that view was not pervasive in most churches. Apparently it was only in the last decades of the second century that the scope of an OT canon was *beginning* to emerge in some Christian communities, but no discussion of debates about the matter from the second century has survived. Robert Grant suggests that an emerging rejection of the Jewish scriptures by Marcion may have led proto-orthodox churches to evaluate not only their acceptance of the OT scriptures, but also their NT scriptures as well.[65] This is, of course, guesswork, but there is no question that second-century churches regularly appealed to the scriptures they inherited from their Jewish siblings, the specific scope and order of which were not yet settled.

Long ago, Samuel Sandmel perceptively noted that public acclaim was an essential feature in the canonical processes and concluded that "canon [is] a logical development, but also determined by fortuitous circumstances. . . . Canon only reflects sanctity which a given era chanced to assign to a given number of books. The books themselves are in part much more important and in part much less important than the act of canonization."[66]

The preference of Jerome and Cyril of Jerusalem for only the books in the HB Tanak appears to have been a minority position in the church in their time except in Palestine, where both men lived and Jewish notions were prevalent. Jerome clearly adopted not only the books in the Jewish canon, but also the Jewish tripartite order, as we see in his *Prologus in libro Regnum*.[67] He also adopted the text of the Hebrew Bible over that of the Greek LXX. His acceptance of only the books in the HB did not prevail until centuries later in the Protestant OT canon.[68] The Apostolic Fathers often quote and refer or allude to several

---

63. This list likely dates to ca. 100–150 CE. It was discovered in Jerusalem in a manuscript (MS 54 fol. 76ᵣₒ) that dates from 1056 CE. Its uniqueness includes its order and number of books (twenty-seven). The order of the books has some parallels with *b. Baba Bathra* 14b, but includes several differences as well. The books and their strange order are as follows: Genesis, Exodus, Leviticus, Joshua, Deuteronomy, Numbers, Ruth, Job, Judges, Psalms, 1–2 Samuel, 1–2 Kings, 1–2 Chronicles, Proverbs, Ecclesiastes, Song of Songs, Jeremiah with Lamentations, The Twelve, Isaiah, Ezekiel, Daniel, 1–2 Esdras, and Esther.

64. Sundberg, *Old Testament of the Early Church*, 154.

65. Grant, "New Testament Canon," here 300.

66. Sandmel, "On Canon," here 206. I owe this quote to S. Talmon, *Text and Canon of the Hebrew Bible*, 431.

67. Jerome, *Preface to the Books of Samuel and Kings*. This text was discussed earlier.

68. Athanasius's thirty-ninth *Festal Letter* lists for the first time the twenty-seven books of the NT, but he also lists a larger OT canon than Protestants accept, i.e., he adds Baruch and the Epistle of Jeremiah. Protestants often ignore Athanasius's OT canon but assume the validity of his NT canon.

apocryphal or deuterocanonical books (especially 2 Maccabees, Judith, Tobit, Sirach, Wisdom of Solomon, 2 Esdras, and *1 Enoch*), but they seldom cite all of the canonical books. Notably missing in their citations are Ruth, Ezra, Nehemiah, Lamentations, Obadiah, Micah, Haggai, Ecclesiastes, Esther, and Song of Songs.[69] It appears that more writings than those included in the later HB canon informed second-century churches; this raises the question of whether today's Christians should at least know or be familiar with the same literature that informed the first generations of Christians, even if they do not include these books in their Bibles or liturgical readings in churches.

The use of the alphabetic numbers twenty-two (Hebrew) or twenty-four (Greek) to limit and identify the scope of the Jewish scriptures can seen in various combinations of books; it appears that the numbers themselves focus more on their sacredness and completeness than on the specific number of the books included in the scripture canons. It is interesting that when some of the Writings were disputed among the rabbis later, no one mentioned how the presence or absence of those disputed books would affect the sacred number of books in the scripture collection. Neither the twenty-two-book canon nor the twenty-four-book canon have exactly same numbers of books as numbered in their respective alphabets.

Lightstone argues that several traditional assumptions about the formation of the Hebrew biblical canon are no longer tenable: they both interfere with an advance in our understanding of canon formation and are incapable of proof. These assumptions include the following: (1) the equation of the Law of Moses, or Torah, with the Pentateuch;[70] (2) the linear model of the growth of the canon in three separate phases; (3) that there was a universal normative Judaism in Late Antiquity that essentially paralleled Pharisaic Judaism of the pre-70 CE days in the land of Israel; (4) that there was a normative first-century-CE biblical canon similar to the canon of Judaism of Late Antiquity; and (5) that there was a so-called Council of Jamnia similar to later church councils in which bishops supposedly decided the scope of a biblical canon.[71] I agree that only after these traditional assumptions have been set aside can there be a careful reassessment of the canon-formation issues.

Dulles also rightly concludes that "if the apostles ever certified a list of biblical books (a most unlikely hypothesis), their testimony was not appealed to or apparently not remembered during the disputes about the canon in subsequent centuries."[72] It is easier to believe that such a tradition was not passed on in the churches than to believe that it was lost or not remembered, as some scholars contend. There is no trace of a biblical canon list in the first century CE like Melito's list in the late second century. Certainly, categories of sacred-scripture collections were known in the first century, namely, Law, Prophets, and on one occasion also

---

69. This observation is from Jeffery, "Canon of the Old Testament," here 40.

70. Lightstone, "Biblical Canon in Judaism," follows the conclusions of J. A. Sanders in *Torah and Canon.*

71. Lightstone, "Biblical Canon in Judaism," 142–43.

72. Dulles, "Authority of Scripture: A Catholic Perspective," here 35.

Psalms (Luke 24:44). In the late first century, Josephus had a different grouping of the Jewish scriptures than the order and identity of scriptures in the Tanak, but we do not know for sure what books he counted as sacred scripture.

All of this suggests fluidity in the full scope of the Jewish scriptures and the church's OT canon in the first and second centuries. We have seen that often the OT scriptures were written to preserve an important story or teaching that was passed on initially in ancient Israel orally and by memory, namely, a story that gave identity to the people of Israel and subsequently also to the earliest Christian community. While some of those writings were widely welcomed at various stages of the development of the Jewish nation, others took much longer. Only after considerable debate were they welcomed as sacred scripture by various elements in Judaism and early Christianity. Some earlier known books were lost or eventually discarded because they no longer met the emerging needs of various communities of faith.

There is a question that cannot be pursued here but is nevertheless quite significant: Did the church focus on the scope of its NT at the same time when it also came to grips with the scope of its OT? Or perhaps that question should be asked in reverse: Did the churches determine the scope of their OT canon after they determined the scope of their NT canon? Which focus led to the other is the question here. It appears that the focus on both OT and NT canons emerged at approximately the same time, though the OT scriptures were, of course, the church's First Testament; yet both were without clear definition in the early stages of the church's development. The early church fathers' lack of attention to the OT canon before the third and fourth centuries may suggest that both canons came into focus at about the same time. There is little question that the scope of the OT scriptures for the church was of considerable interest to Origen in the third century, but most church fathers did not deal with this question until the later fourth and early fifth centuries, when the status of some texts such as Esther, Ecclesiastes, and Song of Songs was being questioned.

Here at the end of my second chapter, I state again that the variety of sacred religious texts that we see at Qumran and circulating in early Christianity decreased after the fourth century CE, when the biblical canon became more stabilized for both Jews and Christians. We must also acknowledge that the biblical canon was not completely settled for Christians even during the Middle Ages, though then it appears more stabilized than in earlier centuries. Several "nonbiblical" texts continued to reappear both in later manuscripts and in church use well into the Renaissance and Reformation era and in some cases even later. It is important here to affirm that there was considerable agreement in the ancient and modern churches on recognizing well over half of the books in the HB and Protestant OT canons. However, still other books not included in those current biblical canons continued to influence some churches for centuries longer, as we see in the surviving OT manuscripts, OT canons, and in the Ethiopian Bible. Well into the Middle Ages, the books, their order, and text varied in many biblical manuscripts. Since the invention of the printing press in 1455 and the beginning of the Reformation and Renaissance era, there has been greater focus on the stability of both the books and texts that comprise the church's OT and NT, but the text of those books is still a work in progress. We know more today about the formation of the Bible than we did earlier and more about the text of its books than we did even a generation ago. It is likely that in the future more will be known as a result of continuing careful work by some biblical scholars today, their own research building upon the research of the generation before them.

Finally, the question of "canon below" and "canon above" is sometimes raised in reference to my work on this subject (Kruger and Chapman); "canon below" is simply a historical approach to the formation of the biblical canon instead of a "canon above," which emphasizes the element of faith and divine activity in the process. I agree with that assessment to some extent, but I have regularly argued that the Bible's canonicity is both historical and faith oriented. Karl Barth once claimed that scripture was written "from faith to faith" but argued forcefully that faith cannot make a book, in his case Romans, less complex than it already is. He argued that the full meaning of Romans could only be fully understood from the context of faith in which it was written, but also that this did not excuse him from doing careful critical-historical homework.[73] He rightly acknowledged that the one who is "concerned with truth must boldly acknowledge that he cannot be simple."[74] That is certainly true, and scripture can only be fully understood within a faith perspective; yet how and when the biblical canon was produced is a complex historical question that requires historical inquiry to understand. We cannot make the subject of canon formation less complex than it already is by an appeal to our faith.

73. See Barth, *Epistle to the Romans* (1968), Second Preface, 2–24, esp. 16–24.
74. Barth, *Epistle to the Romans* (1968), 5.

Chapter 6

Recognizing *Christian* Religious Texts as Scripture

LEE MARTIN McDONALD

In what follows I will focus primarily on the emergence of the New Testament (NT) scriptures, *why* they were written, and whether their authors were consciously aware of writing *sacred scripture* when they composed the texts that eventually formed the current fixed NT canon. I will follow up in the next chapter with a focus on *when* the NT texts were recognized as scripture and eventually as a fixed collection of sacred scriptures that we call the NT canon. I will give an update on recent examinations of the well-known Muratorian Fragment (MF), then conclude with a summary of canon criteria and the modern challenges for canon-formation scholars.

THE EMERGENCE OF *CHRISTIAN* SCRIPTURES

Soon after the church was born, it was involved in an evangelistic and educational ministry that led to its significant growth (Acts 1:8; 2:41–42, 47; 6:7). To advance Jesus' mission, it is possible that even during his lifetime his followers may have produced texts that focused on his major teachings and key activities (I offer a clarification of this below). Within a few years after the death of Jesus, these earlier texts and remembered oral traditions about him were combined with other oral and written traditions in the apostolic era to produce what became known as the canonical Gospels. Before the emergence of the canonical Gospels, various letters were also produced and sent to churches to advance the church's mission, instruct new believers in the church's core teachings, and address the practical implications of this core tradition for Christian living as well as to deal with challenging issues facing churches in the first century. In defense of core Christian beliefs and to advance the church's mission, the second-century church fathers cited mostly New Testament writings, especially the Gospels and some letters of Paul, along with their First Testament (Hebrew Bible: HB or OT). As we will see below, by the first half of the second century (ca. 130–150) some Christian writings (some Gospels and letters of Paul) were *beginning* to be called scripture. By the end of that century, several other Christian writings were also called "scripture" (Acts, other Pauline letters, and some Catholic Epistles). Others were dismissed as heresy or were deemed to be out of step with the proto-orthodox tradition circulating among several second-century churches: the so-called gnostic, apocryphal, and pseudonymous Christian texts. Besides the NT scriptures, other Christian writings were also cited as scripture in early Christianity, especially the *Shepherd of Hermas, Epistle of Barnabas, 1–2 Clement*, the *Letters of Ignatius, Odes of Solomon*, and *Didache*, yet others also. Occasionally these writings were included in various Christian manuscripts alongside other Christian texts (P^{72}) that were recognized as Christian scripture or placed in various scripture lists or catalogs. The first *clear* listing of all the NT writings, and no others, comes from a canon list or catalog produced by Athanasius in his thirty-ninth *Festal Letter* (in 367). His list was later affirmed at the Councils of Hippo (393) and later at Carthage (397 and 416–19), then reaffirmed at the Council of Trent in 1546.[1] Interestingly, the earliest "complete" manuscripts that include all of the NT texts *and no others* first appears in Gregory–von Soden 1424 830 (Gruber MS 152, ca. 9th/10th century) and Gregory–von Soden 175 d95 (Rome: Basiliani 119, ca. 10th–11th c.).[2] This reflects both the agreement and lack thereof that was circulating in churches on the scope of the Christian scriptures for centuries after official council decisions were made. Among the

---

1. It is also the same list for the NT writings as we see in the so-called *Gelasian Decree* that is wrongly attributed to Gelasius, bishop of Rome in 495, but the list was more likely produced anonymously in the sixth century and attributed to the earlier Gelasius. Some scholars suggest that the list was produced in 382 at a Roman council of churches led by Bishop Damasus and that it contained both Old and New Testament books. That list is the same as the one from the Council of Carthage (canon 24) in 416–19 where a series of church councils were held mostly there in 393–424 under Aurelius, the bishop of Carthage (d. ca. 430). Its Old Testament (OT) canon includes some of the apocryphal, or deuterocanonical, books—Tobit, 1–2 Esdras, Judith, and 1–2 Maccabees—and in addition to listing the NT writings, it also includes a long list of Christian apocryphal books to avoid.

2. Schmidt, "Greek New Testament as a Codex," in *CanDb*, 469–84, here 475–79. He lists some sixty manuscripts (MSS) with following descriptions that include all the NT writings. The point is that the circulation of complete MSS of the NT in churches without other Christian texts is much later than earlier council decisions about the scope of the NT.

earliest Christian writings cited in antiquity, the most popular were, first, Gospels—especially Matthew—followed by *some* letters attributed to Paul.

Who Jesus was as the hoped-for Messiah, as well as his teachings and activity, impacted his early followers certainly *before* his death. Because of his popularity in Israel, it is quite possible that one or more of his followers put some of his teachings and deeds in writing during his ministry. These texts told his story, reaffirmed his major teachings, and were included in the later formation of the Gospels.[3] Dunn suggests that the common material in Matthew and Luke, now called Q (from the German *Quelle*, "source"), was likely produced before the death of Jesus and later included in the canonical Gospels after his death. Some of those stories were initially transmitted orally and eventually put into writing and included in the Gospels. Some of that early material about Jesus may also have included some of the special or unique material in Matthew and Luke now commonly referred to as (M) and (L), respectively.[4] Given the popularity of Jesus in Palestine and his impact on his earliest followers, especially in Galilee, it is quite possible that some texts about him were produced before his death and were later included in the surviving NT writings, but others were likely lost (Luke 1:1–2; John 20:30–31).

Elements of the story of Jesus and their implications for faith, mission, and conduct were doubtless shared in churches before they were included in the current Gospels, as we see in Acts 2:42 as well as in the early Christian creeds (1 Cor 15:3–8; Phil 2:6–12; Rom 10:9; and 1 Tim 3:16). Some references to the teachings of Jesus appear in Paul's writings (e.g., 1 Cor 7:10–12; 11:23–25) and were circulating among Jesus' earlier followers before Paul's conversion to the Christian proclamation about Jesus. Several scholars have argued that an earlier form of the Gospel of Mark (*Ur-Markus*) existed before the current Gospel of Mark. That may also be true in the case of the Gospel of Matthew, especially the sayings or teachings of Jesus. In the first half of the second century, Papias of Hierapolis (ca. 60–130) stated that Matthew wrote down "the sayings," or "oracles" (λόγια), of Jesus that were later translated or interpreted. Eusebius preserves Papias's words as follows: "Matthew collected the oracles [τὰ λόγια] or sayings [of Jesus] in the Hebrew language [which may mean Aramaic], and each interpreted them as best he could" (*Hist. eccl.* 3.39.16, LCL). Irenaeus, Tertullian, Origen, and Eusebius likely misunderstood Papias here when they concluded that τὰ λόγια (or "the sayings") were the same as Matthew's Gospel; yet it may be true that Matthew produced a written collection of sayings of

---

3. Dunn, *Jesus Remembered*, 173–254. He suggests the possibility that some of the stories about Jesus and his teachings were circulating in Palestine both orally and in writing *before* his death and that some of these stories were included in the written stories about him after his death (the Gospels), in particular, the sayings now identified as Q material. According to Dunn, what Jesus did and said impacted his early followers *before* his resurrection, but after his death, when hopes seemed dashed, the resurrection of Jesus inspired his followers to continue and to advance his mission. Those stories about Jesus and his teachings were later incorporated into the Gospels.

4. I follow Dunn's suggestion and discuss this possibility in *Story of Jesus in History and Faith*, 65–74.

Jesus that were later included in the Gospel attributed to him, which now also includes the familiar narrative material as well.

The early followers of Jesus made use of several writings or texts that were not later included in the NT Gospels. These are generally called "Agrapha," that is, sayings of Jesus found outside of the Gospels and mostly outside of the NT. In the NT it is clear that some writings about Jesus existed *before* the current NT Gospels were written (Luke 1:1–2), and some apostolic writings were also produced in the first century that have not survived (e.g., 1 Cor 5:9 and Col 4:16). The earliest NT writings date from around 48–49 CE, but other texts now lost doubtless existed before them. It is likely also that several of the early Christian texts were lost as a result of late first-century isolated persecutions (e.g., by Domitian) or empire-wide persecutions in the third and early fourth centuries (e.g., by Decius and Diocletian) that included the destruction of Christian sacred books.[5] It is also possible that some early texts were lost as a result of natural disasters (e.g., earthquakes, fires, floods, etc.), or that later churches preserved only the writings that they believed best identified and advanced their current faith and mission and had continuing relevance for the churches. As we will see below, some writings ceased to have continuing relevance for the following generations of the church and were lost or discarded. From Acts 15:13–21, 23–29 (cf. Gal 2:1–10) we know that James composed a highly significant and influential letter that reflected the early church's decision to welcome Gentiles into the church without requiring them to observe some features in the law (especially circumcision). A summary of this letter exists in Acts, but copies of the original influential letter have not survived antiquity except in Acts 15:13–21 and 23–29. Again, given Jesus' impact on his early followers and the early church's interest in Jesus as the Lord of the church, which included its commitment to teaching its sacred traditions about Jesus (Acts 2:42), it is most likely that some texts existed before the NT writings that we now possess.

Paul's Letters are the earliest writings in the NT and, with the possible exceptions of 2 Peter and the final editions of the Pastoral Epistles,[6] scholars *generally* conclude that the rest of the NT writings were produced in the first century and reflect the earliest known traditions about Jesus as well as the emergence of the early church. The early church fathers cited the Gospels, especially Matthew and John, more frequently than other NT writings. Several of Paul's letters were also regularly cited and read in many first- and second-century churches. Second Peter was under suspicion as a pseudonymous text well into the fourth century, but Athanasius was the first to include it in his NT in his thirty-ninth *Festal Letter*. Eusebius was aware of widespread doubts about 2 Peter's authenticity

5. See a discussion of this in my *New Testament*, 87–90.

6. Based on style and content, it is unlikely that Peter or Paul wrote these letters in their current shape, but it is possible that some elements in 2 Timothy and Titus reflect authentic traditions from Paul (esp. 2 Tim 1:15–18 and 4:6–21).

(*Hist. eccl.* 3.25.3), but he also knew that some churches still found it "useful" (*Hist. eccl.* 3.3.1–4). As the parallels in 2 Peter and the *Apocalypse of Peter* suggest, some dependence appears most likely; although it is possible that the unknown author of the *Apocalypse of Peter* (ca. 110–140) made use of 2 Peter, it is also possible that the same author wrote both texts (ca. 130–140) or that the author of 2 Peter made use of the second-century *Apocalypse of Peter*.[7] Several pseudonymous writings put forward in Peter's name include 2 Peter, *Preaching of Peter*, *Gospel of Peter*, *Acts of Peter*, and *Apocalypse of Peter*; all of these are likely second-century writings. It appears likely that only 1 Peter was written in the first century.

WHY WERE THE NEW TESTAMENT SCRIPTURES WRITTEN?

This question logically starts with the most prominent writings in the NT, the Gospels, since they focus on the Lord of the church, Jesus. It is obvious that the Gospels were not written as objective and unbiased reports about Jesus, but rather as documents written to foster the faith of Jesus' followers and to inform them about his life, teachings, death, resurrection, and exaltation (ascension/return), with the obvious implications of these traditions for his followers. The authors of the Gospels would likely be offended if they were accused of writing unbiased historical reports. They all wrote favorable stories about Jesus not only to inform the audience but also to convince readers and hearers that Jesus was worthy of their faith and trust. They were indeed evangelists telling a familiar story and not simply historians!

The NT authors assumed that the story of Jesus' life, teachings, death, and resurrection was beneficial for persons of faith. Paul, for instance, cites Jesus' teachings on matters related to Christian living and conduct (e.g., 1 Cor 7:10; 11:23–25; 14:37); he especially refers to the importance of Jesus' death for sins and his readers' familiarity with that story (e.g., 1 Cor 2:2; 15:3; Gal 3:1; cf. Heb 10:10) and the importance of Jesus' resurrection for Christian faith (1 Cor 15:4–8; cf. also 1 Tim 3:16; Rev 1:18). The story about Jesus and his significance for faith is arguably the presupposition for all the NT writings, including Paul's Letters. This story forms the foundation and implications for faith, conduct, and mission. The earliest known creedal formulation about Jesus asserts that he is the Lord of the church and that he was raised from the dead (Rom 10:9–10).

---

7. Most scholars conclude that the *Apocalypse of Peter* is a pseudonymous writing dating from the early second century (ca. 100–110). Some scholars argue that its author depended on 2 Peter, thereby establishing an earlier date for the composition of 2 Peter, before 100 CE. Yet alternative and convincing arguments can be made for the reverse, that 2 Peter is dependent on the *Apocalypse of Peter*; for arguments in favor of this possibility, see Grunstaudl, *PETRUS ALEXANDRINUS*. If this is the case, then it is possible to date 2 Peter to 130 CE or even later.

The church's oral traditions about Jesus were seen as foundational for faith, and they existed before the later NT texts about him were written; but Papias preferred the oral traditions over written texts because he did not believe that "things out of books would help me as much as *utterances of a living and abiding voice* [τὰ παρὰ ζώσης φωνῆς καὶ μενούσης]" (Eusebius, *Hist. eccl.* 3.39.4, emphasis added). The preference began to change in favor of written texts about Jesus; this was happening during and following the death of the early eyewitnesses in the apostolic community and those who heard them. The NT writings were largely written to serve the needs of the early churches, including addressing and clarifying the core sacred traditions of the churches, as well as to address the special problems facing them in the first century.

Another motivation for writing the Gospels and producing the NT letters included the early church's aim of preparing texts to foster believers' growth and education; the emerging local congregations were in places not easily accessible to those in the apostolic community. Having these texts available for use (to be read) in churches allowed for a better understanding of the Christian proclamation and its implications in the churches in the widespread Roman Empire. Often texts were sent in lieu of a visit (e.g., 1–2 Corinthians) or to anticipate a forthcoming visit (Romans). The story of Jesus' life and teachings was remembered and transmitted by his followers not simply out of historical interest, but from a missional desire to preserve Jesus' story and to aid in proclaiming his life, actions, and teachings (the Gospels especially) and the story of his death and resurrection. After Jesus' resurrection, what he had said and done, including his fate, was remembered and seen as vitally important for establishing not only the identity of Jesus (Rom 1:3–4), but also the identity of his followers, meaning the church, especially in the clarification of its mission objectives, worship, and teaching ministries.

There was something about Jesus' life and fate that could not be ignored, and it was found necessary to clarify why the early Christians perpetuated the story of a crucified, despised, humiliated, and rejected religious leader. None of that story's repetition would have made much sense or given his followers pause for reflection and reconsideration unless there was something special about him or had something special happened to him. Why would anyone follow a crucified leader? How could Jesus' early followers overcome the scandal of his rejection and crucifixion? How could the tragedies that befell Jesus be understood and appropriated by those who followed him? Paul's focus on the death of Jesus (1 Cor 1:22–25) made no sense without *something else* that is critically important for understanding the perpetuation of the story about Jesus (15:12–19). The something else, of course, is the resurrection of Jesus. It is the reason for the reemergence of faith in Jesus' followers and the birth of the church. His triumph over death is found in all four Gospels and is affirmed in the rest of the NT. What else would have provided the occasion and helped believers perceive the necessity for perpetuating the oral and written story about Jesus and his significance in the early churches? How could Jesus' early followers overcome the scandal of his rejection and crucifixion apart from his triumph over death? How could his death possibly be central to Paul's proclamation (1 Cor 1:22–25) without that something else? Easter faith is the NT's answer to the riddle of the NT, namely, how the "proclaimer became the proclaimed." Thus it was reported that Jesus was alive and appeared to his followers following his crucifixion. The NT writings do not leave that riddle or question unanswered.

Again, the Gospels and the Letters made it easier for those in the apostolic community to have greater contact and influence in the early churches. Those writings aided in perpetuating the church's sacred teachings or traditions and helped believers perceive the implications for their life and mission when it was not possible to hear a "living and abiding voice" from eyewitnesses or those who heard them. The early church's proclamation was based primarily on eyewitness and oral memory of Jesus in the apostolic community (1 Cor 15:5–8; Acts 1:21–22). Long ago Grant suggested that the persecution of Roman Christians that took place in the year 64, when several leading apostles were put to death (Peter and Paul in Rome; in 62 CE, James the brother of Jesus in Jerusalem; on the latter, see Josephus, *Ant.* 20.200–203), might have contributed to the early Christian motivation to preserve in writing the things that had been circulating orally in the early churches.[8] When the eyewitnesses began to die—whether by persecution, illness, or old age—and because of the failure of memory over time, it became necessary to commit their teaching to writing. Many NT writings were composed *after* the deaths of some of the leading early followers of Jesus. Following this line of reasoning, Grant adds that Gospel writing probably began around the year 60 CE, when the apostles and early eyewitnesses were growing old or were increasingly persecuted.[9]

The Gospels were written when it was believed that a stable form of the gospel tradition was needed, one that could resist continuing change, and when eyewitnesses to the church's earliest traditions were still available to ensure that *undue* expansion of those traditions and the church's proclamation would not occur. It is not likely that any of the Gospels would have received widespread approval had any eyewitnesses discredited their reports or if they were contrary to major traditions circulating in the churches. When the evangelists told their story of Jesus, they were clearly using traditions that had already been introduced in and accepted by the earliest community of believers. At first those traditions were communicated orally and later put into written form when eyewitnesses, or those taught by eyewitnesses, were still living. There is no need to conclude, as some critics do, that these traditions were more products of the needs of the later churches than reflections of what they believed had actually happened. The transmission, interpretation, and development of these traditions in the early churches do not necessarily mean that there was *significant* expansion of them.

---

8. Grant, *Introduction to the New Testament*, 108.
9. Grant, *Introduction to the New Testament*, 108.

In other words, the evangelists did not invent stories about Jesus that would only be beneficial to a later generation of Christians, as some scholars have supposed, let alone did a later community of followers of Jesus invent stories to meet their present needs. The early Christians regularly told the story of Jesus in their churches, and these written traditions aided the missional, liturgical, and instructional aims of the early churches.[10] While that story likely expanded over time, especially the creedal statements about Jesus, it is unlikely that core events and teachings about Jesus in those traditions changed much over time. Von Campenhausen offers an important reminder that "the development and advance that takes place in the Church is never such that the origins in Christ and the original faith of the apostles are fundamentally superseded and eliminated." He concludes: "For all Christian Churches, the tradition of the New Testament—understood and interpreted according to its spirit—always remains the standard."[11]

Paul tied his understanding of the gospel to that of the earliest followers of Jesus (Gal 2:1–10); after clarifying the essence of the gospel that was acknowledged by the earliest leaders of the church (1 Cor 15:3–8), he concluded, "Whether then it was I or they, *so we proclaim and so you have come to believe*" (15:11, emphasis added). While oral and written traditions about sayings and activities of Jesus likely existed before the death of Jesus, as noted above, some scholars have concluded from those traditions (Q) that a community of Jesus' followers existed in the first century that either did not know or rejected the significance of the death and resurrection of Jesus for faith. That conclusion, though popular among some, has no biblical or historical support. No such community existed after the death of Jesus, and there is no reference to them in any first-century Christian texts. In the NT there was no hesitation about condemning or reporting aberrant teachings circulating in the churches (e.g., Col 2:20–23; 1 John 4:1–2), but no such views about a Christian faith without Easter faith are found in first-century Christianity.

Luke is different from Matthew, Mark, and John in that Luke also continued the story of Jesus into the early church period. As a result, his two volumes (Luke and Acts) portray the gospel of and about Jesus in the church's witness going all the way from Jerusalem to Rome (Acts 1:8). The Pauline and Catholic Epistles were written to churches in the Greco-Roman world to address practical and catechetical issues facing the churches and especially to present the church's core beliefs and traditions, as well as to provide guidelines for Christian behavior and to deal with the various issues and crises (conflicts and heresies) in the churches. The book of Revelation is apocalyptic and reflects the challenges facing churches in the late first-century Asia Minor, including persecution, heresy, and lethargy in those churches. The book is a call to faithfulness to the risen Christ amid the

10. I have addressed many details about the formation of the Gospels at length in *Story of Jesus in History and Faith*, 77–125.
11. Von Campenhausen, *Tradition and Life in the Church*, 17–18.

crises; it provides hope to all who are faithful to Christ even during their challenges, but also a warning to those who have fallen away.

At the end of the first century, some of the most important crises facing the
early churches included the deaths of the apostles and the failure of Jesus' anticipated soon return (Matt 24:29–31; Mark 8:38; 13:24–27, 32; Luke 21:25–28;
Acts 1:10–11; John 14:1–3; Rev 1:7; 3:11; 22:20; passim; and esp. 2 Pet 3:4); yet
also the growth of heresy in the churches (e.g., Col 1:15; 2 Thess 2:1–12; 1 John
4:2) and local persecutions (Acts 7:54–60; 12:1–5; 2 Tim 4:6–18; Rev 2:10–11;
3:8–9) all contributed significantly to the challenges facing late first-century and
early second-century churches. The severest of the early persecutions can be seen
in the second-century *Letters of Ignatius* and the mid-second-century *Martyrdom
of Polycarp*. Many churches met their challenges by giving greater authority to
the bishop and establishing an ecclesiastical hierarchy. Many also focused on
creeds that reflected the church's sacred traditions as well as a collection of Jewish scriptures. This was accompanied by an emerging collection of *Christian*
texts that later formed the church's second collection of sacred scriptures, the
NT. The NT writings give significant authority to Jesus' teachings (1 Cor 7:10;
11:23–25) and, what is most important, focus on his death, whether in the
plan of God (Luke) or for our sins (Paul), and on his resurrection (Acts 1:22;
2:32–36; Rom 1:3–4; 10:9; 1 Cor 15:3–8, 12–20; Rev 1:18). Paul also connected the resurrection of Jesus with the resurrection of Christians (Rom 8:11;
1 Cor 15:12–22). The story of Jesus was so important that it not only needed to
be proclaimed but also to be preserved and taught to new generations of Jesus'
followers. This surely must have been a factor in the writing and preservation of
the NT writings.

Jesus was recognized as Lord in his resurrection (Rom 1:3–4), and thereafter
whatever he said or did became both supremely authoritative for his followers
and a model for them to follow. From the beginning of the church, his words
were treated as sacred scripture (1 Cor 7:10; 11:23; 14:37; 1 Tim 5:18); even
when the early church fathers quote texts in the NT Gospels, they are generally
quoting only the words of Jesus in them and do not refer to the specific Gospels
by name in which Jesus' words are quoted. His story and teachings became
foundational for the church's mission, worship, and teaching ministries. The
growth in the Gentile mission, the delay of his anticipated return, and the deaths
of the apostles all likely contributed to the church's perceived need to preserve
its sacred traditions about Jesus in writing. Again, it is reasonable to assume that
some expansion and modification of those traditions did take place during their
oral transmission. However, the core traditions in the Gospels and in other NT
writings were kept rather stable despite some expansion both by contemporary
eyewitnesses and by the oral traditions about Jesus that circulated in the church
from its beginning.[12]

12. McDonald, *Story of Jesus in History and Faith*, 77–125.

WERE THE NT WRITERS CONSCIOUSLY
AWARE OF WRITING SCRIPTURE?

Recently some scholars have argued that the NT authors were consciously aware of writing sacred scripture when they composed their NT texts.[13] They contend that several NT texts reflect the authors' conscious proclamation of the "revelation" of God or "word of God"; they suggest that these references are essentially equivalent to the authors' awareness of writing "scripture." Then they transfer this supposed awareness in some NT texts to all other NT texts and conclude from them that *all* NT authors were consciously aware of writing sacred scripture. Such scholars appear to overlook the fact that several NT writings were disputed for centuries in the churches and were not *widely* identified as scripture until well into the fourth century (e.g., 2 Peter, 2–3 John, Jude, Hebrews, Revelation). Also, they do not show awareness that some other writings earlier recognized as sacred scripture were eventually dismissed or rejected from that category. It seems strange to argue that the NT writers recognized their writings as scripture, but that, in many cases, it took more than a hundred years for others in the churches to identify those books as scripture. It is also important to note that no NT author claims to have written sacred scripture, though the author of Revelation comes close to that without saying it, as I will show below.

These scholars also appear to confuse the passages that draw attention to the gospel or revelation that was *proclaimed* by the NT authors with the letters that they wrote. Once this parallel is made from a few texts, they project it on all NT writings. This is an example of an anachronism in which later views of NT writings are projected backward onto NT authors and into the first century. The most commonly cited texts they appeal to in support of their position include Rom 16:25–26; 1 Thess 2:13; and 1 Tim 3:16, but other passages as well are cited to argue that Paul and others affirmed that their *writings* were a "revelation," "prophecy," or "word of God"—and were therefore sacred scripture. In other words, they do not distinguish between what the authors were writing and the gospel that they had *proclaimed* or *preached* earlier to their readers. The designations "revelation," "prophecy," and "word of God" in the NT are generally references to the salvation that is found in Jesus the Christ or the gospel that *was proclaimed* about him. The core of that gospel is often summarized in a number of creedal formulations about Jesus in the NT or summaries of the Christian message (e.g., Rom 10:9–10; Gal 1:2–4; Eph 1:3–14; 1 Cor 14:37; 15:3–8; Phil 2:6–11; cf. 1 Tim 3:16; 1 Pet 1:3–5). I suggest that Paul employed the terms

13. See esp. Kruger, *Question of Canon*, 119–54; earlier, Kruger, *Canon Revisited*, 160–210. He does not distinguish between scripture and canon and argues that when he finds a scriptural text, he also finds a canon. In these texts, he also does not distinguish between "revelation" or "inspiration" from Scripture. Stanley Porter makes a similar claim in his and Pitts's *New Testament Textual Criticism*, 9–20. See also Bokedal, *Christian Biblical Canon*, 330–57, who makes the same argument. See my review and assessment of his work in *Review of Biblical Literature* (February 2016).

"revelation," "prophecy," and "word of God" not as references to his letters, but rather to the gospel that he had earlier *preached* to them. His *proclamation* about Jesus the Christ is "the word of God" and the "revelation" from God, and this proclamation constitutes his gospel. It is far from clear that Paul equates the revelation that he had from the risen Christ with his own letters. Indeed, the opposite seems true when Paul distinguishes what he has said from what the Lord has said (1 Cor 7:10–12, 25; see also 14:37, in which he emphasizes that what he has said is a command of the Lord and not from himself). The *revelation* that Paul has is from the Lord, but he does not always make that claim in his teaching or letters, as we will see below.

While the designation "word of God" is often connected to a prophetic figure offering a word or prophecy from God in the OT Prophets (e.g., Jer 1:1–4; Hos 1:1–2; Joel 1:1; Jonah 1:1–2; passim), it is not commonly understood that way in the NT. In the NT, "word of God" and "revelation" are not the *usual* references to the NT's written texts, but more generally references to the *proclamation* of the gospel or to the gospel itself.[14] In the NT it is acknowledged that God inspired all scripture (2 Tim. 3:16–17), yet that belief does not refer to the NT writings themselves but rather to the church's first scriptures (the OT); only later was the designation extended to the NT scriptures. The author of Revelation comes closest to that position by referring to his writing as a "revelation" from God (Rev 1:1–3; see also 22:18–19), but he also does not call his book "scripture"—though his opening description of his work comes quite close to that.

Even though Paul said, "I believe [δοκῶ] that I have the Spirit" (1 Cor 7:40, my trans.) with regard to the advice he gave to the Corinthians (7:25–39), he did not himself conclude from this that his own letters were "scripture." Kruger contends that it does not matter whether the NT authors used the term "scripture" for their writings since they were aware of their authority.[15] But is the NT authors' failure to refer to their own writings as "scripture" as inconsequential as Kruger suggests? The NT authors do not hesitate to use the term "scripture" for the texts they cite from their First Testament (the OT), yet they do not use such terminology with reference to their own texts. As we have seen, several second-century church fathers called some NT writings "scripture," and they often used the common scriptural formulas to refer to them (e.g., "as the scripture says" or

---

14. These designations are used many times in biblical and apocryphal literature and with various nuances attached to them. The five most common uses of these designations include (1) a simple designation for the Christian message or proclamation (cf. Luke 8:11; Acts 4:31; 1 Cor 14:36; Rev 1:2; and esp. in the Pauline letters); (2) a reference to written OT Scripture passages, as in the case of Matt 15:6 (Mark 7:13; cf. Exod 20:12; Deut 5:16) or John 10:35, in which the designation is a reference to Ps 82:6; (3) a reference to the message or proclamation of Jesus as in Luke 5:1 and 11:28 (cf. also John 5:38; 8:55; 17:6); (4) a reference to the will of God (Rom 9:6 and Col 1:26–27; cf. also Heb 4:12); and (5) a reference to *actions* of God (2 Pet 3:5–7). For a more detailed discussion of "word of God" and "word of the Lord" in both OT and NT, see P. Anderson, "The Word"; also Fretheim, "Word of God," who focuses on the OT use of the designation; and J. N. Sanders, "The Word," in *IBD* 4:868–72.

15. See Kruger, *Question of Canon*, 153.

"as it is written"), but the first-century NT authors do not use these designations with reference to their own writings.

In his letters Paul claims that the gospel he received came by a revelation from God (Gal 1:11–12), but he does not say that his letters are a revelation from God or divinely inspired sacred scripture. In other words, he does not say that his letters are equivalent to the gospel that he proclaimed to his *hearers* earlier. Paul distinguishes the *gospel* that he received by revelation from God and that he also *proclaimed* to his *hearers* from the letters that he subsequently wrote to churches to explain his gospel and its implications for Christian living. Those who miss this distinction may not understand Paul's primary focus when he refers to his revelation from God. If Paul's "hav[ing] the Spirit" (1 Cor 7:40) is equivalent to consciously writing scripture, it is odd that he never says it. In early Christianity those who proclaimed the Christian faith often made a claim to being led by the Spirit, but that does not suggest that they were all consciously aware of writing scripture. If that were the case, we have lost many scriptures from antiquity!

Theophilus of Antioch (ca. 180) reflects a typical belief that the scriptures were inspired when he asserts, "The holy writings teach us, and all the spirit-bearing [inspired] men, . . . that at first God was alone, and the Word in Him" (*Autol.* 2.22, *ANF*). He writes of inspiration thus: "Men of God *carrying in them a holy spirit* [πνευματοφόροι] and becoming prophets, being inspired and made wise by God, became God-taught, and holy and righteous" (*Autol.* 2.9).[16] The author of *2 Clement* believed that *1 Clement* was an inspired document and cites *1 Clement* 23.3–4 with the words "for the prophetic word also says" (λέγει γὰρ καὶ ὁ προφητικὸς λόγος) (*2 Clem.* 11.2). These are the usual words that designate writings as inspired. Clement of Rome (ca. 90–95) told his readers that Paul's letter, 1 Corinthians, was written "with true inspiration" (ἐπ᾽ ἀληθείας πνευματικῶς) (*1 Clem.* 47.3), but later claimed inspiration for himself, saying that his own letter was "written through the Holy Spirit" (γεγραμμένοις διὰ τοῦ ἁγίου πνεύματος) (*1 Clem.* 63.2). Ignatius also emphasized his own inspiration: "I spoke with a great voice—with God's own voice. . . . But some suspected me of saying this because I had previous knowledge of the division among you. But the one in whom I am bound is my witness that I had no knowledge of this from any human being, *but the Spirit was preaching and saying this* [τὸ δὲ πνεῦμα ἐκήρυσσεν, λέγον τάδε]" (Ign. *Phld.* 7.1b–2, LCL, emphasis added).

If these persons were inspired by God to write or speak, as they claim, should their writings also be included in the church's NT scriptures? That might well be the case if the only criterion for scripture and canonicity were inspiration or the leading of the Holy Spirit. Inspiration in the early churches was not limited to the church's sacred texts, but also to those who spoke the truth about God. They did not clearly distinguish between being led by the Spirit from being inspired as later church authorities did. We should also recognize that the inspiration of *all*

---

16. This passage clarifies what Theophilus means by inspiration and perhaps how his and other communities understood it.

the NT writings was not universally obvious to the early church fathers, or even to many later church fathers, as we can see from the various surviving canonical lists or catalogs that reflect the lack of complete agreement on the scope of the NT canon for centuries. By the end of the second century, many church fathers agreed on the scriptural status of the canonical Gospels, Acts, most of Paul's letters, 1 Peter, and 1 John, but not all the NT books received affirmation by that time. Also, some of the so-called noncanonical books were initially welcomed as sacred scripture, but only later were rejected (e.g., *Shepherd of Hermas, Epistle of Barnabas, 1–2 Clement*).

Kruger, interpreting 1 Cor 7:10–12, contends that Paul did not distinguish the authority of his own words from those of Jesus, thus suggesting Paul's own awareness of the scriptural authority of his letter;[17] but on the contrary, Paul appears to want to add to what he is telling the people and appeals directly to a Jesus tradition circulating in the churches for added support of his position. He first presents Jesus' word on the matter at hand and then offers his own advice, which he distinguishes from that of the "Lord" (Paul's favorite term for the risen Jesus). Paul never puts himself on the same level as the church's Lord. He clearly wanted to offer his readers greater support for the advice he was giving them by acknowledging the words of Jesus as the primary authority for what he was telling them. Kruger strangely contends that Paul saw no difference in terms of authority between what the Lord said and what Paul said. When we remember that later in this passage Paul is offering his own *opinion* or judgment (7:25), it seems clear that he does in fact distinguish the authority of the Lord from his own opinion. See, for example, in 1 Cor 11:23–25 and later in 1 Cor 14:37, where he appeals to tradition from the Lord to support his teaching. In 1 Cor 7:10 Paul identifies a command *from the Lord*, which is an otherwise unknown saying of Jesus circulating in the early churches, a saying with which Paul was familiar. Why does Paul emphasize "the Lord" here if he did not recognize a broad preference for the authority of the Lord on church matters? If both the Lord and Paul have the same authority, why does Paul not just give his own view of the matter? He emphasizes that what he has told the people came as a command from the Lord, yet later he expresses his own *opinion* when he is uncertain about what the Lord has said on other matters at hand. Regarding the virgins, he states unambiguously that he has no command from the Lord and that he gives or offers his own "opinion" (γνώμην) on the matter (7:25). After sharing that opinion (7:26–39), he concludes in verse 40, saying: "And I *think* that I have the spirit" (δοκῶ δὲ κἀγὼ πνεῦμα θεοῦ ἔχειν). That does not sound as certain as a command from the Lord (7:10). Paul himself acknowledges that his own advice is not as important as a command from the Lord (v. 12).

In 1 Cor 14:37, after giving guidance to the Corinthian Christians on the appropriate role or practice of prophesying in the church, Paul states (my trans.), "That which I write to you that is a command of the Lord" (ἐπιγινωσκέτω ἃ

---

17. Kruger, *Canon Revisited*, 187 and n. 127.

γράφω ὑμῖν ὅτι κυρίου ἐστὶν ἐντολή). We may ask whether Paul is claiming here that *all* of what he wrote to the Corinthians is a "command from the Lord," as Kruger argues, or whether he is focused on a specific command from the Lord about exercising the gift of prophecy (1 Cor 14:1–33)? We have a clue from 1 Cor 7:25, in which Paul states that he does not have a command from the Lord as he did in 7:10 and in 11:23–25 and in 14:37. We cannot conclude from Paul that everything he says in the Corinthian letters is a conscious command from the Lord, as we will see more clearly in 2 Cor 11:17, below.

So, as before, again we can ask, "Why would Paul emphasize that what he has just said is a specific command from the Lord (14:37) if he were not seeking to enhance and strengthen the authority of the counsel he just gave?" Paul regularly acknowledged his own apostolic authority (e.g., Rom 1:1; 1 Cor 9:1; Gal 1:1; passim), but as we saw, he also clearly distinguished his authority from the authority of the Lord. While he believed that he had the Spirit in what he told the church, it is not clear, as we saw above, that having the Spirit (inspiration) is always equal to writing scripture or on par with a command from the Lord.

No one denies that the apostle Paul believed that the Spirit led him to preach his gospel to both Jews and Gentiles, but did he also believe that he was writing sacred scripture when he wrote his letters to churches? Interestingly, when Paul wrote to the churches, he appealed *more often* to his apostleship derived from his encounter with the risen Lord (Rom 1:1–7; 1 Cor 9:1; 2 Cor 1:1; Gal 1:1–2; Eph 1:1; Col 1:1; Titus 1:1) *rather than* his inspiration as the grounds and authority for his ministry and for writing his letters to the churches. As we saw, he *thought* he had the Spirit in some of his comments (1 Cor 7:40), but that is not as prominent in his letters as the authority of his apostleship.

On acknowledging a text's scriptural status, Carl Holladay correctly observes that "inspiration may not have been the only decisive criterion, but it was a prerequisite for canonicity. No writing could have been included in the NT canon had it not been regarded as inspired."[18] I fully agree. As is also clear, later Christians believed that all sacred scriptural texts, whether OT or NT, were inspired by God, but Bruce correctly adds that "inspiration is no longer a criterion of canonicity: it is a corollary of canonicity."[19] It is nearly impossible to identify the characteristics of inspiration in antiquity, but simply suggesting that inspiration or being led by the Spirit are grounds for recognizing the scriptural status of the NT writings cannot be supported.[20] Everett Kalin argues persuasively that in the church's first five centuries, being led by the Spirit was not something that only biblical writers could assume, and he further states that, to a large extent, every-

---

18. Holladay, *Introduction to the New Testament*, 852–53. He correctly concludes that no NT writing was ever acknowledged as scripture without also having its inspiration affirmed. However, he rightly observes: "Numerous early Christian writings, such as the *Shepherd of Hermas* and the *Apocalypse of Peter*, claimed to be divinely inspired. Some NT writings (Revelation) claimed explicit inspiration in a way that other NT writings (Luke-Acts) did not" (Holladay, *Introduction to the New Testament*, 852).

19. Bruce, *Canon of Scripture*, 268.

20. I address this more in *New Testament*, 342–47.

thing the church believed was true was also believed to be inspired by God.[21] As we saw earlier, several church fathers have also claimed that the Spirit led them when they spoke or wrote about Christian teaching or the church's sacred traditions. Later church councils also claimed that what they concluded and penned at their councils was likewise inspired or led by the Holy Spirit.[22] If the writers of the NT were consciously aware of writing scripture, they do not make that claim; they nowhere call their own writings "scripture." If being led by the Spirit is equal to writing scripture, then (as noted above) there are many lost or omitted scriptures that should also be included in the church's scripture canon.

Again, returning to my primary point here, Paul did not equate his revealed message from the Lord with his own letters, and he did not consciously place his letters on par with the Jewish scriptures, which he frequently cited for support of his positions. Also, he never called his own writings "scripture," though that designation was certainly in his vocabulary; and he cited texts from his acknowledged scriptures frequently with that designation. The acknowledgment of Paul's letters as scripture was a later decision, in the second century, and by later churches.

Kruger also does not adequately distinguish between what is "inspired" and what is "revelatory," or sacred scripture. Not everything that the early Christians believed was inspired by God was also viewed as sacred scripture in the churches. In other words, while all scriptures were believed to be divinely inspired, not all inspired writings or communications were believed to be divine scripture—even in the later churches of the second century and following. Also, as noted above, the designations "word of God" or "word of the Lord" *generally* do not refer to specific biblical texts or scripture in the NT, but more often to a revelation from the Lord, which in most cases refers to the proclamation about Jesus the Christ. There are exceptions, of course, as when Matthew uses the phrase "word of God" and connects it to the Decalogue (Matt 15:3–6; cf. Exod 20:12; Deut 5:16; Exod 21:17; Lev 20:9; cf. also Isa 29:13 LXX). Nevertheless, usually the "word of the Lord" is not a reference to specific written texts in the NT.[23] Similarly, "revelation" *usually* is not a reference to written scripture in the NT so much

---

21. Kalin, "Argument from Inspiration."

22. See my focus on the role and function of inspiration and the Holy Spirit in early Christianity: McDonald, *Biblical Canon*, 416–20; McDonald, *New Testament*, 128–35, 341–46.

23. In a recent dialogue and debate with Charles Hedrick on the theme "Is the Bible the Word of God?," we (McDonald and Hedrick) discussed the references to "word of God" and "word of the Lord" in Scripture and early Christianity. I argued that in the NT those designations are not usually references to previously written scripture so much as references to a specific word from God through a prophetic or apostolic figure. While Hedrick rightly argues that the phrase is not generally a reference to specific biblical texts, there is the exception of Matt 15:3–6. In the NT, "word of God" is generally used for what is "heard" and not something "written." Not infrequently "word of God" in the OT Prophets is a reference to specific written texts (e.g., Mal 1:1; Zech 1:1, 7; 4:8; 6:9; 12:1; Mic 1:1; passim), but it is also often a reference to a revelatory word from God through a prophetic figure intended for a specific situation or action (e.g., Isa 55:11). The phrase "word of the LORD" is also employed to indicate a word from God for a specific occasion (1 Kgs 13:2; cf. 2 Kgs 23:16 and 24:2).

as to a word from God given to address a specific situation, and it is usually a reference to God's revelation about Jesus the Christ, revelation intended for the church (1 Thess 2:13; Rev 1:2–3; and passim).

When Paul wrote, he usually presented himself as an apostle with authority in the churches he founded, but we have no evidence that he viewed this authority as equal to writing scripture when he wrote letters to the churches. Stanley Porter rightly cites Gal 1:1, 11–12 as evidence of Paul's belief that the gospel *proclaimed* by him came to him by revelation,[24] but he assumes that Paul was also saying that his gospel was the same as the letter that he wrote to the Galatians. When explaining his gospel and condemning those who opposed it in that letter, Paul did not claim that his letter to the Galatian Christians was itself scripture, but only that the gospel about God's Son that he had *earlier* proclaimed to the Galatian Christians came to him by divine revelation. Paul specifically summarizes his gospel in 1 Cor 15:3–5 and Rom 10:9–10, but the question is whether he believed, as later churches obviously did, that his letters to the churches were also sacred scripture.

In another passage cited to support Paul's conscious awareness of writing scripture, Porter cites Rom 16:25–27 and concludes that Paul thought his entire Letter to the Romans was on par with the OT prophetic writings;[25] however, that part of the doxology only refers to Paul's "gospel and the *proclamation* of Jesus Christ." The "prophetic writings" also referred to here are the OT prophets, not Paul's writings, and the text itself does not support placing the entire Letter to the Romans on par with those OT "prophetic writings." Paul is only speaking here of the gospel he received by revelation and the "proclamation of Jesus Christ." Porter is well aware that the text itself does not have the best manuscript support and, if it was written by Paul, it could easily have been originally placed at the end of Rom 14:23 or even 15:33. The text goes on to say that Paul's gospel and his proclamation about Jesus Christ "is now disclosed" and affirmed by the "prophetic writings," meaning the Jewish sacred scriptures (see Rom 1:2; 3:21). Here Paul understands that his gospel is a revelation from God and that it is also attested in the Jewish scriptures (1 Cor 15:3–5).[26]

Kruger also appeals to Col 4:16, in which Paul admonishes the church at Colossae to have his letter read to the Christians at Laodicea. The act of reading the text in the church, he claims, places the text on par with the Jewish scriptures,

---

24. S. Porter and Pitts, *New Testament Textual Criticism*, 10.
25. S. Porter and Pitts, *New Testament Textual Criticism*, 10.
26. In support of this, see Dunn, *Romans 9–16*, 914–17. So also Moo, *Epistle to the Romans*, 938–41, who acknowledges that some count this passage as focusing on Paul's Letters or the NT writings, but Moo correctly dismisses that notion. He concludes that Paul's gospel and the proclamation about Jesus Christ are in view here. Fitzmyer, *Romans*, 753–55, does not think that 16:25–27 is an authentic part of Paul's Letter to the Romans, yet claims that it forms a "fitting conclusion" to Romans. So also Byrne, *Romans*, 461, who does not think Paul wrote this doxology since Paul nowhere else has a similar long doxology, yet he adds that the "gospel" here is not Paul's alone (Rom 2:16) but common to the whole church, which now is the revealed mystery earlier proclaimed in the "prophetic writings" (the Jewish scriptures).

which were read in the early churches; this, he claims, is evidence that Paul saw his correspondence as scripture.[27] He appeals to the practice among the Jews, who read their scriptures in their synagogues, and infers that Paul's request for his letter to be read to the Colossian Christians and also be read to the Christians at Laodicea, as well as having his letter to the Laodiceans read at Colossae, constitutes his recognition that those letters are scripture. Kruger assumes that Paul and his readers would think that they would be reading his letters as scripture in the churches instead of simply sharing his advice about the challenging circumstances that both churches were facing. However, the act of reading Paul's Letter to the Colossians in those churches is not equivalent to the Jewish practice of reading scripture in the synagogues. If that were the case, we would also have to say that Paul's letter to the Laodiceans, mentioned in Col 4:16, is lost scripture (such as we see in 1 Cor 5:9), something that Kruger does not consider. Since Colossae and Laodicea were only a few miles apart geographically, it is likely that both churches were facing similar "heretical" issues and that regular communications between both churches logically would take place to deal with them. For this reason, Paul most likely wanted his two letters read to both congregations.

In 1 Thess 2:13, Paul calls his proclamation the word of God and "you accepted it not as a human word but as what it really is, God's word, which is also at work in you believers"; yet again, that designation is more likely a reference to the gospel of and about Jesus that Paul preached and not his Letter to the Thessalonians. Paul was not saying that *his letter* was sacred scripture but simply that the proclamation he shared earlier with the Thessalonians was from God. Clearly Paul accepted his gospel as a revelatory word from God, and he condemned all other proclamations as having human origins (Gal 1:8–9), but there is no evidence that he consciously transferred the authority of his revelation from God to a scriptural authority for *all of his letters*. Paul reminds the Thessalonian Christians that the message of gospel he brought to them came not only in word, but also in the Holy Spirit and with full conviction (1 Thess 1:5), and that they received his word with joy inspired by the Spirit (1:5–6); as a result the "word of the Lord" has sounded forth from them not only in Macedonia and Achaia but also elsewhere (1:8). This gospel that Paul preached and the Thessalonians heard was a "word of the Lord" that they also received and proclaimed. Paul is here describing what he has *already proclaimed* to the Thessalonians, but does this include the letter he sent to them later? The focus here is not on what Paul *wrote*, but on the word that he *preached* and the word the Thessalonians received as the "word of God" (2:13). Paul does not call his letter to them scripture or the word of God; rather, the gospel he had earlier preached to them was the "word of the Lord" (1 Thess 1:8). He regularly affirms that *the gospel* he preached was a revelation from God and not of human origin (Gal 1:11–12). While he no doubt believed that he was led by the Spirit to proclaim his gospel as well as to write his letters, this is not the same as claiming that he was consciously aware

27. Kruger, *Canon Revisited*, 209.

of writing scripture on par with his OT scriptures. That conclusion came later, from several second-century church fathers, but not from Paul.

Several scholars also appeal to 2 Pet 3:16 as evidence that Paul's writings were viewed as scripture *in the first century* and that its author placed them on par with "other scriptures," presumably the OT scriptures. I fully agree here, but 2 Peter is almost universally acknowledged to be a second-century text. To justify the conclusion that Paul's letters were welcomed as scripture in the first century, we have to assume a highly unlikely dating of 2 Peter in the first century. As noted earlier, the earliest evidence for 2 Peter is about 130–150 CE. This letter is not included in some of the earliest canon lists, and its authenticity is even doubted well into the fourth century (Eusebius, *Hist. eccl.* 3.25.3). Athanasius (367) is the first to include it in his list of NT scriptures. Second Peter is not generally referred to by name until the end of the second century, but possibly by 130–40 the author of the *Apocalypse of Peter* appeals to 2 Peter, or 2 Peter appeals to this apocalypse.[28]

As noted above, with the possible exception of the author of Rev 22:18–19, no NT writer claims to have written anything on par with the OT scriptures; the John who wrote Revelation does not call his book "scripture," despite the warning not to change a word in it (a parallel to Deut 4:2; cf. also *Let. Aris.* §311, pointing to the sacredness of his text). That warning was quite common in Jewish and early church fathers when they wanted to preserve the sanctity of texts that often were changed in their transmission. The author of Revelation is clear, however, that what he wrote is a revelation from God and a prophecy (Rev 1:1–3, 10). I have said before that although the author of Revelation does not specifically call his book "scripture," if this is not "scripture," it is very close to it! The John of Revelation does have the primary components that were recognized in scripture, namely, he shares a revelation and prophecy. Changing written texts in transmission was a common even if unwanted practice in classical texts as well,[29] and the author here gives a stern warning about making changes to his revelation from God.

It is not clear why some scholars believe that the NT writers were consciously writing sacred scripture on par with their earlier first scriptures (the OT) when those authors themselves do not make that claim. While later church fathers did make that claim, it is absent from the NT authors themselves; a possible exception is the author of Revelation. The texts mentioned above that Kruger, Bokedal, and Stanley Porter have cited as evidence for a conscious awareness of producing sacred scripture are not convincing; but even if their arguments are correct, what do they say of those NT writings that do not make similar claims about being inspired or claiming to be a revelation from God (Gospels, Acts, most of the Catholic Epistles, and several of Paul's writings)? On what basis can they transfer their arguments from a few NT passages to all the NT writings?

28. See the arguments here in my *New Testament*, 49 fn. 27, and 259–60.
29. McDonald, *Old Testament*, 212, 315; McDonald, *New Testament*, 204–5. See also Kruger, "Early Christian Attitudes," here 69–80; Kruger shows awareness of the common changes in ancient manuscripts.

Perhaps more telling against their claim that the NT writers were consciously aware of writing scripture is when, at the beginning of his boasting about his missionary activities, Paul clearly states (2 Cor 11:21–29): "What I am saying in regard to this boastful confidence, I am saying *not with the Lord's authority, but as a fool*" (11:17, emphasis added). That is, Paul acknowledges that he is speaking "according to the flesh," or "human standards" (11:18). Paul claims that his boasting here is not "according to the Lord" (κατὰ κύριον), but rather is from a "fool" (11:17). He acknowledges that his boasting is "according to the flesh" (κατὰ σάρκα, in v. 18). Paul knows that genuine and appropriate boasting is only boasting *in the Lord*, and that is reflected in his weakness and humility (2 Cor 12:9) rather than in his boasting about his personal achievements or activity. This boasting "according to the flesh" (11:18) is, in the words of Paul, opposed to speaking "in Christ" or "speaking in Christ before God" (κατέναντι θεοῦ ἐν Χριστῷ λαλοῦμεν, in 12:19b). Paul appears consciously aware that he is *not* writing sacred scripture with his boasting and that he is writing "according to the flesh." For Paul, the only basis for boasting is in the Lord and in the weakness and humility in which he received his visions and revelations from the Lord and experienced Christ's power dwelling in him (2 Cor 11:30–12:10). He contends that the Corinthians forced him into his boasting, and he wants to show his opponents that he is not inferior to the "super-apostles," but again, such boasting and sarcasm, he recognizes, *is not from the Lord*, but from the flesh (12:11–13). Here it is difficult to argue that Paul was consciously aware of writing sacred scripture by the Spirit or according to the Lord as he boasted about his achievements and activities "in the flesh." When Paul, for instance, speaks sarcastically, with irony, and in obvious anger, as in 2 Cor 11–12, is he consciously aware of writing sacred scripture on par with the authors of the OT scriptures?

As other examples suggest, Paul was not aware that he was writing sacred scripture. Consider his undoubted anger and sarcasm in Gal 5:12, in which he wishes that those who have troubled his converts "would castrate themselves!" Further, in his disappointment over the divisions among Christians at Corinth, he writes, in evident anger and disappointment, that he is thankful to God that he baptized none of them except Crispus and Gaius (1 Cor 1:14–15); later he *corrects himself*, admitting that he also "baptized the household of Stephanas" and that *he does not know* whether he baptized any others (1:16). This part of his letter expresses his obvious disappointment with the situation in Corinth, and he seems unaware of whom he baptized and then corrects himself. Again, when he needs to correct himself, this does not appear to reflect a person consciously aware of writing scripture in the power of the Spirit or by a revelation from God. What is more important, Paul does not make such a claim *here*. Such examples are not easily harmonized with someone who is consciously writing scripture by revelation or a specific "word of the Lord." Paul no doubt believed that he was saying or doing the right thing in 1 Corinthians, and he even "thinks" that he has the Spirit on a specific matter after offering his opinion (7:12, 25, 40). Nevertheless, he acknowledges that he *did not have a command from the Lord* in what he is about to write, but rather offers his own opinion on the matter. It is the conclusion of the *later church* that what Paul wrote on this occasion was indeed sacred scripture, but it is difficult to draw the conclusion that Paul himself believed he was writing sacred scripture on par with the church's first scriptures (the OT). In his boastfulness and anger against his opponents, he does not give the impression that he is consciously aware of writing sacred scripture.

Kruger also contends that there is a self-awareness on the part of the writers of the New Testament "that they are producing authoritative documents that would function as a rule for the church," and then he goes on to conclude, "[This suggests that] the canonical authors were able to foresee the full shape of the future twenty-seven-book New Testament when they wrote."[30] As additional evidence for this claim, Kruger cites the first statement of Mark 1:1; according to Kruger, Mark is claiming that "the beginning of the gospel of Jesus Christ" is an implicit awareness of the authority of the whole Gospel of (and about) Jesus Christ.[31] The difficulty with this conclusion is the underlying assumption that Mark's Gospel was consciously written as an authoritative document "designed to characterize the work as a whole as the 'Gospel of Jesus Christ.'" There can be little doubt that the authors of the canonical Gospels believed they were telling a true story about Jesus that served as an important foundational proclamation for the church. It was a proclamation of Jesus as the Son of God. From Mark 1:1, Kruger implies that Mark saw his Gospel as sacred scripture and that the other canonical Gospels also were understood by their authors as sacred scripture. He is aware that Mark's absolute use of the term "gospel" (εὐαγγέλιον) as a reference to the human life of Jesus—including his ministry, teaching, fate, and exaltation—is a unique use of that designation in the NT. It is also different from Paul's understanding of the "gospel," which focuses on the death, resurrection, and exaltation/return of Jesus the Christ (Rom 10:9–10; 1 Cor 15:3–5). The other Gospels do not use the term "gospel" to identify their choice of genre for telling the story of Jesus, but by around 150, Justin (*1 Apol.* 64–67) was using "gospel" to identify the canonical Gospels as books. It also seems likely that "gospel" was a designation for a book or genre about Jesus for Marcion and the author of *2 Clement.*[32]

Mark's use of "gospel" in 1:1 as "The beginning of the good news (gospel) of Jesus Christ" though often in its absolute sense (cf. Mark 1:1, 15; 8:35; 10:29; 13:10; 14:9) is unlike Matthew, who uses qualifiers, as in the "gospel *of the kingdom*" (as in Matt 4:23; 9:35; 24:14; cf. also "this gospel" or "good news" in Matt 26:13). Apparently Mark understood the story of Jesus' ministry—including

30. Kruger, *Canon Revisited*, 184.
31. Kruger, *Canon Revisited*, 185–86. I added both the subjective and objective genitive readings of this text because I think the context requires it. The text is both something *from* Jesus and *about* him.
32. See Kelhoffer, "'How Soon a Book' Revisited." Elliott argues that the uniqueness of Mark's designation of "gospel" or Gospel of Jesus Christ, as understood in Pauline and pre-Pauline times, suggests that Mark 1:1–3 was added to Mark's Gospel later. See Elliott, "Mark 1:1–3—A Later Addition to the Gospel?," here 584–85.

his death, resurrection, and ascension/exaltation/return—as an essential part of "gospel of Jesus."[33] He offers a unique and later understanding of the "gospel" *both* as a book[34] *and* the gospel that includes not only what was known and said about Jesus (objective genitive for "gospel of Jesus"), but also the gospel proclaimed by Jesus (subjective genitive), what we see in Mark 1:1. Mark's "gospel" is all about what follows 1:1 in his story of Jesus. He saw that the gospel about Jesus includes Jesus' proclamation of the gospel in word and deed, as well as his fate. From his baptism onward, Jesus' life was also a part of the good news about him. Unlike Paul and his predecessors—who generally understood the heart of the gospel as centrally focused in the death, resurrection, exaltation, and return of Jesus (Rom 1:2–4; 1 Cor 15:1–7; 1 Thess 1:5, 9–10)—Mark's gospel includes Jesus' life, ministry, and miracles, beginning with his baptism by John, then onward to his death and resurrection, *and also* Jesus' proclamation about the kingdom. Anderson concludes that in Mark the "gospel" includes both the message the church proclaimed *about* Jesus as well as the message proclaimed *by* him, including everything he said and did.[35]

Again, the other three canonical Gospels do not use εὐαγγέλιον in its absolute sense, that is, without qualifiers or for their inclusion of Jesus' life, ministry, death, and resurrection, plus the implications of that for faith as central to the gospel. Kruger appears to equate Mark's designation of "gospel" with Paul's reference to his "gospel," though he is aware of the difference between the two; yet he still assumes that they are the same revelation of God and equal to sacred scripture. The problem here is not whether what Mark wrote was to be understood as authoritative in the churches, since he focuses on Jesus, the Lord of the church. It is about whether Mark or Paul viewed their own *writings* as sacred scripture on par with the church's first scriptures (the OT). Since, as noted above, Paul, Mark, and the other NT authors never use the term "scripture" in reference to their own writings, it is best that we do not jump to second-century conclusions that first-century authors did not make. We should also note that Matthew and Luke, who used Mark, did not hesitate to correct Mark's text at several points (e.g., Mark 1:2–3 and parallels in Matt 3:3 and Luke 3:4–6). Would they consciously change Mark if they thought it was sacred scripture? Interestingly, contra Mark and the other evangelists, Paul shows little interest in Jesus' life before the cross, though, as we saw above, he occasionally shows awareness of the relevance of Jesus' words (1 Cor 7:10–12; 11:23–25). He appears to have distinguished his gospel about the Christ of faith from much of the Jesus of history. Paul famously writes: "From now on, therefore, we regard no one from a human point of view; even though we once knew Christ from a human point of view, we know him no longer in that way" (2 Cor 5:16). However,

---

33. Guelich, *Mark 1–8:26*, 8, has raised this question about Mark 1:1.

34. A. Collins, *Mark*, 130–31, rightly observes that Mark used gospel "in a new way, to refer to the content of a written work, in particular a narrative closely related to historical events of an eschatological nature."

35. H. Anderson, *Gospel of Mark*, 67.

Paul did not dismiss the story of Jesus, as his references to commands of Jesus and his institutionalizing of the Last Supper demonstrate; yet he does not focus much on Jesus' earlier life and ministry. It is more likely that he learned many or most of those stories from others in the early church, but they were simply not the central focus of his gospel. Mark's recognition of the authority of the gospel about Jesus and the gospel that Jesus himself proclaimed is not unlike John's Gospel, in which the author says that what he wrote gives grounds for coming to faith that Jesus is the Christ the Son of God (John 20:30–31).

However, and again, does all of this suggest that the NT authors identified their texts as sacred scripture? They certainly did not say so. Can anything be made of the facts that only Mark identifies his story about Jesus as "the gospel" in the absolute sense and the NT authors do not *generally* designate *their writings* as "word of God" or scriptural texts? In the NT, those designations, as noted above, are generally with reference to proclamations of divine revelation of what God has done in Jesus the Christ. That is, the NT authors are generally focusing on the good news that they have proclaimed about the death of Jesus the Christ for sins and his resurrection from the dead (1 Cor 15:3–8). While Mark's story of Jesus' preaching, miracles, and teaching is never called "scripture" in his Gospel, he clearly assumes that what he says about Jesus is highly significant and joyful news, gospel, to those who come in faith to Jesus the Christ.

In a general sense, it was the words of Jesus in the Gospels that were initially cited in a scriptural fashion in the first half of the second century. The Gospels themselves only begin to be called scripture thereafter (ca. 130–150 CE). This recognition of the status of the Gospels from books containing the words of Jesus to books that were scripture was gradual and not immediate. If the first-century authors believed that they were writing scripture when producing the Gospels, it is remarkable that this was not known in the first century or generally acknowledged by the church fathers until the latter part of the second century.

Finally, I note Kruger's references to 2 Pet 1:19–21. He rightly recognizes that the reference to "the prophetic word" (τὸν προφητικὸν λόγον) in verse 19 is a reference to the OT Prophets. Others have argued that it is also a reference to the NT writings,[36] suggesting that the author here is affirming the NT writings as scripture, as he does later when he affirms the scriptural status of the letters of Paul (2 Pet 3:15–16). However, the evidence against this view is more convincing: the author is arguing for the certainty of the *Parousia*, based on eyewitness testimony about the affirmation in the transfiguration, which, as the author claims, supports the OT prophetic witness. This is confirmed by 2:1, in which the author suggests that false prophets from the OT period were also like the false teachers now among them. Bauckham notes that in the second century even Justin never used the designation "the prophetic word" as a reference to the NT writings and reminds us that the author of 2 Peter assures his readers that

36. Arguing thus from this passage are both Plumptre, *St Peter and St Jude*; and Sidebottom, *James, Jude, and 2 Peter*. That is not a widely held view today.

their eschatological hope is based on eyewitness testimony (1:16–18) as well as the OT prophets (1:19–21).[37]

There is no doubt that those who lived in the post-apostolic era gradually came to equate the NT writings as scripture on par with their First Testament (the OT) scriptures; yet again, it is remarkable that those who wrote the NT writings never referred to their own texts as scripture. They affirmed that the gospel they proclaimed was a revelation from God and in accordance with their inherited Jewish scriptures (1 Cor 15:3–5), but they did not regard their own writings as scripture. If one equates revelation and inspiration with scripture, equates scripture with canon, and regards the writings of the NT as revelation and inspiration, it is understandable why Kruger, Bokedal, and Stanley Porter conclude that the NT writers believed that they wrote Christian scriptures in the first century. However, it was not obviously apparent to them since they never use scriptural designations for their own work. The first-century Christian authors did not draw the same conclusions about their own texts that later Christians obviously did, though those texts were useful in the teaching and mission of the churches and supporting the church's sacred traditions that were passed on from the church's beginning, no doubt from the time they were written and were circulated in churches. Throughout the NT, whenever the authors cite *scripture*, they are citing the Jewish scriptures, which they *later* called their OT scriptures—with the one exception of 1 Tim 5:18, in which the words of Jesus are equated with the church's first scriptures.

SUMMARY

The process of recognizing Christian writings as scripture *began* in the first century with their use in the early churches to advance their mission, clarify Christian identity and beliefs, aid churches in resolving conflict, and deal with other issues that concerned them. Those writings were not initially cited with the usual formal scriptural formulas, such as "according to the scriptures" or "as the scripture says," until the second century. The NT writings were also not universally recognized or welcomed as scripture at the same time or by everyone, but by the early fourth century there was a broad agreement about the scriptural status of at least twenty of the twenty-seven NT writings. Several other early Christian writings—such as the *Gospel of the Hebrews*, *1–2 Clement*, the *Didache*, *Epistle of Barnabas*, and *Shepherd of Hermas*—were also earlier welcomed as scripture by some churches well into the fourth centuries and later, and some NT writings were not widely recognized as scripture until the middle to the end of the fourth century and some even later as in the cases mentioned.

In the first century many churches failed to recognize a scriptural status for the writings that later were accepted as belonging in the NT; this is not generally

37. Bauckham, *Jude, 2 Peter*, 224.

discussed by those who affirm the NT authors' awareness of writing scripture in the first century. It would be remarkable if the writers thought that they were writing sacred scripture when no one else in the first century recognized them as doing such; in some cases it took multiple centuries before some Christians recognized all of the NT writings as scripture. Widespread recognition of the scriptural status of all the NT writings came gradually and was happening up to the fifth century, with the possible exception of Revelation, as we see in the variations of books included in some of the fourth- and fifth-century uncial manuscripts, especially codices Vaticanus, Sinaiticus, and Alexandrinus. It is also remarkable that the book coming closest to calling itself scripture in the NT (Revelation) also had the most difficult time being recognized as scripture by the early churches.

In sum, Paul affirmed that the gospel he proclaimed was a revelation from God and in accord with and supported by the church's inherited first scriptures (1 Cor 15:3–5), but he did not call his writings sacred scripture, and neither did anyone else in his generation or before the second century. When the NT authors refer to the "scripture" or "as it is written," they are always referring to OT texts, with the exception of references to the words of Jesus, as we saw in 1 Tim 5:18. His words were regularly recognized in an authoritative scriptural manner (e.g., Matt 28:19–20; 1 Cor 7:10; 14:37). That recognition of the NT writings as scripture took much longer in some cases, yet some NT writings were only beginning to be recognized as scripture in some second-century churches, despite their being read in churches from the beginning. This process of recognizing the status of the NT writings that began in the first century was not finished for most churches until the fourth and fifth centuries, and in some cases even later.

Chapter 7

Forming Christian Scriptures as a Biblical Canon

LEE MARTIN McDONALD

In what follows I will focus primarily on *when* the *Christian* scriptures, now identified as the New Testament (NT), were written and *when* they were recognized as sacred authoritative scriptural texts that eventually formed the fixed NT collection, what we call the NT canon. I will conclude with a summary of recent examinations of the famed Muratorian Fragment, discussing whether it is a second-, third-, fourth-, or even fifth-century catalog of New Testament scriptures.

WHEN DID CHURCHES RECOGNIZE CHRISTIAN TEXTS AS SCRIPTURE?

Because the Gospels report the sayings and deeds of Jesus, the Lord and first canon of the church, they likely *functioned* as catechetical, missional, and apologetic sacred texts in churches from the time they began to be circulated in the first century. They were copied and transmitted throughout the Roman Empire and were by far the most copied and circulated writings in early Christianity, especially the Gospel of Matthew. Paul's writings were also quite popular in many churches because of their perceived value in explaining the Christian proclamation and its practical implications for the mission and conduct of the church. His letters were largely, if not completely, ad hoc texts written in lieu of a visit or in anticipation of a visit in order to clarify his gospel and address specific challenges facing his churches. His letters combined both theological arguments and their implications for Christian faith: they combined both theology and ethics. For Paul, Christian ethics was rooted in theological foundations.

The recognition of the value of several Christian texts no doubt took place in the first century as they were read in churches along with the church's first scriptures, what the church later identified as the Old Testament. The Gospels, especially Matthew and John, likely *functioned like scripture* by the end of the first century because they told the story of Jesus and his teachings, and by the second century several Gospels and some letters of Paul functioned as scripture *before they were called scripture*. In the second century some of these writings *began* to be called "scripture" in its technical sense of divinely inspired sacred scripture (see discussion of 2 Pet 3:15–16 and Basilides below). A text's *function* as scripture regularly precedes its *recognition* as scripture. Most of the known religiously authoritative texts functioned like scripture decades before they were called scripture. Widespread use and function of a text took place before it was called scripture and later included in a collection of the NT scriptures. Some of the so-called noncanonical or apocryphal gospels, Acts, letters, and apocalypses also functioned as scriptural texts in some churches initially because they contained reported words or sayings of Jesus or because they were circulated in the name of an apostle from around the middle to end of the second century. Eventually most of these pseudonymous texts were rejected and not included in the NT canon.

Early instances of citing NT texts as scripture can be seen in *2 Clement*,[1] where the words of Jesus in Mark 2:17 (// Matt 9:13; Luke 5:32) are cited *as scripture* (*2 Clem.* 2.4). The specific text is introduced as follows: "but also another scripture says" (καὶ ἑτέρα δὲ γραφὴ λέγει).[2] The Gospel of Mark itself is not called scripture, but rather the *words of Jesus* in Mark are called scripture. This is similar to 1 Tim 5:18, in which Jesus' *words* are cited as scripture along with citation of Deut 25:4 and Matt 10:10 (// in Luke 10:7): both texts are introduced with the words "For the scripture says" (λέγει γὰρ ἡ γραφή). The author cites the *words of Jesus* but does not name the *books* in which those words are found.[3] Citations of the Gospels by name came later (ca. 150), after apostolic authorship and apostolicity itself had gained greater

---

1. Scholars usually date *2 Clement* vaguely between 120 and 170. It more likely was written ca. 140–150, but it is difficult to establish a widely recognized precise date.

2. See examples in *2 Clement* where the words or commands of Jesus are cited or function as Scripture: 3.4–5; 4.5; 5.2; 6.1; 8.4–5; 9.11; 11.2–4; 12.2; 13.2; 14.1; 17.3, 6; and elsewhere.

3. It is well known that scholars are divided over the authorship and date of 1 Timothy. Traditionally this letter was attributed to Paul and placed among his supposed last three letters, but 1 Timothy was likely composed around 80–90, or possibly even as late as 150–160 CE, and intended to reflect Paul's thinking and influence for a later generation of Christians. In any case, this is likely the first

priority and authority in the early churches. It is especially then that many pseudonymous Christian writings in the names of apostolic figures, including Clement as in *2 Clement* and the *Clementine Homilies* and *Recognitions*, began to appear (ca. 150–200). The words of Jesus continued to hold highest authority and esteem in early Christianity from the beginning, but by 130–150 those words from Jesus were also beginning to be *called* "scripture," even if they *functioned* that way earlier.[4]

It is likely that the author of *2 Clement* recognized one or more of the canonical Gospels as scripture when he quotes the words of Jesus. For example, the author of *2 Clement* writes: "For the Lord says *in the Gospel*" (λέγει γὰρ ὁ κύριος ἐν τῷ εὐαγγελίῳ) (*2 Clem.* 8.5, emphasis added). Depending on how early we date *2 Clement* (140–150 or even 160?), here could be one of the earliest post-apostolic texts that specifically refer to the words of Jesus in a Gospel as sacred scripture. This is like Basilides (ca. 130–140), who cites three of the four Gospels and four letters of Paul as scripture. He specifically mentions Luke, Matthew, and John as scripture (cited in Hippolytus, *Refutation of All Heresies* 7.22.4), along with four of Paul's letters (Romans, 1–2 Corinthians, and Ephesians; see Hippolytus, *Haer.* 7.25.1–3 and 7.26.7), and employs the scriptural formula "as it is written" in reference to them.[5] This is similar to *2 Clement* 14.1, where the author cites Jeremiah 7:11 or Jesus' reference to Jer 7:11 in Matt 21:13. The author of *2 Clement* typically cites the words of Jesus in a scriptural manner (see *2 Clem.* 2.4; cf. also 4.1–5; 5.2; 6.1–2), including words regularly found in the Synoptic Gospels. It is a short move from citing texts containing the words of Jesus and their function like scripture to eventually calling those texts scripture. The author of *2 Clement* often writes *with* scripture[6] and shows familiarity with Matthew, probably also Mark and Luke, as well as several of Paul's letters, Acts, Hebrews, 1 Peter (e.g., cf. *2 Clem.* 11.6 and Heb 10:23; cf. *2 Clem.* 11.7 and 1 Cor 2:9), and possibly also the *Gospel of Thomas* 22 in *2 Clement* 12.2. This may reflect a later date for *2 Clement*, perhaps even as late

---

instance in which Jesus' words are clearly identified as scripture, even though his words no doubt *functioned* that way much earlier, as we saw in 1 Cor 7:10–12 (cf. also Matt 28:19). This is not unlike the later reference in 2 Pet 3:2, which admonishes readers to "remember the words spoken in the past by holy prophets, and *the commandment of the Lord and Savior* spoken through your apostles" (emphasis added). The author here equates the commands of Jesus *spoken* through the apostles with the earlier "holy prophets"—that is, Scripture. Is the phrase "the commands of the Lord" a reference only to the *words* of Jesus, or to all apostolic teachings (the early church traditions), or specifically to all writings by the apostles? Here the text is vague.

4. For a discussion of this and its evidence, see McDonald, "Gospels in Early Christianity."

5. Clement of Alexandria also cites *2 Clement* (*Strom.* 3.13). These references are in Grant, *Formation of the New Testament*, 121–24, who also notes that Mark's Gospel was apparently ignored or unknown at that time.

6. Here I make use of Jacob Neusner's designation for this practice in early Jewish and Christian writings, which is not so much citing Scripture as writing with it, as in much of the NT writings, especially in Hebrews, which gives the usual citation formula only one time in a quote (Heb 10:7 citing Ps 40:7). See Neusner and Green, *Writing with Scripture*.

as 150–160.[7] Interestingly, both *1* and *2 Clement* are listed among Christian scriptures in the *Apostolic Canon* 85 (= Book 8.47 of the *Apostolic Constitutions*, ca. 350–380 CE).

The author of *2 Clement* also shows familiarity with several OT texts, especially Isaiah, and may include several otherwise unknown sayings of Jesus (see 4.5; 5.4; 11.4). Possibly other unknown sayings of Jesus are cited in *1 Clement* 23.3–4; 13.2; 14.3. In the early church, various references to Jesus' teachings in the canonical Gospels reflect the widespread recognition of the "words of the Lord" as a primary scriptural authority; this use reasonably led to the recognition of those texts as scripture. It is interesting that both *1* and *2 Clement* are included in Codex Alexandrinus (5th cent.) following the book of Revelation.

The words of Jesus that the author of *2 Clement* cites as scripture may reflect his awareness of a common oral tradition circulating in the churches rather than his familiarity with specific unknown sources, but some of the texts he cites have close parallels with the Synoptic Gospels. While it is difficult to date *2 Clement* precisely, the parallels with Justin's reference to the Gospels as "memoirs of the Apostles" (*1 Apol.* 64–67) and a specific reference to "the Gospel," as noted above, suggests a possible date of 150 to 160, when the NT Gospels were *beginning* to be cited both as "memoirs of the Apostles" and "Gospels" and in an authoritatively scriptural manner. This, of course, anticipates the later widespread recognition of the Gospels as Christian scripture near the end of the second century (170–180).

Interestingly, the author of *The Clementine Homilies* (or *Klementia*) tells the story of Justa, the name the author gives to the woman in the Gospels with a daughter who was healed by Jesus (Mark 7:24–30 // Matt. 15:21–28). *The Clementine Homilies*, wrongly attributed to Clement of Rome, alter the Gospels by showing that the woman changed from being a Gentile (cf. Mark 7:26) to one who became a proselyte of the Jews and observed Jewish laws (*Clementine Homilies* 13.7.3; cf. also 2.19–21). The author offers a brief summary of her life both before and after meeting with Jesus. This appears to reflect a tendency in the second century (ca. 160), or perhaps no later than when Origen cites it (ca.

---

7. Interestingly, Clement of Alexandria (ca. 180) cites several noncanonical sources in his *Stromata*, including the *Gospel of the Egyptians* (8 times), the *Gospel of the Hebrews* (3 times), and the *Traditions of Matthias* (3 times). He introduces a reference to the *Gospel of the Hebrews* with the scriptural citation formula "it is written" (γέγραπται). For a careful examination of the origin and use of this gospel in early Christianity, see Edwards, "Hebrew Gospel in Early Christianity." See also Edwards's earlier *Hebrew Gospel*. During a debate with a gnostic Christian, Clement of Alexandria quotes from the *Gospel according to the Egyptians* as follows: "When Salome inquired how long death should have power, the Lord (not meaning that life is evil, and the creation bad) said: 'As long as you women give birth to children'" (*Strom.* 3.6.45). Clement concedes, "We do not have this saying [of Jesus to Salome] in the four traditional Gospels, but in the *Gospel according to the Egyptians*." He obviously accepts the saying as an authentic and authoritative saying of Jesus despite it not being in the canonical Gospels. These sources are in Metzger, *Canon of the New Testament*, 132 and 171. Clement of Alexandria accepted the *Epistle of Barnabas* as apostolic and quoted *Barn.* 1.5 and 2.3 in an authoritative manner, like scripture (*Strom.* 2.6 and 2.15.67). He also approvingly cites *1 Clement*, *Shepherd of Hermas*, Sirach, Tatian's *Against the Greeks*, *Preaching of Peter*, *Apocalypse of Peter*, and even the *Sibylline Oracles*.

230), to change Gospel texts in order to bring them into conformity with current views about Jesus.[8] Given the freedom taken to change and enhance the story of the Syrophoenician woman in the Gospels, it is clear that the text of the Gospels was not yet viewed as inviolable at the time *The Clementine Homilies* were written.[9]

In the middle to late second century, the Gospels were *beginning* to be called scripture, but they clearly were already functioning that way earlier because they contained the words and story of Jesus that were cited authoritatively in the early churches from their beginning (1 Cor 7:10; 11:23–25). From the church's beginning, if Jesus spoke about a matter, it was settled for the church. He was the undisputed Lord of the church (Matt. 28:19; Rom 10:9; cf. Matt 16:22 where Peter debates the words of Jesus, something that does not happen in the post-resurrection community of his followers).

As we saw above, in *2 Clement* the "commands" or "commandments" of Jesus functioned as scripture in the same way that we see them functioning in 1 Tim 5:18 and Matt 28:19. Paul's letters functioned authoritatively for some churches by the end of the first century, if not sooner, not only because of his apostolic role in founding those churches (Rom 1:1; 1 Cor 1:1; 9:1; 2 Cor 1:1; Gal 1:1; passim), but also because of their catechetical and apologetic value. Paul's writings were not *generally* called "scripture" before the latter part of the second century, though as we saw above, Basilides was likely the first to designate some of the Gospels and Pauline letters as scripture (ca. 130–135). The author of 2 Pet 3:15–16, perhaps around the same time, also referred to Paul's letters as "scripture."

Paul no doubt intended his writings to be read in his churches (Col 4:16) and even addressed most of them *to the churches* (Rom 1:7; 1 Cor 1:2; 2 Cor 1:1; Gal 1:2; Eph 1:1; Col 1:2; 1 Thess 1:1; 2 Thess 1:1; cf. Col 4:16) and rarely to their leaders (Phil 1:1). Other NT texts also were either cited as scripture or at least appear to have functioned that way in the second century, as we saw above in *2 Clement.*[10] As shown above, NT and early Christian authors often reflect a practice of *writing with scripture* rather than citing texts as scripture. This suggests that ancient authors who cited NT texts without using the usual scriptural

---

8. I owe this suggestion to Patricia A. Duncan, who offered a helpful discussion of this possibility along with several examples of it in her paper: "The Christian Philosopher of the *Klementia*," delivered at the SNTS (Society for NT Studies) meetings in Montreal, 2016. I received a prepublication copy of that paper.

9. According to Duncan, it appears that the author of the *Klementia* blended the original character Justa with the gospel character and used the figure of the healed daughter in the special episode at Tyre (*Klem.* 4–6). The author also added "proselyte" to a later reference to make logical sense of her change in status from Gentile in Matthew and Mark to Jew (*Klem.* 4–6). The change of status for Justa likely reflects an Ebionite origin of the text or perhaps an Elkesite origin from the East. At any rate, the willingness to modify the Gospels here supports the notion that they were not yet viewed as sacrosanct and inviolable texts when *Klementia* was written.

10. Examples: *2 Clem.* 1.1 references Acts 10:42 and 1 Pet 4:5; *2 Clem.* 2.1 parallels Isa 54:1 and Gal 4:27; *2 Clem.* 11.5 cites *1 Clem.* 23.3–4. See also *2 Clem.* 11.6–7 *writing with* NT scriptures, including Heb 10:23 and 1 Cor 2:9; finally, see also *2 Clem.* 16.4; 19.2; 20.5.

citation formulas often made use of them *as scripture* even though they were not yet called scripture. Some churches, especially the Ebionite communities of Christian faith, did not welcome Paul's writings because of his understanding of the role of the law. It appears that a number of churches began welcoming 1 Peter and 1 John as scripture by the late second century primarily because of their theological value and basic agreement with the churches' sacred traditions.[11] Other NT writings took longer to be accepted as scripture in some churches, especially Hebrews, the Pastorals, James, 2 Peter, 2–3 John, Jude, and Revelation.

WHEN DID THE CHURCH FINALIZE ITS NT CANON?

This question is a modern one that was not fully answered in antiquity until the late fourth century *for some* Christians, when church councils began dealing with the matter, but for centuries before and after council meetings, the matter was not generally discussed. Clearly the NT canon shows that the later churches, as we see in the Muratorian Fragment (lines 73–76), wanted to anchor their faith and confidence in documents that were near the time of Jesus and the apostolic community and not in the later time of Hermas. The quest for clearly stated information about the formation of the NT canon is complex, due to the lack of adequate surviving ancient sources that address our modern concerns, but eventually church leaders decided that Christian writings closest to the time of Jesus (as shown in the criteria of apostolicity and antiquity) would be recognized as the church's NT scriptures and be included in the church's NT canon. Such decisions did not take place before the middle to late fourth century, but the texts selected at church councils were not universally normative. As late as the middle to late fourth century, for example, Codex Sinaiticus included the *Epistle of Barnabas* and the *Shepherd of Hermas* among its NT scriptures; both of these were written in the second century, but the date of the pseudonymous *Epistle of Barnabas* may not have been widely known at that time, and it was assumed to have been written by Paul's first-century companion.

Similarly, as noted above, Codex Alexandrinus (5th c.) included in its manuscript *1* and *2 Clement* along with the *Psalms of Solomon*. We see some references to *1 Clement* as sacred scripture well into the twelfth century.[12] There are several examples of later churches welcoming other religious texts for centuries after the majority of churches and church councils had rejected them in favor of a more limited NT canon, as we saw in the Stichometry of Nicephoris (ca. 850). Because of this varied practice and the shortage of relevant ancient sources, there

---

11. See my discussion of the citations of this literature in *New Testament*, 265–75.

12. I owe this recognition to Jeremiah Bailey's paper "The Canon in Clement and Clement in the Canon: 1 Clement as Receiver of the New Testament and as Candidate for Inclusion," which he gave at Houston Baptist University on March 4, 2017; it will soon be published in a separate volume on the canon.

are no simple answers to the question of *when* the churches finalized their NT canon. The early and later church councils often did not reflect the practices of all churches then or even later in their own region or in other regions. While Athanasius's thirty-ninth *Festal Letter* circulated widely in the latter half of the fourth century, not everyone in North Africa agreed with it nor in Syria, where a copy of it was sent, where initially *3 Corinthians* and the *Diatessaron* were welcomed as NT scripture. It is well known that initially and for several centuries the so-called Minor New Testament Epistles (2 Peter, 2-3 John, and Jude), and Revelation were all rejected. The manuscripts produced by the churches at the time of the councils and later often did not exactly reflect the will of those council decisions. The matter of which books to recognize as sacred scripture was resolved for Roman Catholic churches no later than the Council of Trent in 1546, but that was not the case for all churches in the East or West. No Eastern churches had a Council of Trent that finally determined for them the scope of their biblical canon.

After some two thousand years, there is as yet no consensus among historical or biblical scholars on exactly when churches decided the scope of their biblical canons, but there is wide agreement that the process took a long time and that the recognition of the NT canon was *broadly* completed by the late fourth century for most churches but not for all. The canonization of the NT writings was not completed for all churches at the same time, though in time most churches came to full agreement on the scope of the NT canon despite differences in their OT canons. The NT canon was not quickly settled for all churches, especially in the East and especially among the Ethiopian Christians. No single individual made a declaration on the matter that everyone accepted. Athanasius in 367 was the first to acknowledge the scriptural status of 2 Peter, and eventually others fell into line and accepted it as well. The surviving evidence suggests that there was broad agreement on *most* of the books that now comprise the church's NT canon no later than the end of the fourth century and possibly sooner, but seven of the NT writings were still disputed well into the fourth century, and Revelation appears to have had the most difficulty in gaining acceptance, especially in the Eastern churches. Although all Eastern churches finally accepted Revelation into their NT canons, its tenuous acceptance can be seen to this day since it is never read in church liturgies. Similarly, some books that were recognized as scripture earlier did not later remain a part of the church's NT canon (*Shepherd of Hermas, Epistle of Barnabas*, and *1–2 Clement*) but only had temporary recognition as Christian scripture. In the fourth century Eusebius identified books widely accepted or "recognized" or "confessed" (ὁμολογουμένοις), some as doubtful or "disputed" or "spoken against" (ἀντιλεγομένων) writings (James, Jude, 2 Peter, 2–3 John, and possibly Revelation), and those he rejected as "spurious" (νόθοις), that is, *Acts of Paul*, Shepherd, *Apocalypse of Peter, Epistle of Barnabas, Didache,* and possibly Revelation and *Gospel of the Hebrews*. Finally, he completely rejected as heretical ("not even among spurious books") writings such as, but not limited to *Gospel of Peter, Gospel of Thomas, Gospel of Matthias, Acts of Andrew, Acts of John,* and other apostles (*Hist. eccl.* 3.25). The books that did not cohere with the church's sacred traditions were rejected rather early, as we see in Irenaeus's rejection of the *Gospel of Judas* (*Haer.* 1.31.1),[13] as well as the Christian gnostic texts such as the gnostic *Gospel of Truth* (*Haer.* 3.11).

The first scriptures that informed the earliest Christians included *most* of the books that were later included in the Hebrew Bible (HB) and in the church's OT, but as we saw in chapter 5, other Jewish religious writings (the Apocrypha or deuterocanonicals) were also welcomed in many Christian scriptural collections. By the end of the second century, many of the NT writings were beginning to take their place alongside the church's first scriptures, especially the Gospels and some letters of Paul. Some Christians initially welcomed as scripture the *Shepherd of Hermas, Epistle of Barnabas, Didache, 1* and *2 Clement,* the *Gospel of the Hebrews,* the *Odes of Solomon,* and some writings now identified as Christian (NT) Apocrypha, but eventually those were all rejected and left behind.

The early churches were not significantly interested in the scope of their scriptures in the first and second centuries, but that does not mean that they were unfamiliar with collections of Jewish and Christian religious texts that they welcomed as scripture. Only the limits or scope of that collection were not in view at that time. As noted above, Irenaeus's concern was more to secure acceptance of the Gospel of John along with the Synoptics and to disparage the reading of heretical documents such as the *Gospel of Judas* than to construct a complete listing of all NT scriptures. Supporting this, Eusebius tells the story of Bishop Serapion (ca. 200), who initially allowed Christians at Rhossus to read the *Gospel of Peter* in their church without having read it himself; later, after reading it, he reversed himself and forbade its reading in the churches after finding what he believed were docetic teachings in it (*Hist. eccl.* 6.12.3–6). He was evidently unaware of the limitations that Irenaeus earlier put on the scope of the church's gospels. While Irenaeus only welcomed the four canonical Gospels, that was not the case with all church fathers well into the end of the second century. In the third century the four canonical Gospels began to be circulated in one codex volume (P[45]); after that, they were not circulating with other gospels, but often less than all four Gospels were included in NT manuscripts. However, in Tertullian's criticism of Marcion, he ridiculed him for choosing Luke who was not an apostle instead of Matthew and John who were (*Marc.* 4.2.2 and 4.2.5). While accepting the witnesses of Mark and Luke, he did not place them on the same level of authority as Matthew and John who were apostles.

In the second century there was not yet any clear identification of all the books that formed the later church's NT scriptures. Fluidity in the scope of the church's NT scriptures continued for centuries, as we see in the books included in fourth-, fifth-, and sixth-century scripture catalogs and in NT manuscripts

13. His text that identifies and condemns this so-called "gospel" reads in part: "They [Cainites] produce a fictitious history of this kind, which they style the Gospel of Judas" (*Haer.* 1.31.1, *ANF*).

well into the ninth century and even later, despite the considerable overlap of books in most of the surviving manuscripts and canon lists.

The scope of the NT scriptures was settled for most churches by the fourth and fifth centuries, but variations in that collection continued long after that. For example, there are references to rejected books in the sixth-century *Pseudo-Athanasius* catalog and also in the ninth-century Stichometry of Nicephoris, books that had been rejected earlier; yet if later Christians were not reading those earlier rejected books, there would be no need to keep listing them centuries after their formal council rejections. We see the rejected books in catalogs dating from the sixth to the ninth centuries. For example, the manuscript Gregory 1105 from the Lavra Monastery on Mount Athos (an 11th- or 12th-c. minuscule manuscript) includes most NT books in a different order, with the Letters of Paul and Hebrews near the end, but the manuscript ends with a collection of psalms and odes.[14] Perhaps the producer(s) of this manuscript tried to form a NT canon like the OT canon, which included psalms and odes, but it still omits Revelation. This collection is different from the traditional NT canons. Although *most* churches accepted most of the NT books by the latter part of the fourth century, occasionally with the exception of Revelation, some churches continued to read other writings for centuries longer; thus *3 Corinthians*, the *Repose of the Evangelist John* (or *The Rest of the Blessed John*), and the *Petition of Euthalius* were read in the Armenian churches well into the 1800s.

Differences in the books welcomed as scripture can still be seen in the medieval era, when some churches, especially from the East, continued to read and include some noncanonical writings such as *3 Corinthians* and the *Diatessaron*. Likewise, while Christians today regularly view the Bible as a fixed collection of writings that comprise a holy and inspired book (or collection of books, as the name "Bible," which stems from the plural of βίβλος, "book," and implies a sacred collection of books). That notion itself is a late development that emerges in medieval times largely with the production of the thirteenth-century "Paris Bibles."[15] When the notion of a stabilized biblical canon became more common and acceptable among the late fourth-century and fifth-century church fathers, the books of the NT that were earlier marginalized (Hebrews, James, 2 Peter, 2–3 John, Jude, and Revelation) were finally welcomed in the NT canons, but not universally. The Eastern churches took much longer to welcome *only* the NT writings accepted in the West, including Revelation. Besides the Armenian churches, some other churches welcomed the *Diatessaron* in their scriptures well

14. The manuscript includes all the books of the NT except Revelation and the Letters of Paul and Hebrews are near the end of the list, just before the psalms and odes. Acts and the Catholic Epistles follow the canonical Gospels as in many surviving manuscripts. For a helpful listing of the books in a variety of biblical manuscripts, see Swanson, *2 Corinthians*, 341–47. This same collection is added at the end of all his NT volumes.

15. This designation came to be used of the small-lettered pandect Bibles first produced in Paris for student and clergy use in the 13th century. For a helpful discussion of these Bibles, including their contents and name designations, see Liere, *Medieval Bible*, 4–15; and Light, "Bible and the Individual."

into the fourteenth century. Along with the twenty-seven NT books, Ethiopian Christians also welcomed *Synodos* (four sections, a compilation of decisions and documents of early church councils, especially from Nicaea) into their NT canon, as well as the *Book of the Covenant*, the *Ethiopian Clement*, and the *Didascalia*.[16] The widespread acceptance of all of the NT books does not show the habit of some churches that accepted the whole of the NT canon as scripture while continuing to marginalize or ignore several of those books or accept others. For instance, as we saw above, the Eastern Orthodox Christians (Greek and Russian) still do not include the book of Revelation in their liturgies for reading in churches, although they include it in their NT. Eventually there was widespread unity on the scope of the NT canon, but there were still differences over some additional books included in several major uncial codices read in churches. As noted above, we can see these differences in Codex Sinaiticus that includes *Epistle of Barnabas* and *Shepherd of Hermas*; Codex Alexandrinus includes *1–2 Clement* and *Psalms of Solomon*. Also, the fourth-century canon list inserted into the sixth-century Codex Claromontanus includes *Epistle of Barnabas*, *Shepherd of Hermas*, *Acts of Paul*, and *Apocalypse of Peter*.[17]

The NT writings were intentionally circulating and read in churches almost from the time they were penned (Col 4:16). Because the Gospels focused on the teachings and activity of Jesus, the Lord of the early church, they were unquestionably welcomed as authoritative texts in the early churches that had them. However, when they were initially quoted, they were not cited with references to the authors of the Gospels, but only as the words and actions of Jesus in those Gospels, and not identified as documents by their individual authors (Matthew, Mark, Luke, John) generally until the last quarter of the second century. Reading NT Gospels in churches implies, of course, that the Gospels were believed to faithfully transmit the life and teachings and fate of Jesus.

It is unlikely, however, that more than a few churches would have owned copies of all four canonical Gospels, let alone all the letters, Acts, and Revelation before, during, or even after the second century. Before the fifth century, only a handful of NT manuscripts contain more than two books. Although the early third-century Codex P^{45} contains, in fragmented form, all four canonical Gospels and Acts, there is no evidence that most churches had possession of all four canonical Gospels at that time. It is more likely that most second-century churches had only one of the Gospels. Although Justin (ca. 150) refers to mul-

---

16. For a discussion of these, see Isaac, "Bible in Ethiopic," 110–22, especially a summary on 112. I have listed all of the current books in the Ethiopian biblical canon in McDonald, *Old Testament*, 499; McDonald, *New Testament*, 369. It is widely recognized that while the number of books in this biblical canon is always "eighty-one," the actual books included vary and sometimes there are only seventy-eight or fewer books included despite the number eighty-one commonly acknowledged.

17. For a listing of the various NT catalogs and several major fourth- and fifth-century manuscripts, see McDonald, *Old Testament*, 489–97; and McDonald, *New Testament*, 361–68. For a more extended and helpful listing and discussion of these catalogs, see Gallagher and Meade, *Biblical Canon Lists*.

tiple gospels (*1 Apol.* 64–67), it is not clear that he was familiar with the Gospel of John. Irenaeus was aware of the four canonical Gospels and others circulating in his time, but he accepted the reading of only canonical Gospels in the churches and yet read the *Shepherd of Hermas* as scripture (*Haer.* 3.11.8–9; cf. 3.1.1). The Gospel of Matthew was by far the most popular and cited Gospel in the early churches, followed by the Gospel of John. Although other Christian texts were circulating in churches from the beginning, especially several of the letters attributed to Paul, it took much longer for most of the early Christians to recognize all of them *as scripture*, even if some of the Christian writings *functioned* like scripture earlier.

Today all three major branches of the church (Catholic, Orthodox, and Protestant) agree on the scope of the NT canon, but that agreement was neither immediate nor fully settled until well into the nineteenth century for all churches. Churches debated some NT writings and made use of some non-NT Christian writings for centuries.

CRITERIA FOR NEW TESTAMENT CANONICITY: A SUMMARY

The criteria adopted by churches for inclusion of writings in their NT canons were not universally or uniformly employed nor ever clearly and fully stated, but generally they included *apostolicity* (written by an apostle), *orthodoxy* (adherence to the church's sacred beliefs and traditions), *antiquity* (written in the time of the apostolic community), popular use or *catholicity* (widespread use in the majority of churches), and *adaptability* (whether the writings had continuing value and relevance in the churches).[18] There are exceptions to all of these in the writings that survived antiquity, but certainly by the last half of the second century, apostolic authorship was perceived to reflect special authority in the churches. This was the time when many of the pseudonymous writings in the names of apostles began to appear in churches.

Writings that some early Christians welcomed as sacred texts (e.g., *Gospel of the Hebrews, Shepherd of Hermas, Barnabas, 1–2 Clement*) were later excluded from the Christian canon of scriptures. The *Shepherd of Hermas*, for example, was very popular among the early Christians for several centuries, and more ancient manuscript copies of it have been found than of any other NT books except Matthew and John. However, there came a time after several centuries when the criteria of antiquity and apostolicity were applied to it, and *Shepherd of Hermas* was left behind (the MF makes this point).

A related issue has to do with the order of the canonical Gospels at the end of the second century. Irenaeus placed them in what now is the canonical order (Matthew, Mark, Luke, and John), but one of his contemporaries, Clement of

18. I have discussed these criteria at length in *New Testament*, 320–48.

Alexandria, had a different order (Matthew, Luke, Mark, John); later, Origen had Matthew, Mark, Luke–Acts, and John. The canon list from the middle to the end of the fourth century, inserted in the sixth-century Codex Claromontanus, was much like Tertullian's list, naming the Gospels as Matthew, John, Mark, and Luke. The Muratorian Fragment (MF) appears to welcome the traditional order and the four canonical Gospels without comment or defense for the order of the Gospels. Second-century church fathers do not comment on the scope or order of the NT scriptures, and the designations OT and NT had only been introduced in the latter part of that century but still were unfamiliar designations in some fourth-century churches.

The exclusion of some religious texts was based mostly on their lack of agreement with the church's sacred traditions (the *regula fidei*) passed on through its bishops in the churches (Irenaeus, *Haer.* 3.3.3). The identification of heretical writings circulating in churches did not lead the second-century churches to establish a fixed collection of scriptures for the churches, but rather a *regula fidei*, that is, a statement of the church's core beliefs (the criterion of orthodoxy).[19] There was considerable variety in the second-century churches over which religious texts could be read in churches; such differences continued even after later church councils made decisions on the scope of the church's scriptures in the fourth and fifth centuries.

While the issue of the order of the NT books is seldom discussed in antiquity, with few exceptions (MSS 1 and 33), all lists that include the Gospels place them in first place, a practice that is similar to the placing of Torah in first place in the HB and OT canons. Because the Gospels focus on the church's primary authority, Jesus, it is reasonable that they are in first place even though they were not written before many other NT writings. The surviving manuscripts and evidence from the early church fathers show that the order of the NT writings varied. For example, in the manuscripts and catalogs we frequently see that Acts and the Catholic Epistles are right after the Gospels, and Paul's Letters follow them, but sometimes Acts and the Catholic Epistles are at the end of the manuscript. Sometimes, but less often, the Letters of Paul follow the book of Acts, which follows the Gospels. Occasionally Paul's Letters are placed at the end of the NT (Origen), and sometimes Revelation is not last in a NT collection.

The multiple orders of NT books are understandable, given that they were not circulated initially as a complete collection, but rather in individual scrolls, or in smaller codices containing a few NT books, well into and even after the fourth century. Nienhuis and Wall make good arguments for the circulation of the Catholic Epistles in a particular order, the one in the current NT,[20] but this was not the case initially in some of the catalogs, even though most of

19. See Irenaeus's rejection of the *Gospel of Judas* in *Haer.* 1.31.1 and of the *Gospel of Truth* in *Haer.* 3.11.9.
20. See Nienhuis and Wall, *Reading the Epistles*, and esp. 40–69 for their arguments, yet with the concluding proviso that the current order, with all the variations seen in catalogs and manuscripts, still offers "a unified reading strategy" ordered by the church.

the manuscripts that include the Catholic Epistles include them in the current order. Several early NT canon lists in the third to the sixth centuries do not list the Catholic Epistles in their current order.

From the fifth century to the fifteenth, there are also several examples of biblical manuscripts that included noncanonical writings.[21] The councils of the earlier centuries (393 in Hippo; 397 and 416 in Carthage), while recognized by the council members participating, did not reflect the views of all Christians at that time or even later. Likewise, the majority of NT manuscripts were prepared for normal church use either for catechetical instruction or as lectionaries for liturgies; sometimes other writings were included among the current complete NT books.[22] Even after the establishment of a widely recognized NT canon in the fourth and fifth centuries, the notion of a *Bible*, meaning a single book containing all of the church's scriptures, was still a later reality. That reality, as noted above, came in the thirteenth century with the production of the pandect Paris Bibles; these placed smaller alphabetic letters on thin parchment to make them accessible in a smaller and thinner volume for larger numbers of students, professors, and clergy. During that time the Bible became a personal sacred BOOK for them.[23] "Bible" (from *biblia*, "books") came to refer to a single holy book rather than simply "the books" (*ta biblia*) referred to centuries earlier (by Jerome) as the books that comprised the church's scriptures. The "Bible," understood as a single complete book, is a rather late notion. Before the ninth to thirteenth centuries, it was seldom seen as a whole book despite the circulation of a few pandect Old and New Testaments in one volume, as in the codices Vaticanus, Sinaiticus, and Alexandrinus.

THE MURATORIAN FRAGMENT

In 1738–40 Ludovico Antonio Muratori (1672–1750) was in the Ambrosian library in Milan and discovered the well-known fragmented catalog of mostly NT writings, now known as the Muratorian Fragment (MF). It was found among some seventy-six leaves. After extensive investigation, many scholars conclude that the MF is one of the earliest and most important documents that establishes a late second-century date for a first NT canon. The document itself is a seventh- or eighth-century fragment of a Latin text formerly located in Bobbio, Italy; it also contains three treatises from fourth- and fifth-century church fathers (Eucherius, Ambrose, and Chrysostom) as well as five early Christian creeds. Scholars are split over whether the document was originally written in Latin or Greek. Because the manuscript was poorly prepared in Latin, many scholars have argued that it was originally written in Greek and later poorly

21. For multiple examples of this, see Haelst, *Catalogue des papyrus litteraires.*
22. See examples of this in Liere, *Medieval Bible,* 53–78; 93–109 on "The Latin Bible, c. 900 to the Council of Trent, 1546"; and see Bogaert, "The Latin Bible, c. 600–c. 900."
23. See a discussion of this in Light, "Bible and the Individual."

translated into Latin. Scholars have generally argued that the most likely date for the MF is either around 180–200 or as late as the middle to late fourth century. Most scholars agree that the MF originated in or near Rome, but with notable exceptions.[24] Its author is unknown, though recently one scholar has posited that Victorinus of Pettau wrote it in the third century,[25] but his arguments have not gained wide acceptance.

Every word of the MF has been examined carefully, but scholars continue to debate its date, provenance, and influence—and even more recently, whether the document itself is a fourth-century fraud.[26] We cannot debate all of these issues here, but we can say unequivocally that if the MF is a second-century document, it had no known parallel or influence for at least another 150 years. There are no references to it until the late fourth century or early fifth century, when it is cited for the first time by Chromatius of Aquileia in northern Italy, who referred to the MF in the preface to his *Tractatus in Matthaeum* (ca. 398–407). Although Origen produced a list of NT books in the third century (see Origen, *Comm. Matt.* 10.12; *Homilies on Joshua* 7.1; and Eusebius, *Hist. eccl.* 6.25.3–14), it is unlike the MF list. More likely the first known listing or collection of the church's NT writings thus *begins* with Origen in the third century, who was well ahead of his time in this regard; most subsequent lists emerge in the fourth and fifth centuries.

After more than a hundred years of scholarship on the MF, scholars still do not agree on who wrote it or where it was written, but the argument for a late second- or early third-century dating and a Roman provenance are still quite popular. These conclusions are generally based on the reference to the *Shepherd of Hermas* (ca. 140–150), which the MF author claims was written "very recently in our time" (lines 73–74), and on the mention of second-century individuals (Pius, brother of Hermas) or heretical texts to be avoided; these references are at the end of the fragmented text (lines 73–85). However, there are several difficulties surrounding the dating of this document. Those who advocate a second-century date generally assume that it reflects widespread second-century thinking about the scope of the NT canon. However, there is no known evidence of the MF's influence in the second or third centuries, and no other known persons at that time were talking about a NT canon of Christian scriptures. At best there is just an argument for only the four canonical Gospels and no more (Irenaeus). The second-century fathers rejected the writings of Marcion, the gnostics, and Montanists, not on the basis of an already approved list of sacred NT writings but because they were believed to be at odds with the

---

24. Metzger, *Canon of the New Testament*, 193.

25. Armstrong, "Victorinus of Pettau." See my discussion of his arguments in *New Testament*, 283–84.

26. In her "The Muratorian Fragment as Roman Fake," Rothschild has recently argued that the MF is a fourth-century fraudulent document, written to support a fourth-century catalog by situating the MF in the second century (see also her forthcoming volume *Muratorian Fragment*). I have discussed the arguments for the date and provenance of the MF at length in *New Testament*, 274–304.

sacred faith traditions passed on in the churches from its beginning, the *regula fidei*. Those scholars who date the MF in the late second century or early third assume that it reflects all second-century thinking about the scope of the NT, but the evidence from the second century does not support that. No one then was talking about the scope of a NT canon, but rather the scope of the faith passed on in the churches.

If the MF is a second-century document, it has no other parallels until the fourth century when multiple NT canon lists were produced. This coincides with the Diocletian persecution of Christians, which began in May of 303, when Christians were forced to turn over their sacred texts to Roman authorities to be destroyed. Christians thus needed to decide which of their sacred texts to save and which they would turn over to the authorities. At that time, there is evidence that some Christians tried to protect their sacred writings, and many lost their lives as a result of trying to save their sacred texts from destruction (later they were called "martyrs," μάρτυρες), but some Christians turned all of their sacred texts over to the authorities to avoid torture and death, and they were called "traitors" (*traditores* or *lapsi*). Eusebius describes this persecution in considerable detail (*Hist. eccl.* 8.5–6), including some successes and losses (*Hist. eccl.* 8.2.1, 4–5; cf. *Gesta apud Zenophilum*). In this atmosphere, Christians were deciding which texts were most sacred and which needed protection. Obviously not all Christians saved the same texts though there was likely considerable overlap in their selections. In the fourth century, Eusebius identified the NT writings referred to by Irenaeus,[27] Clement of Alexandria,[28] and Origen;[29] but it is not clear that all these church fathers advocated a firmly fixed collection of NT scriptures. Their lists of sacred texts are not precisely the same, but they do overlap considerably.

As noted above, those who accept a second-century dating of the MF often assume that it reflects a widely approved NT canon of Christian scriptures at that time; however, a careful assessment of the available evidence does not support this assumption. Whenever any ancient catalog of Christian scriptures is dated,

27. See Eusebius, *Hist. eccl.* 5.8.2–8 (ca. 320–330, writing at Caesarea-Maritima), but this may be nothing more than Eusebius's listing of references to NT texts in Irenaeus's writings. Nothing in what survives from Irenaeus reflects such a list. Irenaeus does list Matthew, Mark, Luke, John, and refers to Revelation, 1 John, 1 Peter, *Shepherd of Hermas*, and Wisdom of Solomon. Paul is mentioned, but his epistles and Hebrews are not listed. James, 2 Peter, 2–3 John, and Jude are missing from Eusebius's list.

28. Eusebius (*Hist. eccl.* 6.14.1–7) indicates that Clement of Alexandria included "all of the canonical [encovenanted] scriptures" (πάσης τῆς ἐνδιαθήκου γραφῆς), including the disputed writings of Jude and all the Catholic Epistles, *Barnabas, Apocalypse of Peter*, Hebrews as from Paul and translated into Greek by Luke (hence the similarities with Acts). Also, his order of the Gospels is Matthew, Luke, Mark, John. Evidently he also included Revelation.

29. Origen's list is in Eusebius (*Hist. eccl.* 6.25.3–14) and is generally consistent with Rufinus's translation of Origen's *Homily on Joshua* 7.1 and his *Homily on Genesis* 13.2, but the lists are not exactly the same. Origen's list includes Matthew, Mark, Luke and Acts, John, 1 Peter, 2 Peter (doubtful in Eusebius), Revelation, 1 John, 2 and 3 John (doubtful only in Eusebius), Hebrews (included, but he questions its Pauline authorship), Paul (14 letters, but not listed). James and Jude are missing in Eusebius's list but are included in Origen's *Homily on Genesis* 7.1.

it is appropriate to ask whether and to what extent it reflects popular thinking at that time. In the case of the MF, we must ask whether anyone else in the second century held to similar views as those reflected in the MF, or who even discussed a limited NT canon. If that perspective was common or widespread, we might well expect to see other NT catalogs from that time or some discussion of such a catalog or list, but there are no other second-century catalogs comparable to the MF. There likewise is no evidence that any second-century church fathers were interested in the notion of a limited canon of NT scriptures, but rather they focused more on the church's canon of faith (its *regula fidei*), that is, its sacred traditions and beliefs. While Irenaeus produced and argued for a fixed listing of the four canonical Gospels, which could be read in the churches, his list does not include all of the other NT writings, despite his recognition of the scriptural status of several other Christian writings, especially those by Paul (see Eusebius, *Hist. eccl.* 5.8.2–8). Irenaeus appears more interested in recognizing the Gospel of John and rejecting pseudonymous texts such as the *Gospel of Judas* and other heresies than in establishing a complete canon of NT scriptures.

Again, the MF simply has no known parallels in or influence on the rest of the church fathers in the second century.[30] The most relevant and debated parts of the MF list are in lines 47–85:

> It is necessary [47] for us to discuss these one by one, since the blessed [48] apostle Paul himself, following the example of his predecessor [49–50] John, writes by name to only seven churches in the following sequence: to the Corinthians [51] first, to the Ephesians second, to the Philippians third, [52] to the Colossians fourth, to the Galatians fifth, [53] to the Thessalonians sixth, to the Romans [54–55] seventh. It is true that he writes once more to the Corinthians and to the Thessalonians for the sake of admonition, [56–57] yet it is clearly recognizable that there is one Church spread throughout the whole extent of the earth. For John also in the [58] Apocalypse, though he writes to seven churches, [59–60] nevertheless speaks to all.[31] [Paul also wrote] out of affection and love one to Philemon, one to Titus, and two to Timothy; [61] and these are held sacred [62–63] in the esteem of the Church catholic for the regulation of ecclesiastical discipline. There is current also [an epistle] to [64] *the Laodiceans*, [and] another to the Alexandrians, [both] forged in Paul's [65] name to [further] the heresy of Marcion, and several others [66] which cannot be received into the catholic church[32] [67]—for it is not fitting that gall be mixed with honey. [68] Moreover, the Epistle of Jude and two of the above-mentioned [or, bearing the name of] [69] John are counted [or, used] in the catholic [Church];[33] and [the book

30. Joseph Verheyden, an advocate of a second-century dating, acknowledges the MF's lack of influence until the late fourth or early fifth centuries in his "Canon Muratori," here 547–52.

31. This explanation appears to come from a later period, when the reception of Revelation was more widespread.

32. The references to the "catholic church," or "*catholica*" (lines 62–63, 66, and 69), are also more at home in the later fourth-century church than in the second-century churches.

33. This line makes little sense in the second century since both 2 and 3 John were among the doubted or disputed books (*antilegomena*, ἀντιλεγόμενα) as late as the early fourth century (Eusebius, *Hist. eccl.* 3.25).

of] Wisdom, [70] written by the friends of Solomon in his honour. [71] We receive only the apocalypses of John and Peter, [72] though some of us are not willing that the latter be read in church. [73] But Hermas wrote the Shepherd [74] very recently, in our times, in the city of Rome, [75] while bishop Pius, his brother, was occupying the [episcopal] chair [76] of the church of the city of Rome [77]. And therefore it ought indeed to be read; but [78] it cannot be read publicly to the people in church either among [79] the prophets, whose number is complete, or among [80] the apostles, for it is after [their] time. [81] But we accept nothing whatever of Arsinous or Valentinus or Miltiades, [82] who also composed [83] a new book of psalms for Marcion, [84–85] together with Basilides, the Asian founder of the Cataphrygians. . . .[34]

Although there are questions about other parts of the MF, the above lines are pivotal for understanding its context and its anomalies for a second-century text.[35] The following arguments are among the most important factors that suggest a middle-to-late fourth-century or early fifth-century dating of the MF.

1. *No parallels.* It is important first to restate that there are no parallels to this list before the third century (Origen), but especially in the fourth century, in the writings of Eusebius and later in Chromatius of Aquileia (northern Italy, 398–407), who oddly states, following the MF (lines 48–50), that Paul followed *John's* example of writing to *seven* churches. Several other parallels are all from the late fourth or early fifth century.[36]

2. *Anomalies* (lines 69–70). The MF accepts 2 or 3 John, but these letters were both doubted as late as 324–325. The acceptance of two epistles of John without question is different from the doubts about 2 and 3 John expressed by Eusebius in the first third of the fourth century (*Hist. eccl.* 3.25.3). Also, the lack of any defense of the four canonical Gospels, such as we have in Irenaeus in the late second century, is more common in the fourth century. There Eusebius calls the four Gospels the "holy tetrad" (*Hist. eccl.* 3.25.1). At that time most churches accepted only the four canonical Gospels.

3. *"Catholic" church* (lines 62–63, 66, and 68). The references to the "catholic church" or "*catholica*" are also more at home in the later fourth-century churches than in the second-century churches. There are no such references for the whole "catholic" church in the second century, but they are plentiful in the fourth century and later.

4. *The Epistle to the Laodiceans* (lines 64–65). This widely acknowledged pseudonymous letter, produced in Paul's name and purporting to be the letter

34. Like many others, I have made use of B. M. Metzger's translation of the MF in his *Canon of the New Testament*, 305–7.

35. See more detailed discussion of this text in McDonald, *New Testament*, 274–304.

36. Guignard, "Language of the Muratorian Fragment," acknowledges that there is no *clear* evidence that the MF influenced anyone before the end of the fourth century, when it was likely translated into Latin (or constructed in Latin). Victorinus is not an obvious or a clear parallel, as Armstrong claims. Guignard disagrees with Armstrong and points to several problems with his view. See also Geoffrey Hahneman's critique of Armstrong's view, a critique to be published in a forthcoming volume edited by Clare Rothschild (see below).

that Paul wrote to the Laodiceans (Col 4:16), is listed in the MF as a document forged in Paul's name to advance the Marcionite heresy. If the only known pseudonymous text in question is the same as the one mentioned in the MF, and if that text, as appears likely, was formed in the fourth century, this favors a more likely fourth-century date of the MF. Although Tertullian thought that the *Epistle to the Laodiceans*, included in Marcion's list of acknowledged texts, was in fact the Letter to the Ephesians now accepted in the NT (*Marc.* 5.11, 17; cf. also Epiphanius of Salamis, *Pan.* 42.9.4 and 42.12.3), no church father gives evidence that the Letter to the Ephesians was ever rejected in a Pauline corpus. In addition, Ephesians is already mentioned separately in Paul's seven letters. What is rejected in the MF cannot be equated with the Letter to the Ephesians. The only letter widely rejected is the pseudonymous fourth-century *Epistle to the Laodiceans*, and it has no clear attestation before Augustine's reference to it in the late fourth or early fifth century CE. Jerome rejected it in his *De viris illustribus* 5, claiming that it was "rejected by all." That noncanonical rambling letter is likely a fourth- or fifth-century collection of Paul's words from his epistles, supposedly and especially Philippians, according to the MF, and forged in Paul's name to support the Marcionite heresy (lines 64–65). Since the MF already mentions the Epistle to the Ephesians (line 51), we should not confuse Ephesians here with the only other text referred to as the *Epistle to the Laodiceans*, which most likely comes from the fourth century. Pseudo-Augustine, *Liber de divinis scripturis* 50 (5th or 6th c.), noted this pseudonymous letter, and so also did Gregory the Great (*Moralia* 35.20.48, dated ca. 540–604).[37] Since most scholars today agree that this pseudonymous text was most likely produced in the fourth century, its presence in the MF suggests a fourth-century date for the MF.[38]

5. *Wisdom of Solomon in a NT list* (lines 69–70). There are no other parallels in the second century where Wisdom (or Wisdom of Solomon) is found in a NT list. It is only found elsewhere in a NT list in the fourth century, as we see in Eusebius (*Hist. eccl.* 5.8.7) and in Epiphanius (*Pan.* 76.5).

6. The *Shepherd of Hermas* (lines 73–80). Although the MF encourages reading the Shepherd, it was not to be read in church, that is, it was rejected *as scripture* and not listed among the NT scriptures in the earlier part of the MF. However, there are no other parallels to this rejection of the Shepherd as scripture in the second century. In fact, Irenaeus cited the Shepherd as "scripture" in the

37. For a helpful discussion of this pseudonymous letter, see Schneemelcher, *New Testament Apocrypha*, 2:42–44; cf. also 1:36.

38. The *Letter to the Laodiceans* survives in Latin, but possibly it was composed in Greek; it compiles comments from Paul's letters. Reuss identifies and discusses this text in his *History of the Canon*, 254; he observes that the *Letter to the Laodiceans* circulated in the Latin Vulgate and was passed on and translated into the German and Romance languages from the Middle Ages. A version has been found that came from the Albigenses. The ongoing use of noncanonical writings in churches can also be seen in the continuation of *3 Corinthians* in the Armenian Bibles until the mid-1800s. For evidence of this, see Hovhanessian, "New Testament Apocrypha and the Armenian Version." The Laodicean letter often appears after 2 Corinthians and before Galatians. For a discussion of the Bible in Armenia, see Cowe, "Bible in Armenian."

second century (Eusebius, *Hist. eccl.* 5.8.2–8). Allowing the reading of the Shepherd, but *not* in churches as sacred scripture, is much more at home in the fourth century, not in the second century. The *Shepherd of Hermas*, a popular text in the second and third centuries, was even included in the fourth-century NT portion of the Codex Sinaiticus and listed, along with the *Epistle of Barnabas*. It is also in the NT-list dating from around 300–350 inserted in Codex Claromontanus (6th c.). The Shepherd was cited positively by Athanasius in 367 CE (in his 39th *Festal Letter*) to be read, but not listed as scripture; that judgment is like that of the MF. Rufinus (*Commentarius in symbolum apostolorum* 36, from ca. 394 CE) similarly refers to Shepherd as an "ecclesiastical" writing that could be read, but not in church. This text was read publicly before the fourth century but only privately in the fourth century and later, as these fourth-century parallels show.

7. *Hermas and Pius* (lines 75–76). Hermas is not otherwise known or referred to as the brother of Pius, bishop of Rome, before the fourth century. Rothschild has called this relationship the "Fraternity Legend" and observes that the reference to Hermas as the brother of Bishop Pius of Rome (lines 73–76) has its only other known parallels in the fourth century in the *Liberian Catalogue* (*Liber Pontificalis*, ca. 352–366), in Pseudo-Tertullian's *Carmen adversus Marcionitas* (ca. 325), and in the *Letter of Pius to Justus of Vienne* (ca. 4th c.). Collectively these suggest that the Hermas-Pius "Fraternity Legend" most likely originated in the fourth century, not in the second.[39] Also, a strict reading of lines 73–76 suggests a 140–150 date (the time of the writing of the *Shepherd of Hermas* and the term in office of Bishop Pius), but no one presently makes a case for the MF that early since later second-century heresies or heretics are mentioned (lines 81–85) that are not yet a significant concern that early.

8. *Miltiades* (lines 81–83). The references to the rejected works of Miltiades (2nd c. CE) are more clearly at home in the late fourth century than in the second. For example, Tertullian praised Miltiades as an eminent sophist and writer who wrote against heresy in the late second century (*Val.* 5). Later Eusebius (*Hist. eccl.* 5.17.1, 5) praises Miltiades for his writings against Jews, Montanists, Valentinians, and pagans; he also refers positively to Miltiades's *Apology* to secular rulers. None of Miltiades's writings have survived antiquity; yet again, it appears that he was popular in the second century and even in the early fourth century with Eusebius. The rejection of him appears more at home in the later fourth or early fifth centuries.

9. *The Cataphrygians* (line 85). The reference to the works of the "Cataphrygians" is also more at home in the later fourth century than in the second century. Even in the early fourth century, the followers of Montanus (fl. ca. 157–172) are generally called "Montanists," and the term "Cataphrygians" is not yet commonly used for them. Eusebius (ca. 324–25), for example, still speaks of the followers of Montanus as the "Montanists" (Eusebius, *Hist. eccl.* 5.16.10), though in the fourth century he was aware of the emerging title for them and speaks of

---

39. Clare Rothschild makes this argument in "The Muratorian Fragment as Roman Fake."

the "so-called Cataphrygian heresy" (5.16.1). The Montanists were only regularly called "Cataphrygians" in the later fourth and early fifth centuries, especially by Epiphanius (*Haer.* 98; in PG 41:856B) and Jerome (*Comm. Gal.* 3) (PL 26:356C).

10. *The MF is not representative of the second century.* Those who claim a second-century date for the MF typically assume that it was representative of second-century thinking by the church fathers, but there is no evidence for that. Rather, the second-century church fathers were focused on the canon of faith (*regula fidei*), which reflected the church's earliest sacred traditions and creeds. Again, the closest parallels to the MF are in the mid-to-late fourth and possibly early fifth centuries. If the MF is a second-century text, it is not representative of what is known about second-century thought and, as noted above, is without parallel. The special interest in the church at that time was its *regula fidei*, that is, the churches' sacred traditions, rather than a list of NT scriptures. That the MF is representative of second-century thought appears to reflect an unstated scholarly assumption that if one church father held a specific view, then everyone else at the same time in the Roman Empire did as well. That, of course, is seldom the case. Again, there is no evidence that the MF's perspectives are reflected in the second century or were characteristic of second-century thought.

11. *The MF as a fraud.* For several of the above reasons and others besides, Clare Rothschild posits that the MF is a fraudulent text whose author anachronistically produced the MF, not unlike other pseudonymous texts, to support a view about the canon of scriptures circulating in the later fourth century and fraudulently made several second-century references, but not appropriately or clearly. Her arguments are cogent and should be given serious consideration.[40] She advances scholarship not only in dating the MF, but also in asking why the MF was written in the first place. She also claims that the line about Pius and "very recently in our time" are obviously references to the middle second century. The MF refers to heresies in the late second century, yet all these MF comments are more at home in the fourth than in the second century. Rothschild proposes that the author wanted to anchor a fourth-century view anachronistically in the second century, so its author produced this fraudulent document to support a fourth- or early fifth-century view.

12. *Provenance and authorship.* The provenance and authorship are not known, and there is no consensus on these issues, but again, if the MF is a second-century document, it had no known impact in that century, when no known church father discusses the scope of the *Christian* scriptures. It is quite possible that it originated in the West, in or around Rome, but it could also have been produced in the East, thus as a minority view. Only Irenaeus argues for the four canonical Gospels in the second century, and he also accepted *Shepherd of Hermas* as scripture, as noted above.

---

40. See Rothschild, "Muratorian Fragment as Roman Fake." Her position will be more fully developed in her forthcoming work titled *The Muratorian Fragment.* She kindly sent to me an advance copy of her paper on this topic.

THE BIBLE AS A "BOOK"

The formation of a book and its importance for a fixed canon formation have often been largely ignored. Recently Michelle Brown[41] and Harry Gamble[42] appropriately addressed this issue. The notion of a "Bible" (Greek, pl. *biblia* = "books"; from *biblos* = "book") as a single *portable book* was not available until the emergence of a single codex containing all the sacred books. That began with the production of the large codices Vaticanus, Sinaiticus, and Alexandrinus in the fourth and fifth centuries, and later an even larger work: Cassiodorus's nine-volume scripture collection (ca. 490–580).[43] These volumes were not usually called a "Bible"(*biblia*) or the "Holy Bible" (*Hagia Biblia*) until much later.

Amiatinus (ca. 700 CE), following the contents of Cassiodorus's earlier sixth-century pandect nine-volume Bible, produced his complete manuscript of the Latin Vulgate Bible: it contained some 1,040 leaves and weighed some seventy-five pounds! The notion of a complete "Bible," however, was not possible until the widespread production of all the church's scriptures in a single volume. Later Abbot Alcuin prepared two copies of a single Latin volume of the biblical books in Cassiodorus's pandect collection and presented them to Charlemagne during the Carolingian Renaissance in 800 and 801.[44] Besides the Tanak books, the Alcuin OT included several apocryphal books.[45] Nevertheless, the possibility of a "Holy Bible," that is, all sacred books in a single *portable* volume, became a reality with the production of the Latin Paris Bibles (1203–32), following the invention of the magnifying glass and thinner pages, which made it possible to include all of the scriptures in a "pocket-size" portable book. After this, there was considerably more stability in the books in biblical canon lists and scripture collections. Until then, the available evidence suggests that the most common collections of scriptures in churches included *some* of the biblical books in separate manuscripts and in the lectionaries they possessed. The available evidence suggests that few churches possessed all their scriptures in one collection until much later following the production of the Paris Bibles. The Paris Bibles followed the Alcuin Bible, and *most* of them included 2 Ezra (= 3 Ezra), Tobit, Judith, Wisdom, Sirach, Baruch, and 1–2 Maccabees.[46]

Before the Paris Bibles, there were more variations in the church's OT scripture collections in the West, despite the considerable agreement for most of the Tanak books. Variations continued for the apocryphal-deuterocanonical books

41. M. Brown, "Spreading the Word."

42. Gamble, *Books and Readers in the Early Church.*

43. His OT collection included the Tanak books and also Wisdom of Solomon, Sirach, Tobit, Judith, 1–2 Maccabees, Additions to Esther, Additions to Daniel (Hymn of the Three Young Men in Dan 3:24–90; plus Susanna in Dan 13; and Bel and the Dragon in Dan 14).

44. Ganz, "Carolingian Bibles," here 329–34.

45. Wisdom of Solomon, Sirach, Tobit, Judith, 1–2 Maccabees, all of the Additions to Esther, and the Additions to Daniel (as in n. 43). For a careful discussion of this collection, see Bogaert, "Latin Bible," here 510.

46. Light, "Thirteenth Century and the Paris Bible."

in these collections, and that still exists. All church bodies today, both East and West, welcome all the Tanak/HB books despite differences in the disputed books. The collected books in a single portable volume began the common use of the term "Bible" or "Holy Bible" (literally, "Holy Books") for the church's scriptures.

FINAL OBSERVATIONS

The NT writings were largely written and selected to serve as resources for the catechetical, missional, and apologetic needs of the early churches and also to help them resolve issues they were facing at the time of the writing. They also were written to encourage new believers in their faith. Jesus and his teachings were popular among his early followers even before his death; some of his teachings written down before his death may be among the so-called Q material included in Matthew and Luke, which some of his literate followers wrote, preserving some of Jesus' sayings and deeds (especially healings) *before* his death. Later those writings were included in the Gospels along with texts developed in the post-Easter era. Some of Jesus' sayings circulated in various places outside the NT Gospels and are among the so-called Agrapha sayings of Jesus (i.e., those not in the canonical Gospels).

Paul's ad hoc writings were written to clarify the Christian proclamation that he had earlier proclaimed to the churches and to address specific challenges and issues facing his churches. In his letters he regularly included core doctrinal beliefs and their ethical implications for Christian behavior (e.g., Romans, 1–2 Corinthians, Galatians, Philippians, 1 Thessalonians). The value of the Gospels and Paul's Letters was widely recognized in many second-century churches, and some of those writings were *functioning like authoritative scripture* by the end of the first third of that century; others were beginning to be called scripture by around 150–180 CE. Not all the popular Christian religious texts in the second century that functioned like scripture initially were included in the church's NT canon. As we have seen, some of these so-called noncanonical writings functioned as scriptural texts in some churches for centuries before finally being excluded from the church's recognized scriptures. Especially the Gospels were highly valued from the start of their circulation in churches because they focused on the words and deeds of Jesus. More manuscripts of the Gospels have survived antiquity than did any of the NT books or all of them combined.

The Gospels *began* to be called scripture in the second century, but likely *functioned* as scripture soon after they were written because they contained the words and story of Jesus, the church's first and primary authority (Matt 28:19–20; Rom 10:9). Paul's letters functioned authoritatively in many churches by the end of the first century, if not sooner, not only because of Paul's apostolic role in founding those churches, but also because of their practical and apologetic value, which many churches found helpful. They welcomed them and read them in their worship and catechetical gatherings. Some Christians, especially those identified as Ebionite, or Jewish Christians, did not welcome Paul's writings because of his teachings about the limitations of the law in God's salvation. Their views are reflected in the *Clementine Homilies* and the *Odes of Solomon*. Although many second-century churches welcomed Acts, 1 Peter, and 1 John, it took longer for most churches to welcome all the Catholic Epistles and even longer for the book of Revelation.

Although most churches largely agreed on most of the scope of the NT canon by the end of the fourth century, the full scope of the church's NT canon was not settled in all the churches until much later. Some debate continued as late as the Reformation era and even later, as we saw in the Armenian and Ethiopian churches. Frans van Liere acknowledges this reality in the Middle Ages as he concludes:

> Thus, strictly speaking, the biblical canon was not completely "closed" in the Middle Ages [roughly 5th to the 15th centuries]. The canonical books were, of course, held in high authority, and the same authority was generally ascribed to the deuterocanonical books; the reservations that Jerome had expressed regarding these books were often repeated, but in practice were not heeded, in the Middle Ages.[47]

This was the case from early times and well into the Middle Ages. While there is now widespread recognition *at least* of the books in the Protestant OT and the NT canons, in both cases this has not been true throughout church history. At various times and places in both Eastern and Western Christianity, other books beyond the biblical books also informed various Christian churches. Also, the text of the biblical canon, although fluid well into the Reformation era, became more stabilized after the invention of the printing press, but never completely. Text-critical scholars are aware that the texts of several biblical passages are still not certain; no one suggests that the "original" text of the biblical books has yet been found. No manuscripts from antiquity are exactly like the current eclectic Greek New Testaments used by scholars and students. This reflects the fact that canon formation in both HB/OT and NT canons is a complex subject that overlaps many fields of inquiry; more about this subject must doubtless be learned from new studies before any final conclusions can be drawn. The above conclusions are based on the limited resources available to canon scholars today. Such limitations will likely be modified or changed in the future.

Several other important issues need further consideration than is possible here. The lectionaries especially reflect the specific scriptural texts read in the churches after the fourth century, but also the surviving scripture catalogs and manuscripts from the second to the sixth centuries primarily, but not exclusively, are from that period. Later canon lists or catalogs likewise show that while there was considerable agreement on the broader collection of the church's scriptures, there was not *complete* agreement on the scope of the NT canon until much later, following the Reformation period. Students of church history know well

---

47. Liere, *Medieval Bible*, 77.

that Martin Luther marginalized James, 2 Peter, Jude, and Revelation by placing them at the end of his Bible, but they did continue in his Bible. Some apocryphal and gnostic Christian texts that were rejected by various church fathers from the second century onward nevertheless continued to have a life of use in some churches for centuries longer. The continued reception of texts that earlier were rejected by local church councils reflects a broader understanding of the church's scriptures throughout the Middle Ages and well into the nineteenth century. This broader understanding reflects the social-religious context in which several disputed books were produced; it also influenced how they were welcomed and circulated in some communities or rejected in others. Despite the eventual *considerable* agreement in most churches on the scope of the OT and NT canons throughout much of church history, there was also occasional disagreement on the reception and recognition of several books that are presently in the church's scriptures. Finally, despite the occasional differences on the scope of the biblical canon, the church's scriptures continue to offer life, hope, and clarity for its identity and mission in the world.

Chapter 8

The Christian Apocrypha

CRAIG A. EVANS

Almost nothing else has captured the imagination of popular writers and the general public more than the idea that gospels and related literature not included in the Christian canon of scripture may contain secrets and new insights regarding the life and teaching of Jesus. This curiosity, fed by allegations of conspiracies, ancient and modern, lies behind blockbuster novels like *The Da Vinci Code*. Hardly a year goes by without something appearing in the popular media about a new discovery that may change our understanding of who Jesus really was.

From time to time some of these startling announcements emerge from academic settings. A recent example of this was the publication of a fragment of papyrus that became known as the *Gospel of Jesus' Wife*. To the embarrassment of the scholar who published it—in a prestigious journal, no less[1]—the text was quickly shown to be a modern forgery.[2] The papyrus itself is genuine, though probably not old enough for the dialect of Coptic it presents, but the text itself was composed scarcely a decade ago. In a crude sort of way, this modern scandal

---

1. King, "'Jesus said to them, "My wife . . ."'"
2. For a series of studies that debunk the Coptic papyrus fragment called *Gospel of Jesus' Wife*, see *NTS* 61 (2015): 292–394. For an account of this forgery, including the unmasking of the forger, see Sabar, "Tale of Jesus' Wife." Currently the Coptic fragment is in Harvard's custody.

exemplifies a dimension that early Christian circles faced in the second and third centuries. Gospel after gospel appeared, claiming apostolic origins and presenting Jesus and his teachings in a new light. The appearance of texts like these was one of the factors that forced Christian leaders to identify and defend the canonical Gospels and other writings that were truly authoritative.

Second- and third-century apocryphal texts were not limited to gospels and gospel-like writings, of course. Books of acts under various names, epistles, and apocalypses proliferated. Fragments of many of these are still extant. In a few cases we possess the texts in their entirety. Papyri of Late Antiquity recovered from Egypt in the last century and a half have expanded the list of New Testament Apocrypha. Two of these writings will be treated in depth in the following chapter. Here I will survey most of the writings that fall under the broad heading of Christian extracanonical writings.

A SURVEY OF NEW TESTAMENT APOCRYPHAL LITERATURE

A substantial body of extracanonical, or apocryphal, Christian texts has survived from the early centuries of the church. We have gospels and gospel-like writings that provide new teachings and activities relating to Jesus. We have many writings that tell of the acts of various apostles or groups of apostles. We have epistles and we have apocalypses. Most of these materials are available in convenient collections that include introductions, bibliographies, and some or all the texts in modern translation.[3] I begin with the gospels.

Gospels. Most of the extracanonical gospels and gospel-like writings survive only in fragments, either as quotations in patristic writings, or as actual manuscript fragments, usually papyri from Egypt.[4] Among the latter, which are all unnamed, we have P.Oxy. 840 and P.Oxy. 1224. The former is a small leaf of parchment that may have been an amulet. It preserves the concluding part of a teaching about punishment and the beginning of a second story, probably mostly complete, in which Jesus confronts a priest in the temple precincts in a dispute over ritual bathing and purity. The latter, P.Oxy. 1224, is quite fragmentary. It contains a few parallels with the Synoptic Gospels.

Other fragmentary gospels or gospel harmonies include P.Eger. 2 (+ P. Colog. 255), a mid-second-century paraphrase of one or more New Testament

---

3. Among the better known are Elliott, *Apocryphal New Testament*; Schneemelcher, *New Testament Apocrypha*, 2 vols.—based on the 6th German ed. (founded by Edgar Hennecke in 1904), and a 7th German ed. is in preparation; its first volume has appeared in two parts: Schröter and Markschies, *Antike christliche Apokryphen* (2012). See also Lapham, *New Testament Apocrypha*; Gregory et al., *Oxford Handbook of Early Christian Apocrypha*; Burke and Landau, *New Testament Apocrypha: More* [*NTAM*], vol. 1.

4. Many of these are published in Kraus, Kruger, and Nicklas, *Gospel Fragments*; Ehrman and Pleše, *Other Gospels*; and Wayment, *Text of the New Testament Apocrypha*.

Gospels,[5] P.Berol. 11710, P.Cair. 10735, P.Vindob. G 2325, P.Mert. 51, P.Oxy. 210, and P.Oxy. 5072. The last six are small fragments of material that mostly reflect synoptic materials. One more that should be mentioned is P.Oxy. 1081, which appears to be a small fragment of a gnostic gospel, perhaps the *Pistis Sophia*.

Other fragmentary gospels survive as quotations. Among these are the *Gospel of the Egyptians* (not to be confused with the gnostic tractate by that name), which survives in quotations mostly found in Clement of Alexandria (and mostly in his *Stromata*). The so-called Jewish or Ebionite gospels survive in patristic quotations and perhaps in a lost Jewish gospel called τὸ Ἰουδαϊκόν (the Jewish Book), referenced in some three dozen New Testament manuscripts.[6] These include the gospel known to Origen (ca. 185–254), usually identified as the *Gospel of the Hebrews*; the gospel known to Epiphanius (ca. 315–403), usually identified as the *Gospel of the Ebionites*; and the gospel known to Jerome (ca. 342–420), usually identified as the *Gospel of the Nazarenes*. These gospels appear to present Jesus and his teaching in closer harmony with the law of Moses and, in some cases, appear to offer a somewhat lower Christology.[7] Given the fragmentary nature of these gospels, our interpretation must always be cautious and provisional.

There are many second- and third-century gnostic gospels, bearing names like *Gospel of Mary*, *Gospel of Philip*, *Apocryphon* (or *Secret Book*) *of John*, the recently discovered and published *Gospel of Judas*, and various "dialogue" gospels. The first two gained a lot of attention a few years ago because of sensational claims that Jesus was romantically involved with Mary Magdalene. *Gospel of Mary* and *Gospel of Philip* do not claim any such thing; they only present Mary as either on par with the other disciples or perhaps as superior to them. It is in that sense that Jesus "loved" Mary. The *Gospel of Judas* created a sensation when its discovery and publication were announced in 2006.[8] Although a few scholars and popular writers initially claimed that in it Judas Iscariot was presented as a "hero" of sorts, further reflection and corrections of dubious restorations and readings, as well as the recovery of a few more missing fragments, have resulted in the debunking of this careless and misleading portrait and in its place offering a much better exegesis.[9]

Some unknown gospels appear on lists of canonical and noncanonical writings. For example, the fifth-century *Decretum Gelasianum* mentions *Evangelia*

---

5. Nicklas, "'Unknown Gospel' on *Papyrus Egerton* 2"; P.Eger. 2 exhibits several abbreviations and *nomina sacra*. Nicklas does not think P.Eger. 2 is a harmony of the Gospels. Rather, he thinks the text is loosely based on the Gospels and is otherwise a free composition.

6. Pritz, *Nazarene Jewish Christianity*; Klijn, *Jewish-Christian Gospel Tradition*; Tomson and Lambers-Petry, *Image of the Judaeo-Christians*; M. Jackson-McCabe, *Jewish Christianity Reconsidered*.

7. C. A. Evans, "Jewish Christian Gospel Tradition," here 245–58; Paget, *Jewish Christians in Antiquity*, 325–79.

8. Kasser, Meyer, and Wurst, *Gospel of Judas*; Kasser and Wurst, *Gospel of Judas: Together*.

9. See now Jenott, *Gospel of Judas*, as well as some of the essays in the second *National Geographic* edition: Kasser, Meyer, and Wurst, with Gaudard, *Gospel of Judas*, 2nd ed.; and in Popkes and Wurst, *Judasevangelium und Codex Tchacos*.

nomine Andreae ("Gospels in the name of Andrew"; line 276) and an *Evangelium nomine Iacobi minoris* ("Gospel of James the Less"; line 271). All are listed as "apocryphal."

Christian writers produced many other gospels and gospel-like texts that were not theologically idiosyncratic or at least not especially so. These include various infancy gospels, either focused on Jesus himself (many of which became known as recensions of the *Infancy Gospel of Thomas*) or on his mother Mary (e.g., the *Protevangelium of James*).[10] Some of these works are concerned with the trial, crucifixion, burial, and resurrection of Jesus (such as the various works that make up the Pilate cycle). One of these is the *Gospel of Peter*, at least the part that was recovered from Akhmîm. It will be considered in more detail below, along with the much-debated *Gospel of Thomas*. One of the more curious apocryphal writings is the correspondence between Jesus and Abgar V, king of Edessa, Syria (ruled 4 BCE–7 CE and 13–40 CE).[11]

Gospels of one sort or another were produced throughout the Byzantine period and on into the late medieval era. Some of these writings focus on Mary (such as we see in the many versions of the *Miracles of Mary* and the *Assumption of Mary*)[12] or on the Magi who visit the holy family. On the latter theme, one of the most unusual infancy stories is the recently published *Revelation of the Magi*, a fourth-century Syriac pseudepigraphon that exhibits a remarkable ecumenical perspective.[13] Other pseudepigrapha, of course, focus on Jesus and present testimony in the form of reminiscences, visions, or letters from or to various apostles. One of the last gospels to be written is the *Gospel of Barnabas*, which retells some of the story of Jesus from a perspective that is compatible with Islamic beliefs and traditions about Jesus. (This *Gospel of Barnabas* is not related to the second-century *Epistle of Barnabas*, the *Gospel of Barnabas* mentioned in the *Decretum Gelasianum*, or the fifth-century *Acts of Barnabas*.) Although it is debated whether this *Gospel of Barnabas* is an edited and expanded version of an older text, now lost, all critical scholars agree that the extant text cannot date earlier than the fourteenth century. Evidence for this late date is seen not only in the many anachronisms and blunders (for example, the disciples rowing their boat to Nazareth, evidently thought to be a lakeside village; or Jesus born during

10. They appear in the *Decretum Gelasianum*'s list of apocryphal books under the titles *Liber de infantia salvatoris* and *Liber de nativitate salvatoris et de Maria vel obstetrice*.

11. In the *Decretum Gelasianum*'s list of apocryphal books, we find *Epistula Iesu ad Abgarum* and *Epistula Abgari ad Iesum* (lines 328–329). One of these sets of letters is inscribed in eleven lines on a slab in fifth-century Ephesus (cf. I.Eph. 46).

12. Such may be the *Liber qui appellatur Transitus sanctae Mariae* (Book which is called the Transit of Saint Mary), which appears in the *Decretum Gelasianum*'s list of apocryphal books (line 296).

13. Landau, *Revelation of the Magi: The Lost Tale*; Landau, "The Revelation of the Magi." Another recently published infancy pseudepigraphon is the *Apocryphon of Seth*, or *Liber apocryphus nomine Seth* (Apocryphal book in the name of Seth). Produced no later than the fifth century, this pseudepigraphon supplements the story of the Magi and the star. See Toepel, "Apocryphon of Seth," in Bauckham, Davila, and Panayotov, *Old Testament Pseudepigrapha: More Noncanonical Scriptures* [*OTPM*], 1:33–39.

Pilate's administration) and also at least one allusion to Dante's *Divina Commedia* (completed in 1320; the allusion is to part 1, *Inferno*). Recent scholarship has taken great interest in the infancy-gospel tradition.[14]

Acts. The early church also produced many apocryphal accounts of the acts of the apostles, either as groups or as individuals. Among the most popular were the *Acts of Paul*, the *Acts of Paul and Thecla*, the *Acts of Andrew*, the *Acts of John*, the *Acts of Peter*, the *Acts of Peter and Andrew*, the *Acts of Peter and the Twelve Apostles*, the *Acts of Philip*, the *Acts of Thomas*, the Pseudo-Clementines, and other later acts.[15] All of these works extend what little is known of the apostles, as found in the NT Epistles and in the book of Acts. In some of these acts, the apostles' teaching has been modified or updated. Often emphasis fell on the energy and courage of the apostles, complete with amazing miracles and resuscitations.

Only fragments of the *Acts of John* are extant, including a small fragment of papyrus from Oxyrhynchus (P.Oxy. 850). Unorthodox elements probably explain why the full text was not preserved. Eusebius condemns the work (*Hist. eccl.* 3.25.6). Epiphanius says that the work was used by Encratite groups (*Pan.* 2.47.1). Some modern scholars think an incipient form of Gnosticism is reflected in the work.[16]

Tertullian may reference the *Acts of Paul* (*De baptismo* 17.5), but his description does not seem to fit the contents of the text. Clement of Alexandria knows of the work (*Strom.* 6.5). Epiphanius refers to a story from the *Acts of Paul*, evidently with approval (*Comm. Dan.* 3). The work appears in a list of writings evidently accepted as canonical in the sixth-century Codex Claromontanus (D 06, Paris, Bibliothèque nationale de France, Grec 107). However, it appears in the list of rejected works in the seventh-century Catalogue of the Sixty Canonical Books.[17] The work survives in parts and various editions, sometimes under different names, such as the *Acts of Paul and Thecla* and the *Martyrdom of Paul.* The *Acts of Paul and Thecla* is rejected in the fifth- or sixth-century *Decretum Gelasianum* (line 289).[18] Papyrus fragments have been recovered from Egypt (P.Ant. 13;

---

14. For studies on the *Protevangelium of James* and related traditions, see Shoemaker, *Traditions of Mary's Dormition*; Lapham, *New Testament Apocrypha*, 62–65; Zervos, "The *Protevangelium of James*"; Foskett, "Child Mary"; Vuong, "Purpose of the *Protevangelium of James*"; van Oyen, "*Protevangelium Jacobi*"; Aasgaard, "*Protevangelium of James*"; and Shoemaker, *Dormition and Assumption*. Vuong and Hawk are preparing a new translation of the *Protevangelium of James*. For studies on the infancy gospels relating to Jesus' infancy and childhood, see Hock, *Infancy Gospels*; Lapham, *New Testament Apocrypha*, 129–31; Elliott, *Synopsis of the Apocryphal Nativity*; Voicu, "Infancy Apocrypha"; van Oyen, "Rewriting of the Biblical Traditions"; Burke, *Syriac Tradition*; Cousland, *Holy Terror*. Hawk is preparing a new translation of the infancy *Gospel of Pseudo-Matthew.* Burke is preparing a new translation of the *Infancy Gospel of Thomas.*

15. Klauck, *Apocryphal Acts.* Klauck's introduction is concise and quite helpful. See also Stoops, *Apocryphal Acts.*

16. Bremmer, *Acts of John*; Lalleman, *Acts of John*; Pervo with Hills, *Acts of John.*

17. For the Greek and Latin texts of Codex Claromontanus, the Catalogue of the Sixty Canonical Books, Canon Muratori, and other old lists of canonical and noncanonical books, I rely on the works conveniently assembled in Preuschen, *Analecta*; and Zahn, *Urkunden und Belege.*

18. The work is listed as the *Actus Theclae et Pauli.* For the text of the *Decretum*, I rely on von Dobschütz, *Decretum Gelasianum*, 11–13, esp. 12.

P.Hamb.; P.Oxy. 6; P.Oxy. 1602, though misidentified by Grenfell and Hunt, editors of the editio princeps). Thecla's piety and martyrdom are emphasized.[19] A major question centers on whether the *Acts of Paul* was intended to supplement what is known of Paul in Luke's book of Acts or to replace it. Richard Bauckham, against Richard Pervo and others, argues that the author of the *Acts of Paul* sees his work as a sequel, not as a correction or replacement of the Lukan Acts.[20]

The *Acts of Peter* presents interpreters with challenges, not least because of its uncertain text. A small but important fragment has been recovered from Oxyrhynchus (P.Oxy. 849, which corresponds with *Actus Vercellenses*, an important but disputed witness to the *Acts of Peter*). Eusebius regards the work as heretical (*Hist. eccl.* 3.3.2). Philaster of Brescia claims that the Manichaeans made use of the *Acts of Peter* (*Haer.* 88). It is listed as apocryphal in the *Decretum Gelasianum* (line 267: *Actus nomine Petri apostoli* = Acts in the name of the apostle Peter). The role of magic, Peter's contest with Simon Magus, and Peter's crucifixion upside down are major features in this apocryphal work, which influenced several other apocryphal works.[21] One will want to compare the Syriac *History of Simon Cephas.*[22]

The *Acts of Andrew* is referenced critically by Eusebius (*Hist. eccl.* 3.25.6). Augustine claims that the Manichaeans possessed apocryphal books of Acts, including the *Acts of Andrew* (*Contra Faustum* 14.1; 22.79). The *Decretum Gelasianum* lists the *Actus nomine Andreae apostoli* (*Acts in the Name of the Apostle Andrew*) as apocryphal (line 265). Also, P.Oxy. 851, otherwise unidentified, might belong to the *Acts of Andrew.*[23] Who the author was and what relationship this text has to the *Acts of John* and the *Acts of Peter* remain unclear. In any event, the author of the *Acts of Andrew* had interest in magic, martyrdom, and eroticism, among other things.[24] The unrelated *Acts of Peter and the Twelve Apostles* is extant in Coptic in the Nag Hammadi Codices (NHC VI,*1*).[25]

A number of fourth- and fifth-century fathers reference the *Acts of Thomas* (e.g., Epiphanius, *Pan.* 2.47.1; 2.61.1; Augustine, *Serm. Dom.* 1.20.65). It too appears in the list of apocryphal works in the *Decretum Gelasianum* (line 266: *Actus nomine Thomae apostoli* = Acts in the Name of the Apostle Thomas). The work, which reads more like a novel, shows interest in the Thomas-India legend,

19. Bremmer, *Acts of Paul and Thecla*; Lapham, *New Testament Apocrypha*, 139–45; Pervo, *Acts of Paul*; Hills, *Acts of Paul and Thecla*.

20. Bauckham, "The *Acts of Paul*." See also Marguerat, "The *Acts of Paul*." Marguerat does not think the *Acts of Paul* rejects Luke's Acts. Rather, it is intended to "complete the story" of Paul. For the opposing view, see Pervo, "Hard Act to Follow." Implausibly, Rordorf argues that the author of the *Acts of Paul* had no knowledge of Luke's Acts. See Rordorf, "Paul's Conversion"; and the essays recently published by Barrier in *Thecla*.

21. Matthews, "The *Acts of Peter*"; Bremmer, *Apocryphal Acts of Peter*; Baldwin, *Acts of Peter? Text*; Stoops, *Acts of Peter*.

22. Jones, "History of Simon Cephas."

23. Klauck, *Apocryphal Acts*, 120.

24. MacDonald, *Acts of Andrew and Matthias*; Bremmer, *Acts of Andrew*; Lapham, *New Testament Apocrypha*, 67–74; MacDonald, *Acts of Andrew*.

25. Lapham, *New Testament Apocrypha*, 150–54.

the well-known "Hymn of the Pearl" (chaps. 108–113), and a variety of other topics.[26] One scholar has recently argued that the *Acts of Thomas* was read as sacred scripture in some circles.[27] Many other later works in the acts genre— such as the *Acts of Barnabas*,[28] the *Acts of Cornelius the Centurion*,[29] the *Acts of Philip*,[30] the *Acts of Timothy*,[31] and the *Acts of Titus*[32]—circulated in later centuries. The *Epistula Apostolorum* (*Epistle of the Apostles*), which exhibits a variety of genres, probably fits best in the category of acts.[33] The Pseudo-Clementine literature, including the *Homilies* and *Recognitions*, may also be treated under the heading of apocryphal acts.[34]

Some general things can be said about the earliest apocryphal acts. First, they exhibit a marked interest in apologetic, often presented as impressive public displays of God's power working through the apostles and their disciples. Second, it is not always easy to distinguish miracle from magic. No doubt the fuzzy boundary reflects the popular culture of the time. Third, popularizing the stories of Jesus and his apostles through embroidery, expansion, and imagination may well have served an evangelistic purpose, making the Christian experience appear dramatic and exciting. Fourth, the expanded and augmented tales of the apostles provided the respective authors opportunities to express new ideas and to reshape theology and practice.[35]

Epistles. There are several extracanonical epistles, many of which claim to have been authored by apostles. Most of the extracanonical epistles relevant for the present discussion are pseudepigraphal. Many scholars suspect that some of the canonical epistles are pseudepigraphal, such as the two letters attributed to Peter; some of the letters attributed to Paul, especially the Pastorals; and perhaps also the epistles of James and Jude. But our concern here is with extracanonical epistles that claim to be apostolic or otherwise mimic the canonical epistles.

A few of the extracanonical epistles are attributed to Paul. Among these is the *Epistle to Laodiceans*, a short Latin text, which is little more than a pastiche of words and phrases drawn from Paul's letters (esp. from Philippians). *Epistle to Laodiceans* was no doubt inspired by Paul's references in Colossians to "those in Laodicea" (cf. Col 2:1; 4:13, 15–16), to whom apparently he wrote an epistle: "And when this letter has been read among you, have it read also in the church of the Laodiceans; and see that you read also the letter from Laodicea [καὶ τὴν

26. Bremmer, *Apocryphal Acts of Thomas*; Attridge, *Acts of Thomas*.

27. Henry, "*Acts of Thomas* as Sacred."

28. Snyder, "The Acts of Barnabas."

29. Burke and Witakowski, "Acts of Cornelius."

30. Bovon and Matthews, *Acts of Philip*. An *Actus nomine Philippi apostoli* appears on the *Decretum Gelasianum*'s list of apocryphal books.

31. Concannon, "City of the Ephesians"; Concannon, "Acts of Timothy."

32. Pervo, "Acts of Titus."

33. Hills, *Tradition and Composition*; Hill, "*Epistula Apostolorum*: An Asian Tract"; Hannah, "Four-Fold 'Canon'"; Hills, *Epistle of the Apostles*; Pèrés, "Das lebendige Wort."

34. Jones, "Ancient Jewish Christian Rejoinder"; Lapham, *New Testament Apocrypha*, 74–77; Bremmer, *Pseudo-Clementines*.

35. C. A. Evans, "Christians in Egypt," esp. 42–43.

[ἐπιστολὴν] ἐκ Λαοδικείας ἵνα καὶ ὑμεῖς ἀναγνῶτε]" (Col 4:16). The language is somewhat ambiguous, but it is usually understood to mean that the letter sent to the Colossians should be read at Laodicea and the letter sent to the Laodiceans should be read at Colossae. What has become of the letter to the Laodiceans is a mystery. Some think the letter that today is known as Ephesians, but whose address may originally have lacked "in Ephesus [ἐν Ἐφέσῳ]" (Eph 1:1; the words are not present in P⁴⁶ ℵ* B* and other authorities), is the lost letter the Laodiceans. Marie-Émile Boismard rejects this proposal. He thinks Paul's epistle to the Laodiceans has in fact been merged with the apostle's Epistle to the Colossians, so that canonical Colossians contains text for both the original Colossians and the Laodiceans. Boismard, of course, is not talking about the pseudepigraphal Latin epistle.[36] Whatever may have happened to the original epistle to the Laodiceans, the extant Latin *Laodiceans* is a completely different work.[37] The epistle is relatively well crafted and coherent, even if its contents are entirely derivative. Its emphasis falls on Paul as a moral exemplar.[38]

The pseudepigraphal *3 Corinthians* is not a free-standing document but is embedded in the *Acts of Paul*. It is in response to an epistle that the Corinthians addressed to the apostle. The senders of the latter epistle are Stephanus, Daphnus, Eubulus, Theophilus, and Zeno. They beg Paul to come or to write because there are false teachers who deny the resurrection, deny that Jesus came in the flesh, deny that he was born of Mary, and so on. Paul writes back, affirming that Jesus was indeed "born of Mary of the seed of David," that the resurrection is true, and so on. Paul ends his letter with the admonition that the faithful should resist the false teachers.[39] Although *3 Corinthians* was never recognized in the West, a few influential authorities in the East, such as Aphrahat and Ephrem, regarded it as genuine and perhaps even as canonical. It is not included in the Peshitta (Syriac Bible), but it does appear in a few eastern lists of books of scripture.

Among the extracanonical pseudepigraphal Pauline epistles is his supposed correspondence with his contemporary Seneca. Seneca writes to Paul some eight times, and Paul writes to Seneca some six times. (I say "some" because there is evidence that the collection grew over time; how many letters made up the original collection is an open question.) Seneca shows Paul's letters to Nero, whom Seneca at one time tutored and continues to counsel. Seneca also tells Paul that he has read the apostle's epistles to the Galatians, to the Corinthians, and to the "Achaeans," by which is meant 2 Corinthians.

Apart from the allusion to the fire at Rome (July 64 CE) and the suffering inflicted on the Christians as scapegoats, there is very little of substance in this correspondence. The letters were probably composed in the fourth century, perhaps even as part of an exercise in rhetoric. Jerome (*Vir. ill.* 12), Augustine

---

36. Boismard, "Letter to the Laodiceans."
37. Canon Muratori (MF) references an epistle "to the Laodiceans, another to the Alexandrians, forged in Paul's name" (lines 63–65).
38. Tite, *Epistle to the Laodiceans*; Tite, "Pseudo-Historical Letter."
39. Klijn, "Apocrypyal Correspondence"; Webster, "Trapped in a Forger's Rhetoric."

(*Ep.* 153.4), and many others were acquainted with the Seneca-Paul epistles, which they regarded as genuine. Not until the fifteenth century did scholars begin to doubt the authenticity of the correspondence. Recent study suggests that the original collection of epistles was fewer in number and was composed in Greek much earlier, perhaps in the second or third century. The correspondence was later expanded and translated into Latin.[40]

Other pseudepigraphal letters are attributed to characters named or implied in NT writings. One of these is the *Epistle of Dionysius the Areopagite to Timothy*. This letter claims to be written by one of Paul's converts in Athens (Acts 17:34), who later writes to Timothy, informing him of the deaths of the apostles Peter and Paul. The epistle was composed in the fifth or sixth century.[41]

The *Epistle of Titus* (or *Epistula Titi*) claims to have been written by Paul's disciple Titus, to whom the apostle wrote Titus, one of the New Testament's Pastoral Epistles. The *Epistle of Titus* warns of damnation as a punishment for sexual immorality and reminds readers of the story of Susanna and the wicked elders (one of the additions to the book of Daniel). Also known as Pseudo-Titus, the epistle is extant in Latin in the eighth-century Codex Burchardi (folios 84–93v). It exhibits Encratite tendencies in its promotion of celibacy. Its author evidently was acquainted with and may have drawn upon material from the *Acts of Peter* and the *Acts of Andrew*.[42]

Three of the epistles in the collection of writings known as the Apostolic Fathers may be pseudepigraphal, though that is open for debate since they are in fact anonymous. They are the *Epistle of Barnabas*, *1 Clement*, and *Epistle to Diognetus*. Because the *Epistle of Barnabas* 16.1–5 speaks of the destruction of the Jewish temple in Jerusalem and the hope to rebuild it, the epistle is usually dated shortly before the Bar Kokhba revolt (132–135 CE), after which there was no hope of rebuilding. As already mentioned, the epistle is anonymous; it does not claim to be written by Barnabas of Cyprus (Acts 4:36; 15:39), well known as an early leader of the church, who traveled with Paul on the latter's first missionary journey (Acts 9:27; 11:22–30; 12:25; 13:1–14:28) and who joined Paul in the Jerusalem Council and the mission to Antioch (Acts 15:2–35). Most of *Barnabas* is found in Codex Sinaiticus (4th c.), Codex Hierosolymitanus (11th c.), several later Greek manuscripts, and a Latin translation (late 4th c.).[43] *Barnabas* overlaps with and is linked to the *Didache*. Clement of Alexandria cites *Barnabas* several times, sometimes referring to "the apostle Barnabas," implying Barnabas's authorship (e.g., *Strom.* 2.31.2, ὁ ἀπόστολος Βαρνάβας; 2.35.5, Βαρνάβας ὁ ἀπόστολος; etc.). Origen regarded *Barnabas* as a "general epistle"

40. Fürst, "Pseudepigraphie und Apostolizität"; Ramelli, "Correspondence between Seneca and Paul"; Ramelli, "Pseudepigraphon inside a Pseudepigraphon?"
41. Eastman, "Epistle of Pseudo-Dionysius."
42. Santos Otero, "Der apokryphe Titusbrief."
43. On *Barnabas* in Codex Sinaiticus, see Batovici, "Fathers in Codex." He gathers that inclusion of a writing like *Barnabas* in a codex with recognized scripture implies approval and value, but not canonical status.

(*Contra Celsum* 1.63). Eusebius regarded the epistle as "disputed" (*Hist. eccl.* 6.13.6–6.14.1), even "illegitimate" (3.25.4). Jerome referred to *Barnabas* as a work of the "apostle" (*Vir. ill.* 6). *Barnabas* appears in the list of acceptable books in Codex Claromontanus. The epistle sometimes appeared on eastern lists of disputed books. We see this in the eighth-century Stichometry of Nicephorus, where it is "spoken against," and in the seventh-century Catalogue of the Sixty Canonical Books, where *Barnabas* is classified as "apocryphal."[44] One characteristic of the epistle is its many quotations and allusions to the LXX, especially Isaiah, and perhaps, at 4:14, also a passage from Matthew (22:14). It is not clear why it was believed that the epistle had been authored by Barnabas.[45] There has been a resurgence of scholarly interest in *Barnabas* in recent years.[46]

The epistle known as *1 Clement* does not claim to be written by Clement, the bishop of Rome near the end of the first century. The letter begins, "The church of God which sojourns in Rome to the church of God which sojourns in Corinth" (1.1). Names appear at the conclusion of the epistle, where the recipients are enjoined, "Send back to us speedily in peace with joy those sent you by us, Claudius Ephebus and Valerius Bito, along with Fortunatus, so that they may the sooner report to us" (65.1). Clement of Alexandria cites *1 Clement* often and with approval (e.g., *Strom.* 1.15.2; 2.65.2; 2.91.2; etc.). He also explicitly identifies the author as Clement: "Now Clement, in his epistle to the Corinthians [ὁ Κλήμης ἐν τῇ πρὸς Κορινθίους ἐπιστολῇ], . . . says expressly . . ."; then follows a quotation of *1 Clement* 48.5 (*Strom.* 1.38.8; cf. 6.65.4: "Clement in the epistle to the Corinthians"; cf. 5.80.1: "in the letter of the Romans to the Corinthians [τῇ πρὸς Κορινθίους Ῥωμαίων ἐπιστολῇ]"). Elsewhere he identifies Clement as an apostle: "in the epistle to the Corinthians, the apostle Clement [ἐν τῇ πρὸς Κορινθίους ἐπιστολῇ ὁ ἀπόστολος Κλήμης] . . . says . . ." (*Strom.* 4.105.1); then follows a pastiche of phrases from the early chapters of *1 Clement*. Other Fathers who know of or recognize *1 Clement* include Origen, Dionysius of Alexandria, Didymus the Blind (also of Alexandria),[47] Epiphanius, Jerome, and Cyril of Jerusalem. Eusebius refers to the "*Epistle of Clement*, which is recognized by all, which he wrote in the name of the church of the Romans to that of the Corinthians" (*Hist. eccl.* 3.38.1).

First Clement appears in Codex Alexandrinus (5th c.), Codex Hierosolymitanus (11th c.), and in rather early Latin, Syriac, and Coptic translations.[48] The

---

44. Boor, *Nicephori Archiepiscopi Constantinopolitani opscula historica*, 134; Preuschen, *Analecta*, 159.

45. Prigent, *Testimonia dans le Christianisme primitif*; Kraft, *Barnabas and the Didache*; Wengst, *Theologie des Barnabasbriefes*.

46. Loman, "Barnabas in Early Second-Century Egypt"; Paget, "Epistle of Barnabas"; Paget, "Barnabas and the Writings"; Joosten, "Gospel of Barnabas"; Paget, "Barnabas and the Outsiders"; Rothschild, "Barnabas and Secession"; Shepherd, "Barnabas and the Jerusalem Temple."

47. On the possibility that Didymus the Blind regarded *1 Clement* as canonical scripture, see Ehrman, "Canon of Didymus."

48. On *1 Clement* in Codex Alexandrinus, see Batovici, "Fathers in Codex." As stated above (n. 43), he concludes that appearance in a scripture codex, near the end, does not imply canonical status.

Catalogue of the Sixty Canonical Books refers to *1 Clement* as the *"Teaching of Clement"*[49] and classifies the writing as apocryphal. Modern scholarship remains keenly interested in this work.[50] In recent years questions have been raised about the traditional late first-century date, and some have suggested that the work might be a pseudepigraphon.[51] I will deal with that interesting suggestion shortly.

The third epistle included among the writings of the Apostolic Fathers is the anonymous *Epistula ad Diognetum*. The recipient is named in the opening verse: "Since I see, most excellent Diognetus [κράτιστε Διόγνητε], that you are extremely interested in learning about the religion of the Christians . . ." (1.1). The epistle is an outlier in that it is more at home among the second-century apologists. In fact, the early apologist Quadratus has been suggested as its author, but that is only a guess, and not many find it convincing. Study of the epistle is beset by problems, which Michael Holmes has summed up succinctly: "Much about this document remains a mystery. The author is anonymous, the identity of the recipient is uncertain, the date is unknown, the ending is missing, and . . . no ancient or medieval writer is known to have mentioned it."[52]

Charles Hill has recently argued that the epistle was penned by Polycarp,[53] but the evidence, though interesting, is not convincing. It is possible that the recipient's name is only a literary convention, as some think may be the case with respect to Justin Martyr's Trypho the Jew in his *Dialogue with Trypho*. Scholars have also speculated about the identity of Diognetus. Perhaps prompted by the savage persecution and torture of Christians in Lyons in 176, an unnamed apologist has written to Diognetus, tutor of Marcus Aurelius (ruled 161–180), hoping to persuade him to influence the emperor. But was the tutor Diognetus still living after 176? Another candidate that has been suggested is one Claudius Diogenes, who served in Egypt as "procurator of Augustus and interim high priest." In a papyrus dated 202 or 203 the procurator is addressed as "most excellent Diognetus," exactly as we find at the beginning of the epistle.[54] But addressing officials in this manner is not unusual, and in any case it hardly narrows the field. In sum, both proposals are possible, but neither is provable. The recipient of the epistle remains as unknown as its author.

---

49. Preuschen, *Analecta*, 159. The Catalogue titles the work Διδασκαλία Κλήνεντος (*Teaching of Clement*). The Catalogue also mentions the "Teaching of Ignatius" and the "Teaching of Polycarp." These "teachings" probably refer to the well-known epistles.

50. Grant and Graham, *First and Second Clement*; Jaubert, *Clément de Rome*; Hagner, *Testaments in Clement of Rome*; Breytenbach and Welborn, *Encounters with Hellenism*; Rothschild, *New Essays*.

51. See van Unnik, "First Epistle of Clement"; van Unnik maintains a late Domitian date for *1 Clement*. Yet see Welborn, "Date of First Clement"; Welborn, "Preface to 1 Clement"; and Rothschild, "1 Clement as Pseudepigraphon."

52. Lightfoot, Harmer, and Holmes, *Apostolic Fathers*, 292.

53. C. E. Hill, *Lost Teaching of Polycarp*. Hill's other thesis—that Polycarp is the "Elder" in Irenaeus, *Haer.* 4.27–32—is more compelling.

54. Grant, *Greek Apologists*, 178–79. Grant cites Marrou, À *Diognète*, 244–47. For the papyrus that refers to "most excellent Diognetus," see Mitteis and Wilcken, *Grundzüge und Chrestomathie der Papyruskunde*, no. 171 in vol. 1, part 2.

Paul Foster and others date the *Epistle to Diognetus* to the second half of the second century.[55] The reference to the "Gospels" in the plural coheres with the arguments of Irenaeus with respect to the fourfold Gospel canon: "The faith of the gospels is established [καὶ εὐαγγελίων πίστις ἵδρυται], and the tradition of the apostles is preserved" (*Diogn.* 11.6). Although there is no reference to a specific number of the Gospels, as there is emphatically in Irenaeus, the language used here in the epistle seems to imply a set number. Papias knows that there are plural Gospels, but he does not leave us with the impression that there is a set number, whether four or something else. There are other features in the *Epistle to Diognetus* that have attracted scholarly attention.[56]

In my view the three letters in the Apostolic Fathers that have been considered should not be regarded as examples of pseudepigrapha.[57] I say this because all three are in fact anonymous. Pseudepigrapha usually claim apostolic or some other exalted authorship, as we have seen in several writings that have been reviewed in this chapter. The purpose of pseudepigraphal claims of authorship was always to promote the authority of the writing and sometimes was intended, perhaps, to gain acceptance as scripture itself. None of this seems to apply to *Barnabas*, *1 Clement*, or *Diognetus*. There are no claims of special revelation. Indeed, these writings frequently appeal to established tradition. In the case of *1 Clement*, which claims to be a letter from the church of Rome addressed to the church of Corinth, I do not see how a fictional claim of sender and addressee could succeed. It is not likely that the churches of Rome and Corinth would be deceived by such an artifice. The collective memories of these churches would surely recall that no such epistle was sent or received, if none had been. The near quasi-canonical status of *Barnabas* and *1 Clement* was due to beliefs and assumptions about them that arose after their publication. It was not due to claims, explicit or implicit, that the writings themselves made.

There are, of course, other pseudepigraphal epistles. Besides the aforementioned *Epistula Apostolorum* (treated above as an example of the genre acts), we have the *Epistula Petri*, or the *Epistle of Peter to James*, which serves as introduction to the *Kerygmata Petrou*, or the *Sermons of Peter*.[58] Peter enjoins James: "I urgently beseech you not to pass on to any one of the Gentiles the books of my preachings which I here forward to you." The apocryphal *Epistula Petri* may have been intended to provide support for the authenticity of the *Kerygmata Petrou*.

We also have two apocryphal epistles in the Nag Hammadi Codices. One is the *Epistle of Peter to Philip*. It begins: "Peter the apostle of Jesus Christ, to

55. Foster, "The *Epistle to Diognetus*," here 152 in *Writings*.

56. Foster, "The Epistle to Diognetus," in *Expository Times*; Crowe, "Oh Sweet Exchange!"; Rothschild, "Diognetus and the Topos."

57. *Second Clement* is not a letter but an anonymous sermon. The epistles attributed to Ignatius and Polycarp should be viewed as genuine. The epistle from the church of Smyrna to the church of Philomelium (aka *Martyrdom of Polycarp*) should also be viewed as genuine, although chaps. 21 and 22 may be later additions.

58. Lapham, *New Testament Apocrypha*, 44–45.

Philip our beloved brother and our fellow apostle and to the brethren who are with you" (NHC VIII,*2* 132.12–15). The epistolary format is probably secondary, for the balance of the writing is more of an apocalyptic narrative. The claim to be an epistle written by the apostle Peter no doubt was intended to give the writing great authority.[59] The same can be said about the so-called *Apocryphon of James*. It begins: "James writes to [. . .]thos: Peace be with you. . . . Since you asked that I send you a secret book, which was revealed to me and Peter by the Lord, I could not turn you away" (NHC I,*2* 1.1–3, 8–13). Ostensibly a letter, this work really is an account of a revelation. Most gnostic writings claim to be written by apostles or other exalted authorities. But whether the purpose was to gain the status of canonical scripture is another question. More likely these gnostic revelations were intended for insiders, not so much to replace or even rival the better-known public scriptures but to interpret them.

We have several legendary epistles linked to the apocryphal *Acta Pilati*. These include the *Epistula Pilati ad Claudium*, in which the worried prefect explains to the emperor that he, against his will, executed Jesus. We also have Pilate's "Report" (the *Anaphora Pilati*), the *Epistula Pilati ad Herodem*, the *Epistula Herodis ad Pilatum*, and the *Epistula Tiberii ad Pilatum*. In the Pilate-Herod correspondence the two men accuse one another of guilt for the death of Jesus. In the emperor's epistle, Pilate is condemned, along with several Jewish leaders deemed responsible for the death of Jesus.

There are other epistles that fall into the category of legend. Most of these are quite late, usually of medieval origin. One immediately thinks of the *Epistula Lentuli ad Romanos de Christo Jesu*. The pseudepigraphal *Epistle of Lentulus* was supposedly written by Publius Lentulus, a Roman consul during the rule of Augustus, who also served as prefect of Judea before the administration of Pontius Pilate.[60] The epistle is addressed to the Roman senate. It describes Jesus' physical appearance ("stature is straight, his hands and arms beautiful to behold," his beard "divided at the chin") and behavior ("cheerful but without loss of gravity, . . . never known to laugh, but often to weep"). The letter was probably originally written in Greek and then later translated into Latin. It is doubtful that it is older than the thirteenth century. It greatly influenced late medieval portraits of Jesus. The letter is hopelessly unhistorical and anachronistic, not least because there was no known prefect or procurator named Lentulus and certainly not one who served as prefect of Judea before the appointment of Pilate.

Many forgeries of this nature were produced in the late medieval period; indeed, some were produced as recently as the late nineteenth century. These include Jonathan's epistle to the "Masters of Israel," in which he gives an account

---

59. Lapham, *New Testament Apocrypha*, 77–82; van Os, "Role of the Apostles." For an early study, see Meyer, *Letter of Peter to Philip*.

60. Lutz, "Lentulus Describing Christ." Lutz describes some of the Latin MSS that contain the text of the *Epistula Lentuli*. They include, among others, the 15th-century MSS Marston 49 and Marston 247 (both in Yale's Beinecke Library).

of the shepherds of Bethlehem who saw the star and visited the holy family when Jesus was born; Gamaliel's report to the Sanhedrin after he interviewed Joseph, Mary, and others concerning Jesus; High Priest Caiaphas's epistle to the Sanhedrin, in which he gives an account of the trial and execution of Jesus; a second epistle in which Caiaphas reports to the Sanhedrin regarding the resurrection of Jesus; Pilate's report to Emperor Tiberius concerning the arrest, trial, and execution of Jesus; the epistle of Herod Antipas to the Roman senate, to defend himself and his father, Herod the Great, in their mistreatment of Jesus and his family; several epistles by Hillel, in regard to his and his colleagues' treatment of the apostles; and so on. These forgeries and many like them fall well outside of what is regarded as New Testament extracanonical writings, but they do illustrate the lengths to which imagination, curiosity, and reckless apologetic may take us.[61]

Apocalypses. The genre of apocalypse was a favorite among pseudepigraphers, for the genre facilitates the revelation of new teachings directly from a divine source, whose authority could hardly be questioned. Christian extracanonical apocalypses fall into two general groups: apocalypses that occur in the post-Easter setting and apocalypses that occur ostensibly in an Old Testament setting. Examples of the latter are seen in the *Apocalypse of Adam, Testament of Adam, Apocalypse of Daniel, 5 Ezra, 6 Ezra, Apocalypse of Elijah, Apocalypse of Ezra, Apocalypse of Sedrach, Apocalypse of Zechariah, Apocalypse of Zephaniah,* and *Ascension of Isaiah.* Some of these works are normally included in collections of works called the "Old Testament Pseudepigrapha," but I include them here because even if originally Jewish, they have been transformed into Christian apocalypses. (I am not including Jewish works that have only been glossed here and there, such as the *Testaments of the Twelve Patriarchs,* the *Testament of Isaac,* and perhaps the *Apocalypse of Zephaniah.*) The principal point of "Old Testament" apocalypses, as opposed to "New Testament" apocalypses, is that they are *prophetic* as well as revelatory. As such, they were thought to have outstanding apologetic value. For it is one thing for a Christian apocalypse (e.g., *Apocalypse of Peter*) to offer new revelation, perhaps from Jesus; it is quite another matter for Adam, Elijah, Isaiah, or Zechariah to foretell Israel's future and the appearance of Jesus. In a Jewish setting, apocalyptic prophecies of the ministry, suffering, and resurrection of Jesus, thought to have been uttered by OT worthies, would have carried much greater weight. I shall describe them briefly.

The *Apocalypse of Adam* is found among the tractates of the Nag Hammadi Codices (NHC V,5). It seems to be based on Jewish apocalyptic that could date as early as the first century. The gnosticized form that we now have is much later. The work presents itself as a revelation of Adam to his son Seth regarding

---

61. For a survey of this literature, see Goodspeed, *Strange New Gospels.* Even the books themselves that publish translations of these supposed ancient records are spurious. The learned "doctors" given as authors, discoverers, translators, or consultants are fictional. There are also a great many forgeries and hoaxes that have nothing to do with the Bible. See Farrer, *Literary Forgeries*; Charney, *Art of Yregrof* [*Forgery* spelled backward], esp. 253, pointing out that often the goal of forgery is to change history.

the origin of the world and the witness of thirteen kingdoms. The testimony of the third kingdom may allude to the birth of Jesus. There are several NT echoes in the second half of the work. The *Testament of Adam* is a work that evolved over two or three centuries. It is another revelation from Adam to his son Seth. Among other things, Adam foretells the coming of Christ. Many works in several languages circulated under the title *Apocalypse of Daniel*. One is a seventh-century edition from Syria that foretells history, ending with the destruction of the antichrist. Another is a ninth-century work that builds on Jesus' eschatological discourse (Mark 13 and parallels), extending his prophecy on into the time of Charlemagne, coronated in Rome in 800 CE.[62]

The books *5 Ezra* (2 Esd 1–2) and *6 Ezra* (2 Esd 15–16) are expansions of *4 Ezra*, a first-century Jewish apocalypse. The former dates to the second or third century. It presents Ezra the scribe as sharply criticizing the Jewish people, foretelling the coming of a new people (i.e., the Christians). The latter expansion was also written in the second or third century and warns of coming judgment. The *Apocalypse of Elijah* is a composite work composed and assembled over several centuries. Although it originated in Greek, it now survives in both Greek and Coptic. Among other things, the work warns of the coming antichrist. The (Greek) *Apocalypse of Ezra*, whose date of composition is difficult to determine, provides an account of what the biblical Ezra saw in heaven and in hell. He is shown the sins of humanity, and he pleads on humanity's behalf. The work is classified as apocryphal in the Catalogue of Sixty Canonical Books. Although the *Vision of Ezra* is extant in several Latin manuscripts, the original language was Greek. Much like the *Apocalypse of Ezra*, in the *Vision* Ezra descends into hell, where he sees the various forms of punishment inflicted on the wicked. We also have the *Apocalypse of Sedrach*, which is preserved in one fifteenth-century Greek manuscript. The text focuses on the death of God's Son for humanity, humanity's wickedness, and the hope of future paradise.[63]

Finally, the *Ascension of Isaiah* is part of a composite work now known as the *Martyrdom and Ascension of Isaiah*. The oldest part is the *Martyrdom of Isaiah* (1:1–3:12; 5:1–16), a Jewish work that tells how the wicked King Manasseh murdered Isaiah the prophet (probably alluded to in Heb 11:37). Inserted in this first part is the Christian "Testament of Hezekiah" (3:13–4:22), which foretells the death of Jesus, the corruption of the church, and the dominion of Beliar. The second half of the work is the *Ascension*, or "Vision of Isaiah," which

62. Hedrick, *Apocalypse of Adam*; S. Robinson, *Testament of Adam*; S. Robinson, "Updated Arbeitsbericht"; Berger, *Die griechische Daniel-Diegese*; Henze, *Syriac Apocalypse of Daniel*. The *Apocalypse of Daniel* appears in a variety of editions and languages, including Arabic, Armenian, Coptic, Greek, Hebrew, Persian, Slavonic, and Syriac. One will also want to see La Porta, "Seventh Vision of Daniel."

63. Bergren, *Fifth Ezra*; Bergren, *Sixth Ezra*; Hirschberger, *Ringen um Israel*; M. Stone and Strugnell, eds., *Books of Elijah*; Pietersma and Comstock, with Attridge, *Apocalypse of Elijah*; Frankfurter, *Elijah in Upper Egypt*; M. Stone, "Greek Apocalypse of Ezra"; Mueller and Robbins, "Vision of Ezra"; Agourides, "Apocalypse of Sedrach"; Bauckham, "Latin Vision of Ezra"; Bremmer, *Figures of Ezra*.

the prophet receives when he ascends into heaven (6:1–11:43). Isaiah ascends through the seven heavens, sees Christ commissioned for his task of incarnation and ministry on earth, his subsequent birth, the infancy, the crucifixion, and his ascension back into the seventh heaven.[64] There is a *Vision of Isaiah* listed as apocryphal in the Catalogue of the Sixty Canonical Books.

The apocalypses relating to the NT include the *Apocalypse of Peter*, the *Apocalypse of Paul* (or *Visio Pauli*), the *Apocalypse of Thomas*, the *Apocalypse of Bartholomew*, the *Questions of Bartholomew*, the *Apocalypse of Stephen*, the *Apocalypse of the Virgin*, and the *Apocalypse of Zechariah* (i.e., the father of John the Baptist, not the OT prophet.) Among these the first three are the most important.

The *Apocalypse of Peter* was probably composed shortly before the middle of the second century. To some degree its date is tied to the possibility that Bar Kokhba, who during the revolt against Rome (132–135 CE) persecuted Christians (Justin Martyr, *1 Apol.* 31.5–61; Eusebius, *Chronicon: Hadrian Year 17*), is referenced in the parable of the Fig Tree in *Apocalypse of Peter* 2: ". . . In the last days, then shall false Christs come and awake expectation, saying, 'I am the Christ who has now come into the world.' . . . But this deceiver is not the Christ. And when they reject him, he shall slay them with the sword, and there shall be many martyrs." The close match with Justin's description suggests that the false Christ could well have been in reference to Simon Bar Kokhba.[65]

A few church fathers quote the *Apocalypse of Peter* and even reference it by name, including Clement of Alexandria (*Eclogae propheticae* 41.1–2: "Peter in the Apocalypse [Πέτρος ἐν τῇ Ἀποκαλύψει] says . . ."; 48.1: "Peter in the Apocalypse [ὁ Πέτρος ἐν τῇ Ἀποκαλύψει] says . . ."), Theophilus of Antioch (*Ad Autolycum* 2.19), Macarius Magnes (*Apocritica* 4.6.7: ". . . which is said in the *Apocalypse of Peter* . . ."), and Methodius of Olympus (*Symposium* 2.6). The *Shepherd of Hermas*, the *Acts of Paul*, and the *Apocalypse of Peter* appear in the list of accepted books in Codex Claromontanus. So also states the Muratorian Fragment (MF): "Of the apocalypses we accept only those of John and Peter [*apocalypse etiam Iohanis et Petri tantum recipimus*], which some of our people do not want to have read in our churches" (lines 71–73). Eusebius was evidently among those people, for he rejects the *Apocalypse of Peter*: "Among the bastards [τοῖς νόθοις] must be reckoned also the *Acts of Paul*, and the so-called *Shepherd*, and the *Apocalypse of Peter* [ἡ Ἀποκάλυψις Πέτρου]" (*Hist. eccl.* 3.25.4; cf. 3.3.2; 6.14.1). The *Apocalypse of Peter* is listed as a book "spoken against" in the Stichometry of Nicephorus. In the Catalogue of the Sixty Canonical Books it is classified as an "apocryphal" book. Both the *Apocalypse*

---

64. Knibb, "Ascension of Isaiah"; Knight, *Disciples of the Beloved One*; Bremmer et al., *Ascension of Isaiah*.

65. Bauckham, "Fig Tree Parables"; Bauckham, "The *Apocalypse of Peter*," with repr. in Bauckham, *Fate of the Dead*. See also Tigchelaar, "Is the Liar Bar Kokhba?" Although he expresses some reservations, Tigchelaar acknowledges that Bauckham may be correct.

of Paul and the *Acts of Thomas* likely made use of the *Apocalypse of Peter*, which may hint at its authority. The second book of the *Sibylline Oracles*, which has been extensively edited by Christians, also exhibits knowledge of the Petrine apocalypse (see lines 190–338). Taken as a whole, the evidence clearly suggests that in some Christian circles the *Apocalypse of Peter* was regarded as authoritative scripture (as were other writings linked to Peter's name), but in other circles it was categorically rejected.[66]

The *Apocalypse of Paul*, or *Visio Pauli*, was inspired by Paul's account of being caught up into the "third heaven" (2 Cor 12:2–4). The book is classified as apocryphal in the *Decretum Gelasianum* and in the Catalogue of the Sixty Canonical Books. The *Apocalypse of Paul* has made use of the *Apocalypse of Peter*, the *Apocalypse of Elijah*, and the *Apocalypse of Zephaniah*. It warns of judgment awaiting the wicked in hell. Origen seems to have known of the *Apocalypse of Paul*. A gnostic *Apocalypse of Paul* is among the Nag Hammadi texts (NHC V,2). Like the other apocalypse, the gnostic apocalypse is inspired by 2 Cor 12:2–4. Paul ascends through the many heavens, having conversations with those he meets. Along the way, the apostle sees angels whipping and driving souls toward hell (esp. in the fourth heaven). Passing through the seventh heaven, Paul enters the Ogdoad (the "eighth" heavenly realm), where he meets the twelve apostles. They greet him; then Paul enters the ninth heaven, where he greets those present. Finally, Paul enters the tenth heaven, where he greets his "fellow spirits."[67]

The *Apocalypse of Thomas* is classified as apocryphal in the *Decretum Gelasianum*. The apocalypse probably originated in the fifth century. Not until the twentieth century did scholars finally gain possession of the text, which is extant in a short version and a long version. The apostle Thomas is warned by the "Son of God" of the things to come. Evil kings will arise and do wicked things, the heavens will be shaken, people will be terrified, and so forth.[68]

The name of the apostle Bartholomew, one of Jesus' least known disciples, is linked to various apocryphal titles. Jerome speaks of a *Gospel of Bartholomew* (*Comm. Matt. Praefatio*), and in the *Decretum Gelasianum* we read of *evangelia nomine Bartholomaei*, "Gospels in the name of Bartholomew."[69] It is unclear what these gospels were. One of them may have been the text that probably should be called the *Questions of Bartholomew*, which survives in Greek, Latin, and Slavonic manuscripts. This text, probably better classified as an apocalypse, is not to be confused with the Coptic text called *The Book of the Resurrection of*

---

66. Buchholz, *Eyes Will Be Opened*; Lapham, *New Testament Apocrypha*, 99–107; Bremmer and Czachesz, *Apocalypse of Peter*; Kraus and Nicklas, *Petrusevangelium und die Petrusapokalypse*.

67. Lapham, *New Testament Apocrypha*, 107–10; Bremmer and Czachesz, *Visio Pauli*, giving special attention to the *Gnostic Apocalypse of Paul*.

68. Dando, "L'Apocalypse de Thomas"; M. Stone, *Signs of the Judgement*; Herbert and McNamara, *Irish Biblical Apocrypha*, 153–59.

69. The *Decretum* consistently uses the plural *evangelia*. We hear of "Gospels in the name of" Matthias, Barnabas, James the Less, Peter, Thomas, Andrew, and Bartholomew.

Jesus Christ, by Bartholomew the Apostle.[70] In *Questions* the apostle Bartholomew questions Jesus after the resurrection. The principal focus of his questions concerns where Jesus was and what he experienced in the interval between death and resurrection. Jesus explains that he descended "five hundred steps" into Hades and that in doing so created commotion in the underworld (e.g., the agitated dialogues between Beliar and Hades); this reflects the popular *descensus Christi ad inferos* traditions (esp. the *Gospel of Nicodemus = Acts of Pilate* texts).[71] Jesus goes on to relate truths about Adam, the dead, angels, and so forth. As new texts are coming to light, modern scholarship concerned with the Bartholomew apocrypha is only in its early stages.[72]

I conclude this survey with reference to three more relatively unknown Christian apocalypses. The first is the *Apocalypse of Stephen*, which under the name *Revelatio Sancti Stephani* is classified as apocryphal in the *Decretum Gelasianum*. The text apparently is lost. An old Slavonic account of Stephen's martyrdom lacks apocalyptic and visionary material, so it is an unlikely candidate.[73] It is plausibly speculated that the tradition of a *Revelatio Sancti Stephani*, in which references are made to the great Jewish rabbi Gamaliel, may have been generated by relics believed to be linked to the first Christian martyr.[74] There are two versions of the *Apocalypse of the Virgin [Mary]*. In the Greek version Mary, as did Jesus, descends into hell, where she sees punishment of the wicked and where she petitions on their behalf. One Greek manuscript bears the title "The Apocalypse of the All-Holy Theotokos concerning the Punishments" (Biblioteca Apostolica Vaticana, Ottoboni 1). Considering its present form and the way it reflects liturgical practice, the *Apocalypse of the Virgin* cannot be earlier than the ninth century. This apocalypse is gaining new, appreciative attention in critical scholarship.[75]

And finally, we have the *Apocalypse of Zechariah*, which is found in the *Protevangelium of James*. At *Protevangelium of James* 23:3, when threatened with death if he does not reveal the location of his newborn son to the officers of

70. Budge, *Coptic Apocrypha*, 1–48 (Coptic text = British Museum MS Oriental no. 6804), 179–230 (ET). The first five leaves of the text are missing, and there are many lacunae. Budge also includes a Coptic text called "The *Life of Saint Bartholomew the Apostle*," on 49–50 (= British Museum MS Oriental no. 660 fol. 4a). According to this text, Herod Agrippa placed Bartholomew in a "hair sack" and had him cast into the sea. Other legends speak of Bartholomew as either crucified upside down or skinned alive.

71. For a recent assessment of these traditions, see Charlesworth, "Origins of the *descensus ad inferos*."

72. Cherchi, "St. Bartholomew's Gospel"; Pelle, "The *Questions of Bartholomew*"; Suciu, "The *Book of Bartholomew*"; Suciu, "Title of the Coptic *Book of Bartholomew*." There are a few brief references to the Bartholomew literature in *NTAM*, vol. 1.

73. The Slavonic text is summarized in James, *Apocryphal New Testament* (1953), 564–68.

74. Vanderlinden, "*Revelatio Sancti Stephani*"; Dilley, "Invention of Christian Tradition," esp. 596–97. Stephen's bones, it is alleged, were found in the Holy Land in 415 near Kefar Gamala. Vanderlinden's study provides the Latin text.

75. Mimouni, "Apocalypses de la Vierge"; Bauckham, "Apocalypses of the Virgin Mary"; Shoemaker, *Traditions of Mary's Dormition*, 290–350; Shoemaker, "Apocalypse of the Virgin," *NTAM* 1:492–509.

Herod, Zechariah says: "I am a witness of God. Pour out blood! But the Lord will receive my spirit, for you shed innocent blood at the threshold of the temple of the Lord." Shortly after that speech, Zechariah is executed. Alone, his brief utterance scarcely qualifies as an apocalypse. What gives it an apocalyptic flavor is its allusion to Jesus' prophetic utterance: ". . . the blood of all the prophets, shed from the foundation of the world, may be required of this generation, from the blood of Abel to the blood of Zechariah, who perished between the altar and the sanctuary" (Luke 11:50–51, my trans.; cf. Gen 4:8; 2 Chr 24:20–22; Matt 23:35). The aftermath of Zechariah's murder confirms the apocalyptic nature of both his utterance and his death. In *Protevangelium of James* 24:1–3, the officers cannot find the body of Zechariah. Instead, they find that his blood has turned to stone. When the ceiling panels of the temple begin to wail, they are frightened and hear a voice proclaim, "Zechariah has been slain, and his blood shall not be wiped away until his avenger comes!"[76]

It is not clear if this *Apocalypse of Zechariah* is related in any way to the "(Βίβλος) Ζαχαρίου πατρὸς Ἰωάννου [(*Book) of Zechariah, Father of John*]," listed as apocryphal in the Stichometry of Nicephorus and, under the title Ζαχαρίου ἀποκάλυψις (*Apocalypse of Zechariah*), in the Catalogue of the Sixty Canonical Books. In the Stichometry it is said to comprise 500 lines, which is much too long for the apocalypse that is embedded in the *Protevangelium of James*.

Fourth-century fascination with Zechariah, the father of John the Baptist, is witnessed in an inscription on the side of the monumental tomb in the Kidron Valley popularly known as the Tomb of Absalom (aka Absalom's Pillar). Almost twenty years ago two faint inscriptions were detected.[77] The one that is relevant for the present study reads (with some restoration): τόδε μνεμεῖον Ζακκαρίας μάρτυρος πρεσβητέρου θεοσεβεστάτου παππέας Ἰοάννου (Here is the tomb of Zechariah, martyr, old, very pious, father of John). Paleography points to a fourth-century date. The inscription, which serves as an epitaph, alludes to Luke 1:5–23, 57–80, where John's father Zechariah is featured.

The presence of the nearby monumental Tomb of Zechariah may, through confusion, account for the placing of an epitaph dedicated to Zechariah, father of John, on the Tomb of Absalom. It is speculated that in the fourth century, Byzantine Christians looking for holy sites—among whom Emperor Constantine's mother was the most conspicuous—made the identification.

The *Apocalypse of Zechariah* may in some way be related to the inscription because, in the brief version embedded in the *Protevangelium of James*, Zechariah is murdered. Nothing in the Gospel of Luke suggests that Zechariah suffered martyrdom. It is very interesting that, in the *Protevangelium*, Zechariah is said to have been martyred; in the epitaph on the side of the Tomb of Absalom, he

---

76. At *NTAM* 1:xlv, we are promised that the *Apocalypse of Zechariah* (only under the title of the *Martyrdom of Zechariah*) will be treated in the forthcoming vol. 2.

77. Puech, "Le tombeau de Siméon et Zachaarie"; Zias, "Tomb of Absalom."

is called a martyr.[78] The legend of martyrdom seems to have inspired both the *Apocalypse* and the Kidron Valley inscription.

CANON AND CHANCE SURVIVAL

Before bringing this chapter to a close, I will make a few comments about the regional dimension in the survival of the ancient texts under review. We notice that many extant manuscripts come from Egypt, either in Greek or in Coptic. Most of the papyrus documents in our subject area, which usually means our oldest documents, come from Egypt, many of them from one city: Oxyrhynchus. This means that what has survived from Late Antiquity is not necessarily representative of the first three or four centuries of Christendom as a whole. This makes sense, given the dry climate. Some half million pages of papyrus and parchment have been recovered from the trash mounds of Oxyrhynchus, mostly from the top ten feet or so. Countless thousands of documents, buried at lower depths, have perished. Thousands more papyri have been recovered from other sites in Egypt.

At Oxyrhynchus some seventy-two Greek New Testament manuscripts have been identified and published thus far,[79] including the much-talked-about late second-century fragment of the Gospel of Mark (P.Oxy. 5345 = P[137]).[80] Twenty-two of the twenty-seven writings that make up the New Testament have been found at Oxyrhynchus. The missing five are Colossians, 2 Timothy, 2 Peter, 2 John, and 3 John. Some of the New Testament writings are well represented; in descending order of representation, they are the following: Gospel of Matthew (16), Gospel of John (16), Revelation (6), Romans (5), James (4), Gospel of Luke (3), Hebrews (3), Acts (3), Galatians (3), 1 Corinthians (2), 1 Peter (2), 2 Corinthians (1), Ephesians (1), Philippians (1), 1–2 Thessalonians (1), 1 Timothy (1), Titus (1), Philemon (1), 1 John (1), and Jude (1).[81]

At least 25 extracanonical manuscripts (MSS, texts) have been found at Oxyrhynchus to date. We have some 11 MSS of the *Shepherd of Hermas*, all dating from the third and fourth centuries. We have 3 MSS of the *Gospel of Thomas*

---

78. Possibly the story of the priest named Zechariah murdered by the Zealots during the first Jewish revolt (Josephus, *J. W.* 4.343) influenced Christian tradition.

79. I am aided in this tally by Blumell and Wayment, *Christian Oxyrhynchus*. Although this valuable book made its appearance only a few years ago, it is already out of date. For example, since its publication six Oxyrhynchus papyri volumes have appeared, adding several more Christian writings to the list, including five more NT papyri. About half of all NT papyri come from Oxyrhynchus (and given the looting that took place in the early years, it is possible that several other NT papyri, whose find locations are unknown, actually came from Oxyrhynchus). Furthermore, not all the papyri discovered at Oxyrhynchus have appeared in the Oxyrhynchus series published by the Egypt Exploration Society.

80. P.Oxy. 5345 preserves portions of Mark 1:7–9, 16–18. See D. Obbink and D. Colomo, "5345."

81. A few of these papyri are later than the 5th century, thus are not included in the collection edited by Blumell and Wayment, *Christian Oxyrhynchus*.

(P.Oxy. 1, 654, 655), dating from the third century. We have 2 MSS of the *Gospel of Mary* (P.Oxy. 3525; P.Ryl. Gr. 463), dating from the third century.[82] We have fourth-century fragments of the *Acts of John* (P.Oxy. 850) and the *Acts of Peter* (P.Oxy. 849), 2 fragments of the *Acts of Paul and Thecla*, probably dating to the fifth century (P.Oxy. 6, 1602), and a fifth or sixth-century fragment that could be from the *Acts of Andrew* (P.Oxy. 851). We have several other fragments of what could be extracanonical gospels (P.Oxy. 210, 840, 1224, 2949, 4009, 5072), a fragment of the *Didache* (P.Oxy. 1782), a fragment of the gnostic tractate *Sophia of Jesus Christ* (P.Oxy. 1081), and a fragment of the pseudepigraphal work known as *Jannes and Jambres* (P.Oxy. 5290), which is listed as apocryphal in the *Decretum Gelasianum*. All three of the last mentioned probably date to the fourth century.

What can we infer from the bare facts of these finds? The answers are not obvious. Almost all these documents have been recovered from the trash heaps of one city. To what degree these discarded MSS represent the reading preferences and theological views of the Christians who possessed them is not certain. It has been observed that the number of MSS of the *Shepherd of Hermas* equals those of Matthew, exceeds all the rest of the New Testament writings, and is surpassed only by the number of copies of John. True enough, but what does that prove? The *Shepherd of Hermas* must have been popular, and its many copies suggest that it was read in some churches as authoritative scripture.[83] The canon lists support that inference. The MF states, "Hermas wrote the *Shepherd*. . . . It ought to be read, but it cannot be read publicly in the Church" (lines 73–78). Codex Claromontanus places the *Shepherd of Hermas* on its list of acceptable books. But in the *Decretum Gelasianum* it is listed as apocryphal.

Scholars have discussed the sheer number of extracanonical writings. Again, it is not clear what the implications of that observation are. We should expect that Christian reading interests would not be limited to biblical texts, that is, the writings that in time would make up the OT, as well as those that eventually would be recognized as forming the NT. Of the Christian extracanonical writings from Oxyrhynchus thus far identified and published, we have eight named texts and six anonymous texts (whose limited contents cannot guarantee that we are looking at an extracanonical writing rather than a homily or treatise, where biblical material is only quoted). How many extracanonical texts were in circulation by the fifth century?

There may have been as many as thirty gospels, about one dozen books of acts, several epistles, and several apocalypses. Because we do not always know the dates when some of these writings began to circulate nor how widely they

---

82. Tuckett, *Gospel of Mary.*
83. Epp, *New Testament Textual Criticism*, 757: "Too much must not be drawn from such comparative data, but it is clear by any measure available to us that the *Shepherd of Hermas* was very much a part of Christian literature in Oxyrhynchus at an early period." I add that the MS evidence of Oxyrhynchus comports with the generally favorable view of *Hermas* that we see in much of the early patristic literature.

circulated, it is hard to know how many of these texts could have been known to the people of Oxyrhynchus from the second to the fifth centuries. Even if we put the number at a modest fifty (the *Decretum Gelasianum*, which is not exhaustive, lists just over fifty), this would mean that fewer than 30 percent of the extracanonical texts have been recovered from the trash heaps of Oxyrhynchus thus far. If we possessed fuller data, the real percentage would probably be much lower. In contrast, about 80 percent of the writings that would eventually make up the New Testament have been recovered from the trash heaps of Oxyrhynchus, and more may be found, potentially increasing the percentage of New Testament writings found at Oxyrhynchus.

All these calculations are tentative and provisional, of course; they will no doubt change as additional texts come to light and as progress is made in dating these texts and determining their provenance. But for what it is worth, the percentages seem to suggest that the Christians of Oxyrhynchus in general valued the New Testament writings much more than they did the extracanonical writings. The smaller number of copies of several NT writings may suggest that Christians were reluctant to throw out these books, even if they were badly worn. In any event, we must bear in mind the utter uncertainty of it all.

In light of that last remark, I am reminded of what Revel Coles, well known for his work with the papyri of Oxyrhynchus, says in his introductory essay, "Oxyrhynchus: A City and Its Texts": "Documents vastly outnumber literary texts; nevertheless the literary quantity is huge, and two-thirds of the literature that found its way into the town's rubbish is from works unknown today, by unknown writers." Coles goes on to remark, "In broad statistical terms, the inhabitants of this relatively remote place might have had access to three times the quantity of classical Greek literature to be found on the shelves of the university libraries of today."[84] What Coles says about classical Greek literature could well apply to the burgeoning Christian literature of the second to fifth centuries.

In the next chapter I shall turn my attention to two extracanonical gospels that garnered a lot of attention in scholarly and popular contexts. One is the *Gospel of Peter*, a large excerpt of which was recovered more than one century ago at Akhmîm (or Panopolis) in Egypt. This text needs to be discussed in greater detail because some scholars think it is early and independent of the canonical Gospels and may have even served as the principal source for their respective passion and resurrection narratives. The second text that warrants more detailed discussion is the *Gospel of Thomas*, whose Greek fragments discovered at Oxyrhynchus have already been mentioned. The *Gospel of Thomas* is important for many reasons, not least because some scholars believe it also is early and independent of the canonical Gospels, may have influenced several New Testament writings, and perhaps should even be considered for inclusion in the Christian canon of scripture.

---

84. R. A. Coles, "Oxyrhynchus: A City and Its Texts," with quotations from 9.

Chapter 9

The Gospels of Peter
and Thomas

CRAIG A. EVANS

Most scholars will probably agree that the two extracanonical gospels that have drawn the lion's share of attention for the last thirty or forty years have been the *Gospel of Peter* and the *Gospel of Thomas*. The first attracts attention because of its unusual account of the resurrection of Jesus and the question of its relationship to the canonical resurrection narratives, and the second because of its possible relevance for the study of Q and the quest for dominical tradition that is independent of the canonical Gospels. Both of these extracanonical gospels have become storm centers of scholarly debate, with scholars on one side saying that these writings are not early and not independent, and scholars on the other side saying precisely the opposite.[1] *Gospel of Peter* and *Gospel of Thomas* are also well known to the general public and often find their way into popular literature. Some have suggested adding *Gospel of Thomas* to the canon of NT scripture! I begin with the *Gospel of Peter*.

---

1. One of the most influential voices promoting the idea that several extracanonical gospels are early and independent of the NT Gospels is John Dominic Crossan. See Crossan, *Four Other Gospels*; Crossan, *Historical Jesus*, appendix 1, "An Inventory of the Jesus Tradition," 427–50. See also Koester, *Ancient Christian Gospels*.

THE *GOSPEL OF PETER*

The early church knew of the *Gospel of Peter* no later than the end of the second century. Codex Claromontanus does not place *Peter* on its list of accepted books. The *Decretum Gelasianum* includes *Peter* on its list of "apocryphal" books. Church historian Eusebius categorically rejects the *Gospel of Peter* as spurious. While discussing the literature attributed to the apostle Peter, Eusebius states:

> Of Peter, one epistle, that which is called his first, is admitted, and the ancient presbyters used this in their own writings as unquestioned, but the so-called second Epistle we have not received as canonical, but nevertheless it has appeared useful to many, and has been studied with other Scriptures. On the other hand, of the *Acts* bearing his name, and the Gospel named according to him [καὶ τὸ κατ᾽ αὐτὸν ὠνομασμένον Ἐυαγγέλιον] and Preaching called his and the so-called Revelation, as we have no knowledge at all in Catholic tradition, for no orthodox writer of the ancient time [ἀρχαίων] or of our own has used their testimonies. (*Hist. eccl.* 3.3.2, LCL)

Whereas Eusebius concedes that 2 Peter (i.e., the "so-called second Epistle"), which he and others do not accept, seems to be useful to some and so "has been studied with other Scriptures," he emphatically rejects the *Acts*, the *Gospel*, the *Preaching*, and the *Apocalypse*, all named after Peter. Eusebius does so because he and like-minded leaders in the church "have no knowledge at all in Catholic tradition" (i.e., καθολικός, "universal") about these writings named after the great apostle. They lack this knowledge because no church leader from early times quotes it or refers to it. The criterion at work here is largely one of antiquity, but widespread or universal usage is also in view. These various writings, named after Peter, simply were not known until more recent times. Therefore they are suspect and should be rejected.

In a second passage Eusebius refers to the testimony of Serapion, bishop of Antioch in the late second and early third centuries (cf. *Hist. eccl.* 5.19.1; 5.22.1), who wrote a tract condemning the *Gospel of Peter*. Eusebius begins with a reference to Serapion's "literary studies" and then quotes a passage from the tract concerning *Peter*:

> Now it is likely, indeed, that other memoirs also, the fruit of Serapion's literary studies, are preserved by other persons, . . . and another book has been composed by him, a statement (titled) *Concerning what is called the Gospel of Peter* [περὶ τοῦ λεγομένου κατὰ Πέτρον Ἐυαγγελίου], which he has written refuting the false statements in it, because of certain people in the community of Rhossus, who on the ground of the said writing turned aside to heterodox teachings. It will not be unreasonable to quote a short passage from this (Serapion's) work, in which he puts forward the view he held about the book, writing as follows: "For our part, brethren, we receive both Peter and the other apostles as Christ, but the writings which falsely bear their names we reject, as men of experience, knowing that such were not handed down to us. For I myself, when I came among you, imagined

that all of you clung to the true faith; and, without going through the Gospel put forward by them in the name of Peter [καὶ μὴ διελθὼν τὸ ὑπ' αὐτῶν προφερόμενον ὀνόματι Πέτρου Εὐαγγέλιον], I said: 'If this is the only thing that seemingly causes irritation among you, let it be read.' But since I have now learned, from what has been told me, that their mind was lurking in some hole of heresy, I shall give diligence to come again to you. Therefore, brethren, expect me quickly. But we, brethren, gathering to what kind of heresy Marcianus belonged (who used to contradict himself, not knowing what he was saying, as you will learn from what has been written to you), were enabled by others who studied this very Gospel, that is, by the successors of those who began it, whom we call Docetists (for most of the ideas belong to their teaching)—using [the material supplied] by them, were enabled to go through (it) and discover that the most part indeed was in accordance with the true teaching of the Savior [διελθεῖν καὶ εὑρεῖν τὰ μὲν πλείονα τοῦ ὀρθοῦ λόγου τοῦ Σωτῆρος], but that some things were added, which also we place below for your benefit." (*Hist. eccl.* 6.12.1–6, LCL)

This is a remarkably unclear and convoluted statement. Its basic meaning, however, seems clear enough: Serapion decided no longer to permit the *Gospel of Peter* to be read because it contains some questionable material. But it is hard to be more precise. In what way the *Gospel of Peter* is heretical and in what way it either contains docetic elements or could have been utilized by Docetists is not clear. There really is nothing obviously docetic in the surviving Akhmîm excerpt that supports Docetism or that those inclined toward Docetism would find particularly useful. It makes one wonder if the Akhmîm fragment, discovered during a French excavation in 1886–87, is the *Gospel of Peter* of which Serapion and (later) Eusebius speak. The small fragments discovered at Oxyrhynchus—P.Oxy. 2949 and P.Oxy. 4009—are not of much help simply because it is far from certain that they really are from the *Gospel of Peter*, at least as the Akhmîm text reads.[2]

Three major works on the *Gospel of Peter* have been published in recent years. The first is a collection of studies edited by Thomas Kraus and Tobias Nicklas.[3] In his essay in this collection, Peter van Minnen wisely cautions against the assumption that the sixth- or seventh-century text of the Akhmîm fragment reflects "the original, early character of the *Gospel of Peter*."[4] His point is well taken, for textual divergence is very much in evidence in literature of this nature. Kraus's essay, which treats the language of the Akhmîm text, lends additional

2. On this important point, see Foster, "So-Called *Gospel of Peter*?" As Foster rightly recognizes, it is not at all clear that P.Oxy. 2949, P.Oxy. 4009, and other early artifacts have anything to do with the *Gospel of Peter*, and therefore they do not really help anchor the Akhmîm gospel fragment to the second century or to Serapion's testimony. For a polemical response, see Lührmann, "Handschrift des Petrusevangeliums?" Lührmann's criticisms and "corrections" of Foster's study are for the most part off target and unfair. For a rejoinder, see Foster, "Disputed Early Fragments."

3. Kraus and Nicklas, *Evangelium nach Petrus*. A few years earlier, Kraus and Nicklas produced a critical edition of the Greek text. See Kraus and Nicklas, *Petrusevangelium und die Petrusapokalypse*, 3–77 + plates.

4. See van Minnen, "Akhmîm *Gospel of Peter*," 53–60, with quotation from 60.

justification to van Minnen's principal concern.[5] Although most essays in this important collection rightly challenge some of the older scholarship on *Gospel of Peter* (for exaggerating its antiquity, independence, and the like), they do conclude that the Akhmîm gospel excerpt probably is a Byzantine-era edition of the *Gospel of Peter* and that this apocryphal gospel probably did originate in the second century.

These principal conclusions received support from the lengthy and learned monographs by Paul Foster and Jeremiah Johnston.[6] Foster concludes that "the *Gospel of Peter* appears to be posterior to the canonical [G]ospels where there are parallel passages. In those cases where there is unparalleled material, there is little reason to suppose that this is due to anything other than the author's own creativity." Foster further finds that *Peter* is literarily dependent on all three Synoptic Gospels, but this "literary dependence does not equate to slavish copying of sources, or even a desire to preserve the narrational microstructure of any one" of the Synoptic Gospels.[7] Given what has been observed with regard to much of this apocryphal literature, Foster's point seems unassailable.

Foster also rightly rejects Paul Mirecki's proposed early date for the *Gospel of Peter*. Mirecki asserts: "The *Gospel of Peter* . . . circulated in the mid-1st century under the authority of the name of Peter. An earlier form of the gospel probably served as one of the major sources for the canonical [G]ospels."[8] Mirecki's remarkable statement is breathtaking, especially so in the context of a major reference work, where claims and conclusions normally reflect mainstream scholarly views. Very few scholars with competence in the field date *Gospel of Peter* so early or accept the speculative hypothesis that an early form of *Peter* was used by the authors of the canonical Gospels. Foster, of course, rejects both these unsupported claims. After reviewing the evidence and the scholarly discussion, Foster believes "a date of composition during the period 150–190 CE seems the most sensible suggestion."[9]

Echoing van Minnen, Foster underscores the point that "scholars have too quickly made the identification between the text mentioned by Serapion and the first document in the Akhmîm Codex," but even so, it "remains the most likely explanation."[10] To be sure, but can we move beyond "most likely"? In his groundbreaking study, Johnston addresses the question of the Akhmîm excerpt's identification as the *Gospel of Peter* and asks if additional and better evidence can be adduced for dating the work and, at the same time, confirming the identification of the excerpt as belonging to the *Gospel of Peter*. In my view

5. Kraus, "'Sprache des Petrusevangeliums?,'" esp. 63–68.

6. Foster, *Gospel of Peter*; also dealing with *Gospel of Peter* is Johnston, *Resurrection of Jesus*.

7. Foster, *Gospel of Peter*, 146. In the history of the transmission of the text, many changes may have taken place, further obscuring verbal agreement.

8. Mirecki, "Peter, Gospel of," esp. 278; also quoted in Foster, *Gospel of Peter*, 169. Mirecki's claims are also rejected by Johnston, *Resurrection of Jesus*, 117 n. 12. For an influential publication that promoted the antiquity and independence of the *Gospel of Peter*, see Crossan, *Cross That Spoke*.

9. Foster, *Gospel of Peter*, 172.

10. Foster, *Gospel of Peter*, 171.

Johnston has succeeded in both tasks. He argues that the Akhmîm gospel fragment probably is the *Gospel of Peter* and probably should be dated to the middle
of the second century. Johnston does this "not by appeals to P.Oxy. 2949 or
P.Oxy. 4009 (or other related materials), but by comparative analysis, an analysis that demonstrates that the fragment exemplifies an apologetic that addresses
quite specifically second-century pagan criticisms of the resurrection narratives
of the earlier [G]ospels."[11]

Johnston makes an impressive case for seeing the resurrection narrative of the
Gospel of Peter as an extension of Matthean apologetic (witnesses at the tomb on
Easter morning) and for seeing the anti-Jewish polemic of the *Gospel of Peter* as
a reflection of contemporary hostility toward the Jewish people in the aftermath
of the destructive and costly Bar Kokhba uprising in 132–135 CE.[12] In the *Gospel of Peter*, Johnston also sees the presence of literary and storytelling traits that
became fashionable in the second century.[13] Johnston's work, though still quite
recent, is receiving scholarly affirmation.[14]

Here it will be helpful to say a bit more about how the *Gospel of Peter* extends
the resurrection narratives of the canonical Gospels, especially the apologetic
of the Gospel of Matthew. My comments very much reflect Johnston's work.
My focus is on the part of the *Gospel of Peter* that elaborates on Matthew in
the burial and resurrection scenes. There are in fact three distinct movements
in the apologetic: the burial, the posting of a guard, and the resurrection. There
certainly are other components, including some remarkable conversations
involving Herod, Pilate, Jewish leaders, and the like—all typical for the type
of literature produced in the second century—but the three components under
review should be sufficient to show how the author of the *Gospel of Peter* has
enhanced Matthean apologetic, so as to answer second-century skepticism. I
begin with the burial scene:

> [3]Now stood there Joseph friend of Pilate and of the Lord, and knowing that
> they were about to crucify him he came to Pilate and requested the body
> of the Lord for burial. [4]And sending to Herod Pilate requested the body.
> [5]And Herod said, "Brother Pilate, even if no one had requested him, we
> should bury him, since the Sabbath draws on. For it is written in the Law:
> 'The sun should not set on one that has been murdered [πεφονευμένῳ].'"

11. Johnston, *Resurrection of Jesus*, 5, and 135–53 on the *Gospel of Peter* as response to pagan and
Jewish skepticism with regard to the canonical Gospels' Easter narratives.

12. Johnston, *Resurrection of Jesus*, 119–35.

13. Johnston, *Resurrection of Jesus*, 173–79. Bowersock (*Fiction as History*, 99–119) believes that
the Christian story of Jesus' death, burial, and resurrection was well known by the end of the first
century and that Greco-Roman novelists made use of some of these elements. Johnston (*Resurrection
of Jesus*) argues plausibly that the author of the *Gospel of Peter* fictionalized and romanticized the
canonical Passion Narrative along very similar lines.

14. Kraus, "EvPet [Petrusevangelium] 12,50–14,60," esp. 338 and 338 n. 10; Fowler, Review
of J. J. Johnston, *Resurrection of Jesus*. Kraus refers to Johnston's 2012 prepublication dissertation;
Fowler refers to the 2016 published version cited in the preceding notes. Kraus confirms the importance of comparing the *Gospel of Peter* with the second-century Greco-Roman romance novels.
Fowler recognizes the validity of Johnston's comparative analysis and its compelling results.

And he delivered him to the people on the day before unleavened bread, their feast. (2:3–5)[15]

[15]Now it was midday, and darkness covered all Judea; and they were worried and uneasy, lest the sun had already set, since he was still alive. It is written for them that "the sun is not set upon him that has been murdered [πεφονευμένῳ]." (5:15)

[21]And then they drew the nails from the hands of the Lord, and they laid him upon the ground. And all the earth was shaken, and there was great fear. [22]Then the sun shone, and it was found to be the ninth hour. [23]But the Jews rejoiced and gave his body to Joseph, in order that he might bury it. . . . [24]But taking the Lord he washed and wrapped him in linen and brought him to his own tomb called Joseph's Garden. (6:21–23a, 24)

What stands out in 2:3–5; 5:15; and 6:21–24 is the emphasis on burying Jesus according to Jewish law and custom. The custom, of course, grows out of the command in Deut 21:22–23 that no corpse, not even the corpse of a man executed and hanged on a tree (or stake), was to be left unburied overnight. The corpse was to be buried or placed in a tomb before sunset. The passage from Deuteronomy is explicitly referenced in 2:5. The paraphrase of Deut 21:22–23 at Qumran (11QT[a] 64.7–13 = 4Q524 14.2–4; cf. Josephus, *J. W.* 4.317; Josephus, *Ag. Ap.* 2.211; Gal 3:13), in which the sequence of death-then-hanging is reversed to hanging-then-death, reflects the practice of crucifixion in Israel in the Roman period.

This concern is emphasized in *Gospel of Peter* 5:15, in which the darkness raised the possibility that the sun had set while the body of Jesus had not yet been taken down from the cross and placed in a tomb. Failure to do this, according to Deuteronomy, would result in a curse on the land. The Deuteronomy passage is once again paraphrased: "It is written for them that 'the sun is not set upon him that has been murdered.'" The *Gospel of Peter* tells us that the "darkness covered all Judea" (5:15). The Synoptic Gospels, however, only say that "the darkness covered the land," without specifying the geographic extent of the darkness. It is likely that *Peter* qualifies the geographical reach with the words "all Judea" to underscore that divine judgment was falling on the Jewish people, not on the Roman authority that only reluctantly agreed to execute Jesus.

After the earthquake in 6:21, the sun appears. Accordingly, we are told, "The Jews rejoiced." The day had not ended; there was still time to bury Jesus. The emphasis on the burial sets the stage for the resurrection event. It also makes clear to readers outside the land of Israel—unacquainted with Jewish law and local Roman policy as it relates to the Jewish people in their homeland—that crucifixion victims in Israel during peacetime were in fact taken down and buried; they were not left hanging on crosses unburied. This is a very important

15. The verse numbers of the *Gospel of Peter* are confusing because two systems are in use. One system divides *Peter* into fourteen paragraphs; the other divides *Peter* into sixty verses, from beginning to end. The verse numbers do not restart at the beginning of each paragraph. In the discussion I will refer only to the verse numbers.

point in the apologetic of the *Gospel of Peter*. The apologetic is buttressed further by telling readers that the body of Jesus was taken to Joseph's "own tomb" (ἴδιον τάφον), a tomb "called Joseph's Garden" (καλούμενον Κῆπον Ἰωσήφ) (6:24). This adds a touch of first-hand knowledge, which again enhances the apologetic interests of the author of the *Gospel of Peter*.

The inspiration for reference to a garden likely comes from John 19:41, which speaks of a garden (κῆπος) where Jesus was crucified. Giving a name to the garden may have been suggested to the author of the *Gospel of Peter* by conflating John 18:1, 26, which speaks of a garden (κῆπος) where Jesus prayed, with Matt 26:36 and Mark 14:32, which provide the place of prayer with the name "Gethsemane" (hence the tradition of the "Garden of Gethsemane"). If Jesus was crucified in a place where there was a garden and the place where his body was placed belonged to Joseph, who provided the tomb, then perhaps the tomb was called the "Garden of Joseph."

There are other features that should be mentioned. First, *Gospel of Peter* states that "they drew the nails from the hands of the Lord." In the post-resurrection setting, the Gospel of John (20:25) mentions the "mark of the nails," while in Colossians (2:14) we hear of the handbill "against us" that has been nailed to the cross. But the NT Gospels do not mention nails in the crucifixion of Jesus or their removal when Jesus is taken down from the cross. *Gospel of Peter's* specific reference to the crucifixion nails seems to reflect second-century Christian interest in the nails, as we see in Ignatius, *To the Smyrnaeans* 1.2, "truly nailed in the flesh for us under Pontius Pilate and Herod the tetrarch"; in the *Epistle of Barnabas* 5.13, "Pierce my flesh with nails"; and in Justin Martyr, *Dialogue with Trypho* 97.3, "When they crucified him, driving in the nails, they pierced his hands and feet." Justin Martyr, of course, mentions feet as well as hands, in order to parallel the righteous man's lament in Psalm 21:17 LXX (cf. Justin, *1 Apol.* 35.7, "a description of the nails fixed to the cross in his hands and feet").[16] One should also see Irenaeus, *Adversus haereses* 1.14.6, ". . . at that sixth hour, at which he was nailed to the tree . . ."; and 2.24.4, ". . . on which the person rests who is fixed by the nails"; and Origen, *Contra Celsum* 2.55, ". . . his hands were pierced with nails; who beheld this?" (cf. 2.59).

Second, the paraphrases of Deut 21:22–23 in *Gospel of Peter* 2:5 and 5:15 are quite innovative. Both times the verb used is πεφονευμένῳ, "(has) been murdered."[17] The Greek translation of Deut 21:23 uses κρεμάμενος. One would have expected Herod to say, κεκρεμασμένῳ, "(has) been hanged, suspended,"[18] the word used for judicial execution. For Herod to speak of Jesus as "murdered" implies that Jesus was innocent, and his accusers—Herod and the Jewish people—knew it. The execution of Jesus was not just; it was a crime, which is exactly how it is portrayed in the *Gospel of Peter*. This too adds a great

16. As noted by Foster, *Gospel of Peter*, 337–38.
17. Cf. Exod 20:15 LXX, οὐ φονεύσεις, "You shall not murder" (NETS).
18. As pointed out by Foster, *Gospel of Peter*, 245.

deal to the apologetic thrust of the *Gospel of Peter*. Here is another indication of the widening gap between the Jesus movement, as understood and represented by the author of the *Gospel of Peter*, and the Jewish people. Herod and the Jews are vilified. In contrast, Pilate is placed in a neutral or even positive light. Pilate is a "friend" of Joseph (of Arimathea), who is also a "friend of the Lord." In the narrative world of the *Gospel of the Peter*, these friends stand over against the Jewish people. This perspective reflects the second century, especially post–Bar Kokhba, not the middle of the first century, not prior to the first Jewish rebellion against Rome.

A third observation is what might be called the upgrading of language in the *Gospel of Peter*. Whereas all four NT Gospels speak of "the body of Jesus" (Matt 27:58; Mark 15:43; Luke 23:52; John 19:40), the *Gospel of Peter* speaks of "the body of the Lord" (2:3). If the NT Gospels made use of *Peter*, as Mirecki and others think, we would expect at least one of them, if not all four, to refer to *the Lord* instead of *Jesus*. It clearly is *Gospel of Peter* that depends on the canonical Gospels and so has christologically upgraded the canonical language. One might compare the scene of Peter's third denial of Jesus. Mark 14:72 and Matt 26:75 say that Peter remembered the saying of *Jesus*, but Luke says, "Peter remembered the word of *the Lord*" (Luke 22:61, emphasis added). Commentators rightly understand this as Lukan redaction. We see the same thing here in the *Gospel of Peter* (and at 6:21, when the nails were drawn from the hands "of the Lord").

A fourth observation concerns the overt use of Deut 21:22–23 in *Peter's* account of the burial of Jesus. The NT Gospels do not quote the passage or refer to it, but it may be alluded to in John and presupposed in Matthew. The only place in the New Testament where any part of the passage is quoted is in Gal 3:13. There Paul appeals to Deut 21:23b as part of his theology concerning the value of Jesus' death on the cross. He does not appeal to the first part of the verse, "You shall bury him that same day." Matthew simply states, "When it was evening" (27:57). No part of the passage from Deuteronomy is quoted, and nothing is said about placing the body in the tomb before the end of the day. Indeed, Matthew's language could be understood to mean that the day had already ended and the deadline missed.

John comes close to an allusion to Deut 21:23 when the evangelist explains that because "it was the day of Preparation, in order to prevent the bodies from remaining on the cross on the sabbath (for that sabbath was a high day), the Jews asked Pilate that their legs might be broken, and that they might be taken away" (John 19:31, my trans.). Yet John does not actually say that the bodies had to come down because the end of the day approached, only that the approaching new day (which would commence at sunset) was a sabbath, "a high day." In Acts the apostle Peter states that they "put him [Jesus] to death by hanging him on a tree" (Acts 10:39). Again, nothing is said about taking Jesus down and placing him in a tomb before the end of the day.

In sum, the New Testament does not explicitly appeal to the requirement that a corpse be buried before night; there appears to be no apologetic with respect to this point. The only apologetic is seen in Paul's theology of atonement, a feature that is frequently referenced in second-century Christian theology and apologetic (e.g., Justin Martyr, *Dial.* 96, 111; Tatian, *Diatessaron* 20 §36; Irenaeus, *Haer.* 3.18.3; Tertullian, *Marc.* 3.18) and has nothing to do with burial itself. As part of his Passion Narrative apologetic, the author of the *Gospel of Peter* has made the point that Jesus was buried in a known and named tomb, before sundown, as Jewish scripture commands. The inspiration for the addition of this element likely came from John 19:31, the only NT Gospel to mention that bodies were not to remain on the cross (because of the approaching sabbath, not sundown). The apologetic appeal to Deuteronomy 21:23 is a distinctive feature of the *Gospel of Peter*.

Dependence on Matthew becomes clear in the story of the posting of the guard at the tomb of Jesus and the communication with Pontius Pilate. The relevant part of the *Gospel of Peter* reads thus:

> [29]The elders were afraid and went to Pilate entreating him and saying, [30]"Give us soldiers, that we might guard his tomb for three days, lest his disciples come and steal him and the people suppose that he has been raised from the dead, and do us harm." [31]And Pilate gave them Petronius the centurion, with soldiers, to guard the tomb. And elders and scribes went with them to the tomb. [32]And having rolled a large stone, all who were there, with the centurion and the soldiers, placed (it) at the door of the tomb [33]and put on it seven seals, and after pitching a tent they kept guard. (8:29–33)

Of the NT Gospels, only Matthew reports the request for and posting of a guard at the tomb of Jesus. The *Gospel of Peter* embellishes the story at several points. *Peter* tells us that the Jewish leaders ask Pilate for a guard out of fear, because if something happens to make the people believe Jesus has been raised from the dead, they will "do us harm." In Matthew, Pilate simply says, "You have a guard" (ἔχετε κουστωδίαν) (27:65). *Gospel of Peter* (8:31) elaborates on the story, saying, "Pilate gave them Petronius the centurion, with soldiers [Πετρώνιον τὸν κεντυρίωνα μετὰ στρατιωτῶν]." *Peter*'s centurion and soldiers are more impressive than Matthew's "custodians," for they will guarantee proper security against tampering or theft.

Providing the centurion with a name, Petronius, once again implies eyewitness testimony and so strengthens the apologetic. Supplying names for the anonymous is a tendency not limited to but very much at home in the second century and beyond. For example, in the *Acts of Pilate* (*Gesta Pilati*), or *Gospel of Nicodemus A*, the centurion who pierced the side of Jesus is given the name Longinus (*Acts Pil.* 16:7; and in the related *Epistula Pilati ad Herodem* 2). In the same legendary materials (*Acts Pil.* 4:4; *Epistula Pilati ad Herodem* 2–4), we learn that the name of Pilate's wife is (Claudia) Procula (or Procla). We also learn that the woman whom Jesus healed of the hemorrhage (Luke 8:42–48) is named Veronica (*Acts Pil.* 7:1; *Vindicta Salvatoris* 22); later, during Jesus' painful cross-bearing trek to Golgatha (Luke 23:26–31), she wipes his face with a linen cloth, which retains the image of Jesus' face (*Vindicta Salvatoris* 24, 32–33; *Mors Pilati* 2).[19] In the *Narrative of Joseph of Arimathea* ('Υφήγησις 'Ιωσήφ), the names of the two robbers crucified with Jesus are said to be Gestas and Demas. Their crimes are described (*Narr. Jos.* 2). The *Acts of Pilate* (*Acta Pilati*), or *Gospel of Nicodemus* B 17:1–2, and *Anaphora Pilati* 9 provide names for some of the holy ones raised up in Matthew 27:51–53. The imaginary prefect of Judea named Lentulus, as noted already, will send a report about Jesus to the Roman senate (the so-called *Epistula Lentuli*).

To return to the *Gospel of Peter*, we are told that the centurion and soldiers with the elders and scribes "rolled a large stone [λίθον μέγαν]" and "placed (it) at the door of the tomb." Matthew (27:66) speaks of a stone (λίθον), not a *large* stone, and says the officials sealed (ἠσφαλίσαντο) the stone, another Matthean addition to the Passion Narrative. The *Gospel of Peter* again embellishes the story by saying that the officials (lit.) "smeared it [the large stone] with seven seals" (ἐπέχρισαν ἑπτὰ σφραγῖδας) (v. 33a), that is, seven drops of wax, impressed with seals. If the stone is rolled aside, the wax seals will be broken.[20] One may well wonder if the "seven seals" of the *Gospel of Peter* were inspired by the seven seals of the NT Apocalypse (Rev 5:1: "sealed with seven seals" [κατεσφραγισμένον σφραγῖσιν ἑπτά]). In the NT Apocalypse it is the "Lion of the tribe of Judah," the "Root of David," the "Lamb" (i.e., Jesus) who is able to break open the seals (cf. Rev 5:5; 6:1), even as he is able in the *Gospel of Peter* to break the seven seals that are intended to prevent the opening of his tomb. Whatever their inspiration, *Peter*'s seven seals represent another secondary embellishment of the Passion Narrative.[21]

We are also told that the officials then "pitched a tent and kept guard" (σκηνὴν ἐκεῖ πήξαντες ἐφύλαξαν) (8:33b). The pitching of a tent further embellishes Matthew's story of the guard posted at the tomb of Jesus to keep watch. It implies that the guard will be spending the night, keeping watch for up to three days (8:30), probably in reference to Jesus' prophecy that is no longer extant. *Peter*'s vague third person in the verbs—"They placed [ἔθηκαν] the stone. . . . They put on it [ἐπέχρισαν] seven seals, and after pitching a tent they kept guard [ἐφύλαξαν]" (8:32–33)—suggests that the Jewish elders as well as the soldiers participated in the vigil at the tomb (and their presence is confirmed in 8:38). The author of the *Gospel of Peter* apparently does not realize that no

---

19. Nicklas, "Gedanken zum Verhältnis." Although Nicklas focuses on the Veronica traditions, his observations have relevance for critical study of the type of literature in which these traditions appear.

20. See Dan 6:18 LXX (6:16–17 ET), where Daniel is thrown into the lions' pit; the mouth of the pit is shut with a large stone and sealed (ἐσφραγίσατο) with the king's signet ring, "so that Daniel might not be removed." The same idea seems to be in play in Bel and Dragon 14–15.

21. A visionary work, *4 Bar.* 3:10, has also been suggested because God has sealed the earth with seven seals. In the *Acts of Pilate*, Joseph of Arimathea, who buried Jesus and is criticized and threatened for doing so, is locked in a room, with seals placed on the door. In Joseph's case, however, he is miraculously transported from the locked room without breaking the seals (*Acts of Pilate* 12:2; 15:6).

Jew, and certainly not Jews identified as "elders," would spend the night in a cemetery, given the Jewish concern to avoid impurity, not to mention fear of evil spirits believed to haunt cemeteries. The author of the *Gospel of Peter* apparently has also lost sight of the reason for the urgency to bury Jesus in the first place: the approaching "first day of unleavened bread, their feast" (2:5). The Jewish elders would have returned to their homes, readying themselves for the holy day; guarding the tomb would be left to the soldiers who, the author of *Peter* would have assumed, were Roman soldiers and so would have no interest in a Jewish holy day.

The embellishments, mostly of distinctive Matthean features, as well as the obvious lack of historical and cultural verisimilitude, once again place the *Gospel of Peter* in the second century and argue for its dependence on the first-century canonical Gospels. Had the *Gospel of Peter* originated in the middle of the first century and had the canonical Gospels made use of it, one would expect mention of a guard in more than one Gospel (Matthew) and the appearance of some of the other apologetic details.

In the Resurrection Narrative we find the *Gospel of Peter*'s most unusual features again greatly embellish Matthew's apologetic. The relevant portions of *Peter* read:

> [34]Early in the morning, when the Sabbath had dawned, there came a crowd from Jerusalem and the surrounding countryside to see the tomb that had been sealed. [35]Now in the night in which the Lord's day dawned, when the soldiers, two by two in every watch, were keeping guard, a loud sound rang out in heaven, [36]and they saw the heavens opened and two men come down from there in a great brightness and draw near to the tomb. [37]That stone which had been laid against the entrance to the tomb started of itself to roll and gave way to the side, and the tomb was opened, and both the young men entered. (9:34–37)

> [38]When now those soldiers saw this, they awoke the centurion and the elders (for they also were there keeping watch). [39]And while they were relating what they had seen, they saw again three men come out from the tomb, and two of them sustaining the other, and a cross following them, [40]and the heads of the two reaching to heaven, but that of him who was led by them by the hand overpassing the heavens. [41]And they heard a voice out of the heavens saying, "Have you preached to them that sleep?" [42]And from the cross there was heard the answer, "Yes." (10:38–42)

> [43]Those ones therefore took counsel with each other to go and report these things to Pilate. [44]And while yet deliberating, again the heavens were seen opened and a man having descended and having entered the tomb. [45]Seeing these things, they about the centurion hurried to Pilate at night, abandoning the tomb that they had been guarding. And they related all that they had seen, agonizing greatly and saying, "Truly he was a son of God!" [46]Answering, Pilate said, "I am clean of the blood of the Son of God; but this was decided by you." [47]Then coming, all were begging him and urging him to summon the centurion and soldiers, that they not tell what they had seen. [48]"For it is better," they said, "to make ourselves guilty of a great sin

before God, and not fall into the hands of the people of the Jews and be stoned." [49]Therefore Pilate commanded the centurion and the soldiers to say nothing. (11:43–49)

Almost every element in these three paragraphs contributes to *Gospel of Peter's* embellishment of Matthew's Easter story. *Peter's* version is especially focused on the number and nature of eyewitnesses at hand to witness the resurrection event. The opening verse tells readers that a "crowd from Jerusalem and the surrounding countryside" come to "see the tomb," as if on cue. Everyone seems to know that Sunday morning is the third day, when, according to Jesus' earlier prophecy, he would be raised up. All come to see if it is so. All we have in Matthew is what the Jewish leaders say to Pilate, to justify the posting of a guard. The posting of the guard makes it possible to have on hand hostile witnesses, even if, because of their fear, they witness very little (Matt 28:4).

Somewhat awkwardly the narrative in the next verse regresses to the soldiers watching the tomb. It is "the Lord's day" (ἡ κυριακή), *Peter* tells his readers (9:35; cf. 12:50). This term is not found in the canonical Gospels; it is a late expression that begins to emerge at the end of the first century (Rev 1:10; *Didache* 14.1) and becomes standard diction in the second century (*Acts of Peter* 29; *Acts of Paul* 7), not just as a way of referring to Sunday but as a conscious replacement of the Sabbath (Ign. *Magn.* 9.1–2; cf. Eusebius, *Hist. eccl.* 3.27.5).

We are told that soldiers keep guard "two by two in every watch" (ἀνὰ δύο δύο κατὰ φρουράν), which again underscores the value of their testimony (cf. Deut 17:6, ἐπὶ δυσὶν μάρτυσιν; 19:15, ἐπὶ στόματος δύο μαρτύρων). The "two by two" language matches more closely the NT Gospel tradition, especially as it is found in Luke (cf. Mark 6:7, δύο δύο; Luke 10:1, ἀνὰ δύο δύο). The point is that the soldiers are not all dozing through the night; at least two are awake and on watch at any given time.

As the Lord's day dawned, "a loud sound rang out in heaven" (9:35). Possibly that "sound" (φωνή) should be understood as *voice*. After all, a heavenly voice will be heard later in the narrative (10:41).[22] The loud sound/voice alerts the soldiers to the dramatic events about to unfold. (It is curious that the loud sound evidently was not loud enough to awaken the centurion and elders; the frightened soldiers had to wake them.) They see "the heavens opened and two men . . . in a great brightness" descend. The opening of the heavens recalls the baptism of Jesus (Matt 3:16; Luke 3:21; John 1:32, 51) and in general reflects apocalyptic imagery (cf. Rev 4:1). *Peter's* "two men . . . in great brightness" is borrowed from Luke's "two men . . . in dazzling apparel" (Luke 24:4; cf. 9:29 RSV: "His countenance was altered, and his raiment became dazzling white").

22. In the *Anaphora Pilati* 8, Pilate reports to Rome that on the first day of the week "exalted men appeared in the air, like lightning that strikes in winter. . . . A multitude of angels without number cried out and said, 'Glory be to God in the highest. . . .' At the sound of their voice [ἐκ τῆς φωνῆς] all the mountains and hills were shaken and the rocks split apart." Here is an allusion to Matt 28:2–5.

The single young man of Mark 16:5 and Matt 28:2, 5 (where he is identified as an angel) will later make his appearance in *Gospel of Peter* (in 11:44 and 13:55).

The two men who descended from heaven enter the tomb. Meanwhile the soldiers awaken the centurion and the elders. This will make it possible for the whole group of watchers to witness the resurrection take place. While the soldiers describe what they have seen, the two men and a third emerge from the tomb. *Peter* tells his readers that the heads of the two men reach heaven, while the head of the third (who is Jesus, of course) overpasses heaven (v. 40).

The supernatural height of the risen Jesus is part of what scholars call polymorphic Christology, which apparently developed in the second century.[23] The specific tradition of Jesus' great height is seen in second-century Christian literature. In the *Shepherd of Hermas* the seer says, "I saw an array of many men coming, and in the midst a man of such lofty stature that he stood taller than the tower" (83:1). This is very similar to the scene in the *Gospel of Peter*, where the risen Christ stands between the two angels who assist him, but his head reaches beyond heaven itself. Second-century *5 Ezra* 2:43–48 (= 2 Esd 2:43–48) describes "a young man of great stature, taller than any of the others, . . . more exalted than they. . . . 'He is the Son of God.'" In the late second-century *Acts of John* the apostle John relates that "sometimes he [the risen Jesus] appeared to me as a small man and unattractive, and then again as one reaching to heaven" (89).

The scene in the *Gospel of Peter* very much reflects these second-century traditions. The question about preaching to the dead ("to them that sleep") and the reply of "Yes" (10:41–42) together allude to the tradition of Christ's descent into hell, an idea that is hinted at in NT literature (Eph 4:8–20; 1 Pet 3:18–20, 22) and is greatly embellished in the second century and beyond (*Odes of Solomon* 4:10–20; *Epistula Apostolorum* 27; *Acts Pil.* 18:1; *Acts of Thomas* 10 and 32; *Teaching of Silvanus* NHC VII,4 104.2–14).[24]

The third paragraph (*Gos. Pet.* 11:43–49) is typical of the type of material found in the *Acts of Pilate*. The witnesses of Jesus' resurrection decide to report to Pilate. The centurion does so. While the witnesses are deliberating, "again the heavens were open and a man" descends and enters the tomb (11:44). This time we have an echo of the Markan and Matthean tradition. This second angelic descent prompts the centurion to hurry to Pilate. They say, "Truly he was a son of God!" (11:45), which was originally on the lips of the centurion alone (Mark 15:39; Matt 27:54). It is no longer a private confession, but a universal one.

Pilate asserts that he is "clean of the blood of the Son of God." This, of course, is an embellishment of Pilate's declaration in Matt 27:24, "I am innocent of this man's blood." In *Gospel of Peter*, Pilate's self-exculpatory "This was decided by you" alludes to the Jewish acceptance of responsibility in Matt 27:25, "His

---

23. Foster, *Gospel of Peter*, 165–68; Johnston, *Resurrection of Jesus*, 155–69. For a new proposal on the origin of the concept—that it may be seen as a prophetic fulfillment of Ps 18 LXX (18:6 LXX, "like a giant")—see Galbraith, "Whence the Giant Jesus?"

24. Charlesworth, "Origins of the *descensus ad inferos*," 378–83.

blood be on us and on our children!" In the *Gospel of Peter*, the Jewish leaders declare that "it is better to make ourselves guilty of a great sin before God, and not fall into the hands of the people of the Jews and be stoned" (v. 48). Such a statement, which obviously heightens the guilt of the Jewish leadership, wildly lacks verisimilitude. But the lack of verisimilitude was not obvious to either the author of the *Gospel of Peter* or his readers. It is clearly the product of the second century, whose Christian writers and readers knew little of first-century Jewish piety and therefore could entertain such an outlandish utterance.

Perhaps the most spectacular feature of the *Gospel of Peter* is its description of the cross that emerges from the tomb: "and a cross following them" (10:39). The tradition of a cross that accompanies Jesus also emerged in the second century. In the late second-century *Epistula apostolorum*, in both the Ethiopic and Coptic versions, at 16:4–5 Jesus is envisioned as returning to earth in judgment and accompanied by his cross: "Borne upon the wings of the clouds in glory, my cross going before me, I shall come to earth to judge the living and the dead" (Ethiopic); "with the wings of the clouds carrying me in glory, the sign [σημεῖον] of the cross [σταυρός] before me, I shall come down to the earth to judge the living and the dead" (Coptic, with Greek loanwords noted in brackets). Similarly in the Ethiopic *Apocalypse of Peter* (1:6), Jesus tells the apostle Peter: "I will come in a cloud of heaven with great power in my glory while my cross goes before my face" (alluding to Dan 7:13).[25]

The principal goal of the author of the *Gospel of Peter* was not to advance a new doctrine or a new Christology. All his material and editing, so far as we can judge from the extant Akhmîm excerpt, reflects canonical and extracanonical traditions that the leadership of the second-century church found acceptable. Even Bishop Serapion's belated decision to forbid the reading of the *Gospel of Peter* in church had more to do with what he thought Docetists were doing with it. And it is possible that Docetists or others possessed a significantly altered version of *Gospel of Peter*, one that did contain material that the "orthodox" of the late second century would have found objectionable.

The goal of the author of the *Gospel of Peter*, as Jeremiah Johnston recently demonstrated, was to provide the resurrection event with numerous credible witnesses, even if they were unsympathetic, and in doing so, to provide what he imagined was irrefutable proof for the resurrection of Jesus in the face of hostile skepticism emanating from both the synagogue and, especially, pagan critics like Celsus.[26] For example, Celsus asks:

> But who really saw [the resurrection]? A hysterical woman, as you admit and perhaps one other person—both deluded by his sorcery, or else so wrenched with grief at his failure that they hallucinated him risen from the dead by a sort of wishful thinking. . . . If this Jesus were trying to convince anyone of his powers, then surely he ought to have appeared first to the

25. Translation by Buchholz, *Eyes Will Be Opened*, 167.
26. Johnston, *Resurrection of Jesus*, 137–51.

Jews who treated him so badly—and to his accusers—indeed to everyone, everywhere. (*apud* Origen, *Contra Celsum* 2.55, 63)[27]

According to the *Gospel of Peter*, this is exactly what the risen Jesus did: He appeared to the Jews—his accusers—who treated him so badly and, indeed, to everyone else involved in his crucifixion. Therefore the witnesses featured in the canonical Gospels take a back seat to the Jewish elders and Roman soldiers. The women do eventually arrive at the tomb and find it empty (12:50–54), just as the canonical Gospels relate. They meet the young man, who explains that Jesus is risen (13:55–56). They flee (13:57). Our fragment of the *Gospel of Peter* ends with the grieving disciples and Peter and Andrew's decision to return to fishing (vv. 58–60). If the fragment had preserved a few more verses, it is most probable that we would read about the eleven apostles meeting the risen Jesus. The *Gospel of Peter* has not deleted the canonical tradition of witnesses; it has dramatically supplemented that tradition. *Peter* thus meets the requirements of a skeptic like Celsus: *All* see the risen Jesus: his accusers, those who crucified him and guarded his tomb, women, his disciples, even crowds from Jerusalem and the surrounding countryside.

Matthew's Gospel, with its story of the posting of a guard, which later reported to the Jewish leadership what had happened, gave the author of the *Gospel of Peter* what he needed in order to develop a convincing apologetic. The discovery of the empty tomb by frightened women, the subsequent discovery of the tomb by two male disciples, and an appearance or two to confused, doubting male disciples—these features hardly amount to a body of testimony that skeptics like Celsus and Porphyry could find convincing. In order to refute this kind of skepticism, the *Gospel of Peter* greatly augments and embellishes the Resurrection Narrative.[28]

The author of the *Gospel of Peter* gave dramatic and creative voice to an apologetic designed to fend off the charge that the resurrection of Jesus lacked credible witnesses. A few frightened women and grief-stricken disciples were not convincing. What was needed were several witnesses, many of whom were not followers, who indeed see the risen Jesus exit the tomb in terrifying power. This is what the author of the *Gospel of Peter* provides. His creative rewrite of the canonical Gospels' respective accounts of the passion and resurrection of Jesus was so compelling and so effectively answered some of the growing skepticism that it was read in church in some regions, at least for a time on Bishop Serapion's watch. Not until the bishop and others became convinced that the *Gospel of Peter* either contained or in some way could be interpreted in ways

---

27. I follow the translation in Hoffmann, *Celsus on the True Doctrine*, 61–62, 67–68.

28. Porphyry, like Celsus before him, was familiar with the Gospel narratives, including accounts of the resurrection. We do not know if he was acquainted with the embellished eyewitness tradition of the *Gospel of Peter*. One may wonder, for it is interesting that Porphyry, reasoning as had Celsus but going beyond him, asks why the risen Christ did not appear to the Roman governor, to Herod, to the Jewish high priest, or even to Roman senators! (*apud* Macarius Magnes, *Apocriticus* 2.14–15).

that supported false teaching did the bishop finally forbid further public reading of the work. The *Gospel of Peter* did not expand the Gospel canon, but it did expand a key element of the Gospel canon's proclamation.

The next text under review evidently was never read publicly in church. As we shall see, its author(s) and readers probably never intended it to be public. After all, its contents are secret. But this gospel did compete, in its own way, with the better-known public gospels.

THE *GOSPEL OF THOMAS*

As it so happens, we have physical artifacts that may shed light on the question of the canon, particularly with respect to the practice of reading sacred texts in public in church. The most helpful data that we have relates to the *Gospel of Thomas*, the most talked-about extracanonical gospel, which some even advocate adding to the New Testament canon of scripture.

Thus far three Greek fragments of the *Gospel of Thomas* have come to light, though at the time of their discovery no one knew that they belonged together and were part of a work called the *Gospel of Thomas* mentioned by church fathers beginning in the third century. All three Greek fragments were discovered at Oxyrhynchus (P.Oxy. 1, P.Oxy. 654, and P.Oxy. 655). Given how widespread patristic testimony is (ranging from the 3rd c. to the 6th c.),[29] *Gospel of Thomas* must have been known in several regions and not just in Egypt. It was only with the 1945 discovery of the apparently full text of *Thomas*, in what is now Codex II (tractate 2) of the Coptic Nag Hammadi library, that scholars realized what the Greek fragments were.

Coptic *Thomas* was found to comprise a prologue and 114 logia. There is no narrative. Jesus speaks or responds to questions. There is no birth account, no miracle stories, and no passion week or resurrection account. *Thomas* is regarded as a Sayings Gospel and is compared to Q, the sayings source on which Matthew and Luke evidently drew, as well as to a few other gnostic sayings documents. *Thomas* exhibits numerous parallels with the Synoptic Gospels, as well as with the Fourth Gospel and several other New Testament writings.

Because some of the Thomasine sayings are briefer than their synoptic counterparts, some scholars think *Thomas* originated early and independently of the NT Gospels. Because *Thomas* is a collection of sayings, perhaps a bit like Q, some argue that *Thomas* is primitive and predates the NT narrative Gospels. Some scholars date *Thomas*, at least its earliest form, to the middle of the first century and even link it to James and Jerusalem. They do this by assuming that *Thomas* underwent a series of expansions as it moved from the middle of

---

29. Gathercole, *Gospel of Thomas*, 35–59. Gathercole has assembled 47 named testimonia to the *Gospel of Thomas* that date from the third to the sixth centuries. I will reference a few of these below.

the first century to its final form sometime in the second century, or that the author(s) of *Thomas* had access to different synoptic sources, for which there is otherwise no evidence.[30] This tactic makes it possible to excise materials that obviously reflect the second century or are obviously dependent on NT writings. Such a tactic, of course, is gratuitous and amounts to special pleading in that the extant evidence is modified through imagination and preference to fit the theory.[31]

Writing about 225, Hippolytus of Rome speaks of a group that say "the kingdom of heaven" is "to be sought within man, about which they expressly pass on a statement in the Gospel entitled 'according to Thomas,' as follows: 'He who seeks me will find me in children seven years old'" (*Haer.* 5.7.20–21). The saying seems to match *Gospel of Thomas* §4: "The person old in days will not hesitate to ask a little child of seven days concerning the place of life—and he shall live." It may also allude to *Thomas* §3: "The kingdom of God is within you and it is without."

A few years later Origen speaks of groups that have produced new gospels, including the "'Gospel according to Thomas,' . . . and the 'Gospel according to Matthias' and many others" (καὶ τὸ κατὰ Θωμᾶν εὐαγγέλιον καὶ τὸ κατὰ Ματθίαν καὶ ἄλλα πλείονα) (*Hom. Luc.* 1.1). One century later Eusebius, the great church historian and apologist, speaks of "heretics who put forward in the names of the apostles [τὰς ὀνόματι τῶν ἀποστόλων πρὸς τῶν αἱρετικῶν προφερομένας] . . . gospels as if of Peter, or Thomas, or Matthias, or of any others in addition to them" (*Hist. eccl.* 3.25.6). A few years later Cyril of Jerusalem speaks of "falsely attributed" gospels, claiming that the "Manichees wrote the 'Gospel according to Thomas'" (*Catecheses* 4.36; cf. 6.31). Both *Matthias* and *Thomas* are classified as apocryphal in the *Decretum Gelasianum*. *Matthias* also appears as apocryphal in the Catalogue of the Sixty Canonical Books.

The *Decretum Gelasianum* not only classifies *Thomas* as apocryphal; it also adds the note, "which the Manichaeans use [*quibus Manichaei utuntur*]," recalling Cyril's assertion. The remark is probably intended to be prejudicial. Yet the *Decretum* falls short of claiming that the Manichaeans wrote *Thomas*. That the Manichaeans found it acceptable for reading and study is not surprising, but there is no reason to think they wrote it.

Near the end of the fourth century, Didymus the Blind warns of apocryphal gospels, such as "according to Thomas" and "according to Peter," reminding readers that a bishop once said, "We prevent the study of the apocrypha, because of those who are not able to distinguish what has been combined in

---

30. For two prominent examples, see Patterson, *Thomas and Jesus*; DeConick, *Original Gospel of Thomas*; DeConick, *Thomas in Translation*.

31. See Schröter, *Erinnerung an Jesu Worte*, 135. Schröter rightly complains of the tendency to hypothesize the existence of various pre-synoptic sources in order to avoid the conclusion that *Thomas* is in fact dependent on the Synoptic Gospels.

them by heretics" (*Commentarii in Ecclesiasten* 8.3–7). Also writing in the late fourth century, Jerome and Ambrose mention a gospel "according to Thomas" (Jerome, *Commentariorum in Matthaeum Praefatio*; Ambrose, *Expositio Evangelii secundum Lucam* 1.2).

The lateness of these testimonies supports the conclusion that the *Gospel of Thomas* was not written until the second half of the second century. The suggestion that *Thomas* was unknown until the early third century because it was composed in eastern Syria, perhaps in Edessa, is not convincing.[32]

Although some scholars continue to maintain that *Thomas* in its original form was independent of the NT Gospels,[33] several scholars disagree. Recent studies by Simon Gathercole and Mark Goodacre have concluded that *Thomas*, in its original Greek form, as well as in its later Coptic version, is dependent on the Synoptic Gospels.[34] They find that *Thomas* knows of all sources and traditions that found their way into the NT Gospels, including Double Tradition, Triple Tradition, Tradition unique to Matthew, and Tradition unique to Luke. This also includes clear-cut examples of Matthean and Lukan redaction.

In the first example, Luke's improvement on Mark's awkward syntax appears in *Thomas*, in a saying preserved in Greek. The Greek of *Thomas* is an exact match with the Greek of Luke:

> οὐ γάρ ἐστιν κρυπτὸν ἐὰν μὴ ἵνα φανερωθῇ, "For there is nothing hidden except that it be made manifest." (Mark 4:22, my trans.)

> οὐ γάρ ἐστιν κρυπτὸν ὃ οὐ φανερὸν γενήσεται, "For there is nothing hidden that will not be made manifest." (Luke 8:17, my trans.)

> [οὐ γάρ ἐστ]ιν κρυπτὸν ὃ οὐ φανε[ρὸν γενήσεται], "[For there i]s nothing hidden that will not be [made manifest]." (P.Oxy. 654, lines 29–31 = *Gos. Thom.* §5)

In the next two examples, the Greek text of *Thomas* is not extant, but it is still apparent that *Thomas* has followed Matthean redaction in the first example (where "mouth" is inserted) and Lukan redaction in the second example (where "division" and "divided" have been added):

---

32. See C. A. Evans and Patterson, "Doubting Thomas." Patterson (on 34–35) explains that *Thomas* is "a Syrian, or eastern Syrian gospel, and so it did not circulate widely in the west. . . . It wasn't a text that was relevant for Christians in the west and so it didn't gain currency in the west." It should be noted that Edessa, the principal city of eastern Syria, was not isolated but rather "was a junction of important caravan roads." These roads went "from Antioch to Edessa" and carried "in addition to material goods, religious and philosophical thoughts" and, I might add, literature. Quotations are from Uro, *Thomas*, 30.

33. Meyer, *Hidden Sayings of Jesus*; Patterson, *Thomas and Jesus*; Pagels, *Beyond Belief.*

34. Gathercole, *Composition of the Gospel of Thomas*; Goodacre, *Thomas and the Gospels*. Both Gathercole and Goodacre build on Tuckett's earlier study, which also concluded that the author of *Thomas* was familiar with the Synoptic Gospels. See Tuckett, "Thomas and the Synoptics"; Tuckett, "Thomasevangelium."

There is nothing outside a man which by going into him can defile him; but the things which come out of a man are what defile him. (Mark 7:15 RSV)

Not what goes into the *mouth* defiles a man, but what comes out of the *mouth*, this defiles a man. (Matt 15:11 RSV, emphasis added)

Whatever goes into your *mouth* will not defile you. Rather, that which comes out of your *mouth*, that is what will defile you. (*Gos. Thom.* §14, emphasis added)

Do not think that I have come to bring peace on earth; I have not come to bring peace, but a sword. (Matt 10:34 RSV)

Do you think that I have come to give peace on earth? No, I tell you, but rather *division*; for henceforth in one house there will be five *divided*. . . . They will be *divided*. . . . (Luke 12:51–53 RSV, emphasis added)

Perhaps people will think that I have come to bring peace upon the world. They do not know that I have come to bring *divisions* on the earth. . . . (*Gos. Thom.* §16, emphasis added)

In the following example, we again have *Thomas* preserved in the original Greek. The Thomasine logion reflects Luke, where the evangelist uses the word "acceptable" (δεκτός) in order to agree with his quotation of Isa 61:1–2:

οὐκ ἔστιν προφήτης ἄτιμος εἰ μὴ ἐν τῇ πατρίδι αὐτοῦ καὶ ἐν τοῖς συγγενεῦσιν αὐτοῦ καὶ ἐν τῇ οἰκίᾳ αὐτοῦ, "a prophet is not without honor, except in his home country and among his relatives and in his house." (Mark 6:4, my trans.)

οὐκ ἔστιν προφήτης ἄτιμος εἰ μὴ ἐν τῇ πατρίδι καὶ ἐν τῇ οἰκίᾳ αὐτοῦ, "a prophet is not without honor, except in (his) home country and in his house." (Matt 13:57, my trans.)

προφήτης ἐν τῇ ἰδίᾳ πατρίδι τιμὴν οὐκ ἔχει, "a prophet has no honor in his home country." (John 4:44, my trans.)

οὐδεὶς προφήτης δεκτός ἐστιν ἐν τῇ πατρίδι αὐτοῦ, "no prophet is *acceptable* in his home country." (Luke 4:24, my trans., emphasis added)

οὐκ ἔστιν δεκτὸς προφήτης ἐν τῇ π(ατ)ρίδι αὐτ[ο]ῦ, οὐδὲ ἰατρὸς ποιεῖ θεραπείας εἰς τοὺς γεινώσκοντας αὐτό(ν), "a prophet is not *acceptable* in his home country, nor does a physician heal those who know him." (P.Oxy. 1, lines 9–14 = *Gos. Thom.* §31, italics added)

In the final example *Thomas* follows Luke, which speaks of lending and expecting a return:

Give to him who begs from you, and do not refuse him who would borrow from you. (Matt 5:42 RSV)

Give to everyone who begs from you; of him who takes away your goods *do not ask them again.* (Luke 6:30, my trans., emphasis added)

If you *lend to those from whom you hope to receive* . . . (Luke 6:34 RSV, emphasis added)

And lend, *expecting nothing in return.* (Luke 6:35 RSV, emphasis added)

If you have money, *do not lend it at interest,* but give it to the one from whom *you will not get it back.* (*Gos. Thom.* §95, emphasis added).

There are several more examples where synoptic material, either wording or order, has influenced the *Gospel of Thomas.* There are also numerous examples of *Thomas* reflecting second-century Syrian traditions, some of which probably did not emerge until the second half of the second century. These traditions confirm the Syrian provenance of *Thomas,* argue for a late date, and support the evidence suggesting that *Thomas,* like other second-century Christian writings, is familiar with the NT Gospels. Indeed, *Thomas* seems influenced by about half of the writings of the New Testament.[35]

The authority behind the *Gospel of Thomas* is, of course, none other than the apostle Thomas, of "doubting Thomas" fame (John 20:26–29). In second-century Syria, Thomas was highly regarded as an authoritative apostle and considered perhaps the twin brother of Jesus. In the *Gospel of Thomas* we are told, "These are the secret words that the living Jesus spoke and that Didymos Judas Thomas wrote down" (*Gos. Thom.* Prologue [NHC II,*2*] 32.10–11). The apostle Thomas is often called Judas Thomas in Syrian Christian literature (e.g., Syriac John 14:22; *Thomas the Contender* [NHC II,*7*] 138.1–3) and sometimes Didymus, "Twin," as well (e.g., *Acts of Thomas* 1:2; 11:5; 39:1, "twin brother of Christ"). The Syrian Christian belief that Judas Thomas was the (twin) brother of Jesus likely was based, at least in part, on Mark 6:3, where it is noted that among the brothers of Jesus was one "Judas." Perhaps this brother was Judas Thomas the disciple. As Jesus' twin, Thomas was privileged with much deeper insight.

Explicit claims of apostolic authorship, where the apostolic figure is embedded in the gospel narrative itself, are characteristic of second- and third-century pseudepigraphal literature.[36] In the *Gospel of Peter,* for example, Peter speaks in the first person: "I, Simon Peter, and my brother Andrew took our nets and

35. See the list of parallels in C. A. Evans, Webb, and Wiebe, *Nag Hammadi Texts and the Bible,* 88–144. The attempt to reverse the evidence, that is, to claim that half the writings of the NT have quoted, have alluded to, or have knowledge of *Thomas* will then need to explain why *Thomas,* supposedly so widely known, remains unacknowledged until the third century.

36. On this important point, see Schröter, "Apocryphal and Canonical Gospels," esp. 30–31. Schröter (35) rightly concludes that *Thomas* did not originate "before the second half of the second century."

went to the sea" (*Gos. Pet.* 14.60). We find the same thing in a gnostic apocalypse: "As the Savior was sitting in the temple, . . . he said to me, 'Peter'" (*Apocalypse of Peter* [NHC VII,*3*] 70.13–20). James the brother of Jesus speaks in the first person in a gnostic apocalypse: "The Lord spoke to me. . . . 'I have given you a sign of these things, James, my brother'" (*1 Apocalypse of James* [NHC V,*3*] 24.10–14). The explicit claim of apostolic authorship that we see in the *Gospel of Thomas* reflects this second-century setting.

There are also verbal matches with distinctive Syrian forms of the dominical tradition, which again point to a second-century Syrian setting for the *Gospel of Thomas*. Some of these parallels are with Tatian's *Diatessaron*, a harmony of the four NT Gospels that was especially influential in Syria. For example, the Synoptic Gospels speak of Jesus coming into his home *country* (Matt 13:54, 57; Mark 6:4; Luke 4:24), but in the *Diatessaron* and the later Syriac Gospels (Old Syriac Mark 6:4; Old Syriac Matt 13:57; Peshitta Matt 13:54; Peshitta Luke 4:15), Jesus comes into his own *town* (cf. *Gos. Thom.* §31). As another example, the Synoptic Gospels say the seed "fell *along* the path" (Matt 13:4; Mark 4:4; Luke 8:5), but in the *Diatessaron*, it fell "*on* the path" (cf. *Gos. Thom.* §9). In the Synoptic Gospels, Jesus tells his disciples to proclaim what they "hear in your ear" (Matt 10:27 NIV), but in the *Diatessaron* and in Syrian tradition (Old Syriac and Peshitta Matt 10:27) and in *Thomas* (§33) it is "ears."

There are several examples where Syrian dominical tradition, probably influenced by Tatian's *Diatessaron*, agrees with the form of the tradition found in *Thomas*. For example, in Greek, Matthew's Jesus says, "Do not think that I have come to bring peace to the earth; I have come not come to bring peace, but a sword" (Matt 10:34). But in Syriac Matthew he says, "I came not to bring peace but *division* of minds and a sword" (emphasis added), and in the Pseudo-Clementine *Recognitions*, a work that circulated in Syria, Jesus says, "I have not come that I might cast peace on the earth but rather *war*" (emphasis added). Both distinctive Syrian elements—division and war—appear in the Thomasine form of the saying: "They do not know that it is *division* I have come to cast upon the earth: fire, sword, and *war*" (*Gos. Thom.* §16a, emphasis added).

In *Gospel of Thomas* §§12–13 we have what appears to be the attempt to subordinate Peter and Matthew to Thomas. In what is a new form of Peter's famous confession (Matt 16:13–20; Mark 8:27–30), neither Peter nor Matthew can properly answer Jesus' question about who he is. But Thomas can, and he is privileged with secret revelation, which he cannot share with his fellow disciples. Taken with the prologue, in which we are told that Thomas has written down the secret words of Jesus, *Thomas* §§12–13 justifies the view of the people who wrote, studied, and circulated *Thomas* that the *Gospel of Thomas* is superior to the popular and widely read Gospel of Matthew.

All these factors—that *Thomas* remains unknown and unmentioned until the third century, that it sees itself as a rival of the well-established Matthew, that *Thomas* is familiar with the synoptic tradition and many other NT writings, that *Thomas* appears to be influenced by the *Diatessaron* and other distinctive second-century Syrian traditions—make it unlikely that *Thomas* was composed before the second half of the second century. Indeed, given its familiarity with distinctive *Diatessaron* readings, it is probable that the *Gospel of Thomas* was composed no earlier than the late 170s.

The late date of *Gospel of Thomas*—not to mention the oddness of its presentation of Jesus, who appears to be a champion of Encratite views (radical celibacy, vegetarianism, asceticism, and the like), as well as its utter lack of verisimilitude—no doubt worked against any claim of canonical authority and status. But did the author of *Thomas* and its readers even entertain canonicity? It seems clear that they viewed the *Gospel of Thomas* as in some sense a rival of the Gospel of Matthew, or at least saw the apostle Thomas as superior to the apostles Peter and Matthew, who were highly regarded in the West; but was *Thomas* intended for public reading in the churches and so, in that sense, a canonical writing? This is an important question, and the nature of the physical evidence seems to provide an answer.

Recently Larry Hurtado, a well-known textual critic and expert in early Christian literature as artifacts, has studied the three extant Greek fragments of *Thomas* mentioned above.[37] Here I summarize his findings. The papyrus P.Oxy. 1 (= *Gos. Thom.* §§26–30 + 77b) is part of a single leaf from a codex. It is written in a small hand and presents no spacing, punctuation, or reader's aids. Hurtado concludes that the codex had been prepared for private study. Then P.Oxy. 654 (= *Gos. Thom.* §§1–7) is a text written on the back, or outer, side of an opisthograph bookroll, whose inner side contained a land survey written at the end of the second century or the beginning of the third century. Although there are paragraph markers and some punctuation (which appear to have been added by someone other than the original copyist), Hurtado believes that this fragment, in a poor-quality hand, was also intended for private study. He concludes the same with regard to P.Oxy. 655 (= *Gos. Thom.* §§24 + 36–39), which comprises fragments of a papyrus bookroll.

In a study published a few years later, AnneMarie Luijendijk agrees with most of Hurtado's findings.[38] However, she thinks that, because of the punctuation and paragraph markers, P.Oxy. 654 may have been intended for public reading out loud. Perhaps, but the fact that the text is on the back side of an opisthograph makes it unlikely that it was intended for reading in a church assembly. Nevertheless, the possibility that the text might be read aloud in a small, select group (in keeping with the theme of "secrecy" of *Thomas*) cannot be ruled out.

---

37. Hurtado, "Greek Fragments of the *Gospel of Thomas*." See also Attridge, "Greek Fragments"; Grenfell, Drexel, and Hunt, *New Sayings of Jesus*; Grenfell and Hunt, *Oxyrhynchus Papyri: Part IV*; and Fitzmyer, "Oxyrhynchus Logoi."
38. Luijendijk, "*Thomas* in the Third Century."

The *Gospel of Thomas* also survives in a fourth-century Coptic translation. It is extant as the second tractate in one of a dozen codices recovered near Nag Hammadi, Egypt, shortly after the Second World War.[39] A popular and oft-told account of the discovery of these leather-bound codices, around December of 1945, would have us believe that a couple of Egyptian villagers, in search of black earth for their vegetable garden, found the books in a jar, not too far from the bank of the Nile River. James Robinson and his students and colleagues have been major proponents of this version.[40] However, it is much more likely that the story is a piece of imaginative apologetic, told by the local villagers to avoid criminal charges for looting and grave robbery.[41] The original details relating to the find, as Jean Doresse learned—without intimidating Egyptian officials present—in a series of visits in 1947, 1948, 1949, and 1950, was that the codices were looted from Coptic Christian burial sites.[42] This is plausible, for other books, many gnostic, have been recovered from Coptic burial sites, including the aforementioned Akhmîm Codex (aka Codex Panopolitanus), which contains an excerpt of the *Gospel of Peter*; the celebrated Tchacos Codex, which contains almost the whole text of the *Gospel of Judas* plus three other gnostic tractates; and perhaps also the Askew Codex, the Bruce Codex, and the Berlin Gnostic Codex (BG 8502).[43] There is speculation, taken as gospel in some circles, that the Nag Hammadi Library and other gnostic codices were part of a Pachomian monastery and were hidden following the *Festal Letter* of 367 by Athanasius. That speculation has been subjected to trenchant criticism. There simply is no evidence that these codices ever had anything to do with a Christian church, school, or monastery.[44] The theory that the Nag Hammadi Codices were once

---

39. Nag Hammadi Codex (NHC) II,2. The Coptic text and numerous modern-language translations are widely available. Still quite handy is Guillaumont et al., *Gospel according to Thomas*, giving the Coptic text (with Greek loanwords) and English translation on facing pages. One will also want to see Lambdin, "Gospel of Thomas."

40. The story about finding the jar, complete with fear of jinn, is ubiquitous. One may wish to see J. Robinson, "From the Cliff to Cairo"; Meyer, *Gnostic Discoveries*, 13–31.

41. For a succinct account of the story and a compelling critique, see Goodacre, "How Reliable Is the Story?"; Denzey Lewis and Blount, "Rethinking the Origins." Rodolphe Kasser and Martin Krause strongly disagree with much of James Robinson's story of the find. See J. Robinson et al., *Introduction* (vol. 12 of the *Facsimile Edition*), 3 n. 1. In my opinion the studies by Goodacre, Denzey Lewis, and Blount have obliterated Robinson's account of the discovery of the Nag Hammadi Codices.

42. Doresse, *Secret Books*, 128–34.

43. So Denzey Lewis and Blount, "Rethinking the Origins," 404–5. See also Johnston, *Resurrection of Jesus*, 17–18 n. 21. The Bruce Codex (= Bruce 96 in the Bodleian Library, Oxford)—a gnostic codex containing what might be the *Books of Jeu* (mentioned in the *Pistis Sophia*), purchased by James Bruce in 1769 in Upper Egypt—had also been looted from a Coptic burial site. The Askew Codex, which contains the *Pistis Sophia*, is housed in the British Library (= BL Additional MS 5114). It was acquired by Anthony Askew in the eighteenth century. The Berlin Codex, discovered at Akhmîm, was purchased in Cairo in 1896. Among other tractates, it contains the *Gospel of Mary*. The Theban Magical Library, which was discovered by Egyptian peasants in the early nineteenth century, may have been looted from a tomb. For a recent study of the contents and murky history of this interesting collection of magical and alchemical texts, see Dosoo, "Theban Magical Library."

44. Emmel, "Coptic Gnostic Texts," here esp. 36; Denzey Lewis and Blount, "Rethinking the Origins," 409–10.

part of a Pachomian monastery and therefore may have enjoyed quasi-canonical status is highly dubious.[45]

Why were gnostic books, as well as other books, buried in Christian graves and burial caves? It is possible that books were thought to offer postmortem protection, just as iron and, especially, crucifixion nails were thought to offer protection. In effect, the books were amulets.[46] Burial with a book may also have been viewed as a mark of distinction. The *content* of the book may have been of little importance. There is yet another possibility. The gnostic books, written in Sahidic Coptic of the fourth and fifth centuries, may have been part of an Egyptian cultural renaissance, in which Egyptians, whether they could speak or not speak the Coptic used in Egypt, took pride in the language of Egypt's ancient and glorious past. As Stephen Emmel has recently put it, these books were commissioned by Egyptians who "wanted these books *in Coptic*, rather than in Greek,"[47] even if these Egyptians were not fluent in Coptic.

And finally, it is worth noting that no Christian book of scripture contains the *Gospel of Thomas*. For early examples, P[75] contains only Luke and John (and perhaps, we may conjecture, a companion volume may have contained Matthew and Mark), and P[45] contains the four Gospels and Acts. Thus it is with all of the later New Testament manuscripts. It should also be pointed out that no gnostic codex—and we now have several—contains a NT Gospel or any other NT (or OT) writing. Taken as a whole, the physical evidence—the extant artifacts, not what we speculate may have existed—provides no support whatsoever for the notion that *Thomas* was viewed as a fifth Gospel or was read in churches. Even in Egypt, where *Thomas* evidently was popular in some circles (in Oxyrhynchus, in any event), there simply is no evidence that it was regarded as scripture.

SHOULD THE NEW TESTAMENT BE UPDATED?

This brings us to the recent and eccentric proposal emanating from the Jesus Seminar, based in California, that the New Testament canon of scripture should be expanded, to include, among others, the *Gospel of Thomas*. In a book titled *A New New Testament*, the canon of the New Testament has been expanded from twenty-seven to forty books.[48] This curious publication quite surely reveals the kind of thinking that dominated the Jesus Seminar's deliberations back in the 1980s and 1990s, which came to fruition in the Seminar's principal publica-

---

45. As argued years ago by Brakke, "Canon Formation"; and more recently Denzey Lewis and Blount, "Rethinking the Origins," 410–12. Athanasius was not concerned with Gnosticism or gnostic texts; he was concerned with Arian (followers of Arius) and Melitian (followers of Melitius of Lycopolis) heresies.

46. On books and texts as possessing magical power, see Hezser, *Jewish Literacy*, 209–26.

47. Emmel, "Coptic Gnostic Texts," 46–48, with quotation from 47.

48. Taussig, *A New New Testament*. The dedication page credits Robert Funk, co-founder of the Jesus Seminar, as the one "who first thought about *A New New Testament*." The Foreword (xi–xv) is by the other co-founder, John Dominic Crossan.

tions: *The Five Gospels* (1993) and *The Acts of Jesus* (1998). In these books the authentic words and deeds of Jesus, as imagined by the members of the Jesus Seminar, are indicated by red and pink type; the doubtful and clearly inauthentic words and deeds are indicated by gray and bold black type.

The writings that Taussig and company have added to the New Testament are the *Prayer of Thanksgiving* (NHC VI,7), the *Gospel of Thomas* (NHC II,2), four portions of the *Odes of Solomon* (extant in various Syriac MSS), the *Thunder: Perfect Mind* (NHC VI,2), the *Gospel of Mary* (BG 8502,1; P.Oxy. 3525; P.Ryl. 463), the *Gospel of Truth* (NHC I,3), the *Prayer of the Apostle Paul* (NHC I,1), the *Acts of Paul and Thecla* (various Greek and Coptic MSS), the *Letter of Peter to Philip* (VIII,2), and the *Apocryphon of John* (NHC II,1; III,1; IV,1; BG 8502,2). Most of the added books come from the Nag Hammadi Codices (NHC) and the Berlin Gnostic Codex (BG 8502). The *Odes of Solomon* is an early second-century Syrian Christian work, and the *Acts of Paul and Thecla* is a fanciful romance. Although the *Gospel of Thomas* is numbered among the mostly gnostic materials in the Nag Hammadi Codices, some argue that it too is a second-century Syrian Christian work.[49]

The book *A New New Testament* raises a myriad of questions. First, why have Taussig and his colleagues drawn so heavily on gnostic writings? Why not include some of the so-called Apostolic Fathers? After all, some of these writings do appear in early Christian codices and collections of scripture. *Thomas* and the gnostic writings never do. Also, if we include the *Acts of Paul and Thecla*, then why not some of the other extracanonical books of Acts? Second, does it really make sense to lump together the canonical writings—whose authors embrace the OT, the God of the OT, and Israel's heritage—with gnostic writings? These gnostic documents reject or radically reinterpret the Old Testament; denounce as evil the physical world and the God of the OT, who made it; embrace a second god; and in general show little respect for Israel's heritage, sometimes even giving expression to anti-Semitic sentiments. How does gnostic bitheism fit within the monotheism of the traditional New Testament writings and the Jewish matrix out of which they arose?

Third, would the authors of many of these gnostic writings, including the *Gospel of Thomas*, even want their writings lumped together with those of the "Great Church"? This question leads to a fourth and related question. Many of the gnostic writings, including the *Gospel of Thomas*, refer to themselves as "secret," that is, not for public reading and wide distribution. This understanding flies in the face of the earliest understanding of canonical scripture in the early church, in which what was to be read in assemblies was what was regarded as canonical (the rule of authority, against which all theology was to be measured). Gnostic authors and readers did not want their secret texts to be read in public. In what sense, then, were they "canonical," as the first generations of Christians understood this concept?

---

49. McDonald, *New Testament*, 336, raises some of these questions.

As one would expect in a work produced by members and sympathizers of the Jesus Seminar, the latest possible dates for the canonicals are advanced, while the earliest possible dates for the extracanonicals are assumed. This allows for a great deal of overlap between the writing times of the canonicals and the extra-canonicals. Taussig and his colleagues explain to readers that the time period from which they made their selections is 50 to 175 CE. This is a bit risky, for one or two of their new writings could well fall outside this range. Although it is popular to date the *Gospel of Thomas* to the first century (e.g., 70–90 CE), a careful reading suggests a date not much earlier than 180 CE. This writing shows its familiarity with distinctive synoptic traditions and redaction, with *Diatessaron* readings, with Tatian's radical Encratism, and with other Syrian traditions that emerged in the second half of the second century, as shown above. And how confident are we that the gnostic documents, found in late fourth-century codices, all date to times before 175 CE?

Taussig's proposed new New Testament is an interesting thought experiment and is in some ways reflective of today's academic sectarianism and presumption.[50] What motivates the quest for a new New Testament, we are told, is the hope to break the "churches' strangleholds on what they deem unarguable truth about a certain kind of Jesus."[51] Indeed, this concern does seem to lie behind the production of many of the works reviewed in the preceding chapter, works counted as NT Apocrypha. But the Jesus we find in the writings that the church selected—over the course of centuries, in ad hoc settings and in formal councils—seems to be a Jesus that is deeply rooted in his Jewish first-century setting, a setting that ongoing historical and archaeological work continues to confirm and clarify. The NT Gospels that narrate the life, teaching, death, and resurrection of this Jesus exhibit verisimilitude, which archaeologists appreciate. The apocryphal writings do not, which is why archaeologists ignore them.[52]

The Jesuses found in the apocryphal writings, including those included in the proposed expanded New Testament, tend to be far removed from the early

---

50. In Taussig, *A New New Testament*, 555–58, we are told that a Council convened for several meetings from August 2011 till February 2012. The names and credentials of the nineteen Council members are listed. Their task was "to determine which works from the first two centuries should be added to the traditional New Testament to form" a new New Testament (Taussig, *A New New Testament*, 555). Evidently these nineteen Council members think their number, learning, and wisdom constitute a gravitas that outweighs that of the many councils held and numerous treatises written in the first five centuries of the church.

51. Taussig, *A New New Testament*, xix. Talk of "strangleholds," as well as the discussion of the canon process (xxiii–xxvi), caricatures the actual history of the formation of the Christian canon. One will want to read McDonald, *Old Testament*; McDonald, *New Testament*. In a sense, the Jesus Seminar's understanding of the Christian canon is not too far removed from the conspiracy theories presupposed by books like *The Da Vinci Code*. The underlying premise of this novel is that both Christology and the canon of scripture were manipulated by a handful of church leaders, who unfairly excluded equally valid writings and interpretations.

52. Major works on Jesus and archaeology rely heavily on the NT Gospels and make no use of the extracanonical gospels. For an example, see James H. Charlesworth, ed., *Jesus and Archaeology* (Grand Rapids: Eerdmans, 2006). Of the thirty-one contributors, one-third are archaeologists and about one-third are Jewish scholars. Not one of these contributors relies on extracanonical sources.

Jewish Jesus. But perhaps this is what some modern scholars and clergy prefer. A Jesus whose teachings and lifestyle resemble those of Cynics and Buddhists is today very attractive in some settings. A Jesus who is not divine, who performed no miracles, whose death saves no one, and who was not raised from the dead—this is a scandal-free Jesus. He is a Jesus who causes no embarrassment for the modern academic who takes his cue from modern secularism and skepticism.[53] This is the thinking that seems to lie behind the proposed new New Testament. It is very unlikely, however, that any church will adopt it. The old New Testament has been read and studied for two millennia, and it has served the church well. I am confident that will continue.

SUMMING UP

The writings that make up the collection of sacred scripture known as the New Testament, which in combination with the Old Testament make up the Christian canon of scripture, were vetted formally and (mostly) informally over a period of at least five hundred years. The early church's decisions on which books are authoritative and should be read publicly and on which books should be regarded as apocryphal and were not to be read publicly—these decisions were not made in haste. Arguments for and against were heard, differences of opinion were aired, and eventually decisions were made. In the end, the church opted for what might be described as a "minimal" canon, including only writings of which almost everyone approved. Informed, critical review of the church's decision, in the light of historical and archaeological verisimilitude, strongly supports the conclusion that the church decided wisely.

---

53. This was very much the thinking of the old Comparative Religions school of thought (or what in Germany was called the *Religionsgeschichtliche Schule*).

Conclusion

JOHN J. COLLINS, CRAIG A. EVANS,
AND LEE MARTIN McDONALD

We have argued that the disputed writings not included in the later rabbinic scripture canon or the Christians' First Testament (or Old Testament), namely, the so-called Apocrypha (deuterocanonical books) and Pseudepigrapha, functioned initially as sacred texts in some Jewish and Christian communities, whether Jewish or Christian. Although most of them were eventually excluded from the biblical canon of Judaism, they had considerable influence in early Christianity, which was significantly shaped by an apocalyptic perspective present in the Judaism of the late Second Temple period, in the first centuries BCE and CE. While the rabbis rejected most of the extracanonical literature, and especially the apocalyptic writings, early Christianity focused more on apocalyptic aspects of first-century Judaism rather than the law. Several of the disputed writings have been preserved in Catholic, Orthodox, and Ethiopian churches down to the present.

Generally speaking, those who do not recognize the OT Apocrypha or deuterocanonical and pseudepigraphal writings as sacred scripture nonetheless recognize the value of this literature for understanding the historical-social contexts in which Judaism and early Christianity emerged. Even those writings usually called the NT Apocrypha contributed in various ways to the church's developing sense of what was authoritative and what was not, plus a sense of what that distinction meant for the church. These writings make it clear that literature thought to derive from an apostle—and in some cases from Jesus himself—was believed to be authoritative. When a text was shown or widely thought to be spurious, only then was the writing in question repudiated. The appearance of these writings, mostly in the second and third centuries, helped the pastors and leaders of the early church think through the question of canon and authority.

The rabbis and early church fathers did not initially welcome or cite all the writings that eventually were included in the biblical canons of Judaism and Christianity. Variations in scripture collections and their orders and divisions continued for centuries in both communities of faith. Greater, but not absolute, stability in the books and the order included in the church's scriptures resulted from the introduction of the fourth- and fifth-century early pandect (all-inclusive) scriptures of the church, which included all of the accepted books at that time, as in the Greek codices Vaticanus, Sinaiticus, and Alexandrinus. Still greater stability is found in the Latin pandect "Paris Bibles" (13th c.).

We have seen (above) that for centuries some rabbis had doubts about Esther, Song of Songs, Ecclesiastes, and Sirach. Although most Christians eventually welcomed all the books that were included in the Hebrew Bible, some early church fathers questioned the inclusion of Esther and some welcomed *1 Enoch*, as well as other books not now included in the canon. *Enoch* was widely received in churches until the mid-third century. After that, it faded in the West, but it still is present in the Ethiopian scriptures. Yet questions remained for centuries after local church councils made decisions about the scope of their scriptures. Several HB books that were included in the church's OT canon are seldom cited by the church fathers, and for centuries several NT books were seldom cited or included in emerging canon lists.

Review of the many writings that circulated in the second and third centuries CE and later reveals great levels of interest in the life and teaching of Jesus and his apostles. Behind this profusion of texts were several motivating factors, including curiosity, doctrinal concerns, and apologetics. Despite the antiquity and wide circulation of the four canonical Gospels, more gospels were written in the second and third centuries. Some of these newer works elaborate on themes found in the older canonical Gospels. One, the *Gospel of Peter*, offers an imaginative retelling of the passion and resurrection by building upon and extending the apologetic found in the Gospel of Matthew. Its purpose seems to be to defend the resurrection witness against the skepticism of second-century critics like Celsus.

The extracanonical books of acts were, for the most part, intended to lionize the apostles and some of their converts (such as Thecla) in the eyes of both the church and the pagan public, showing the nobility, authority, and courage of these early missionaries, evangelists, and defenders of the faith. These apocryphal portraits were designed to impress Christians and pagans alike, since the leaders of the early church exemplified the virtues that were most admired in late antique Greco-Roman society, legend, and myth. At the same time some of these books of acts were intended to distinguish the apostles from the magicians and charlatans well known and well represented (and often mistrusted and despised) in Late Antiquity. The purpose here was to show that—unlike the trickery and chicanery of the magicians, whose motives and purposes were deceitful and nefarious—the Christian apostles were empowered by the Spirit of God, and their works of power were truthful and beneficial.

Of course, some of these extracanonical writings were designed to promote new teachings. What is not clear is whether the authors of these writings intended them to be included in the authoritative collection of sacred literature to be read publicly in churches. It is probable that at least a few were written and circulated with that intention. But other writings, especially those that are lumped together as "gnostic," were likely never intended to be read in public, and so they were never candidates for canonical status. These writings contained, it was believed, "secret" teachings and so were to be read by a select, limited number of people and never in public. Writings that strayed too far from the church's Judaic roots, which included respect for the First Testament (Old Testament), the God of Israel, the patriarchs, and the history and destiny of Israel itself—such texts were viewed with mistrust and so not surprisingly were excluded.

Extracanonical letters and apocalypses functioned similarly. They too could be vehicles of new revelation, new polity, and new ethics and practice. Of course, sometimes these writings intended to offer nothing completely new; they only wanted to fill in gaps or clear up things that seemed unclear. But these writings, especially the apocalypses, did make it possible for their authors to elaborate on what in the earlier and widely recognized literature is only incipient or present as a hint. The second- and third-century apocalypses do greatly elaborate details relating to eschatology, the antichrist, heaven, hell, and the second coming of Jesus Christ. Opponents, both secular and ecclesiastical, could be condemned, and a persecuted church could be assured and comforted.

Another feature that is common in the extracanonical literature is its explicit claim to exalted authorship. Unlike the writings that the early church accepted as authoritative, some of which are anonymous or at least make no explicit interior claim of apostolic authorship, the extracanonical writings—gospels, books of acts, letters, and apocalypses—almost always make an explicit claim of apostolic authorship and sometimes even claim to have been composed by Jesus himself (before or after the resurrection). These explicit and exaggerated claims were often recognized, even in antiquity, as indicators of pseudepigraphy. Of course, apostolic claims of authorship did not always imply the intent to gain canonical status (as already noted with respect to gnostic writings), but they sometimes did. The early church, as seen in explicit statements in the writings of the Fathers as well as in the canon lists, did not regard these explicit claims as decisive, and that also applies to the so-called NT *antilegomena* (ἀντιλεγόμενα), whose claims of apostolic authorship, as in the case of 1–2 Peter, did not silence opposition and criticism.

As we have seen, several NT writings were questioned and not regularly included in various Christian collections of sacred scripture for centuries, but they eventually were included (Hebrews, Pastorals, 2 Peter, 2–3 John, Jude, and Revelation). The Syriac-speaking Christians, for example, did not initially welcome the "Minor Catholic Epistles" (2 Peter, 2–3 John, Jude) and Revelation, but for centuries many in the Syrian traditions accepted the *Diatessaron* and *3 Corinthians* as Christian scripture. Many Eastern Orthodox Christians include the disputed writings (called deuterocanonical or noncanonical OT scriptures; Protestants regularly refer to them as Apocrypha), interspersing them among their other OT scriptures according to genre. The Russian Orthodox Christians conclude their OT generally with 1–3 Maccabees and 3 Esdras (*4 Ezra*). Most churches eventually rejected the Christian Apocrypha, but not all and not all at the same time. The books and their orders varied in the Christian OT and NT canons for centuries. Further study of these challenging issues will hopefully clarify the formation of the Jewish and Christian Bibles and the processes and perceptions that led Jews and Christians to the decisions about the scope and function of their sacred scriptures.

These considerations raise the question of the usefulness of speaking about a fixed biblical canon at all since the notion is not present in late Second Temple Judaism or in the earliest churches, nor is it mentioned in any of the Christian scriptures. The early churches recognized a special status of books that reinforced the church's earliest sacred traditions and enabled them to advance the church's mission. Some books were useful for a time and later were set aside, but many continued as useful and were welcomed into the early church's scriptures, though not uniformly for centuries.

Future studies of canon formation and textual function might well and profitably focus on an examination of the Bibles of later churches that for centuries seldom possessed all of the books in both the OT and NT until the later pandect Bibles produced in Latin in the thirteenth-century Paris Bibles (noted earlier), and especially after the invention of the printing press and moveable type. A recent survey of the surviving manuscripts of antiquity, which are likely less than 1 percent of what was produced,[1] suggests that the functional scriptures of most churches for many centuries do not reflect a complete Bible such as was determined by church councils, but often fewer books and sometimes other books not approved in church councils. Likewise, the books in surviving translations also vary on the fringes of both OT and NT canons, in or out. The lectionaries read in various churches also reflect the writings that functioned as scripture in the churches that had them, but none of the lectionaries, earlier or today, reflect all the books included in Christian Bibles, whether Protestant, Catholic, or Orthodox. For example, while Revelation is included in all three major Christian churches (Catholic, Orthodox, and Protestant), it is seldom included in their lectionaries and specifically is not read in Orthodox worship services.

---

1. Hurtado, *Earliest Christian Artifacts*, 24–25.

Future studies of the ancient sacred religious writings will doubtless need to focus on several of the issues addressed in our chapters, as well as areas not addressed in our treatment here. We in the West have generally focused on the Catholic and Protestant traditions. Much more attention should be given to the churches of the East, especially the Eastern Orthodox primarily in Greece and Istanbul, the Oriental Orthodox of Syria, the Coptic Orthodox in Egypt, and the Ethiopian and Armenian churches. The Orthodox churches depend quite heavily on the traditions of more openness in terms of the books that comprised their scriptures in their initial centuries. Their traditions are deeply rooted in prominent Eastern church fathers, especially Melito, Eusebius, Athanasius, and subsequent Eastern, Russian, and Oriental Orthodox church fathers.

While all scholars agree that a biblical canon has to do with the books that comprise the church's scripture collections, there has been no universal agreement on the scope of the Old Testament scriptures or the *text* of both OT and NT scriptures. Text-critical scholars are aware that the surviving manuscripts reflect much agreement, yet they often include noncanonical books and contain considerable variants in both the OT and NT manuscripts. Most scholars have abandoned the goal of producing an *original* text of the church's scriptures, but all recognize how the surviving texts reflect a wealth of information regarding the context in which they were produced. While some variants are easily corrected and seen simply as a slip of hand or eye, some were intentional and often reflect later and accepted theological views circulating in the churches (e.g., John 3:13; 1 John 5:7–8). Most of these variants also tend toward adding to or clarifying the emerging orthodoxy of the church.

Future studies of the function or use of canonical and noncanonical Jewish and Christian religious texts might well deal with some of the questions in more detail, issues that we have not addressed above but have noted. Several helpful summaries of the available evidence are found in the *Oxford Encyclopedia of the Books of the Bible*[2] and *The New Cambridge History of the Bible*.[3] However, more detailed examinations, such as the first four volumes of *The Textual History of the Bible*,[4] have also proved valuable in reflecting the history of scriptural use and reception. On their way are more volumes that will doubtless be useful for understanding how the ancient Jewish and Christian religious texts functioned in Jewish and Christian communities of faith.

---

2. Michael D. Coogan, ed. in chief, *The Oxford Encyclopedia of the Books of the Bible* (New York: Oxford University Press, 2011), 2 vols.

3. James Carleton Paget and Joachim Schaper, eds., *From the Beginnings to 600* (vol. 1 of *The New Cambridge History of the Bible*; Cambridge: Cambridge University Press, 2013); Richard Marsden and E. Ann Matter, eds., *From 600 to 1450* (vol. 2 of *The New Cambridge History of the Bible*; Cambridge: Cambridge University Press, 2012); Euan Cameron, ed., *From 1450 to 1750* (vol. 3 of *The New Cambridge History of the Bible*; Cambridge: Cambridge University Press, 2016); John Riches, ed., *From 1750 to the Present* (vol. 4 of *The New Cambridge History of the Bible*; Cambridge: Cambridge University Press, 2015).

4. Armin Lange and Emanuel Tov, eds., *Textual History of the Bible* (Leiden: Brill, 2016–).

The formation of scripture and canon in antiquity is a prominent issue in contemporary biblical inquiry and deserves greater attention than what our chapters have been able to offer in this volume. We have endeavored to clarify why and when some writings were recognized as the scriptures of Judaism in Late Antiquity and of early Christianity, but also why some were initially recognized as scripture but later were not. Our focus was only on *some* of the complex and challenging issues facing scholars pursuing the function and stabilization of biblical literature in antiquity. We hope that this discussion, as well as new discoveries yet to be made, will lead to further inquiry.

Bibliography

Aasgaard, R. "The *Protevangelium of James* and the *Infancy Gospel of Thomas*: Orthodoxy from Above or Heterodoxy from Below?" Pages 75–97 in *The Other Side: Apocryphal Perspectives on Ancient Christian "Orthodoxies."* Edited by T. Nicklas et al. NTOA 117. Göttingen: Vandenhoeck & Ruprecht, 2017.

Abegg, Martin, Peter Flint, and Eugene Ulrich. *The Dead Sea Scrolls Bible.* San Francisco: Harper, 1999.

Agourides, S. "Apocalypse of Sedrach." *OTP* 1:605–13.

Alexander, Philip. *The Mystical Texts.* New York: T&T Clark International, 2006.

———. "3 (Hebrew Apocalypse of) Enoch." *OTP* 1:223–315.

Anderson, G. W. "Canonical and Non-canonical." Pages 113–59 in *From the Beginnings to Jerome.* Edited by P. R. Ackroyd et al. Vol. 1 of *The Cambridge History of the Bible.* Cambridge: Cambridge University Press, 1970.

Anderson, Hugh. *The Gospel of Mark.* NCB. London: Oliphants, 1976.

Anderson, Paul N. "The Word." Pages 893–98 in vol. 5 of *NIBD.*

Armstrong, J. J. "Victorinus of Pettau as the Author of the Canon Muratori." *VC* 62 (2008): 1–35.

Asale, Bruk A. "The Ethiopian Orthodox Tweahedo Church Canon of the Scriptures: Neither Open nor Closed." *The Bible Translator* 67, issue 2 (September 14, 2016): 202–22. This issue, "Biblical Canons in Church Traditions and Translations," edited by Jean-Claude Loba Mkole. UBS 67.2 (Sage, 2016).

Attridge, H. W. *The Acts of Thomas.* Early Christian Apocrypha 3. Salem, OR: Polebridge, 2010.

———. "Appendix: The Greek Fragments." Pages 103–9 in *Nag Hammadi Codex II,2–7 together with XII,2 Brit. Lib. Or. 4926 (1), and P. Oxy 1, 654, 655.* Edited by B. Layton. Vol. 1 of *Gospel according to Thomas, Gospel according to Philip, Hypostasis of the Archons, and Indexes.* NHS 20. Leiden: Brill, 1989.

Baillet, M. *4Q482–4Q520.* Vol. III of *Qumrân Grotte 4.* DJD 7. Oxford: Clarendon, 1982.

Baldwin, M. C. *Whose Acts of Peter? Text and Historical Context of the Actus Vercellenses.* WUNT II/196. Tübingen: Mohr Siebeck, 2005.

Bar-Ilan, M. "Writing in Ancient Israel and Early Judaism: Ancient Books in the Late Second Commonwealth and Rabbinic Period." Pages 21–37 in *Mikra: Text,*

Translation, Reading, and Interpretation of the Hebrew Bible in Ancient Judaism and Early Christianity. Edited by M. J. Mulder. CRINT 2/1. Minneapolis: Fortress, 1990.

Barr, James. *Holy Scripture: Canon, Authority, Criticism*. Philadelphia: Westminster, 1983.

Barrier, J. W., et al., eds. *Thecla: Paul's Disciple and Saint in the East and West*. SECA 12. Leuven: Peeters, 2017.

Barth, Karl. *The Epistle to the Romans*. First ed. of *Der Römerbrief* in 1918. 2nd German ed., 1922. ET of 2nd German ed., by E. C. Hoskyns in 1933. Page references are to the 6th English ed. Oxford: Oxford University Press, 1968.

Barton, John. *Oracles of God: Perceptions of Ancient Prophecy in Israel after the Exile*. Oxford: Oxford University Press, 1986. Reprint, New York: Oxford University Press, 2007.

Batovici, D. "The Apostolic Fathers in Codex Sinaiticus and Codex Alexandrinus." *Bib* 97 (2016): 581–605.

Bauckham, Richard J. "The *Acts of Paul*: Replacement of Acts or Sequel to Acts?" Pages 159–68 in *The Apocryphal Acts of the Apostles in Intertextual Perspectives*. Edited by R. F. Stoops Jr. Semeia 80. Atlanta: Scholars Press, 1997.

———. "The *Apocalypse of Peter*: A Jewish Christian Apocalypse from the Time of Bar Kokhba." *Apocrypha* 5 (1994): 7–111. Repr. as pages 160–258 in *The Fate of the Dead: Studies on the Jewish and Christian Apocalypses*. NovTSup 93. Leiden: Brill, 1998.

———. *The Fate of the Dead: Studies on the Jewish and Christian Apocalypses*. NovTSup 93. Leiden: Brill, 1998.

———. "The Four Apocalypses of the Virgin Mary." Pages 332–62 in *The Fate of the Dead: Studies on the Jewish and Christian Apocalypses*. NovTSup 93. Leiden: Brill, 1998.

———. *Jude, 2 Peter*. WBC 50. Waco, TX: Word, 1983.

———. "The Latin Vision of Ezra." *OTPM* 1:498–528.

———. "The Two Fig Tree Parables in the *Apocalypse of Peter*." *JBL* 104 (1985): 269–87.

Bauckham, R. J., J. R. Davila, and A. Panayotov, eds. *Old Testament Pseudepigrapha: More Noncanonical Scriptures* [*OTPM*]. Vol. 1. Grand Rapids: Eerdmans, 2013.

Bautch, Kelley Coblentz. *A Study of the Geography of 1 Enoch 17–19: "No One Has Seen What I Have Seen."* JSJSup 81. Leiden: Brill, 2003.

Beckwith, Roger T. *The Old Testament Canon of the New Testament Church*. Grand Rapids: Eerdmans, 1985.

Berger, Klaus. *Die griechische Daniel-Diegese: Eine altkirchliche Apokalypse*. StPB 27. Leiden: Brill, 1976.

Bergren, T. A. *Fifth Ezra: The Text, Origin, and Early History*. SBLSCS 25. Atlanta: Scholars Press, 1990.

———. *Sixth Ezra: The Text and Origin*. Oxford: Oxford University Press, 1998.

Berthelot, Katell, and Daniel Stökl Ben Ezra, eds. *Aramaica Qumranica: Proceedings of the Conference on the Aramaic Texts from Qumran in Aix-en-Provence, 30 June–2 July 2008*. STDJ 94. Leiden: Brill, 2010.

Blumell, Lincoln H., and Thomas A. Wayment, eds. *Christian Oxyrhynchus: Texts, Documents, and Sources*. Waco, TX: Baylor University Press, 2015.

Boccaccini, Gabriele, ed. *Enoch and the Messiah Son of Man: Revisiting the Book of the Parables*. Grand Rapids: Eerdmans, 2007.

Bogaert, Pierre-Maurice. "The Latin Bible." Pages 505–26 in *From the Beginnings to 600*. Edited by James Carleton Paget and Joachim Schaper. Vol. 1 of *The New Cambridge History of the Bible*. Cambridge: Cambridge University Press, 2013.

———. "The Latin Bible, c. 600–c. 900." Pages 69–92 in *From 600 to 1450*. Edited by Richard Marsden and E. Ann Matter. Vol. 2 of *The New Cambridge History of the Bible*. Cambridge: Cambridge University Press, 2012.

Boismard, M.-E. "Paul's Letter to the Laodiceans." Pages 45–57 in *The Pauline Canon.* Edited by S. E. Porter. PAST 1. Leiden: Brill, 2004.

Bokedal, Tomas. *The Formation and Significance of the Christian Biblical Canon: A Study in Text, Ritual and Interpretation.* London: T&T Clark, 2014.

Boor, Carl de, ed. *Nicephori Archiepiscopi Constantinopolitani opuscula historica.* Bibliotheca Scriptorum Graecorum et Romanorum Teubneriana. Leipzig: Teubner, 1880.

Bousset, Wilhelm. *Die Religion des Judentums in neutestamentlichen Zeitalter.* Berlin: Reuther & Reichard, 1903.

———. *Volksfrömmigkeit und Schriftgelehrtentum: Antwort auf Herrn Perles' Kritik meiner "Religion des Judentums im N. T. Zeitalter."* Berlin: Reuther & Reichard, 1903.

Bovon, F., and C. R. Matthews. *The Acts of Philip: A New Translation.* Waco, TX: Baylor University Press, 2012.

Bowersock, G. W. *Fiction as History: Nero to Julian.* Sather Classical Lectures 58. Berkeley: University of California Press, 1994.

Boyarin, Daniel. *A Radical Jew: Paul and the Politics of Identity.* Berkeley: University of California Press, 1994.

Brakke, David. "Canon Formation and Social Conflict in Fourth-Century Egypt: Athanasius of Alexandria's Thirty-Ninth Festal Letter." *HTR* 87 (1994): 395–419.

Bremmer, J. N., ed. *The Apocryphal Acts of Andrew.* SECA 5. Leuven: Peeters, 2000.

———, ed. *The Apocryphal Acts of John.* Studies on the Apocryphal Acts of the Apostles 1. Kampen: Kok Pharos, 1995.

———, ed. *The Apocryphal Acts of Paul and Thecla.* Studies on the Apocryphal Acts of the Apostles 2. Kampen: Kok Pharos, 1996.

———, ed. *The Apocryphal Acts of Peter: Magic, Miracles and Gnosticism.* SECA 3. Leuven: Peeters, 1998.

———, ed. *The Apocryphal Acts of Thomas.* SECA 6. Leuven: Peeters, 2001.

———, et al., eds. *The Ascension of Isaiah.* SECA 11. Leuven: Peeters, 2016.

———, et al., eds. *Figures of Ezra.* SECA 13. Leuven: Peeters, 2018.

———, ed. *The Pseudo-Clementines.* SECA 10. Leuven: Peeters, 2010.

Bremmer, J. N., and I. Czachesz, eds. *The Apocalypse of Peter.* SECA 7. Leuven: Peeters, 2003.

———, eds. *The Visio Pauli and the Gnostic Apocalypse of Paul.* SECA 9. Leuven: Peeters, 2007.

Breytenbach, C., and L. L. Welborn, eds. *Encounters with Hellenism: Studies on the First Letter of Clement.* AGJU 53. Leiden: Brill, 2003.

Brown, Michelle P. "Spreading the Word: The Single-Volume Bible." Pages 176–203 in *In the Beginning: Bibles before the Year 1000.* Edited by Michelle P. Brown. Washington, DC: Smithsonian Institution, 2006.

Brown, Raymond E., and Raymond F. Collins. "Canonicity." Pages 1034–54 in *The New Jerome Biblical Commentary.* Edited by Raymond E. Brown, Joseph A. Fitzmyer, and Roland E. Murphy. Englewood Cliffs, NJ: Prentice Hall, 1990.

Bruce, F. F. *The Books and the Parchments: How We Got Our English Bible.* 5th ed. London: Marshall Pickering, 1991.

———. *Canon of Scripture.* Downers Grove, IL: InterVarsity, 1988.

Bruce, James. *Travels to Discover the Source of the Nile, in the Years 1768, 1769, 1770, 1771, 1772 and 1773.* 5 vols. London: Robinsons, 1790.

Buchholz, Dennis D. *Your Eyes Will Be Opened: A Study of the Greek (Ethiopic) Apocalypse of Peter.* SBLDS 97. Atlanta: Scholars Press, 1988.

Budge, E. A. Wallis. *Coptic Apocrypha in the Dialect of Upper Egypt.* London: Longmans, 1913.

Burke, Tony. *Infancy Gospel of Thomas.* Early Christian Apocrypha 10. Salem, OR: Polebridge Press, forthcoming.

————. *The Syriac Tradition of the Infancy Gospel of Thomas: A Critical Edition and English Translation.* Gorgias Eastern Christian Studies 48. Piscataway, NJ: Gorgias Press, 2017.

Burke, T., and B. Landau, eds. *New Testament Apocrypha: More Noncanonical Scriptures* [*NTAM*]. Vol. 1. Grand Rapids: Eerdmans, 2016.

Burke, T., and W. Witakowski. "The Acts of Cornelius the Centurion." *NTAM* 1:337–61.

Byrne, Brendan. *Romans.* Sacra Pagina 6. Collegeville, MN: Liturgical Press, 1996.

Campenhausen, Hans von. *Tradition and Life in the Church: Essays and Lectures in Church History.* London: Collins, 1968.

Carleton Paget. *See* Paget.

Carr, David M. *The Formation of the Hebrew Bible: A New Reconstruction.* Oxford: Oxford University Press, 2011.

————. "The Song of Songs as a Microcosm of the Canonization and Decanonization Process." Pages 173–89 in *Canonization and Decanonization.* Edited by A. van der Kooij and K. van der Toorn. Studies in the History of Religion 82. Leiden: Brill, 1998.

————. *Writing on the Tablet of the Heart: Origins of Scripture and Literature.* Oxford: Oxford University Press, 2005.

Chapman, Stephen B. "The Canon Debate: What It Is and Why It Matters." *Journal of Theological Interpretation* 4, no. 2 (2010): 273–94.

————. "Canon, Old Testament." Pages 97–109 in vol. 1 of *The Oxford Encyclopedia of the Books of the Bible.* Edited by M. D. Coogan. Oxford: Oxford University Press, 2011.

————. "Reclaiming Inspiration for the Bible." Pages 167–206 in *Canon and Biblical Interpretation.* Edited by C. B. Bartholomew, Scott Hahn, Robin Parry, Christopher Seitz, and Al Wolters. Scripture and Hermeneutics 7. Grand Rapids: Zondervan, 2006.

————. "Second Temple Jewish Hermeneutics: How Canon Is Not an Anachronism." Pages 281–96 in *Invention, Rewriting, Usurpation: Discursive Fights over Religious Traditions in Antiquity.* Edited by Jörg Ulrich, Anders-Christian Jacobsen, and David Brakke. Early Christianity in the Context of Antiquity 11. Frankfurt am Main: Peter Lang, 2011.

————. "What Are We Reading? Canonicity and the Old Testament." *Word & World* 29, no. 4 (Fall 2009): 334–47.

Charles, Robert Henry, ed. *The Apocrypha and Pseudepigrapha of the Old Testament.* 2 vols. Oxford: Clarendon Press, 1913.

Charlesworth, James H. ed. *Apocalyptic Literature and Testaments.* Vol. 1 of *The Old Testament Pseudepigrapha* [*OTP* 1]. Garden City, NY: Doubleday, 1983.

————. "Exploring the Origins of the *descensus ad inferos.*" Pages 372–95 in *Earliest Christianity within the Boundaries of Judaism: Essays in Honor of Bruce Chilton.* Edited by A. J. Avery-Peck, C. A. Evans, and J. Neusner. Brill Reference Library of Judaism 49. Leiden: Brill, 2016.

————, ed. *Expansions of the "Old Testament" and Legends, Wisdom and Philosophical Literature, Prayers, Psalms, and Odes, Fragments of Lost Judeo-Hellenistic Works.* Vol. 2 of *The Old Testament Pseudepigrapha* [*OTP* 2]. Garden City, NY: Doubleday, 1985.

Charney, N. *The Art of Yregrof [Forgery]: The Minds, Motives and Methods of Master Forgers.* London: Phaidon, 2015.

Cherchi, P. "A Legend from St. Bartholomew's Gospel in the Twelfth-Century." *RB* 91 (1984): 212–18.

Clivaz, C., et al., eds. *Infancy Gospels: Stories and Identities.* WUNT 281. Tübingen: Mohr Siebeck, 2011.

Cohen, Shaye J. D. "The Significance of Yavneh: Pharisees, Rabbis, and the End of Jewish Sectarianism." *Hebrew Union College Annual* 55 (1984): 17–53.

Coles, R. A. "Oxyrhynchus: A City and Its Texts." Pages 3–16 in *Oxyrhynchus: A City and Its Texts*. Edited by A. K. Bowman et al. Graeco-Roman Memoirs 93. London: Egypt Exploration Society, 2007.

Collins, Adela Yarbro. *Mark*. Hermeneia. Minneapolis: Fortress, 2007.

Collins, Adela Yarbro, and John J. Collins. *King and Messiah as Son of God*. Grand Rapids: Eerdmans, 2008.

Collins, John J. *Apocalypse, Prophecy, and Pseudepigraphy: On Jewish Apocalyptic Literature*. Grand Rapids: Eerdmans, 2015.

———. *The Apocalyptic Imagination: An Introduction to Jewish Apocalyptic Literature*. 3rd ed. Grand Rapids: Eerdmans, 2016.

———. *Apocalypticism in the Dead Sea Scrolls*. London: Routledge, 1997.

———. "The 'Apocryphal' Old Testament." Pages 165–89 in *From the Beginnings to 600*. Edited by James C. Paget and Joachim Schaper. Vol. 1 of *The New Cambridge History of the Bible*. Cambridge: Cambridge University Press, 2013.

———. "The Background of the Son of God Text." Response to E. M. Cook. *Bulletin for Biblical Research* 7 (1997): 51–62.

———. "Before the Canon: Scriptures in Second Temple Judaism." Pages 225–41 in *Old Testament Interpretation: Past, Present, and Future*. Edited by James Luther Mays, David L. Petersen, and Kent Harold Richards. Nashville: Abingdon, 1995.

———. *Beyond the Qumran Community: The Sectarian Movement of the Dead Sea Scrolls*. Grand Rapids: Eerdmans, 2010.

———. "Canaanite Myth and Daniel 7: Illusion or Allusion?" Forthcoming in the Festschrift for John Day, edited by Stuart Weeks.

———. "Canon, Canonization." Pages 460–63 in *The Eerdmans Dictionary of Early Judaism*. Edited by J. J. Collins and Daniel C. Harlow. Grand Rapids: Eerdmans, 2010.

———. *Daniel. A Commentary on the Book of Daniel*. Hermeneia. Minneapolis: Fortress, 1993.

———. *The Dead Sea Scrolls. A Biography*. Princeton: Princeton University Press, 2013.

———. "A Herald of Good Tidings: Isaiah 61:1–3 and Its Actualization in the Dead Sea Scrolls." Pages 225–40 in *The Quest for Context and Meaning: Studies in Biblical Intertextuality in Honor of James A. Sanders*. Edited by Craig A. Evans and Shemaryahu Talmon. Leiden: Brill, 1997.

———. "The Interpretation of Psalm 2." Pages 49–66 in *Echoes from the Caves: Qumran and the New Testament*. Edited by Florentino García Martínez. STDJ 85. Leiden: Brill, 2009.

———. *Introduction to the Hebrew Bible*. 1st ed. Minneapolis: Fortress, 2004. 2nd ed., 2014. 3rd ed., 2018.

———. *The Invention of Judaism: Torah and Jewish Identity from Deuteronomy to Paul*. Oakland: University of California Press, 2017.

———. "Journeys to the World Beyond in Ancient Judaism." Pages 178–97 in *Apocalypse, Prophecy, and Pseudepigraphy*.

———, ed. *The Origins of Apocalypticism in Judaism and Christianity*. Vol. 1 of *The Encyclopedia of Apocalypticism*. New York: Continuum, 1998.

———. "The Penumbra of the Canon: What Do the Deuterocanonical Books Represent?" Pages 1–17 in *Canonicity, Setting, Wisdom in the Deuterocanonicals*. Edited by Géza G. Xeravits, József Zsengellér, and Xavér Szabó. Deuterocanonical and Cognate Literature Studies 22. Berlin: de Gruyter, 2014.

———. *The Scepter and the Star: Messianism in Light of the Dead Sea Scrolls*. 2nd ed. Grand Rapids: Eerdmans, 2010.

———. *Seers, Sibyls and Sages in Hellenistic-Roman Judaism*. JSJSup 54. Leiden: Brill, 1997.

———. "What Have We Learned from the Dead Sea Scrolls?" Pages 1–16 in *Scriptures and Sectarianism: Essays on the Dead Sea Scrolls*. Grand Rapids: Eerdmans, 2016.

Collins, John J., and Daniel C. Harlow, eds. *The Eerdmans Dictionary of Early Judaism*. Grand Rapids: Eerdmans, 2010.

Concannon, C. W. "The Acts of Timothy." *NTAM* 1:395–405.

———. "In the Great City of the Ephesians: Contestations over Apostolic Memory and Ecclesial Power in the Acts of Timothy." *Journal of Early Christian Studies* 24 (2016): 419–46.

Coogan, Michael D. *The Old Testament: A Historical and Literary Introduction to the Hebrew Scriptures*. 3rd ed. Oxford: Oxford University Press, 2014.

Cook, E. M. "4Q246." *Bulletin for Biblical Research* 5 (1995): 43–66.

Cousland, J. R. C. *Holy Terror: Jesus in the Infancy Gospel of Thomas*. LNTS 560. London: Bloomsbury T&T Clark, 2018.

Cowe, S. Peter. "The Bible in Armenian." Pages 143–61 in *From 600–1450*. Edited by Richard Marsden and E. Ann Matter. Vol. 2 of *The New Cambridge History of the Bible*. Cambridge: Cambridge University Press, 2012.

Cowley, R. W. "The Biblical Canon of the Ethiopian Orthodox Church Today." *Ostkirchliche Studien* 23 (1974): 318–24.

Cross, Frank M. *From Epic to Canon*. History and Literature in Ancient Israel. Baltimore: Johns Hopkins University Press, 1998.

———. "The Stabilization of the Canon of the Hebrew Bible." Pages 219–29 in *From Epic to Canon: History and Literature in Ancient Israel*. Baltimore: Johns Hopkins University Press, 1998.

Crossan, J. D. *The Cross That Spoke: The Origins of the Passion Narrative*. San Francisco: Harper & Row, 1988.

———. *Four Other Gospels: Shadows on the Contours of Canon*. New York: Harper & Row, 1985. Repr., Sonoma: Polebridge, 1992.

———. *The Historical Jesus: The Life of a Mediterranean Jewish Peasant*. San Francisco: HarperCollins, 1991.

Crowe, B. D. "Oh Sweet Exchange! The Soteriological Significance of the Incarnation in the Epistle to Diognetus." *ZNW* 102 (2011): 96–109.

Dando, M. "L'Apocalypse de Thomas." *Cahiers d'études cathares* 28/37 (1977): 3–58.

Daschke, Dereck. *City of Ruins: Mourning the Destruction of Jerusalem through Jewish Apocalypse*. Biblical Interpretation 99. Leiden: Brill, 2010.

Davies, Philip R. "The Jewish Scriptural Canon in Cultural Perspective." Pages 36–52 in *CanDb*.

Davila, James R. *The Provenance of the Pseudepigrapha: Jewish, Christian, or Other?* JSJSup 105. Leiden: Brill, 2005.

———. "Quotations from Lost Books in the Hebrew Bible: A New Translation and Introduction, with an Excursus on Quotations from Lost Books in the New Testament." *OTPM* 1:673–98.

Day, John. *God's Conflict with the Dragon and the Sea: Echoes of a Canaanite Myth in the Old Testament*. University of Cambridge Oriental Publications 35. Cambridge: Cambridge University Press, 1985.

Dean, James E., ed. *Treatise on Weights and Measures: The Syriac Version*. Chicago: University of Chicago Press, 1935.

DeConick, April D. *The Original Gospel of Thomas in Translation: With a Commentary and New English Translation of the Complete Gospel*. LNTS 287. London: T&T Clark International, 2006.

———. *Recovering the Original Gospel of Thomas: A History of the Gospel and Its Growth*. LNTS 286. London: T&T Clark International, 2005.

De Hamel, Christopher. *The Book: A History of the Bible*. New York: Phaidon, 2001.

———. "Books for Students." Pages 108–40 in *A History of Illuminated Manuscripts*. London: Phaidon, 1994.

De Jonge, Marinus. *Pseudepigrapha of the Old Testament as Part of Christian Literature: The Case of the "Testaments of the Twelve Patriarchs" and the Greek "Life of Adam and Eve."* Leiden: Brill, 2003.

———. *The Testaments of the Twelve Patriarchs: A Study of Their Text, Composition, and Origin*. Assen: van Gorcum, 1953.

Denzey Lewis, N., and J. A. Blount. "Rethinking the Origins of the Nag Hammadi Codices." *JBL* 133 (2014): 399–419.

De Regt, Lenart J. "Canon and Biblical Text in the Slavonic Tradition in Russia." *The Bible Translator* 67, issue 2 (September 14, 2016): 222–39. This issue, "Biblical Canons in Church Traditions and Translations," edited by Jean-Claude Loba Mkole. UBS 67.2 (Sage, 2016).

DeSilva, David A. *The Jewish Teachers of Jesus, James, and Jude: What Earliest Christianity Learned from the Apocrypha and Pseudepigrapha*. Oxford: Oxford University Press, 2014.

Dilley, P. C. "The Invention of Christian Tradition: 'Apocrypha,' Imperial Policy, and Anti-Jewish Propaganda." *GRBS* 50 (2010): 586–615.

Dobschütz. *See* von Dobschütz.

Doresse, Jean. *The Secret Books of the Egyptian Gnostics: An Introduction to the Gnostic Coptic Manuscripts Discovered at Chenoboskion*. New York: Viking, 1960.

Dorival, Gilles. "L'apport des Pères de l'Église à la question de la clôture du Canon de l'Ancien Testament." Pages 81–110 in *The Biblical Canons*. Edited by J.-M. Auwers and H. J. de Jonge. BETL 163. Leuven: Leuven University Press, 2003.

———. "Has the Category of 'Deuterocanonical Books' a Jewish Origin?" Pages 1–10 in *The Books of the Maccabees: History, Theology, Ideology*. Edited by Géza G. Xeravits and József Zsengellér. JSJSup 118. Leiden: Brill, 2007.

Dosoo, K. "A History of the Theban Magical Library." *Bulletin of the American Society of Papyrologists* 53 (2016): 251–74.

Douglas, Michael. "The Teacher Hymn Hypothesis Revisited: New Data for an Old Crux." *DSD* 6 (1999): 239–66.

Dulles, Avery. "The Authority of Scripture: A Catholic Perspective." Pages 14–40 in *Scripture in the Jewish and Christian Traditions*. Edited by F. E. Greenspahn. Nashville: Abingdon, 1982.

Dunn, James D. G. *Jesus Remembered*. Christianity in the Making 1. Grand Rapids: Eerdmans, 2003.

———. *Romans 9–16*. WBC 38B. Dallas: Word, 1988.

Dunne, John A. *Esther and Her Elusive God: How a Secular Story Functions as Scripture*. Eugene, OR: Wipf & Stock, 2014.

Du Toit, Jaqueline S. *Textual Memory: Ancient Archives, Libraries and the Hebrew Bible*. Sheffield: Sheffield Phoenix Press, 2010.

Eastman, D. L. "The Epistle of Pseudo-Dionysius the Areopagite to Timothy concerning the Deaths of the Apostles Peter and Paul." *NTAM* 1:464–80.

Edrei, Arye, and Doron Mendels. "A Split Jewish Diaspora: Its Dramatic Consequences." *JSP* 16 (2007): 91–137.

Edwards, James R. *The Hebrew Gospel and the Formation of the Synoptic Tradition*. Grand Rapids: Eerdmans, 2009.

———. "The Hebrew Gospel in Early Christianity." Pages 116–52 in *"Non-Canonical" Religious Texts in Early Judaism and Early Christianity*. Edited by Lee Martin McDonald and James H. Charlesworth. Jewish and Christian Texts in Contexts and Related Studies 14. London: T&T Clark, 2012.

Ehrman, Bart D. "The New Testament Canon of Didymus the Blind." *VC* 37 (1983): 1–21.

Ehrman, Bart D., and Z. Pleše, eds. *The Other Gospels: Accounts of Jesus from Outside the New Testament.* Oxford: Oxford University Press, 2011.

Elliott, J. K., ed. *The Apocryphal New Testament: A Collection of Apocryphal Christian Literature in an English Translation based on M. R. James.* Oxford: Clarendon, 1993.

―――. "Mark 1:1–3—A Later Addition to the Gospel?" *NTS* 46 (2000): 584–88.

―――. *A Synopsis of the Apocryphal Nativity and Infancy Narratives.* NTTSD 34. Leiden: Brill, 2006.

Emmel, Stephen. "The Coptic Gnostic Texts as Witnesses to the Production and Transmission of Gnostic (and Other) Traditions." Pages 33–49 in *Das Thomasevangelium: Entstehung—Rezeption—Theologie.* Edited by J. Frey, E. E. Popkes, and J. Schröter. BZNW 157. Berlin: de Gruyter, 2008.

Epp, Eldon Jay. *Perspectives on New Testament Textual Criticism: Collected Essays, 1962–2004.* NovTSup 116. Leiden: Brill, 2005.

Eshel, Esther. "The Identification of the 'Speaker' of the Self-Glorification Hymn." Pages 619–35 in *The Provo International Conference on the Dead Sea Scrolls.* Edited by D. W. Parry and E. Ulrich. STDJ 30. Leiden: Brill, 1999.

Evans, C. A. "Christians in Egypt: A Preliminary Survey of Christian Literature Found in Oxyrhynchus." Pages 26–51 in *"Non-Canonical" Religious Texts in Early Judaism and Christianity.* Edited by J. H. Charlesworth and L. M. McDonald. Jewish and Christian Texts in Contexts and Related Studies 14. London: T&T Clark International, 2012.

―――. "The Jewish Christian Gospel Tradition." Pages 241–77 in *Jewish Believers in Jesus: The Early Centuries.* Edited by Oskar Skarsaune and Reidar Hvalvik. Peabody, MA: Hendrickson, 2007.

―――. "The Scriptures of Jesus and His Earliest Followers." Pages 185–195 in *CanDb.*

Evans, C. A., and S. J. Patterson. "Doubting Thomas: Is the *Gospel of Thomas* an Authentic Witness to Jesus?" *Midwestern Journal of Theology* 8 (2009): 3–40.

Evans, C. A., R. L. Webb, and R. A. Wiebe. *Nag Hammadi Texts and the Bible: A Synopsis and Index.* NTTS 18. Leiden: Brill, 1993.

Farrer, J. A. *Literary Forgeries.* London: Longmans, Green, 1907.

Fishbane, Michael. *Biblical Myth and Rabbinic Mythmaking.* New York: Oxford University Press, 2003.

―――. "From Scribalism to Rabbinism." Pages 439–56 in *The Sage in Israel and the Ancient Near East.* Edited by John G. Gammie. Winona Lake, IN: Eisenbrauns, 1990.

Fitzmyer, Joseph A. "The Oxyrhynchus Logoi of Jesus and the Coptic Gospel according to Thomas." Pages 355–433 in *Essays on the Semitic Background of the New Testament.* London: Geoffrey Chapman, 1971.

―――. *Romans: A New Translation with Introduction and Commentary.* AB 33. New York: Doubleday, 1993.

Flint, Peter W., ed. *The Bible at Qumran: Text Shape and Interpretation.* Grand Rapids: Eerdmans, 2001.

―――. "Noncanonical Writings in the Dead Sea Scrolls." Pages 80–126 in *The Bible at Qumran: Text, Shape, and Interpretation.* Edited by P. W. Flint. Grand Rapids: Eerdmans, 2001.

Foskett, M. F. "The Child Mary in the Protevangelium of James." Pages 195–204 in *"Non-Canonical" Religious Texts in Early Judaism and Christianity.* Edited by J. H. Charlesworth and L. M. McDonald. Jewish and Christian Texts in Contexts and Related Studies 14. London: T&T Clark International, 2012.

Foster, P. "Are There Any Early Fragments of the So-Called *Gospel of Peter?*" *NTS* 52 (2006): 1–26.

————. "The Disputed Early Fragments of the So-Called *Gospel of Peter*—Once Again." *NovT* 49 (2007): 402–6.

————. "The Epistle to Diognetus." *ExpTim* 118 (2007): 162–68.

————. "The *Epistle to Diognetus*." Pages 147–56 in *The Writings of the Apostolic Fathers*. Edited by P. Foster. T&T Clark Biblical Studies. London: T&T Clark, 2007.

————. *The Gospel of Peter: Introduction, Critical Edition and Commentary*. TENTS 4. Leiden: Brill, 2010.

Fowler, K. Review of J. J. Johnston, *The Resurrection of Jesus in the "Gospel of Peter."* "Booklist" 20, *JSNT* 39/5 (2017): 111.

Frankfurter, D. *Elijah in Upper Egypt: The Apocalypse of Elijah and Early Egyptian Christianity*. Studies in Antiquity and Christianity. Minneapolis: Fortress, 1993.

Fretheim, Terence E. "Word of God." *ABD* 6:961–68.

Frey, J., E. E. Popkes, and J. Schröter, eds. *Das Thomasevangelium: Entstehung—Rezeption—Theologie*. BZNW 157. Berlin: de Gruyter, 2008.

Funk, R. W., *The Acts of Jesus: What Did Jesus Really Do? The Search for the Authentic Deeds of Jesus*. San Francisco: HarperCollins, 1998.

Funk, R. W., R. W. Hoover, and the Jesus Seminar. *The Five Gospels: The Search for the Authentic Words of Jesus*. New York: Macmillan, 1993.

Fürst, A. "Pseudepigraphie und Apostolizität im apokryphen Briefwechsel zwischen Seneca und Paulus." *JAC* 41 (1998): 77–117.

Galbraith, D. "Whence the Giant Jesus and His Talking Cross? The Resurrection in *Gospel of Peter* 10.39–42 as Prophetic Fulfillment of LXX Psalm 18." *NTS* 63 (2017): 473–91.

Gallagher, Edmon L. "Augustine on the Hebrew Bible." *JTS* 67 (2016): 97–114.

————. "The Blood from Abel to Zechariah in the History of Interpretation." *NTS* 60 (2014): 121–38.

————. "The End of the Bible? The Position of Chronicles in the Canon." *Tyndale Bulletin* 65 (2014): 181–99.

————. "Jerome's *Prologus Galeatus* and the OT Canon of North Africa." Pages 99–106 in *Studia Patristica* 69. Edited by Markus Vinzent. Leuven: Peeters, 2013.

————. "The Old Testament 'Apocrypha' in Jerome's Canonical Theory." *Journal of Early Christian Studies* 20 (2012): 213–33.

————. "Writings Labeled 'Apocrypha' in Latin Patristic Sources." Pages 1–14 in *Sacra Scriptura: How "Non-Canonical" Texts Functioned in Early Judaism and Early Christianity*. Edited by J. H. Charlesworth and L. M. McDonald. Jewish and Christian Texts in Contexts and Related Studies 20. London: Bloomsbury, 2014.

Gallagher, Edmon L., and John Meade. *The Biblical Canon Lists from Early Christianity: Texts and Analysis*. Oxford: Oxford University Press, 2017.

Gamble, Harry Y. *Books and Readers in the Early Church: A History of Early Christian Texts*. New Haven: Yale University Press, 1995.

Gammie, John G., and Leo P. Perdue, eds. *The Sage in Israel and the Ancient Near East*. Winona Lake, IN: Eisenbrauns, 1990.

Ganz, David. "Carolingian Bibles." Pages 325–37 in *From 600–1450*. Edited by Richard Marsden and E. Ann Matter. Vol. 2 of *Cambridge History of the Bible*. Cambridge: Cambridge University Press, 2012.

García Martínez, Florentino, and Eibert J. Tigchelaar. *The Dead Sea Scrolls Study Edition*. 2 vols. Leiden: Brill, 1997–98.

Gathercole, S. J. *The Composition of the Gospel of Thomas: Original Language and Influences*. SNTSMS 151. Cambridge: Cambridge University Press, 2012.

————. *The Gospel of Thomas: Introduction and Commentary*. TENTS 11. Leiden: Brill, 2014.

Gerstenberger, Erhard S. *Israel in the Persian Period: The Fifth and Fourth Centuries BCE.* Atlanta: Society of Biblical Literature, 2011.

Goff, Matthew J. *Discerning Wisdom: The Sapiential Literature of the Dead Sea Scrolls.* VTSup 116. Leiden: Brill, 2007.

Goodacre, M. "How Reliable Is the Story of the Nag Hammadi Discovery?" *JSNT* 35 (2013): 303–22.

———. *Thomas and the Gospels: The Case for Thomas's Familiarity with the Synoptics.* Grand Rapids: Eerdmans, 2012.

Goodspeed, E. J. *Strange New Gospels.* Chicago: University of Chicago Press, 1931. Reprinted as *Modern Apocrypha.* Boston: Beacon, 1956.

Grant, Robert M. *Formation of the New Testament.* New York: Harper & Row, 1965.

———. *Greek Apologists of the Second Century.* Philadelphia: Westminster, 1988.

———. *A Historical Introduction to the New Testament.* New York: Simon & Schuster, 1972.

———. "The New Testament Canon." Pages 284–307 in *From the Beginnings to Jerome.* Edited by P. R. Ackroyd and C. F. Evans. Vol. 1 of *The Cambridge History of the Bible.* Cambridge: Cambridge University Press, 1970.

Grant, Robert M., and H. H. Graham. *First and Second Clement.* Vol. 2 of *The Apostolic Fathers: A New Translation and Commentary.* New York: Thomas Nelson, 1965.

Green, R. P. H., trans. *Saint Augustine: On Christian Teaching.* Oxford World's Classics. Oxford: Oxford University Press, 1997.

Gregory, Andrew, et al., eds. *The Oxford Handbook of Early Christian Apocrypha.* Oxford: Oxford University Press, 2015.

Grenfell, B. P., L. W. Drexel, and A. S. Hunt, eds. *New Sayings of Jesus and a Fragment of a Lost Gospel from Oxyrhynchus.* London: Frowde, 1904.

Grenfell, B. P., and A. S. Hunt, eds. *The Oxyrhynchus Papyri: Part IV.* London: Egypt Exploration Fund, 1904.

Grunstaudl, Wolfgang. *PETRUS ALEXANDRINUS.* WUNT 2/353. Tübingen: Mohr Siebeck, 2013.

Guelich, Robert A. *Mark 1–8:26.* WBC 34A. Dallas: Word, 1989.

Guignard, Christophe. "The Original Language of the Muratorian Fragment." *JTS* 66 (2015): 596–624.

Guillaumont, A., et al., eds. *The Gospel according to Thomas: Coptic Text, Established and Translated.* Orig., 1959. 2nd ed. Leiden: Brill, 1976.

Haelst, Joseph van. *Catalogue des papyrus litteraires juifs et chretiens.* Universite de Paris IV. Serie Papyrologie 1. Paris: Publications de la Sorbonne, 1976.

Hagner, D. A. *The Use of the Old and New Testaments in Clement of Rome.* NovTSup 34. Leiden: Brill, 1973.

Hamilton, Alastair. *The Apocryphal Apocalypse.* Oxford: Oxford University Press, 1999.

Hannah, D. D. "The Four-Fold 'Canon' in the *Epistula Apostolorum.*" *JTS* 59 (2008): 598–633.

Harrington, Daniel J. "The Old Testament Apocrypha in the Early Church and Today." Pages 196–210 in *CanDb.*

Hawk, Brandon. *Gospel of Pseudo-Matthew.* Early Christian Apocrypha 8. Salem, OR: Polebridge, forthcoming.

Hedrick, Charles W. *The Apocalypse of Adam: A Literary and Source Analysis.* SBLDS 46. Chico, CA: Scholars Press, 1980.

Henry, J. K. "The *Acts of Thomas* as Sacred Text." Pages 152–70 in *Sacra Scriptura: How "Non-Canonical" Texts Functioned in Early Judaism and Early Christianity.* Edited by J. H. Charlesworth, L. M. McDonald, and B. A. Jurgens. Jewish and Christian Texts in Contexts and Related Studies 20. London: Bloomsbury T&T Clark, 2014.

Henze, Matthias. *Mind the Gap: How the Jewish Writings between the Old and New Testament Help Us Understand Jesus.* Minneapolis: Fortress, 2017.

———. *The Syriac Apocalypse of Daniel: Introduction, Text and Commentary.* STAC 11. Tübingen: Mohr Siebeck, 2001.

Herbert, M., and M. McNamara. *Irish Biblical Apocrypha.* Edinburgh: T&T Clark, 1989.

Hezser, Catherine. *Jewish Literacy in Roman Palestine.* TSAJ 81. Tübingen: Mohr Siebeck, 2001.

Hill, Charles E. "The *Epistula Apostolorum*: An Asian Tract from the Time of Polycarp." *Journal of Early Christian Studies* 7 (1999): 1–53.

———. *From the Lost Teaching of Polycarp: Identifying Irenaeus' Apostolic Presbyter and the Author of Ad Diognetum.* WUNT 186. Tübingen: Mohr Siebeck, 2006.

Hills, J. V. *The Acts of Paul and Thecla.* Early Christian Apocrypha 7. Salem, OR: Polebridge, forthcoming.

———. *The Epistle of the Apostles.* Early Christian Apocrypha 2. Salem, OR: Polebridge, 2009.

———. *Tradition and Composition in the Epistula Apostolorum.* Minneapolis: Fortress, 1990.

Himmelfarb, Martha. "*3 Baruch* Revisited: Jewish or Christian Composition, and Why It Matters." *Zeitschrift für Antikes Christentum / Journal of Ancient Christianity* 20, Themenheft: *Die antiken christlichen Apokalypsen in den antiken christlichen Apokryphen* (2016): 41–62.

Hirschberger, V. *Ringen um Israel: Intertextuelle Perspektiven auf das 5. Buch Esra.* SECA 14. Leuven: Peeters, 2018.

Hock, R. F. *The Infancy Gospels of James and Thomas.* Scholars Bible 2. Santa Rosa, CA: Polebridge, 1995.

Hoffmann, R. J. *Celsus on the True Doctrine.* New York: Oxford University Press, 1987.

Hogan, Karina Martin. "The Meanings of *tôrah* in 4 Ezra." *JSJ* 38 (2007): 530–52.

———. *Theologies in Conflict in 4 Ezra: Wisdom Debate and Apocalyptic Solution.* JSJSup 130. Leiden: Brill, 2008.

Holladay, Carl R. *A Critical Introduction to the New Testament: Interpreting the Message and Meaning of Jesus Christ.* Expanded CD-Rom Version. Nashville: Abingdon, 2005.

Hovhanessian, Vahan S. "New Testament Apocrypha and the Armenian Version of the Bible." Pages 63–87 in vol. 2 of *The Canon of the Bible and the Apocrypha in the Churches of the East.* Edited by V. S. Hovhanessian. Bible in the Christian Orthodox Tradition. New York: Peter Lang, 2012.

Hultgren, Stephen. "4Q521, the Second Benediction of the Tefilla, the Hasidim, and the Development of Royal Messianism." *RevQ* 23 (2008): 313–40.

———. "4Q521 and Luke's Magnificat and Benedictus." Pages 119–32 in *Echoes from the Caves: Qumran and the New Testament.* Edited by F. García Martínez. STDJ 85. Leiden: Brill, 2009.

Hurtado, Larry W. *The Earliest Christian Artifacts: Manuscripts and Christian Origins.* Grand Rapids: Eerdmans, 2006.

———. "The Greek Fragments of the *Gospel of Thomas* as Artefacts: Papyrological Observations on Papyrus Oxyrhynchus 1, Papyrus Oxyrhynchus 654 and Papyrus Oxyrhynchus 655." Pages 19–32 in *Das Thomasevangelium: Entstehung—Rezeption—Theologie.* Edited by J. Frey, E. E. Popkes, and J. Schröter. BZNW 157. Berlin: de Gruyter, 2008.

Isaac, Ephraim. "The Bible in Ethiopic." Pages 110–22 in *From 600 to 1450.* Edited by Richard Marsden and E. Ann Matter. Vol. 2 of *The New Cambridge History of the Bible.* Cambridge: Cambridge University Press, 2012.

Jackson-McCabe, M., ed. *Jewish Christianity Reconsidered: Rethinking Ancient Groups and Texts.* Minneapolis: Fortress, 2007.

James, M. R. *The Apocryphal New Testament*. Oxford: Clarendon, 1924. Corrected ed., 1953.

Jaubert, A. *Clément de Rome: Epître aux Corinthiens*. Sources chrétiennes 167. Paris: Cerf, 1971.

Jeffery, A. "The Canon of the Old Testament." Pages 32–45 in vol. 1 of *The Interpreter's Bible*. Edited by G. A. Buttrick. New York: Abingdon, 1952.

Jenott, L. *The Gospel of Judas: Coptic Text, Translation, and Historical Interpretation of the "Betrayer's Gospel."* STAC 64. Tübingen: Mohr Siebeck, 2011.

Johnston, Jeremiah J. *The Resurrection of Jesus in the "Gospel of Peter": A Tradition-Historical Study of the Akhmîm Gospel Fragment*. T&T Clark Jewish and Christian Texts 21. London: Bloomsbury T&T Clark, 2016.

Jones, F. S. "An Ancient Jewish Christian Rejoinder to Luke's Acts of the Apostles: Pseudo-Clementine *Recognitions* 1.27–71." Pages 223–45 in *The Apocryphal Acts of the Apostles in Intertextual Perspectives*. Edited by R. F. Stoops Jr. Semeia 80. Atlanta: Scholars Press, 1997.

———. "The History of Simon Cephas, the Chief of the Apostles." *NTAM* 1:371–94.

Jonge. *See* De Jonge.

Joosten, J. "The Date and Provenance of the Gospel of Barnabas," *JTS* 61 (2010): 200–215.

Kalin, Everett R. "Argument from Inspiration in the Canonization of the New Testament." ThD diss., Harvard University, 1967.

Käsemann, Ernst. "The Beginnings of Christian Theology." *Journal for Theology and the Church* 6 (1969): 17–46.

Kasser, R., M. Meyer, and G. Wurst, eds. *The Gospel of Judas*. Washington, DC: National Geographic Society, 2006.

Kasser, R., M. Meyer, and G. Wurst, with F. Gaudard, eds. *The Gospel of Judas*. 2nd ed. Washington, DC: National Geographic Society, 2008.

Kasser, R., and G. Wurst, eds. *The Gospel of Judas: Together with the Letter of Peter to Philip, James, and a Book of Allogenes from Codex Tchacos; Critical Edition*. Washington, DC: National Geographic Society, 2007.

Kelhoffer, James A. "'How Soon a Book' Revisited: ΕΥΑΓΓΕΛΙΟΝ as a Reference to 'Gospel' Materials in the First Half of the Second Century." *ZNW* 95 (2004): 1–34.

Kerber, Daniel. "The Canon in the Vulgate Translation of the Bible." Pages 168–83 in *Biblical Canons in Church Traditions and Translations*. Edited by Jean-Claude Loba Mkole. UBS 67, no. 2.

King, Karen L. "'Jesus said to them, "My wife . . ."': A New Coptic Papyrus Fragment." *HTR* 107 (2014): 131–59.

Klauck, H.-J. *The Apocryphal Acts of the Apostles: An Introduction*. Waco, TX: Baylor University Press, 2008.

———. *Apocryphal Gospels: An Introduction*. London: T&T Clark, 2003.

Klijn, A. F. J. "The Apocryphal Correspondence between Paul and the Corinthians." *VC* 17 (1963): 2–23.

———. *Jewish-Christian Gospel Tradition*. VCSup 17. Leiden: Brill, 1992.

Knibb, M. A. "Martyrdom and Ascension of Isaiah." *OTP* 1:143–76.

Knight, J. *Disciples of the Beloved One: The Christology, Social Setting and Theological Context of the Ascension of Isaiah*. JSPSup 18. Sheffield: Sheffield Academic Press, 1996.

Knohl, Israel. *Messiahs and Resurrection in "The Gabriel Revelation."* London: Continuum, 2009.

Koester, Helmut. *Ancient Christian Gospels: Their History and Development*. London: SCM Press, 1990.

Kraft, Robert Alan. *Barnabas and the Didache*. Vol. 3 of *The Apostolic Fathers: A Translation and Commentary*. Edited by R. M. Grant. New York: Thomas Nelson, 1965.

———. "The Pseudepigrapha in Christianity." Pages 3–33 in *Exploring the Scripturesque: Jewish Texts and Their Christian Contexts*. JSJSup 137. Leiden: Brill, 2009.

———. "The Pseudepigrapha in Christianity Revisited." Pages 35–60 in *Exploring the Scripturesque: Jewish Texts and Their Christian Contexts*. JSJSup 137. Leiden: Brill, 2009.

Kraus, T. J. "EvPet 12,50–14,60: Leeres Grab und was dann? Kanonische Traditionen, *Novelistic Development* and romanhafte Züge." *Early Christianity* 5 (2013): 335–61.

———. "'Die Sprache des Petrusevangeliums?' Methodische Anmerkungen und Vorüberlegungen für eine Analyse von Sprache und Stil." Pages 61–76 in *Das Evangelium nach Petrus: Text, Kontexte, Intertexte*. Edited by T. J. Kraus and T. Nicklas. TUGAL 158. Berlin: de Gruyter, 2007.

Kraus, T. J., M. J. Kruger, and T. Nicklas, eds. *Gospel Fragments: The "Unknown Gospel" on Papyrus Egerton 2, Papyrus Oxyrhynchus 840, Other Gospel Fragments*. Oxford Early Christian Gospel Texts. Oxford: Oxford University Press, 2009.

Kraus, T. J., and T. Nicklas, eds. *Das Evangelium nach Petrus: Text, Kontexte, Intertexte*. TUGAL 158. Berlin: de Gruyter, 2007.

———, eds. *Das Petrusevangelium und die Petrusapokalypse: Die griechischen Fragmente mit deutscher und englischer Übersetzung*. GCS 11. Berlin: de Gruyter, 2004.

Kruger, Michael J. *Canon Revisited: Establishing the Origins and Authority of the New Testament Books*. Wheaton, IL: Crossway, 2012.

———. "Early Christian Attitudes toward the Reproduction of Texts." Pages 63–80 in *The Early Text of the New Testament*. Edited by Charles E. Hill and Michael J. Kruger. Oxford: Oxford University Press, 2014.

———. *The Question of Canon: Challenging the Status Quo in the New Testament Debate*. Downers Grove, IL: InterVarsity Press, 2013.

Lalleman, P. J. *The Acts of John: A Two-Stage Initiation into Johannine Gnosticism*. SECA 4. Leuven: Peeters, 1998.

Lambdin, T. O. "Gospel of Thomas." Pages 117–30 in *The Nag Hammadi Library*. Edited by J. M. Robinson. Leiden: Brill, 1977.

Landau, B. "The Revelation of the Magi." *NTAM* 1:19–38.

———. *Revelation of the Magi: The Lost Tale of the Wise Men's Journey to Bethlehem*. New York: HarperOne, 2010.

Lapham, F. *An Introduction to the New Testament Apocrypha*. London: T&T Clark International, 2003.

La Porta, S. "The Seventh Vision of Daniel." *OTPM* 1:410–34.

Laurence, Richard. *The Book of Enoch the prophet: an apocryphal production, supposed to have been lost for ages; but discovered at the close of the last century in Abyssinia; now first translated from an Ethiopic ms. in the Bodleian Library*. Oxford: Parker, 1821.

———. *Libri Enoch prophetae versio aethiopica*. Oxford: Parker, 1838.

Lawson, R. P., ed. *Origen: Song of Songs, Commentary and Homilies*. Ancient Christian Writers 26. New York: Paulist Press, 1957.

Layton, B., ed. *Gospel according to Thomas, Gospel according to Philip, Hypostasis of the Archons, and Indexes*. Vol. 1 of *Nag Hammadi Codex II,2–7 together with XII,2 Brit. Lib. Or. 4926 (1), and P. Oxy 1, 654, 655*. NHS 20. Leiden: Brill, 1989.

Leiman, Sid Z., ed. *The Canon and Masorah of the Hebrew Bible: An Introductory Reader*. New York: Ktav, 1974.

———. *The Canonization of the Hebrew Scripture: The Talmudic and Midrashic Evidence*. Hamden, CT: Archon Books, 1976.

———. "Inspiration and Canonicity: Reflections on the Formation of the Biblical Canon." Pages 56–63 and 315–18 in *Jewish and Christian Self-Definition*, vol. 2: *Aspects of Judaism in the Graeco-Roman Period*. Edited by E. P. Sanders, A. I. Baumgarten, and A. Mendelson. Philadelphia: Fortress, 1981.

Lewis, Jack P. "Jamnia Revisited." Pages 146–62 in *CanDb*.

Liere, Frans van. *An Introduction to the Medieval Bible*. New York: Cambridge University Press, 2014.

———. "The Latin Bible, c. 900 to the Council of Trent, 1546." Pages 93–109 in *From 600–1450*. Edited by Richard Marsden and E. Ann Matter. Vol. 2 of *The New Cambridge History of The Bible*. Cambridge: Cambridge University Press, 2012.

Light, Laura. "The Bible and the Individual: The Thirteenth Century." Pages 228–46 in *The Practice of the Bible in the Middle Ages: Production, Reception, and Performance in Western Christianity*. Edited by Susan Boynton and Diane J. Reilly. New York: Columbia University Press, 2011.

———. "The Thirteenth Century and the Paris Bible." Pages 380–91 in *From 600–1450*. Edited by Richard Marsden and E. Ann Matter. Vol. 2 of *The New Cambridge History of the Bible*. Cambridge: Cambridge University Press, 2012.

Lightfoot, J. B., J. R. Harmer, and M. W. Holmes. *The Apostolic Fathers*. Rev. ed. Grand Rapids: Baker, 1989.

Lightstone, J. N. "The Formation of the Biblical Canon in Judaism of Late Antiquity: Prolegomenon to a General Reassessment." *Studies in Religion* 8 (1979): 135–43.

Lim, Timothy H. "'All These He Composed through Prophecy.'" Pages 61–73 in *Prophecy after the Prophets: The Contribution of the Dead Sea Scrolls to the Understanding of Biblical and Extra-Biblical Prophecy*. Edited by Kristin De Troyer and Armin Lange, with the assistance of Lucas L. Schulte. CBET 52. Leuven: Peeters, 2009.

———. "Authoritative Scriptures and the Dead Sea Scrolls." Pages 303–22 in *The Oxford Handbook of the Dead Sea Scrolls*. Edited by Timothy H. Lim and John J. Collins. Oxford: Oxford University Press, 2010.

———. *The Formation of the Jewish Canon*. AYBRL. New Haven: Yale University Press, 2013.

Loman, J. "The Letter of Barnabas in Early Second-Century Egypt." Pages 247–65 in *The Wisdom of Egypt: Jewish, Early Christian, and Gnostic Essays in Honour of Gerard P. Luttikhuizen*. Edited by A. Hilhorst and G. H. Kooten. AGJU 59. Leiden: Brill, 2005.

Lücke, Friedrich. *Versuch einer vollständigen Einleitung in die Offenbarung Johannis und in die gesamte apokalyptische Literatur*. Bonn: Weber, 1832.

Lührmann, Dieter. "Kann es wirklich keine frühe Handschrift des Petrusevangeliums geben? Corrigenda zu einem Aufsatz von Paul Foster." *NovT* 48 (2006): 379–83.

Luijendijk, A. "Reading the *Gospel of Thomas* in the Third Century." Pages 241–67 in *Reading New Testament Papyri in Context = Lire les papyrus du Nouveaue Testament dans leur contexte*. Edited by C. Clivaz and J. Zumstein. BETL 242. Leuven: Peeters, 2011.

Lutz, C. E. "The Letter of Lentulus Describing Christ." *Yale University Library Gazette* 50 (1975): 91–97.

MacDonald, Dennis R. *The Acts of Andrew*. Early Christian Apocrypha 1. Santa Rosa, CA: Polebridge, 2005.

———. *The Acts of Andrew and the Acts of Andrew and Matthias in the City of the Cannibals*. SBLTT 33: Christian Apocrypha Series 1. Atlanta: Scholars Press, 1990.

Machiela, Daniel A. *The Dead Sea Genesis Apocryphon [1Q20]: A New Text and Translation with Introduction and Special Treatment of Columns 13–17*. STDJ 79. Leiden: Brill, 2009.

Marcus, Joel. "John the Baptist and Jesus." Pages 179–97 in *When Judaism and Christianity Began: Essays in Memory of Anthony J. Saldarini*. Edited by Alan J. Avery Peck, Daniel J. Harrington, and Jacob Neusner. JSJSup 85. Leiden: Brill, 2004.

Marguerat, D. "The *Acts of Paul* and the Canonical Acts: A Phenomenon of Rereading." Pages 169–83 in *The Apocryphal Acts of the Apostles in Intertextual Perspectives*. Edited by R. F. Stoops Jr. Semeia 80. Atlanta: Scholars Press, 1997.

Marrou, H. I. À *Diognète*. Paris: Cerf, 1965.

Mason, Steve. "Josephus and His Twenty-Two Book Canon." Pages 110–27 in *CanDb*.

Matthews, Christopher R. "The *Acts of Peter* and Luke's Intertextual Heritage." Pages 207–22 in *The Apocryphal Acts of the Apostles in Intertextual Perspectives*. Edited by R. F. Stoops Jr. Semeia 80. Atlanta: Scholars Press, 1997.

McDonald, Lee Martin. *The Biblical Canon: Its Origin, Formation, and Authority*. Grand Rapids: Baker Academic, 2011.

———. *Forgotten Scriptures: The Selection and Rejection of Early Religious Writings*. Louisville: Westminster John Knox, 2009.

———. "The Gospels in Early Christianity: Their Origin, Use, and Authority." Pages 150–78 in *Reading the Gospels Today*. Edited by S. E. Porter. Grand Rapids: Eerdmans, 2004.

———. "Lost Books." Pages 581–87 in vol. 1 of *The Oxford Encyclopedia of the Books of the Bible*. Edited by M. D. Coogan. New York: Oxford University Press, 2011.

———. *The New Testament: Its Authority and Canonicity*. Vol. 2 of *The Formation of the Biblical Canon*. 4th ed. London: Bloomsbury T&T Clark, 2017.

———. *The Old Testament: Its Authority and Canonicity*. Vol. 1 of *The Formation of the Biblical Canon*. London: Bloomsbury T&T Clark, 2017.

———. "The Parables of Enoch in Early Christianity." Pages 329–63 in *Parables of Enoch: A Paradigm Shift*. Edited by D. L. Bock and J. H. Charlesworth. T&T Clark Jewish and Christian Texts Series 11. London: Bloomsbury, 2013.

———. "The Reception of the Writings and Their Place in the Biblical Canon." Pages 397–413 in *The Oxford Handbook of the Writings of the Hebrew Bible*. Edited by Donn Morgan. Oxford: Oxford University Press, 2018.

———. Review of Tomas Bokedal, *The Formation and Significance of the Christian Biblical Canon: A Study in Text, Ritual and Interpretation*. In *Review of Biblical Literature* (February 2016). Online: http://www.bookreviews.org/BookDetail.asp?TitleId=9700.

———. "The Scriptures of Jesus: Did He Have a Biblical Canon?" Pages 827–62 in *Jesus Research: New Methodologies and Perceptions*. Edited by James H. Charlesworth, with Brian Rhea and Petr Pokorný. The Second Princeton-Prague Symposium on Jesus Research. Grand Rapids: Eerdmans, 2014.

———. *The Story of Jesus in History and Faith*. Grand Rapids: Baker Academic, 2013.

McDonald, Lee Martin, and Charles W. Hedrick. "Is the Bible the Word of God?" Part 1 of 3 parts. *Fourth R* 29, no. 3 (2016): 3–11.

McDonald, Lee Martin, and James A. Sanders, eds. *The Canon Debate [CanDb]*. Peabody, MA: Hendrickson, 2002.

Metzger, Bruce M. *The Canon of the New Testament: Its Origin, Development, and Significance*. Oxford: Clarendon, 1987.

———. "Introduction to Apocryphal/Deuterocanonical Books." Pages iii–xv in *The New Oxford Annotated Bible with the Apocryphal / Deuterocanonical Books: New Revised Standard Version*. Edited by B. M. Metzger and R. E. Murphy. New York: Oxford University Press, 1991.

Meyer, Marvin W. *The Gnostic Discoveries: The Impact of the Nag Hammadi Library*. San Francisco: HarperCollins, 2005.

———. *The Gospel of Thomas: The Hidden Sayings of Jesus*. San Francisco: HarperCollins, 1992.

———. *The Letter of Peter to Philip*. SBLDS 53. Chico, CA: Scholars Press, 1981.

Milik, J. T. *The Books of Enoch: Aramaic Fragments from Qumrân Cave 4*. Oxford: Clarendon Press, 1976.

Mimouni, S. C. "Les Apocalypses de la Vierge: État de la question." *Apocrypha* 4 (1993): 101–12.

Mirecki, P. A. "Peter, Gospel of." *ABD* 5:278–81.
Mitteis, Ludwig, and Ulrich Wilcken. *Grundzüge und Chrestomathie der Papyruskunde.* Vol. 1, part 2. Leipzig: Teubner, 1912.
Moo, Douglas. *The Epistle to the Romans.* NICNT. Grand Rapids: Eerdmans, 1996.
Moore, George Foot. "Christian Writers on Judaism." *HTR* 14 (1921): 197–254.
———. *Judaism in the First Centuries of the Christian Era: The Age of the Tannaim.* 3 vols. Cambridge: Harvard University Press, 1927–30.
Morgan, Donn F. *Between Text and Community: The "Writings" in Canonical Interpretation.* Minneapolis: Fortress, 1990.
Mroczek, Eva. *The Literary Imagination in Jewish Antiquity.* Oxford: Oxford University Press, 2016.
Mueller, J. R., and G. A. Robbins. "Vision of Ezra." *OTP* 1:581–90.
Najman, Hindy. *Losing the Temple and Recovering the Future: An Analysis of 4 Ezra.* Cambridge: Cambridge University Press, 2014.
———. "The Vitality of Scripture within and beyond the Canon." *JSJ* 43 (2012): 497–518.
Nersessian, Vrej. *The Bible in the Armenian Tradition.* London: British Library, 2001.
Neusner, Jacob, and W. S. Green. *Writing with Scripture: The Authority and Uses of the Hebrew Bible in the Torah of Formative Judaism.* Minneapolis: Fortress, 1989.
Newsom, Carol A. *Daniel.* OTL. Louisville: Westminster John Knox, 2014.
———. "The Reuse of Ugaritic Mythology in Daniel 7: An Optical Illusion?" Pages 85–100 in *Biblical Essays in Honor of Daniel J. Harrington, S.J., and Richard J. Clifford, S.J.: Opportunity for No Little Instruction.* Edited by Christopher G. Frechette, Christopher R. Matthews, and Thomas D. Stegman, S.J. Mahwah, NJ: Paulist Press, 2014.
———. "'Sectually Explicit' Literature from Qumran." Pages 167–87 in *The Hebrew Bible and Its Interpreters.* Edited by W. H. Propp, B. Halpern, and D. N. Freedman. Winona Lake, IN: Eisenbrauns, 1990.
Nicholson, Ernest W. *Deuteronomy and the Judaean Diaspora.* Oxford: Oxford University Press, 2014.
Nickelsburg, George W. E. *1 Enoch 1.* Hermeneia. Minneapolis: Fortress, 2001.
———. *Resurrection, Immortality, and Eternal Life in Intertestamental Judaism and Early Christianity.* 2nd ed. Harvard Theological Studies 66. Cambridge, MA: Harvard University Press, 2006.
Nickelsburg, George W. E., and James C. VanderKam. *1 Enoch 2.* Hermeneia. Minneapolis: Fortress, 2012.
Nicklas, Tobias. "Gedanken zum Verhältnis zwischen christlichen Apokryphen und hagiographischer Literatur: Das Beispiel der Veronica-Traditionen." *NedTT* 62 (2008): 45–63.
———. "The 'Unknown Gospel' on Papyrus Egerton 2 (+ Papyrus Cologne 255)." Pages 9–120 in *Gospel Fragments: The "Unknown Gospel" on Papyrus Egerton 2, Papyrus Oxyrhynchus 840, Other Gospel Fragments.* Edited by T. J. Kraus, M. J. Kruger, and T. Nicklas. Oxford Early Christian Gospel Texts. Oxford: Oxford University Press, 2009.
Nicklas, Tobias, C. R. Moss, C. M. Tuckett, and J. Verheyden, eds. *The Other Side: Apocryphal Perspectives on Ancient Christian "Orthodoxies."* NTOA 117. Göttingen: Vandenhoeck & Ruprecht, 2017.
Niebuhr, Karl-Wilhelm. "4Q521, 2 II—Ein eschatologischer Psalm." Pages 151–68 in *Mogilany 1995.* Edited by Z. J. Kapera. Kraków: Enigma, 1996.
Nienhuis, David B., and Robert W. Wall. *Reading the Epistles of James, Peter, John, and Jude as Scripture: The Shaping and Shape of a Canonical Collection.* Grand Rapids: Eerdmans, 2013.

Obbink, D., and D. Colomo. "5345." Pages 4–7 + plate II in vol. 83 of *The Oxyrhynchus Papyri*. Edited by P. J. Parsons and N. Gonis. London: The Egypt Exploration Society, 2018.

Oikonomos, Elias. "Deuterocanonicals in the Orthodox Church." Pages 17–32 in *The Apocrypha in Ecumenical Perspective*. Edited by Siegfried Meuer. UBS Monograph 6. New York: United Bible Societies, 1991.

Orlov, Andrei A. *The Enoch-Metatron Tradition*. TSAJ 107. Tübingen: Mohr Siebeck, 2005.

Pagels, Elaine. *Beyond Belief: The Secret Gospel of Thomas*. New York: Random House, 2003.

Paget, J. N. B. Carleton. "Barnabas and the Outsiders: Jews and Their World in the Epistle of Barnabas." Pages 177–202 in *Early Christian Communities between Ideal and Reality*. Edited by M. Grundeken and J. Verheyden. WUNT 342. Tübingen: Mohr Siebeck, 2015.

———. *Christians and Jewish Christians in Antiquity*. WUNT 251. Tübingen: Mohr Siebeck, 2010.

———. "The Epistle of Barnabas." *ExpTim* 117 (2006): 441–46.

———. "The Epistle of Barnabas and the Writings That Later Formed the New Testament." Pages 229–49 in *The Reception of the New Testament in the Apostolic Fathers*. Edited by A. F. Gregory. Oxford: Oxford University Press, 2007.

Patterson, S. J. *The Gospel of Thomas and Jesus*. Sonoma, CA: Polebridge, 1993.

Pelle, S. "A Quotation from the *Questions of Bartholomew* in an Early Medieval Latin Sermon." *Apocrypha* 25 (2014): 133–49.

Pentiuc, Eugen J. *The Old Testament in Eastern Orthodox Tradition*. New York: Oxford University Press, 2014.

———. "The Old Testament: Canon." Pages 341–43 in J. A. McGuckin, ed., *The Concise Encyclopedia of Orthodox Christianity*. Oxford: Wiley-Blackwell, 2014.

Pérés, J.-N. "Das lebendige Wort: Zu einem Agraphon in der Epistula apostolorum." Pages 125–32 in *Christian Apocrypha: Receptions of the New Testament in Ancient Christian Apocrypha*. Edited by J.-M. Roessli and T. Nicklas. Novum Testamentum Patristicum 29. Göttingen: Vandenhoeck & Ruprecht, 2014.

Perles, Felix. *Bousset's "Religion des Judentums" im neutestamentlichen Zeitalter kritisch untersucht*. Berlin: Peiser, 1903.

Perrin, Andrew B. *The Dynamics of Dream-Vision Revelation in the Aramaic Dead Sea Scrolls*. JAJSup 19. Göttingen: Vandenhoeck & Ruprecht, 2015.

Pervo, R. I. *The Acts of Paul: A New Translation with Introduction and Commentary*. Eugene, OR: Cascade, 2014.

———. "The Acts of Titus." *NTAM* 1:406–10.

———. "A Hard Act to Follow: The Acts of Paul and the Canonical Acts." *Journal of Higher Criticism* 2, no. 2 (1995): 3–32.

Pervo, R. I., with J. V. Hills. *The Acts of John*. Early Christian Apocrypha 6. Salem, OR: Polebridge Press, 2015.

Pietersma, A., and S. T. Comstock, with H. W. Attridge. *The Apocalypse of Elijah: Based on Chester Beatty 2018*. SBLTT 19: Pseudepigrapha Series 9. Chico: Scholars Press, 1981.

Plisch, U.-K. *The Gospel of Thomas: Original Text with Commentary*. Stuttgart: Deutsche Bibelgesellschaft, 2008.

Plumptre, E. H. *The General Epistles of St Peter and St Jude*. CBSC. Cambridge: Cambridge University Press, 1892.

Popkes, E. E., and G. Wurst, eds. *Judasevangelium und Codex Tchacos: Studien zur religionsgeschichtlichen Verortung einer gnostischen Schriftensammlung*. WUNT 297. Tübingen: Mohr Siebeck, 2012.

Porter, F. C. Review of G. F. Moore, *Judaism in the First Centuries of the Christian Era: The Age of the Tannaim. Journal of Religion* 8 (1928): 30–62.

Porter, Stanley E., and Andrew W. Pitts. *Fundamentals of New Testament Textual Criticism.* Grand Rapids: Eerdmans, 2015.

Preuschen, E. *Analecta: Kürzere Text zur Geschichte der alten Kirche und des Kanons.* Freiburg and Leipzig: Mohr, 1893.

Prigent, P. *Les Testimonia dans le Christianisme primitif: L'Épître de Barnabé I–XVI et ses sources.* Paris: Libraire Lecoffre, 1961.

Pritz, R. A. *Nazarene Jewish Christianity: From the End of the New Testament Period until Its Disappearance in the Fourth Century.* StPB 37. Leiden: Brill, 1988. Repr., Jerusalem: Magnes, 1992.

Puech, Émile. "[4Q521.] Apocalypse Messianique." Pages 1–38 in *Textes Hébreux (4Q521–4Q528).* Vol. XVIII of *Qumrân Grotte 4.* Edited by É. Puech. DJD 25. Oxford: Clarendon, 1998.

———. "[4Q246.] 4QApocryphe de Daniel ar." Pages 165–84 in *Parabiblical Texts.* Part 3 of vol. XVII of *Qumran Cave 4.* Edited by G. Brooke et al. DJD 22. Oxford: Clarendon, 1996.

———. "Le tombeau de Siméon et Zacharie dans la vallée de Josaphat." *RB* 111 (2004): 563–77 + plates II–IV.

Qimron, Elisha, and John Strugnell, eds. *Miqsat Maʿase Ha-Torah.* Vol. V of *Qumran Cave 4.* DJD 10. Oxford: Clarendon Press, 1994.

Rajak, Tess. *Translation and Survival: The Greek Bible of the Ancient Jewish Diaspora.* Oxford: Oxford University Press, 2009.

Ramelli, I. L. E. "The Pseudepigraphal Correspondence between Seneca and Paul: A Reassessment." Pages 319–36 in *Paul and Pseudepigraphy.* Edited by S. E. Porter and G. P. Fewster. PAST 8. Leiden: Brill, 2013.

———. "A Pseudepigraphon inside a Pseudepigraphon? The Seneca-Paul Correspondence and the Letters Added Afterwards." *JSP* 23 (2014): 259–89.

Reed, Annette Yoshiko. "The Modern Invention of 'Old Testament Pseudepigrapha.'" *JTS* 60 (2009): 403–36.

Regt. *See* De Regt.

Reuss, E. W. *History of the Canon of the Holy Scriptures in the Christian Church.* Translated by D. Hunter. Edinburgh: Hunter, 1891.

Robinson, J. M. "From the Cliff to Cairo: The Study of the Discoverers and Middlemen of the Nag Hammadi Codices." Pages 21–58 in *Colloque internationale sur les textes de Nag Hammadi (Québec, 22–23 août 1978).* Edited by B. Barc. Quebec City: Les presses de l'Université Laval, 1981.

Robinson, J. M., et al., eds. *The Facsimile Edition of the Nag Hammadi Codices.* 12 vols. Leiden: Brill, 1972–84.

———, eds. *Introduction.* Vol. 12 of *The Facsimile Edition of the Nag Hammadi Codices.* Leiden: Brill, 1984.

Robinson, S. E. *The Testament of Adam: An Examination of the Greek and Syriac Traditions.* SBLDS 52. Chico, CA: Scholars Press, 1982.

———. "The Testament of Adam: An Updated Arbeitsbericht." *JSP* 5 (1989): 95–100.

Rordorf, W. "Paul's Conversion in the Canonical Acts and in the *Acts of Paul.*" Pages 137–44 in *The Apocryphal Acts of the Apostles in Intertextual Perspectives.* Edited by R. F. Stoops Jr. Semeia 80. Atlanta: Scholars Press, 1997.

Rothschild, Clare K. "Diognetus and the Topos of the Invisible God." Pages 213–26 in *New Essays on the Apostolic Fathers.* Edited by C. K. Rothschild. WUNT 375. Tübingen: Mohr Siebeck, 2017.

———. "Epistle of Barnabas and Secession through Allegory." Pages 191–212 in *New Essays on the Apostolic Fathers.* Edited by C. K. Rothschild. WUNT 375. Tübingen: Mohr Siebeck, 2017.

———. "1 Clement as Pseudepigraphon." Pages 61–68 in *New Essays on the Apostolic Fathers.* Edited by C. K. Rothschild. WUNT 375. Tübingen: Mohr Siebeck, 2017.

———. *The Muratorian Fragment.* WUNT. Tübingen: Mohr Siebeck, forthcoming.

———. "The Muratorian Fragment as Roman Fake." *NovT* 60 (2018): 55–82.

———, ed. *New Essays on the Apostolic Fathers.* WUNT 375. Tübingen: Mohr Siebeck, 2017.

Sabar, Ariel. "The Unbelievable Tale of Jesus' Wife." *The Atlantic* 160 (July/August 2016): 64–78.

Sanders, James A. "Canon: Hebrew Bible." *ABD* 1:837–52.

———. "Judaism." In Thomas Hatina and Stanley E. Porter, eds. Leiden: Brill, forthcoming.

———. *The Monotheizing Process: Its Origins and Development.* Eugene, OR: Cascade, 2014.

———. "The Scrolls and the Canonical Process." Pages 1–23 in vol. 2 of *The Dead Sea Scrolls after Fifty Years: A Comprehensive Assessment.* Edited by P. W. Flint and J. C. VanderKam. Leiden: Brill, 1999.

———. "'Spinning' the Bible." *Bible Review* 14, no. 3 (1998): 22–29 and 44–45.

———. *Torah and Canon.* Philadelphia: Fortress, 1972.

Sanders, J. N. "The Word." Pages 868–72 in vol. 4 of *IDB.*

Sandmel, Samuel. "On Canon." *CBQ* 28 (1966): 189–207.

Santos Otero, A. de. "Der apokryphe Titusbrief." *ZKG* 74 (1963): 1–14.

Schaff, Philip, trans. and ed. Revised by David S. Schaff. *The Creeds of Christendom: With a History and Critical Notes.* 6th ed. 3 vols. Grand Rapids: Baker Books, 1998. A revision of the edition by Harper & Row, 1931.

Schmidt, Daryl D. "The Greek New Testament as a Codex." Pages 469–84 in *The Canon Debate.* Edited by L. M. McDonald and J. A. Sanders. Peabody: Hendrickson, 2002.

Schneemelcher, W., ed. *New Testament Apocrypha.* Vol. 1, *Gospels and Related Writings.* Rev. ed. Louisville: Westminster/John Knox Press, 1991.

———, ed. *New Testament Apocrypha.* Vol. 2, *Writings Relating to the Apostles: Apocalypses and Related Subjects.* Rev. ed. Louisville: Westminster/John Knox Press, 1992.

Schröter, J. "Apocryphal and Canonical Gospels within the Development of the New Testament Canon." *Early Christianity* 7 (2016): 24–46.

———, ed. *The Apocryphal Gospels within the Context of Early Christian Theology.* BETL 260. Leuven: Peeters, 2013.

———. *Erinnerung an Jesu Worte: Studien zur Rezeption der Logienüberlieferung in Markus, Q und Thomas.* WMANT 76. Neukirchen: Neukirchener Verlag, 1997.

Schröter, J., and C. Markschies, eds. *Antike christliche Apokryphen in deutscher Übersetzung.* One vol. in 2 Teilbänden: *Evangelien und Verwandtes.* Tübingen: Mohr Siebeck, 2012.

Schwarz, Baruch J. "Torah." Pages 696–98 in *The Oxford Dictionary of the Jewish Religion.* Edited by R. J. Zwi Werblowsky and Geoffrey Wigoder. New York: Oxford University Press, 1997.

Seitz, Christopher R. *The Goodly Fellowship of the Prophets: The Achievement of Association in Canon Formation.* ASBT. Grand Rapids: Baker Academic, 2009.

———. *Prophecy and Hermeneutics: Toward a New Introduction to the Prophets.* Studies in Theological Interpretation. Grand Rapids: Baker Academic, 2007.

Shepherd, A. "The Letter of Barnabas and the Jerusalem Temple." *JSJ* 48 (2017): 531–50.

Shoemaker, S. J. *The Ancient Traditions of the Virgin Mary's Dormition and Assumption.* OECS. Oxford: Oxford University Press, 2002.

———. "The Apocalypse of the Virgin." *NTAM* 1:492–509.

———. *The Dormition and Assumption Apocrypha.* SECA 15. Leuven: Peeters, 2018.

Sidebottom, E. M. *James, Jude, and 2 Peter.* NCB. London: Thomas Nelson, 1967.

Silver, Daniel J. *Story of Scripture: From Oral Tradition to the Written Word.* New York: Basic Books, 1990.

Singer, S. *The Authorized Daily Prayer Book.* 9th American ed. New York: Hebrew Publishing, 1931.

Smith, Morton. "Ascent to the Heavens and Deification in 4QM^a." Pages 181–88 in *Archaeology and History in the Dead Sea Scrolls.* Edited by L. H. Schiffman. Sheffield: JSOT Press, 1990.

———. "Two Ascended to Heaven." Pages 290–301 in *Jesus and the Dead Sea Scrolls.* Edited by James H. Charlesworth. New York: Doubleday, 1991.

Snyder, G. E. "The Acts of Barnabas." *NTAM* 1:317–36.

Stackert, Jeffrey. *Prophet like Moses: Prophecy, Law, and Israelite Religion.* Oxford: Oxford University Press, 2014.

Steinberg, Julius. *Die Ketuvim: Ihr Aufbau und ihre Botschaft.* BBB 152. Hamburg: Philo, 2006.

Steinberg, Julius, and Timothy J. Stone, eds. *The Shape of the Writings.* Siphrut 16. Winona Lake, IN: Eisenbrauns, 2015.

Stokes, Ryan E. "The Throne Visions of Daniel 7, 1 Enoch 14, and the Qumran *Book of Giants* (4Q530): An Analysis of Their Literary Relationship." *DSD* 15 (2008): 340–58.

Stone, Michael E. *Fourth Ezra: A Commentary on the Book of Fourth Ezra.* Hermeneia. Minneapolis: Fortress, 1990.

———. "Greek Apocalypse of Ezra." *OTP* 1:561–79.

———. *Signs of the Judgement, Onomastica Sacra and The Generations from Adam.* Armenian Texts and Studies 3. Chico, CA: Scholars Press, 1981.

Stone, Michael E., J. C. Greenfield, and E. Eshel. *The Aramaic Levi Document: Edition, Translation, Commentary.* SVTP 19. Leiden: Brill, 2004.

Stone, Michael E., and Matthias Henze. *4 Ezra and 2 Baruch: Translations, Introductions, and Notes.* Minneapolis: Fortress, 2013.

Stone, Michael E., and J. Strugnell, eds. *The Books of Elijah: Parts 1–2.* SBLTT 18: Pseudepigrapha Series 8. Missoula, MT: Scholars Press, 1979.

Stone, Timothy J. *Compilational History of the Megilloth: Canon, Contoured Intertextuality and Meaning in the Writings.* Forschungen zum Alten Testament 2. Reihe. 59. Tübingen: Mohr Siebeck, 2013.

Stoops, Robert F., Jr. *The Acts of Peter.* Early Christian Apocrypha 4. Santa Rosa, CA: Polebridge Press, 2012.

———, ed. *The Apocryphal Acts of the Apostles in Intertextual Perspectives.* Semeia 80. Atlanta: Scholars Press, 1997.

Strugnell and Qimron. *See* Qimron and Strugnell.

Stuckenbruck, Loren T. "Apocrypha and Pseudepigrapha." Pages 179–203 in *Early Judaism: A Comprehensive Overview.* Edited by John J. Collins and Daniel C. Harlow. Grand Rapids: Eerdmans, 2012.

———. "Daniel and the Early Enoch Traditions." Pages 368–86 in vol. 2 of *The Book of Daniel: Composition and Reception.* Edited by John J. Collins and Peter W. Flint. VTSup 83. FIOTL 2. Leiden: Brill, 2001.

———. *1 Enoch 91–108.* CEJL. Berlin: de Gruyter, 2007.

———. *The Myth of Rebellious Angels: Studies in Second Temple Judaism and New Testament Texts.* Grand Rapids: Eerdmans, 2014.

———. "The Origins of Evil in Jewish Apocalyptic Tradition: The Interpretation of Genesis 6:1–4 in the Second and Third Centuries B.C.E." Pages 1–35 in *The Myth of Rebellious Angels.*

Stuckenbruck, Loren T., with Mark D. Mathews. "The Apocalypse of John, 1 Enoch, and the Question of Influence." Pages 281–325 in *The Myth of Rebellious Angels*.

Suciu, A. "The *Book of Bartholomew*: A Coptic Apostolic Memoir." *Apocrypha* 26 (2015): 211–37.

———. "The Recovery of the Lost Fragment Preserving the Title of the Coptic *Book of Bartholomew*: Edition and translation of Cornell University Library, Misc. Bd. MS. 683." *Apocrypha* 26 (2015): 239–59.

Sundberg, A. C., Jr. *The Old Testament of the Early Church*. Cambridge: Harvard University Press, 1964.

Swanson, Reuben, ed. *2 Corinthians: New Testament Greek Manuscripts; Variant Readings Arranged in Horizontal Lines against Codex Vaticanus*. Carol Stream, IL: Tyndale House Publishers, 2005.

Talmon, Shemaryahu. *Text and Canon of the Hebrew Bible: Collected Essays*. Winona Lake, IN: Eisenbrauns, 2010.

Taussig, Hal, ed. *A New New Testament: A Bible for the Twenty-First Century*. Boston: Houghton Mifflin Harcourt, 2013.

Tigchelaar, E. "Is the Liar Bar Kokhba? Considering the Date and Provenance of the Greek (Ethiopic) *Apocalypse of Peter*." Pages 63–77 in *The Apocalypse of Peter*. Edited by J. N. Bremmer and I. Czachesz. SECA 7. Leuven: Peeters, 2003.

Tite, P. L. *The Apocryphal Epistle to the Laodiceans: An Epistolary and Rhetorical Analysis*. TENTS 7. Leiden: Brill, 2012.

———. "Dusting Off a Pseudo-Historical Letter: Re-Thinking the Epistolary Aspects of the Apocryphal Epistle to the Laodiceans." Pages 289–318 in *Paul and Pseudepigraphy*. Edited by S. E. Porter and G. P. Fewster. PAST 8. Leiden: Brill, 2013.

Toepel, A. "The Apocryphon of Seth." *OTPM* 1:33–39.

Tomson, P. J., and D. Lambers-Petry, eds. *The Image of the Judaeo-Christians in Ancient Jewish and Christian Literature*. WUNT 158. Tübingen: Mohr Siebeck, 2003.

Trotter, Jonathan R. "The Tradition of the Throne Vision in the Second Temple Period: Daniel 7:9–10, *1 Enoch* 14:18–23, and the *Book of Giants* (4Q530)." *RevQ* 25 (2012): 451–66.

Tuckett, Christopher M. *The Gospel of Mary*. Oxford Early Christian Gospel Texts. Oxford: Oxford University Press, 2007.

———. "Thomas and the Synoptics." *NovT* 30 (1988): 132–57. Reprinted as pages 359–82 in *From the Sayings to the Gospels*. WUNT 328. Tübingen: Mohr Siebeck, 2014.

———. "Das Thomasevangelium und die synoptischen Evangelien." *BThZ* 12 (1995): 186–200.

Ulrich, Eugene C. *The Dead Sea Scrolls and the Developmental Composition of the Bible*. Esp. pages 187–99. VTSup 169. Leiden: Brill, 2015.

———. "The Jewish Scriptures: Texts, Versions, Canons." Pages 97–119 in *Early Judaism: A Comprehensive Overview*. Edited by J. J. Collins and Daniel C. Harlow. Grand Rapids: Eerdmans, 2012.

———. "The Non-Attestation of a Tripartite Canon in 4QMMT." *CBQ* 65 (2003): 202–14.

———. "The Notion and Definition of Canon." Pages 21–52 in *CanDb*.

Uro, R. *Thomas: Seeking the Historical Context of the Gospel of Thomas*. London: T&T Clark International, 2003.

VanderKam, James C. *Enoch and the Growth of an Apocalyptic Tradition*. CBQMS 16. Washington, DC: Catholic Biblical Association of America, 1984.

———. "Questions of Canon Viewed through the Dead Sea Scrolls." Pages 91–109 in *CanDb*.

Vanderlinden, S. "*Revelatio Sancti Stephani* (BHL 7850–56)." *REByz* 4 (1946): 178–217.

van Minnen, P. "The Akhmîm *Gospel of Peter.*" Pages 53–60 in *Das Evangelium nach Petrus: Text, Kontexte, Intertexte.* Edited by T. J. Kraus and T. Nicklas. TUGAL 158. Berlin: de Gruyter, 2007.

van Os, B. "The Role of the Apostles in the Letter of Peter to Philip." *Annali di storia dell'esegesi* 29 (2012): 155–60.

van Oyen, G. "The *Protevangelium Jacobi*: An Apocryphal Gospel?" Pages 271–304 in *The Apocryphal Gospels within the Context of Early Christian Theology.* Edited by J. Schröter. BETL 260. Leuven: Peeters, 2013.

———. "Rereading the Rewriting of the Biblical Traditions in the *Infancy Gospel of Thomas* (Paidika)." Pages 482–505 in *Infancy Gospels: Stories and Identities.* Edited by C. Clivaz et al. WUNT 281. Tübingen: Mohr Siebeck, 2011.

van Unnik, W. C. "Studies on the So-Called First Epistle of Clement: The Literary Genre." Pages 115–81 in *Encounters with Hellenism: Studies on the First Letter of Clement.* Edited by C. Breytenbach and L. L. Welborn. AGJU 53. Leiden: Brill, 2003.

Verheyden, Joseph. "The Canon Muratori: A Matter of Dispute." Pages 487–556 in *The Biblical Canons.* Edited by J.-M. Auwers and H. J. de Jonge. BETL 163. Leuven: Peeters, 2003.

Vermès, Géza. *The Complete Dead Sea Scrolls in English.* Rev. ed. London: Penguin, 2004.

———. *Jesus the Jew.* Philadelphia: Fortress, 1981.

Vermès, Géza, and Martin D. Goodman. *The Essenes according to the Classical Sources.* Sheffield: JSOT Press, 1989.

Voicu, S. J. "Ways to Survival for the Infancy Apocrypha." Pages 401–17 in *Infancy Gospels: Stories and Identities.* Edited by C. Clivaz et al. WUNT 281. Tübingen: Mohr Siebeck, 2011.

von Dobschütz, E. *Das Decretum Gelasianum: De libris recipiendis et non recipiendis.* TUGAL 38.4. Leipzig: Hinrichs, 1912.

Vuong, L., and B. Hawk. *Protevangelium of James.* Early Christian Apocrypha 9. Salem, OR: Polebridge Press, forthcoming.

———. "Purity, Piety, and the Purpose of the *Protevangelium of James.*" Pages 205–21 in *"Non-Canonical" Religious Texts in Early Judaism and Christianity.* Edited by J. H. Charlesworth and L. M. McDonald. Jewish and Christian Texts in Contexts and Related Studies 14. London: T&T Clark International, 2012.

Wayment, Thomas A. *The Text of the New Testament Apocrypha (100–400 C.E.).* London: Bloomsbury T&T Clark, 2013.

Webster, C. "Trapped in a Forger's Rhetoric: *3 Corinthians,* Pseudepigraphy, and the Legacy of Ancient Polemics." Pages 153–61 in *"Non-Canonical" Religious Texts in Early Judaism and Christianity.* Edited by J. H. Charlesworth and L. M. McDonald. Jewish and Christian Texts in Contexts and Related Studies 14. London: T&T Clark International, 2012.

Welborn, L. L. "On the Date of First Clement." *BR* 29 (1984): 35–54.

———. "The Preface to 1 Clement: The Rhetorical Situation and the Traditional Date." Pages 197–216 in *Encounters with Hellenism: Studies on the "First Letter of Clement."* Edited by C. Breytenbach and L. L. Welborn. AGJU 53. Leiden: Brill, 2003.

Wengst, K. *Tradition und Theologie des Barnabasbriefes.* Arbeiten zur Kirchengeschichte 42. Berlin: de Gruyter, 1971.

Westcott, Brooke Foss. *The Bible in the Church.* New York: Macmillan, 1891.

Wildeboer, G. *The Origin of the Canon of the Old Testament: An Historico-Critical Enquiry.* Translated by B. W. Bacon. London: Luzac & Co., 1895. Republished by the Cornell University Library Digital Collections, Lexington, KY: 2010.

Williams, Rowan, *Arius: Heresy and Tradition.* London: Darton, Longman & Todd, 1987.

Wise, Michael O. "*Mî kamoni ba'elîm*: A Study of 4Q491c, 4Q471b, 4Q427 7 and 1QH^a 25.35–26.10." *DSD* 7 (2000): 173–219.

———. "The Origins and History of the Teacher's Movement." Pages 92–122 in *The Oxford Handbook of the Dead Sea Scrolls*. Edited by Timothy H. Lim and John J. Collins. Oxford: Oxford University Press, 2010.

Wyrick, Jed. *The Ascension of Authorship: Attribution and Canon Formation in Jewish, Hellenistic, and Christian Traditions*. Cambridge, MA: Harvard University Press, 2004.

Yee, Gale A., Hugh R. Page Jr., and Matthew J. M. Coomber, eds. *Fortress Commentary on the Bible: The Old Testament and Apocrypha*. Minneapolis: Augsburg Fortress, 2014.

Zahn, T. *Urkunden und Belege zum ersten und dritten Ban. Erste Hälfte* in vol. 2 of *Geschichte des neutestamentlichen Kanons*. Erlangen and Leipzig: Deichert, 1890.

Zervos, G. T. "The *Protevangelium of James* and the Composition of the Bodmer Miscellaneous Codex: Chronology, Theology, and Liturgy." Pages 177–94 in *"Non-Canonical" Religious Texts in Early Judaism and Christianity*. Edited by J. H. Charlesworth and L. M. McDonald. Jewish and Christian Texts in Contexts and Related Studies 14. London: T&T Clark International, 2012.

Zias, J. "The Tomb of Absalom Reconsidered." *NEA* 68 (2005): 148–65.

Index of Ancient Writings

Index of Modern Authors

Index of Subjects

gospel
core of, 106
as good news, 42–44, 85, 116–17
preaching, 42, 108, 118, 156, 168,
179
the term, 116
Gospel of Barnabas,, 148
Gospel of Jesus' Wife, 145
Gospel of Judas, 128, 132n19, 136,
147
Gospel of Mary, 147, 165, 189n43, 191
Gospel of Peter, 101, 128, 148, 166,
167–82, 186, 189, 196
dating of, 170–71
importance of, 4–5, 167–82
Gospel of the Hebrews, 119, 124n7,
127–28, 131, 147
Gospel of Thomas, 123, 128, 148, 164–
67, 182–92
dating of, 164–65
importance of, 4–5
Gospel of Truth, 128, 191
Gospels, 118
four canonical, 98–99, 109, 116–17,
123–24, 128–37, 140, 142, 146,
166–67, 170–71, 177–78, 181,
196
the "holy tetrad," 137
Synoptic, 4, 123–24, 146, 170, 172,
182–84, 187
gospels, extracanonical, 4, 145–48, 165–
67, 182, 192n52. See also *Gospel of
Peter; Gospel of Thomas*
gospels, fragmentary/gospel harmonies,
146–47, 187
gospels, gnostic, 128, 147
Greece, Hellenistic. See Hellenism
Greek language, 2, 4, 8–11, 17, 21–23,
33, 35, 48, 63–66, 72, 78–84,
86n48, 88, 93–94, 130, 133,
135n28, 138, 141, 149n17,
153–54, 157, 159, 161–62, 182,
184–85, 187–91, 196
Greek literature, 166
Greek New Testament, 98n2, 143,
164
Greek Old Testament. See Septuagint,
Greek
Greek Orthodox churches. See Orthodox
Christianity
Greek philosophy, 23
Gregory 1105 (manuscript), 129
Gregory the Great, 138

Hagiographa. *See* Writings (Ketuvim)
harmonies, gospel, 146–47, 187
Hasmonean dynasty, 14–18, 37
heaven, 23–31, 38, 42–47, 159–61,
177–80, 183, 197
a throne in, 44–47
Hebrew Bible, 2–3, 7, 22, 25–27, 30,
35, 43, 48–96, 98, 128, 196
canon, forming/criteria for establishing, 71–96
dating of, 62
divisions and order of, 75–84
recognizing as sacred scripture, 49–70
See also Old Testament
Hebrew language, 2, 8, 18, 22–24,
32–33, 35–39, 42–44, 63, 67–68,
77–78, 82, 87, 92, 94, 99, 159n62
Hebrews, letter to, 77–78, 106, 123,
126, 129, 135nn27–29, 164
authorship of, 4
hell, 159, 161–62, 179, 197. *See also*
punishment
Hellenism, 2, 17, 19, 40
Hellenistic period, 23, 57n19
heresy, 12, 80, 98, 104–5, 113, 127–28,
134, 136–40, 150, 169, 183–84
heretical writings, 132
See also specific heresies, e.g., gnostics;
Marcionites; Montanists
Hermas, 126, 139. See also *Shepherd of
Hermas*
hermeneutics, 18, 58, 64, 89–90
Herod Agrippa, 162n70
Herod Antipas, 44, 157–58, 171, 173–
75, 181n28
Herod the Great, 158, 162–63
Hezekiah, King, 54
high priests/high priesthood, 14–16, 43,
47, 155, 158, 181n28
Hillel, 16, 158
Hippolytus of Rome, 91, 123, 183
Hodayot, 44–46, 88
holiness, 108, 129, 133, 141–42
Holy Spirit, 13, 80, 83, 91, 108, 111,
113, 197
cessation of prophecy, notion of, 22, 72
Homily on Genesis (Origen), 135n29
Homily on Joshua (Origen), 135n29
hope, 42, 46–47, 50–51, 57–60, 64, 72,
91, 144, 153, 159, 186, 192
Christian, 105
eschatological, 119
messianic, 76

Judah, 22, 41, 51, 53, 176
Judaism, 33
  anti-Semitism, 191
  Apocrypha, Jewish, 54, 66
  "axial transformation" in, 14
  a canon in, 9–11, 13–19
  Christianity's beginnings within, 58
  Christianity's break with, 34
  Christianity's continuity with, 33–34
  communities, Jewish, 63, 89–90,
    195, 199
  by definition, 33
  early, 51
  Eastern Dispersion, 90
  identity, Israelite/Jewish, 50–51, 54,
    60–61, 71, 89, 95
  Jesus as Jewish, 192–93
  Jewish community, 89–90
  Jewish literature, 38, 48, 56, 75
  Karaite Jews, 68
  mainline Jewish tradition, 26, 32
  messianic expectations, 44
  normative, 32, 93–94
  revolts against Rome, 31, 153, 160,
    164n78, 171, 174
  sects, Jewish, 31, 54, 92
  uniformity of, 33
  See also diaspora; Hebrew Bible; Israel;
    Second Temple period/Second
    Temple Judaism; Torah; specific top-
    ics and descriptions, e.g., Pharisees;
    synagogues
Jude, letter of, 4, 126–27, 129, 135,
  144, 151, 164
judges, 51
judgment, divine, 24–25, 28, 45, 47, 51,
  159, 161, 172, 180
Justa, 124–25
justice, 42
Justin Martyr, 155, 160, 173, 175

Karaite Jews, 68
Ketuvim (Writings). See Writings
kingdom of heaven, 183
King James Bible, 83
kingship, 41
  Jesus as king, 41
  kings of Israel, 52–53, 62
  See also monarchy

"Laments" (book), 53
land, 23, 25, 27, 51, 59–60, 64, 69,
  71–72, 86, 172

entrance into, 60
  See also Canaan
languages, 87–88
  vernacular, 88
  See also specific languages, e.g., Aramaic
    language
Laodicea, 112–13, 136–38, 151
Late Antiquity, 32, 55, 72, 77, 94, 146,
  164, 196–97, 200
Latin language, 8, 10, 22–23, 68,
  133–34, 137n36, 138n38, 141n7,
  151–54, 157, 159, 161–62
Latin Paris Bibles. See Paris Bibles
Latin Vulgate Bible. See Vulgate Bible,
  Latin
Latter Prophets, 50, 55–57, 60–63,
  71–72
law, 23
  centrality of Jewish, 34
  Gentiles and, 100
  God as lawgiver or legislator, 57n19
  priestly, 38
  Ten Commandments, 90n58
"Law and the Prophets," 9–10, 55, 63,
  65, 74, 76–77, 84, 88
law of Moses, 14, 29–30, 33, 37, 54, 57,
  61–62, 69, 94, 147. See also Torah
lectionaries, 133, 141, 143, 198
Leningrad Codex, 75
Leviathan, 27
Levi document, Aramaic, 38
libraries, 2, 16, 21–22, 37, 51n5, 166
life after death, 28, 30. See also resurrection of the dead
light and darkness (Two Spirits of Light
  and Darkness), 39
liturgies, 46, 50, 74, 80–81, 94, 104,
  127, 130, 133, 162
  Jewish, 87
Lord, the term, 109. See also under Jesus
  Christ: as Lord
"lost books," 53–54, 90
Lotan, 27
love, 90–91, 136, 147
Luther, Martin, 81, 143–44

Maccabean revolt, 37–38, 40, 43
magic, 150–51, 189n43, 190n46, 197
Malachi/book of Malachi, 56, 59n25,
  60, 64, 72–73, 76–79
Malachim, 67
Manasseh, King, 159
Manichaeans, 150

CPSIA information can be obtained
at www.ICGtesting.com
Printed in the USA
BVHW072312280820
587569BV00001B/23